VOLUME 1

THEMES IN IMMIGRATION HISTORY

EDITED BY
George E. Pozzetta

GARLAND PUBLISHING, INC.
New York & London
1991

Introduction Copyright © 1991 by George E. Pozzetta
All Rights Reserved

Library of Congress Cataloging-in-Publication Data

Themes in immigration history/ edited by George E. Pozzetta.
p. cm.—(American immigration and ethnicity: v. 1)
ISBN 0-8240-7401-7 (alk. paper)
1. Minorities—United States—History. 2. Immigrants—United States—History. 3. United States—Emigration and immigration—History. I. Pozzetta, George E. II. Series.
E184.A1T48   1990
305.8'00973—dc20   90-49051

Printed on acid-free, 250-year-life paper
Manufactured in the United States of America

INTRODUCTION

Once I thought to write a history of the
immigrants in America. Then I discovered
that the immigrants were American history.

Oscar Handlin,
The Uprooted (1951)

When it first appeared forty years ago, Oscar Handlin's startling observation occasioned disbelieving reactions; today, changes in historical scholarship have moved immigrants much closer to the central position posited by Handlin than perhaps even he ever considered possible. Once relegated to the fringes of historical investigation, immigrants now speak to the main themes of American history with an eloquence that belies the lack of attention they received earlier. In large part this is true because of what has happened to the field of immigration studies. Drawing from the momentum of the new social history, with its perspective "from the bottom up" and its insistence on exploring the experiences of ordinary people, the scholarly inquiry into immigration and ethnicity has produced an astounding outpouring of books and articles over the past several decades.

This rich and complex historical literature has drawn heavily from the methodologies and insights of the other social sciences and humanities, and the wider investigation into immigration has criss-crossed disciplinary boundaries at a rapid pace. The major journals of History, Political Science, Anthropology, Sociology, and Geography, for example, regularly carry essays dealing with the immigrant experience, and hundreds of articles appear in the more specialized local, regional, and topical publications of each discipline. Simply finding the relevant essays on any given topic within the general field has become a substantial challenge to researchers. This collection, therefore, represents an effort to bring together a selected cross section of the most significant articles on immigration and ethnicity. It is not definitive, no compilation treating with such broad-ranging and dynamic topics can ever be, but it is indicative of the scholarship that has shaped—and continues to shape—these important subjects. The major themes and issues of the field are discussed below, and each volume contains an individualized listing of supplemental readings for additional guidance. Taken together the collected essays contained within these volumes explore the manifold ways in which "immigrants were American history."

The liberation of immigration studies from its previously marginalized position has flowed from a number of critical interpretive and conceptual advances. One of the most important of these has been the effort to place immigration to America in the context of broader patterns of movement. Alerted by Frank Thistlethwaite's pioneering work, which showed how European migration to America was only part of a much larger transatlantic population and technological exchange, researchers now realize that an American-centered perspective is too restrictive to comprehend the full dimensions of migration. Immigrants from all quarters of the globe often envisioned America as only one destination among many, and then not necessarily a permanent one. Outmoded conceptions of "America fever" and exclusive one-way movement have given way to more complex understandings of the various manners by which America attracted and retained immigrants. The best works have taken into account the ability of multinational labor markets, economic cycles, transportation networks, as well as individual familial strategies, to propel immigrants outward in multi-step journeys.

At the same time as Thistlethwaite called for attention to large scale movements, he also urged that scholars be sensitive to the highly particularized nature of small scale migrations. Instead of studying "an undifferentiated mass movement" of individuals from loosely defined nation states, he insisted that immigrants be seen as emanating from "innumerable particular cells, districts, villages, towns, each with an individual reaction or lack of it to the pull of migration." This perspective necessarily involved linking the homeland with the new land in very precise ways, accounting for the specific influences of such factors as chain migration, kinship networks, travel agents, steamship companies, and repatriation flows, as well as the highly individualized economies of local regions.

Rudolph J. Vecoli's seminal work on Italian peasants in Chicago has pushed the study of premigration backgrounds in new directions. By pointing out that old world cultures survived the ocean crossing and significantly influenced adaptations in America, Vecoli stimulated a broad-based inquiry into the various ways in which immigrant traditions articulated with new world realities. The resulting scholarship has shifted the emphasis of investigation away from attention to the forces of assimilation and cultural break-down to those of cultural persistence and ethnic continuity. Immigrants did not succumb passively to pressures for conformity, but rather followed patterns of resistance and accommodation to the new land by which they turned themselves into something new—ethnic Americans. The ethnic culture that they created has proved to be a dynamic quality that has had influence into the third and fourth generation and beyond.

Such a viewpoint has led to different conceptions of assimilation and accultura-tion. Less often have scholars viewed these processes as easy, straight-line move-ments from "foreign" to "American." Nor have they continued to be captivated by images of a vast "Melting Pot" at work that has thoroughly erased differences. Rather, newer studies have posited a syncretic outcome in which both immigrants and the mainstream society have been changed, and the overall process of immigrant integration has emerged as more contingent and unpredictable than previously imagined. Attempts to preserve immigrant languages, value structures, and tradi-tion, for example, could not, and did not, result in the exact replication of old-world ways. In a process of "invention" and "negotiation," immigrants adapted their ethnic cultures to meet changing historical circumstances and to resolve the problems of duality inherent in their straddling of Old and New Worlds. At the same time, the host society was changing, or "reinventing," its own cultural traditions, in part because of the need to accommodate the presence of diverse clusters of immigrants.

Much of the most stimulating new research carried out along these lines has adopted the urban immigrant community as its setting. Community studies have not only examined the institutional structures of settlements, but have also typically attempted to penetrate into the "interior worlds" of newcomers to discover the mentalities, values, and life strategies that shaped immigrant destinies. Such inquiries have probed deeply into the families, kin groups, and neighborhoods that formed the core of immigrant districts. Their conclusions have revised older conceptions of immigrant neighborhoods that emphasized the social pathology of family breakdown, crime, and deviant behavior. Immigrant communities emerge as remarkably vibrant and complex entities that provided effective cushions between the often strange and harsh dominant society and newly arrived residents. They also were far from the homogenous bodies so often envisioned by outsiders, but rather were replete with various "subethnic" divisions based upon distinctions of class, religion, ideology, and local culture. The process of immigrant adaptation to America, therefore, was as often marked by tension and conflict *within* ethnic concentrations as it was by friction between the group and the receiving society.

Internal divisions were also features of immigrant communities in rural and small town locations. However, the distinctive physical and cultural contexts encountered in such settings meant that immigrants usually experienced different adjustment patterns from those of their urban-dwelling cousins. More isolated from mainstream contact and better able to establish a local hegemony, immigrant settlements in these settings often maintained traditional languages and folkways for longer periods of time and with less change than was possible in city neighborhoods. The ethnic culture that rural immigrants crafted correspondingly reflected these particular conditions.

Eschewing a reliance on sources generated by the host society and utilizing a broad range of foreign language materials, researchers have demonstrated the existence of a remarkable range of civic, labor, religious, recreational, cultural, and fraternal organizations created by immigrants. Each of these played important roles in mediating the difficult adjustment to new-world conditions, and the presence of these institutions points to the need of recognizing immigrants as active agents in determining their own futures. To be sure, they were often circumscribed in their actions by poverty, nativism, discrimination, and limited skills, but they typically responded with imaginative adaptations within the limits imposed upon them. Many formal immigration institutions such as labor unions and mutual aid societies, for example, employed collective strategies to overcome the constraints restricting immigrant lives. Informal familial and kin networks often assisted these initiatives with adjustments of their own to ease the process of insertion into America.

The most fundamental institution of all, the immigrant family, reveals these patterns clearly. Families did not disintegrate under the pressures of immigration, urbanization, and industrialization, but rather proved to be remarkably flexible and resilient. Family structures and values responded to the multiple challenges imposed by migration—both in urban centers and rural spaces—by expanding their roles to accommodate a variety of new demands. Immigrant women, in their capacities as mothers and daughters, played critical functions in these transformations. Recent work, however, has attempted to move the study of immigrant women beyond the family context and to view women as historical actors who were able to influence the larger society in many different ways. The broader challenge has been to reveal how women confronted the multiple dilemmas posed by migration, and, more generally, to insert the issue of gender into the wider interpretations of the immigrant experience.

Since most immigrants entered America in quest of work, and after the 1860s usually industrial work, their relationship to the labor performed assumed a special importance. The vast majority arrived with preindustrial cultural values and confronted a complex urban-industrial economy. This encounter was a crucial factor not only in understanding the patterns of immigrant assimilation and social mobility, but also in comprehending the nature of American industrialization and the processes by which an American working class came into being. Through their collective labor as workers, their actions as union members, and their varied responses to exploitation and insecurity, immigrants were critical elements in the shaping of a modern American economy and labor force. Researchers are continuing to explore the exact nature of this dialectical relationship as they attempt to link immigrant values and expectations with the demands of the workplace.

Just as scholars have pursued the immigrant into the factory, home, and mutual aid society, so too have they entered the doors of immigrant churches in their investigations. The denominational pluralism that has characterized American society is a direct outgrowth of the nation's ethnic pluralism. Older works concentrated on examining the institutional histories of different immigrant religions and on the conflict engendered by such issues as parochial education and the formation of national parishes. More recently scholars have moved the study of America's religious tapestry out of church buildings and diocesan boardrooms and into the streets and neighborhoods. By examining the "popular piety" of immigrants, researchers hope to understand more clearly the ways in which new arrivals integrated the actual practice of religion into their everyday lives.

Investigators have already learned much about the relationships between ethnicity and political behavior. Indeed, one of the most surprising findings of the "new political history" was the discovery that ethnocultural considerations—often in the form of religious indentifications—were critical influences in shaping American voting patterns. Election outcomes in many parts of the nation often hinged on such factors. Indeed, perhaps no aspect of the American political arena has been immune to the force of ethnicity. Currently, researchers have been interested in determining how immigrants shaped a political culture of their own as they adapted to the American environment. Arriving from dissimilar backgrounds and frequently containing within their ranks followers of many different political ideologies, immigrants cannot be neatly classified into simple categories. Whether as supporters of urban machines, leftist critics of American capitalism, or as second and third generation politicians pushing group demands, immigrants and their progeny have been essential ingredients in the American political equation.

The American educational system similarly underwent profound transformation due to the immigrant presence. Many newcomers approached this powerful institution with ambivalent feelings since education in America offered both an opportunity for future progress and a danger to valued traditions. For their part, schools and school officials were forced to cope with unprecedented problems of space, curriculum, rules of discipline, attendance, and staffing. Immigrants ultimately found it necessary to judge the worth of education defined in new-world terms, both in relation to themselves and their children. They reacted in various ways, ranging from the formation of separate educational initiatives that sought to maintaine cherished values to the avoidance of formal educational institutions altogether. One thing was certain: both sides of the equation were changed by the contact.

America responded to the immigrant presence in varied ways. During periods of crisis, the host society often reacted by promoting rigid programs of Americanization that sought to strip away foreign customs and values. Research has shown that even programs of assistance and outreach, such as those offered by settlement houses and philanthropic agencies, often contained strong doses of social control. Immigrants were not unaware of these elements and frequently reacted to these and such programs as bilingual education and affirmative action have engendered sharp public division. The present collection of essays, therefore, should be seen as providing the first installment of an important research agenda that needs to be open-ended in scope, responsive to new methodologies and interpretations, and cognizant of its relevance to contemporary American society.

The editor wishes to thank Leonard Dinnerstein, Victor Greene, Robert Singerman, Jeffrey Adler, Robert Zieger, and especially Rudolph Vecoli and Donna Gabaccia, for their helpful advice on this project.

GEORGE E. POZZETTA

AMERICAN IMMIGRATION & ETHNICITY

A 20-Volume Series of Distinguished Essays

EDITED BY
George E. Pozzetta

VOLUME 1

THEMES IN IMMIGRATION HISTORY

ERRATA
Replacement Pages

ISBN 0-8240-7401-7

initiatives with caution and skepticism. Of course, newcomers could seldom shield themselves so easily from the nativist outbursts that have periodically gripped the nation. Anti-immigrant hostility, with its attendant discriminatory practices and negative stereotyping, has been a feature of America's past, particularly during periods when the nation has felt threatened.

Since the United States continues as the world's greatest immigrant receiving nation, the need for clear-eyed scholarship dealing with immigration, assimilation, and ethnic group development remains high. An informed understanding of these critical issues is necessary to underpin effective public policy. The vigorous national debate over immigration and the treatment of ethnic minorities that has persisted since the 1960s suggests that little consensus among policy makers currently exists. More pointedly, the cultural politics surrounding immigration legislation, renewed outbreaks of nativism, and such programs as bilingual education and affirmative action have engendered sharp public division. The present collection of essays, therefore, should be seen as providing the first installment of an important research agenda that needs to be open-ended in scope, responsive to new methodologies and interpretations, and cognizant of its relevance to contemporary American society.

The editor wishes to thank Leonard Dinnerstein, Victor Greene, Robert Singerman, Jeffrey Adler, Robert Zieger, and especially Rudolph Vecoli and Donna Gabaccia, for their helpful advice on this project.

GEORGE E. POZZETTA

SUPPLEMENTAL READING

Thomas Archdeacon, "Problems and Possibilities in the Study of American Immigration and Ethnic History," *International Migration Review*, 19 (Spring 1985), 112–134.

———, *Becoming American: An Ethnic History* (New York: Free Press, 1983).

John Bodnar, *The Transplanted: A History of Immigrants in Urban America* (Bloomington: Indiana University Press, 1985).

Oscar Handlin, *The Uprooted: The Epic Story of the Great Migrations that Made the American People* (Boston: Little Brown and Co., 2nd ed., 1973).

Marcus Lee Hansen, *The Atlantic Migration, 1607–1860* (Cambridge: Harvard University Press, 1940).

———, *The Immigrant in American History* (Cambridge: Harvard University Press, 1941).

John Higham, *Send These to Me: Immigrants in Urban America* (Baltimore: The Johns Hopkins University Press, 1984).

Michael J. Piore, *Birds of Passage: Migrant Labor and Industrial Societies* (Cambridge: Cambridge University Press, 1979).

Franklin Scott, *The Peopling of America: Perspectives on Immigration* [AHA Pamphlets #241] (Washington, D.C., 1972).

Maxine Seller, *To Seek America: A History of Ethnic Life in the United States* (New York: Jerome Ozer, 1988, 2nd ed.).

Philip Taylor, *The Distant Magnet: European Emigration to the U.S.A.* (New York, 1972).

Peter Temin, "Labor Scarcity in America," *Journal of Interdisciplinary History*, 1 (Winter 1971), 251–264.

Stephan Thernstrom, ed., *Harvard Encyclopedia of American Ethnic Groups* (Cambridge: Harvard University Press, 1980).

Frank Thistlethwaite, "Migration from Europe Overseas in the Nineteenth and Twentieth Centuries," *Rapports: XIe Congress International des Sciences Historiques*, 5 (Stockholm, 1960), 32–60.

David Ward, *Poverty, Ethnicity, and the American City, 1840–1925: Changing Conceptions of the Slum and the Ghetto* (Cambridge: Cambridge University Press, 1989).

Virginia Yans-McLaughlin, *Immigration Reconsidered: History, Sociology and Politics* (New York: Oxford University Press, 1990).

SUPPLEMENTAL READING

Tomas Almaguer, "Racial Discrimination and Class Conflict in Capitalist Agriculture: The Oxnard Sugar Beet Worker's Strike of 1903," *Labor History*, 25 (Summer 1984), 325–350.

Mie Liang Bickner, "The Forgotten Minority: Asian American Women," *Amerasia Journal*, 11 (Spring 1974), 1–17.

Melvin Dubofsky, "Organized Labor and the Immigrant in New York City, 1900–1918," *Labor History*, 2 (1961), 182–201.

Melvin Dubofsky, "Success and Failure of Socialism in New York City, 1900–1918," *Labor History*, 9 (Fall 1968), 361–375.

Charlotte Erickson, "Emigration from the British Isles to the U.S.A. in 1831," *Population Studies*, 35 (1981), 175–197.

Frances H. Early, "The French Canadian Family Economy and Standard-of-Living in Lowell, Massachusetts, 1870," *Journal of Family History*, 7 (Summer 1982), 180–199.

Howard M. Gitelman, "No Irish Need Apply: Patterns of and Response to Ethnic Discrimination in the Labor Market," *Labor History*, 14 (1973), 56–68.

Philip Gleason, "Confusion Compounded: The Melting Pot in the 1960s and 1970s," *Ethnicity*, 6 (1979), 10–20.

Philip Gleason, "The Melting Pot: Symbol of Fusion or Confusion?" *American Quarterly* SVI (Spring 1974), 20–46.

Bruce C. Levine, "Immigrant Workers, 'Equal Rights,' and Antislavery: The Germans of Newark, New Jersey," *Labor History*, 25 (Winter 1984), 26–52.

Hubert Perrier, "The Socialists and the Working Class in New York, 1890–1896," *Labor History*, 22, No. 4 (Fall 1981), 485–511.

Thaddeus Radzialowski, "Immigrant Nationalism and Feminism: Glos Polek and the Polish Women's Alliance in America, 1898–1980," *Review Journal of Philosophy and Social Science*, 2 (1972), 183–203.

Robert Swierenga, "Dutch Immigrant Demography, 1820–1880," *Journal of Family History*, 5 (Winter 1980), 390–405.

Peter Temin, "Labor Scarcity in America," *Journal of Interdisciplinary History*, 1 (Winter 1971), 251–264.

CONTENTS

Samuel L. Baily, "The Adjustment of Italian Immigrants in Buenos Aires and New York, 1870–1914," *American Historical Review*, 88:2 (April 1983), 281–305. 1

Ronald H. Bayor, "Italians, Jews and Ethnic Conflict," *International Migration Review*, 6 (Winter 1972), 377–391. 27

John Bodnar, "Immigration, Kinship and the Rise of Working-Class Realism in Industrial America," *Journal of Social History*, 14:1 (Fall 1980), 45–65. 43

A. W. Carlson, "One Century of Foreign Immigration to the United States: 1880-1979," *International Migration*, 23:3 (September 1985), 309–334. 65

Roger Daniels, "Chinese and Japanese in North America: The Canadian and American Experiences Compared," *The Canadian Review of American Studies*, 17:2 (Summer 1986), 173–187. 91

Oscar Handlin, "Historical Perspectives on the American Ethnic Group," *Daedalus* (Spring 1961), 220–232. 106

Marcus L. Hansen, "The History of American Immigration as a Field for Research," *American Historical Review*, 32 (April 1927), 500–518. 120

R. F. Harney, "The Commerce of Migration," *Canadian Ethnic Studies, 9:1 (1977)*, 42–53. 140

James A. Henretta, "Social History as Lived and Written," *American Historical Review*, 84:5 (December 1979), 1293–1322. 153

John Higham, "Hanging Together: Divergent Unities in American History," *Journal of American History*, 61 (June 1974), 5–28. 183

John Higham, "The Mobilization of Immigrants in Urban America," *Norwegian-American Studies*, 31 (1986), 3–33. 207

David A. Hollinger, "Ethnic Diversity, Cosmopolitanism and the Emergence of the American Liberal Intelligentsia," *American Quarterly*, 27:2 (May 1975), 133–151. 239

Herbert S. Klein, "The Integration of Italian Immigrants into the United States and Argentina: A Comparative Analysis," *American Historical Review*, 88:2 (April 1983), 306–329. 258

Moses Rischin, "Beyond the Great Divide: Immigration and the Last Frontier," *Journal of American History*, 55 (December 1968), 42–53. 282

Jonathan D. Sarna, "The Spectrum of Jewish Leadership in Ante-Bellum America," *Journal of American Ethnic History*, 1:2 (Spring 1982), 59–67. 295

Arthur Meier Schlesinger, "The Significance of Immigration in American History," *American Journal of Sociology*, 27 (July 1921–May 1922), 71–85. 305

Timothy L. Smith, "New Approaches to the History of Immigration in Twentieth-Century America," *American Historical Review*, 71:4, (July 1966), 1265–1279. 321

Rudolph J. Vecoli, "*Contadini* in Chicago: A Critique of *The Uprooted*," *Journal of American History*, 51:3 (December 1964), 404–417. 336

Acknowledgments 351

The Adjustment of Italian Immigrants in Buenos Aires and New York, 1870–1914

SAMUEL L. BAILY

AMEDEO CANUTI AND GIUSEPPE TRIMORA left Italy for the Americas at the turn of the past century. Amedeo was born in the tiny Adriatic fishing village of Sirolo in 1865. When the town's fishing industry came upon hard times during the latter part of the nineteenth century, he and his three brothers went to Buenos Aires. In 1894 Amedeo was recorded in the membership lists of a leading mutual aid society as a literate, twenty-nine-year old sailor who lived with six fellow villagers at 175 Calle La Madrid in the Boca, the center of Argentina's maritime industry. He later married and moved with his family to the nearby town of Quilmes, where he became the owner of a grocery store. Giuseppe's background was somewhat different. As an unmarried Sicilian of thirty-two, he migrated to New York in 1896. The census of 1900 records him as living with eighty other individuals, all but five of whom were Italian, in a tenement house at 228 Elizabeth Street in the heart of one of the city's many Sicilian colonies. Giuseppe could not read, write, or speak English. He listed his occupation as laborer, but at the time of the census he had been unemployed for several months.[1]

Amedeo and Guiseppe were joined by millions of their countrymen who migrated to Argentina and the United States before World War I. Some remained permanently in their adopted country. Others returned home. Still others went back and forth many times. By 1914, however, nearly a million Italians lived in Argentina and a million and a half in the United States. In each country, the Italian immigrants settled primarily in the urban areas, especially in the rapidly growing commercial and industrial port cities of Buenos Aires and New York. When World War I broke out, three hundred and twelve thousand Italians—one-third of the total in Argentina—lived in Buenos Aires, and three hundred and seventy

I wish to thank the American Philosophical Society, the Rutgers University Research Council, and the Social Science Research Council for financial support, which made possible four trips to Argentina and two to Italy to gather data for this study of Italian immigration to Buenos Aires and New York. I also would like to thank Michael Adas, Jane Orttung, Adrienne Scerbak, Mark Wasserman, the members of the Rutgers Social History group, and especially Joan G. Baily for their insightful comments on earlier drafts of this article. They are not, of course, responsible for any shortcomings that may still remain.

[1] Alfredo Canuti, Interview with Samuel L. Baily, Numana, Italy, May 12, 1980; Colonia Italiana, "Libri d'inscrizione dei soci, 1894," Archiv d'Unione e Benevolenza, Buenos Aires; and U.S. Federal Census Schedules, Manuscript, 1900, New York City, enumeration district 128, A2, B2.

thousand Italians—one-quarter of the total in the United States—lived in New York.

What happened to Amedeo, Guiseppe, and the hundreds of thousands of Italians who went to Buenos Aires and New York at the turn of the century is the central focus of this essay. As these immigrants looked for jobs and housing and attempted to make a better life for themselves and their children, how did they interact with each other and with those already living in the two cities? What were the similarities and differences in the patterns of adjustment? And why?[2]

Scholars in various disciplines have devoted considerable attention to Italian migration to the Americas.[3] Although this cumulative scholarly effort has increased our understanding of the process of Italian migration, it has fallen short in several important respects. Among the most important, the coverage of the subject is uneven. Much more has been written about the United States and Italy than about Argentina, Brazil, or Canada. The literature on the United States, moreover, is not only extensive but also more developed in terms of local and topical studies. A second shortcoming is that this work, with few exceptions, is not comparative. Although the Italians immigrated in substantial numbers to several American countries, few scholars have analyzed more than one receiving country. Furthermore, many students of Italian migration have focused on isolated parts of the subject, unmindful of the interrelatedness of the various aspects of the experience. Some, for example, have written exclusively about the receiving society as though nothing of importance had happened before the immigrants got off the boat. Others have accounted for the development of the process solely in economic terms, with little or no mention of social, cultural, psychological, political, or other noneconomic variables. Finally, authors have frequently confused their readers by using such broad, imprecise, and in general poorly defined terms as assimilation, absorption, and integration.

My own work during the past decade and a half has impressed upon me the

[2] In this essay, I am dealing with the Italians as a group, not as individuals. Amedeo Canuti and Giuseppe Trimora illustrate some of the characteristics of their respective groups of Italian immigrants, but certainly not all.

[3] The literature on Italian migration is extensive. Some representative works on Italians in the United States and Argentina include Robert F. Foerster, *The Italian Immigration of Our Times* (Cambridge, Mass., 1919), and "The Italian Factor in the Race Stock of Argentina," *Quarterly Publications of the American Statistical Association*, 16 (1919): 347–60; Luciano J. Iorizzo and Salvatore Mondello, *The Italian Americans* (New York, 1971); Alexander DeConde, *Half Bitter, Half Sweet: An Excursion into Italian American History* (New York, 1971); Silvano M. Tomasi and Madeline H. Engel, eds., *The Italian Experience in the United States* (New York, 1970); Humberto S. Nelli, *Italians in Chicago, 1880–1930* (New York, 1970); Andrew F. Rolle, *The Immigrant Upraised: Adventurers and Colonists in an Expanding America* (Norman, Okla., 1968), and *The Italian Americans: Troubled Roots* (New York, 1980); Edwin Fenton, *Immigrants and Unions—A Case Study: Italians and American Labor, 1870–1920* (New York, 1975); George E. Pozzetta, "The Italians of New York City, 1890–1914" (Ph.D. dissertation, University of North Carolina, 1971); Carla Bianco, *The Two Rosetos* (Bloomington, Ind., 1974); Leonard Covello, *The Social Background of the Italo-American School Child* (Totowa, N.J., 1972); Thomas Kessner, *The Golden Door: Italian and Jewish Immigrant Mobility in New York City, 1880–1915* (New York, 1977); Grazia Dore, *La Democrazia italiana e l'emigrazione in America* (Brescia, 1964); Gino Germani, *Política y sociedad en una época de transición* (Buenos Aires, 1962), and "Mass Immigration and Modernization in Argentina," in Irving Louis Horowitz, ed. *Masses in Latin America* (New York, 1970), 289–330; Antonio Franceschini, *L'Emigrazione italiana nell'America del Sud* (Rome, 1908); Emilio Zuccarini, *I Lavori degli italiani nell República Argentina* (Buenos Aires, 1910); Carl Solberg, "Mass Migrations in Argentina, 1870–1970," in William H. McNeill and R. S. Adams, eds., *Human Migration* (Bloomington, Ind., 1978), 146–70; Gianfausto Rosoli, ed., *Un Secolo di emigrazione italiana* (Rome, 1978); and Ercole Sori, *L'Emigrazione italiana dall'Unità alla Seconda Guerra Mondiale* (Bologna, 1979).

difficulty of grasping the complexity of the Italian migration experience.[4] The literature to date provides a base upon which to build, not only because it contains specific information but also because the shortcomings suggest new approaches and directions for future study. Several recent works, whose authors have already approached the subject in new ways, are particularly useful, and I gratefully acknowledge my indebtedness to them.[5] My intent here is to provide a broad comparative overview of one phase of the process of Italian migration, the immigrants' adjustment to Buenos Aires and New York, to identify the important explanatory variables in the process, and to suggest a framework or model that can be applied to immigrant adjustment in other cities.

Because adjustment is an early phase of assimilation, the meaning of "assimilation" must be established. Scholars have, however, used the term in different ways.[6] Is it a process or a fixed condition? How does it differ from absorption or integration? When does it begin or end? How can it be measured? And what is its outcome? I use the term "assimilation" to refer to the long-term, open-ended process of interaction that begins when the immigrants first come into contact with a new environment and with the people living there. Adjustment is the first phase of this process, in which the immigrants develop the knowledge, skill, and organization that enable them to function effectively. The advantage to focusing on adjustment lies in the ease with which it can be identified and in the ability to measure it accurately by how quickly and how easily immigrants are able to find housing and employment, to improve their circumstances, and to develop organizations to protect their interests.

ALMOST ALL OF THE ITALIANS who went to Buenos Aires and New York did so primarily to earn more money than they had in Italy—either to send back home or to improve their living conditions in the New World, or perhaps a combination of both. To earn more, however, they first had to find work and housing. The

[4] This essay forms part of a larger study in progress on Italians in Buenos Aires and New York City during the period of mass migration from 1875 to 1925. For some of my thoughts on the subject, see "The Italians and Organized Labor in the United States and Argentina, 1880–1910," *International Migration Review* [hereafter, *IMR*], 1 (1967): 55–66, "The Italians and the Development of Organized Labor in Argentina, Brazil, and the United States, 1880–1914," *Journal of Social History*, 3 (1969): 123–34, "The Role of the Press and the Assimiliation of Italians in Buenos Aires and São Paulo, 1893–1913," *IMR*, 12 (1978): 321–40, "Marriage Patterns and Immigrant Assimilation in Buenos Aires, 1882–1923," *Hispanic American Historical Review*, 60 (1980): 32–48, "Chain Migration of Italians to Argentina: Case Studies of the Agnonesi and the Sirolesi," *Studi Emigrazione* (Rome), 19 (1982): 73–91, and "Las Sociedades de ayuda mutua y el desarrollo de una comunidad italiana en Buenos Aires, 1858–1918," *Desarrollo Económico* (Buenos Aires), 21 (1982): 485–514.

[5] Josef J. Barton, *Peasants and Strangers: Italians, Rumanians, and Slovaks in an American City, 1890–1950* (Cambridge, Mass., 1975); Rudolph M. Bell, *Fate and Honor, Family and Village: Demographic and Cultural Change in Rural Italy since 1800* (Chicago, 1979); John W. Briggs, *An Italian Passage: Immigrants to Three American Cities, 1890–1930* (New Haven, 1978); Robert F. Harney, "Ambiente and Social Class in North American Little Italies," *Canadian Review of Studies in Nationalism*, 2 (1975): 208–24; Frank Sturino, "Inside the Chain: A Case Study of South Italian Migration to North America, 1880–1930" (Ph.D. dissertation, University of Toronto, 1981); Mark D. Szuchman, *Mobility and Integration in Urban Argentina: Córdoba in the Liberal Era* (Austin, Texas, 1980); and Rudolph J. Vecoli, "Contadini in Chicago: A Critique of *The Uprooted*," *Journal of American History*, 51 (1964): 404–17.

[6] For a useful evaluation of the literature on assimilation, see Charles Price, "The Study of Assimilation," in J. A. Jackson, ed., *Migration* (New York, 1969), 181–237. Also see S. N. Eisenstadt, *The Absorption of Immigrants* (London, 1954); Milton M. Gordon, *Assimilation in American Life* (New York, 1964); Gino Germani, "Assimila-

3

temporary migrant, who was interested in maximizing his short-term savings, was willing to live in the least expensive housing, no matter how crowded or unhealthy, and to accept any job.[7] Those who decided to remain for some time, however, sought to improve their living and working conditions and to form organizations to protect their interests.[8] Here I am focusing primarily on the permanent migrant. The cumulative search by thousands of Italians in Buenos Aires and New York for jobs and housing, for better living and working conditions, and for collective forms of protection created patterns that can be studied and compared. To the degree that Italians in one city obtained better positions, experienced more occupational and residential upward mobility, and formed more effective community organizations than those in the other city, they "adjusted" more rapidly and successfully to their new environment. Just what were these "patterns"?

Buenos Aires and New York were the leading ports and economic centers of their respective countries at the turn of the century. Although Buenos Aires was a provincial town of one hundred and eighty thousand inhabitants in 1869, it became during the next forty-five years a major metropolis with a population of one million six hundred thousand. In 1870, New York was already a leading industrial and commercial city with a population of just under a million people. By 1914, it had grown to more than five million.[9] The success of the Italians in their economic pursuits in these two cities is an important indicator of adjustment.

Foreign workers and owners dominated the commercial and industrial sectors of the Buenos Aires economy. As early as 1887, Italians, who accounted for 32 percent of the population, made up 53 percent of the workers in industry, 57.5 percent of the owners of industrial establishments, 39 percent of the workers in commerce, and 16 percent of the owners of commercial establishments. Native Argentines, who made up 47 percent of the population, represented only slightly more than 20 percent of both workers and owners in commerce, 16 percent of the workers in industry, and less than 10 percent of the owners of industrial establishments. During the next three decades, Italian workers and owners in industry gradually declined to between 35 and 40 percent, largely because second-generation Italians were recorded as Argentines. In commerce, however, although the percentage of Italian workers remained the same, that of owners more than

---

tion of Immigrants in Urban Areas," *Working Papers,* Instituto Torcuato Di Tella (Buenos Aires, 1966); John Goldlust and A. H. Richmond, "A Multivariate Model of Immigrant Adaptation," *IMR,* 8 (1974): 193–227; J. J. Mangalam and H. K. Schwarzweller, "General Theory in the Study of Migration: Current Needs and Difficulties," *ibid.,* 3 (1968): 3–17, and "Some Theoretical Guidelines toward a Sociology of Migration," *ibid.,* 4 (1970): 5–20.

[7] To avoid the cumbersome he/she, him/her, and his/hers, I use he, him, and his throughout to refer to any individual immigrant, either male or female.

[8] Many scholars make the distinction between temporary migrants (sojourners) and permanent migrants (immigrants). The definition of these terms is, however, often imprecise. I use "temporary migrant" to refer to those migrants who left Italy with the intention of returning or who returned within five years. "Permanent migrant" refers to those who left Italy with the intention of remaining abroad or who did, in fact, remain there for more than five years. See J. D. Gould, "European Inter-Continental Emigration—The Road Home: Return Migration from the U.S.A.," *Journal of European Economic History,* 9 (1980): 41–112; and Betty Boyd Caroli, *Italian Repatriation from the United States, 1900–1914* (New York, 1973).

[9] Ira Rosenwaike, *Population History of New York City* (Syracuse, N.Y., 1972), 63, 93, 102; and Guy Bourdé, *Urbanisation et immigration en Amérique Latine: Buenos Aires* (Paris, 1974), 174.

doubled. Throughout the period, the percentage of Italian immigrants active in these areas stayed above that of native Argentines.[10]

In New York, the situation was fundamentally different in large part because the Italians there formed such a small percentage of the total population and, as such, had little chance of dominating any sector of the economy. Although Italians never represented as large a percentage of workers or owners in industry and commerce as did native Americans, they formed a substantial proportion of the workers in personal and domestic service. In 1900, when they accounted for 4.2 percent of the population, they represented 17 percent of the workers in service positions. Most notably, 55 percent of the male barbers and hairdressers and 97 percent of the bootblacks were Italian. Italians were also slightly overrepresented in manufacturing and mechanical pursuits; they accounted for 5.5 percent of the total, including 34 percent of the shoemakers and 18 percent of the masons. And 9 percent of the retail merchants and 16 percent of the peddlers were Italian.[11] Thus, although Italians in New York were numerous in a few occupations, they never dominated any sector of the economy as Italians did in industry and to a lesser extent commerce in Buenos Aires.

The relative distribution of Italians in white- and blue-collar occupations also differed in the two cities. Both in 1880 and in 1905, approximately three-quarters of the Italians in New York were blue-collar workers, most of whom were in unskilled or semi-skilled construction, transportation, factory, or domestic service jobs. White-collar peddlers, shopkeepers, and barbers accounted for most of the remaining one-quarter. High white-collar occupations provided only 2 percent of the total. The only significant group of professionals were musicians and teachers of music.[12] Most Italians in Buenos Aires also held blue-collar jobs, but a substantially higher proportion (30 to 35 percent in Buenos Aires versus 13 to 22 percent in New York) were skilled workers. Although approximately one-quarter entered white-collar occupations, as was the case in New York, the distribution differed; many more Italians in Buenos Aires were owners of small industrial and commercial establishments as opposed to peddlers and barbers. Furthermore, although the percentage of high white-collar jobs was small in Buenos Aires, it was twice as large as that in New York (4 percent compared to 2 percent); there were significant numbers of Italians in Buenos Aires among the health, education, and fine arts professionals and among engineers.[13]

[10] Manual arts are included in industry. Some of the figures for Argentina are estimates based on Buenos Aires, *Censo general de la Ciudad de Buenos Aires, 1887*, 2 (Buenos Aires, 1889): 36, 306, 379, and *Censo general de la Ciudad de Buenos Aires, 1909*, 1 (Buenos Aires, 1910): 132, 135, 150, 155.

[11] U.S. Senate, 61st Congress, 3d Session, *Reports of the Immigration Commission* [hereafter, U.S. Immigration Commission, *Reports*], 41 vols. (Washington, 1911), 28: 168–76; and U.S. Bureau of the Census, *Special Reports: Occupations at the Twelfth Census* (Washington, 1904), 634–38.

[12] U.S. Immigration Commission, *Reports*, 23: 168–76; U.S. Bureau of the Census, *Special Reports: Occupations*, 634–38; and Kessner, *The Golden Door*, 52.

[13] These figures are estimates based on the data in República Argentina, *Segundo Censo nacional de la República Argentina, 1895*, 2 (Buenos Aires, 1898): 47–50, and *Tercer Censo nacional de la República Argentina, 1914*, 10 vols. (Buenos Aires, 1916), 4: 201–12. Also see Herbert S. Klein, "La Integración de inmigrantes italianos en la Argentina y los Estados Unidos: Un Análisis comparativo," *Desarrollo Económico* (Buenos Aires), 21 (1981): 3–27. Another important set of figures to compare is relative real wages and buying power. Some information exists for both Argentina and the United States, but the comparison is hazardous, and I have not yet worked

5

Figure 1: Bank ("Banca Italiana") and Bar of Liccione, Pittaro, and Co., corner of Hester and Mulberry Streets, New York, 1893. (The bank's earlier headquarters are shown on the front cover.) Pittaro is second from left and G. Liccione is second from right. When this photograph was taken, the new proprietors had not yet taken down the sign above the store from the previous owner, Henry Elias, a brewer. University of Minnesota, Twin Cities, Immigration History Research Center Collection, Vito Pittaro Papers.

The Italian immigrant groups in both cities experienced some upward occupational mobility but of a different sort. Although there was a substantial increase in semi-skilled (7 to 16 percent) and skilled (13 to 22 percent) Italian workers in New York between 1880 and 1905, there was a decline among white-collar workers (25 to 18 percent). In Buenos Aires, the percentage of both skilled and white-collar Italian workers increased slightly between 1895 and 1914. And a few immigrants were able to move into the leadership ranks of the army, the church, and politics. Thus, there was some upward mobility among Italians in New York, but it was confined to blue-collar workers; in Buenos Aires, however, mobility—however slight—extended to white-collar occupations as well.[14]

Italians in Buenos Aires also played a more significant role in local workers' and

out a satisfactory analysis. See Roberto Cortes Conde, *El Progreso Argentino, 1880–1914* (Buenos Aires, 1979), 240–69; Paul H. Douglas, *Real Wages in the United States, 1890–1926* (New York, 1966); Clarence D. Long, *Wages and Earnings in the United States, 1860–1890* (Princeton, 1960); and Albert Rees, *Real Wages in Manufacturing, 1890–1914* (Princeton, 1961).

[14] The Buenos Aires figures are estimates based on República Argentina, *Segundo Censo nacional de ... 1895*, 47–50, and *Tercer Censo nacional de ... 1914*, 4: 201–12. Also see Kessner, *The Golden Door*, 52; U.S. Bureau of the Census, *Special Reports: Occupations*, 634–38; José Luis de Imaz, *Los Que Mandan* (Albany, N.Y., 1970); Dario Canton, *El Parlamento Argentino en épocas de cambio* (Buenos Aires, 1965); and Robert A. Potash, *The Army and Politics in Argentina* (Stanford, 1969). Many second-generation Italians moved rapidly into positions of leadership in Argentine society. One of them, Carlos Pellegrini, was president of the country from 1890 to 1892.

employers' organizations than did those in New York. Organized labor in Buenos Aires was almost completely the product of the various immigrant groups. In the 1880s and 1890s the immigrants attempted several times to organize national confederations, and by the first decade of the twentieth century they had succeeded in establishing two rival organizations. Italians made up about 40 percent of the organized workers, provided the most important leadership within the movement, and were much more active in labor organizations and in strikes than were native Argentines. In New York, the Italians were slow to organize. The Immigration Commission concluded that southern Italians were less organized than native workers or foreigners in general. Although by 1914 Italian stevedores, garment workers, bricklayers, and barbers had achieved some success at organizing, they never played a leadership role in New York or on the national level.[15]

The same pattern held true for employers' organizations. Italians were influential in the development and growth of the Argentine Industrial Union. From its founding in 1887, at least 20 percent of the administrative council and one of its officers was a first- or second-generation Italian, and an Italian was president of the Industrial Union in twenty-one of the thirty-one years between 1905 and 1935. In New York, Italians played no role in the development of the National Association of Manufacturers, and not one of the presidents or members of the executive committee was a first- or second-generation Italian during the first twenty years of the organization's existence (1895–1914).[16]

The patterns of Italian participation in economic life in Buenos Aires and New York were strikingly different. In Buenos Aires, Italians—who accounted for a much larger percentage of the total population—naturally represented a higher percentage of the workers. Yet they were more effective than those in New York in areas where numbers alone did not make the difference. They formed a higher percentage of the skilled and white-collar workers than their relative proportion of the population, as a group experienced greater upward mobility especially among skilled and white-collar workers, were more active than the native Argentines in the economy, and were a major force in the development of workers' and employers' organizations. Italians in New York, in contrast, were less successful than their counterparts in Buenos Aires at obtaining jobs in the upper levels of the occupational structure and at organizing to protect their economic interests.

Housing was another major concern of the Italian immigrants to both cities. Most immigrants started out in the crowded, low-rent districts in the center of the metropolitan area, where living conditions were poor. To improve their situation, many Italians moved to homes they could buy and to residences outside the center

---

[15] Baily, "Italians and Organized Labor" (1967), 55–66; U.S. Immigration Commission, *Reports*, 7: 417–19, and 23: 368–75; Pozzetta, "The Italians of New York City, 1890–1914," 337–64; and Fenton, *Immigrants and Unions—A Case Study*, 574.

[16] Eugene G. Sharkey, "Union Industrial Argentina, 1887–1920: Problems of Industrial Development" (Ph.D. dissertation, Rutgers University, 1978), 46–89. Professor Sharkey very kindly shared with me data on the nationality of the UIA leadership, which is not included in his dissertation. Also see Albert K. Steigerwalt, *The National Association of Manufacturers, 1895–1914: A Study in Business Leadership* (Ann Arbor, Mich., 1964), 175–83.

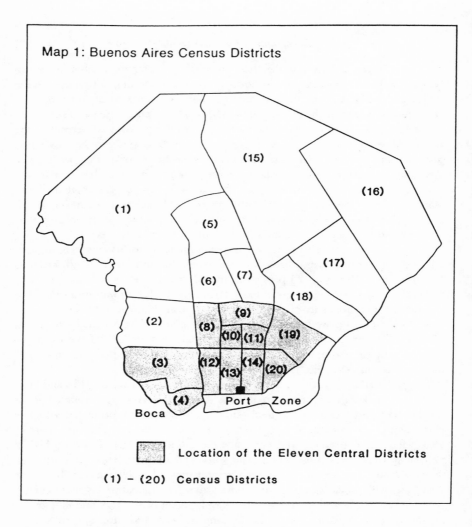

Map 1: Buenos Aires Census Districts

(15)

(16)

(1)

(5)

(17)

(6)   (7)

(18)

(2)   (9)

(8)

(10)(11)   (19)

(3)   (12)   (14)   (20)

(13)

(4)   Port   Zone

Boca

Location of the Eleven Central Districts

(1) – (20)   Census Districts

city. Italians in Buenos Aires were more dispersed throughout the city in 1887 and in 1904 than those in New York. In 1904, they—like the rest of the population— lived predominantly in the eleven census districts located within a three-mile radius of the downtown business center, and they accounted for at least 14 percent of the total population in every district (see Map 1). They did, nevertheless, cluster somewhat within this area; while 41 percent lived in the five districts on the perimeter of the downtown business center (3, 4, 8, 9, and 19), only 29 percent resided in the six most central districts (12, 13, 14, 20, 10, and 11). Italians in New York, however, concentrated in only a few areas. By the 1870s, a substantial number lived in the sixth and fourteenth wards of Manhattan, and they gradually spread out into several neighboring wards and into Harlem, in the area between Second Avenue and 110th Street (see Map 2). In 1890, 64 percent lived in the Bowery colony and another 10 percent in Harlem. Gradually they moved to other

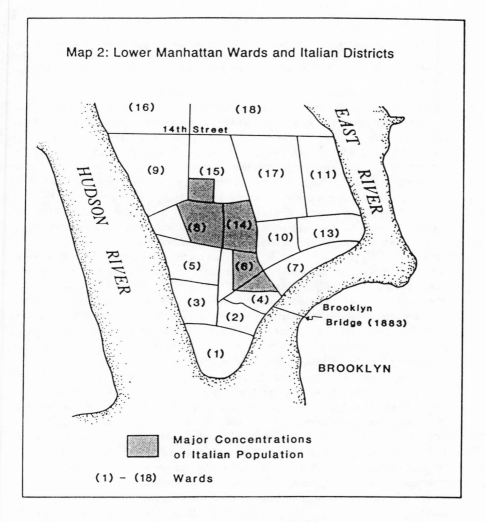

Map 2: Lower Manhattan Wards and Italian Districts

Major Concentrations
of Italian Population

(1) – (18)   Wards

areas of the city, but before World War I they for the most part remained in these areas of Manhattan.[17]

The living conditions of the Italians in both cities were generally poor. Most suffered from the effects of overcrowding, inadequate sanitary facilities, and unsatisfactory health conditions. A description of New York immigrant housing by the Tenement House Department could equally well have been applied to Buenos Aires.

Many cases have been found where plumbing fixtures have been removed and the pipes left open. . . . [T]he tenants have used the dumbwaiter shaft as a chute for the disposal of

[17] Buenos Aires, *Censo general* . . . , *1887*, 33, 65, and *Censo general de la Ciudad de Buenos Aires, 1904* (Buenos Aires, 1906), 6, 84; República Argentina, *Tercer Censo nacional de . . . 1914*, 2: 129–48; Kessner, *The Golden Door*, 127–60; U.S. Industrial Commission, *Reports*, 15 (Washington, 1902): 471–74; and U.S. Bureau of the Census, *Vital Statistics of New York and Brooklyn, 1885–1900* (Washington, 1901), 230–37.

rubbish, fecal matter and garbage. . . . [T]he water closets have been stopped up for weeks. . . . Often the roofs are not repaired, and after a storm the water soaks through the plastered ceilings. . . . Bedrooms are often festooned with cobwebs hanging from the ceiling.[18]

Yet the Italians in Buenos Aires were somewhat better off. In the Argentine capital, less than one-quarter lived in crowded tenement houses, compared to more than three-quarters in New York. In addition, the population density per acre of the Italian districts in New York was approximately 50 percent higher than it was in Buenos Aires. The remaining, nontenement-house working-class living quarters in Buenos Aires may not have been much better, but at least they were less crowded.[19]

Property ownership was also higher among the Italians in Buenos Aires. In 1887 and in 1904 approximately 12 percent owned their own homes, and by 1914 this figure had risen to 17.6 percent. Even in the areas of heaviest concentration, such as the Boca (district 4), the percentage of Italian homeowners was substantial: 8 percent in 1904 and 11 percent in 1914. Data on property ownership in New York are fragmentary but suggestive. The Immigration Commission's survey of 524 households in 1909 indicates that only 1.3 percent of the Italian immigrants owned their homes. Even if that figure were doubled or tripled, to account for the possible underrepresentation of property owners in the sample, it would still be far lower than the percentage for Buenos Aires. Clearly, in the years before World War I, New York Italians were much less successful in achieving the goal of property ownership than were those in Buenos Aires.[20]

Although Italians in both cities changed their residences frequently, they may not have improved their living conditions by doing so. Many immigrants left New York and Buenos Aires for places in other parts of their adopted country, and others relocated within their own neighborhood. We cannot trace those who left either city, nor can we make any meaningful judgments about the significance of intraneighborhood moves. We can, however, measure the movement to the outer areas of the two cities, where conditions were less congested and the opportunity to purchase a home was greater.[21] In Buenos Aires, Italians at first resided almost completely within the central area; as of 1904, 70 percent still remained there (districts 3, 4, 8, 9, 10, 12, 13, 14, 19, and 20). By 1914, however, only 47 percent lived in the center, and 53 percent lived in the outlying districts. Although Italians in New York first settled in Manhattan and gradually spread out to Brooklyn and the other boroughs of the city, they moved from the center at a later date than

[18] City of New York, Tenement House Department, *First Report*, 1 (New York, 1903): 6–7; Luigi Villari, *Gli Stati Uniti d'America e l'emigrazione italiana* (New York, 1975), 212–22; and James R. Scobie, *Buenos Aires: Plaza to Suburb, 1870–1910* (New York, 1974), 146–59.

[19] Kessner, *The Golden Door*, 132; Buenos Aires, *Censo general . . . , 1904*, 84; and Charles S. Sargent, *The Spatial Evolution of Greater Buenos Aires, Argentina, 1870–1930* (Tempe, Ariz., 1974), 150.

[20] The data of the Immigration Commission are limited to heads of Italian households; they do not apply to the Italian population as a whole. Thus, the percentage of all Italians who owned their own homes in New York may have been as low as or lower than the 1.3 percent figure used in the sample. See U.S. Immigration Commission, *Reports*, 26: 209; Kessner, *The Golden Door*, 150–52; and Buenos Aires, *Censo general . . . , 1887*, 104, and *Censo general . . . , 1904*, 84.

[21] U.S. Immigration Commission, *Reports*, 26: 244; Kessner, *The Golden Door*, 142; and Società Italiana Unione e Benevolenza, "Elenco dei soci, 1895–1902," Archiv d'Unione e Benevolenza, Buenos Aires.

those in Buenos Aires. In 1900, 66 percent lived in Manhattan, and ten years later 59 percent still resided there. Only after World War I did more than half of New York's Italians live outside of Manhattan.[22]

Several factors influenced patterns of settlement and dispersion. Italians, especially those who worked long hours for low pay, lived near their places of employment. Italians in New York, therefore, lived below 14th Street in Manhattan, where, as late as 1906, 67 percent of all factory jobs were located. In Buenos Aires, industry and commerce were concentrated in the central area, yet, because the city was not an island, the Italians could spread out and still be close to their jobs. As industry and commerce expanded to other parts of each city, the Italians followed.[23] Although the transportation system influenced where an immigrant might move when he decided to relocate, it did not necessarily determine the timing of his move. Elevated trains began to run from the Battery to Harlem in 1881, which clearly facilitated the development of the Harlem colony. By the early 1900s, however, the subway system connected Brooklyn, Queens, and the Bronx with Manhattan, yet the major outward movement in New York did not occur until after World War I. Although in Buenos Aires the rail system linked various parts of the city, not until the introduction of the electric streetcar and the drastic reduction of fares in the early 1900s did Italians in large numbers begin to move to the outlying districts.[24]

Old World ties also proved important in determining patterns of settlement. Italians in both cities frequently settled and then moved in village- and language-based clusters.[25] Migrants from Agnone to Buenos Aires, for example, lived in District 14, especially in two nearby clusters on Calle Córdoba. Those from Bagnara also lived in District 14, but in a four-block area between Calles Reconquista and 25 de Mayo. Amedeo Canuti and other Sirolesi lived in three clusters within the Boca (District 4). A second colony of Sirolesi developed in Quilmes, about eleven miles and several train stops away from the Boca. Amedeo and one of his brothers moved to Quilmes, but the other brothers remained in the Boca.[26]

Similarly, Italians in New York generally settled by villages. In 1890 the Neapolitans populated the area of Mulberry Bend, the Genovesi Baxter Street near the Five Points area, and the Sicilians, like Giuseppe Trimora, Elizabeth Street between Houston and Spring Streets. In 1920, more than two hundred families from Cinisi, Sicily, lived in the area of 6th Street and Avenue A. Other clusters from

[22] Buenos Aires, *Censo general . . . , 1904*, 6, 84; República Argentina, *Tercer Censo nacional de . . . 1914*, 2: 129–49; and U.S. Bureau of the Census, *Thirteenth Census of the United States . . . , 1910*, 1 (Washington, 1913): 824, 827–28, and *Fourteenth Census of the United States . . . , 1920*, 2 (Washington, 1922): 47, 747–49.

[23] Kessner, *The Golden Door*, 150; Scobie, *Buenos Aires: Plaza to Suburb*, 70–113, 135–46; and Sargent, *Greater Buenos Aires, Argentina*, 22–25.

[24] Kessner, *The Golden Door*, 148–49; Scobie, *Buenos Aires: Plaza to Suburb*, 160–80; and Sargent, *Greater Buenos Aires, Argentina*, 66–76.

[25] These clusters are normally referred to as "chains." The term "chain migration" is subject to differing interpretations, yet most agree on the essential point: informal personal networks of individuals, kinship groups, villagers, and language clusters in the sending and receiving areas were a major influence on how most individual Italians chose their destinations, how they got there, where they settled, how they got jobs, and with whom they associated. For a fuller discussion of this idea, see Baily, "Chain Migration of Italians to Argentina," 73–75.

[26] Baily, "Chain Migration of Italians to Argentina," 73–91.

Cinisi lived in the Bowery, Harlem, and Brooklyn.[27] Presumably, the relationship between the Cinisi colonies in Manhattan and Brooklyn was similar to that of the Sirolo colonies in the Boca and Quilmes.

Although the availability of jobs, inexpensive transportation, and village chains primarily determined patterns of residence and movement, they do not by themselves explain the earlier movement of Italians to outlying areas of Buenos Aires. Circumstantial evidence indicates that the greater ability of the immigrants in Buenos Aires to save does more to account for the early relocation of Italians in the outlying districts of the city. Because more Italians in Buenos Aires held more prestigious, better-paying jobs, they were presumably in a better position to save. Since the main purpose of the move outward was often to buy a house with some land, relocation was postponed until accumulated savings permitted such a purchase. In New York most Italian immigrants were unable to accumulate the necessary savings until after World War I; thus, the move outward came later.[28]

Italians in Buenos Aires were more dispersed, lived in somewhat better physical circumstances, were more successful in acquiring property, and were residentially upwardly mobile at an earlier date than those in New York. This difference must not be overstated. Most Italians in both cities lived in very poor circumstances. Nevertheless, there was a difference. And that difference meant that Italians in Buenos Aires were more likely to have found better housing.

Immigrant institutions often played an important role in the adjustment of the Italians to their new environment. Both in New York and Buenos Aires, the Italians established mutual aid societies, social and recreational clubs, hospitals, banks, chambers of commerce, churches, and newspapers · to help them meet their needs.[29] To the extent that these organizations involved the immigrants, had the necessary resources, and developed representative leadership, they could provide social and economic services and a structure that served to integrate and strengthen the community. The stronger and more united the community, the better able it was to defend the interests of its members within the new society.

Mutual aid societies were the most important of these immigrant institutions; more Italians in both New York and Buenos Aires joined these societies than any other kind of organization. Some societies recruited members exclusively from a specific village or area of Italy. Others were more broadly based, bringing together individuals from all parts of Italy. Still others were formed by workers in the same occupation. All of them sought to provide essential death, sickness, and unemployment benefits for their members as well as a congenial social environment.

Both the New York and Buenos Aires mutualist movements began in the mid-

[27] U.S. Industrial Commission, *Reports*, 474; Pozzetta, "The Italians of New York City, 1890–1914," 995–97; John Horace Mariano, *The Italian Contribution to American Democracy* (New York, 1975), 19–22; and Robert E. Park and Herbert A. Miller, *Old World Traits Transplanted* (New York, 1921), 146–58.
[28] Kessner, *The Golden Door*, 151; and Robert E. Shipley, "On the Outside Looking In: A Social History of the *Porteña* Worker during the 'Golden Age' of Argentine Development, 1914–1930" (Ph.D. dissertation, Rutgers University, 1977), 173–96. The availability of credit was another factor that influenced the timing of the move outward, but I have not been able to gather sufficient data to make a meaningful comparison of the two cities. See Scobie, *Buenos Aires: Plaza to Suburb*, 182–91; and Anton F. Mannel, "New York City Population Trends Related to Mortgage Lending" (Ph.D. dissertation, Rutgers University, 1941), 86–117.
[29] Pozzetta, "The Italians of New York City, 1890–1914," 231–304; and Zuccarini, *I Lavori degli Italiani*.

nineteenth century and expanded with each new wave of immigrants. Although many of the largest and most important societies in Buenos Aires were established before 1880, more were founded during the last two decades of the nineteenth century than at any other time. In New York, growth was very gradual, and by far the greatest number of them were established in the decade or so prior to World War I. By 1910 in Buenos Aires there were seventy-five mutual aid societies with approximately fifty-two thousand members out of an Italian population of some two hundred and eighty thousand. In New York at about the same time there were as many as two thousand societies with an estimated total membership of forty thousand out of an Italian population of three hundred and forty thousand.[50]

The two movements differed in ways that significantly affected their ability to serve their Italian communities. Divisiveness, based on personal rivalries and Old World ties, typified the mutual aid movement in New York. The overwhelming majority of the societies were small (under five hundred members), poorly financed and managed, and restricted to immigrants from the same town or region of Italy. Although a few societies opened their membership to all Italians, these few never attained the size, wealth, or influence necessary to establish effective leadership of the mutualist movement. Most of the societies were made up of artisans, but the top officers frequently were successful businessmen. Louis V. Fugazy, a noted banker and labor agent, was the prime mover in more than one hundred mutual aid societies and was president of fifty. Beginning in 1905, many societies joined the National Order of the Sons of Italy, and that organization thus gradually gained influence within the community. But the Sons of Italy was really a loose confederation of societies, and it too lacked the resources to be of significant help to most immigrants.[31]

In Buenos Aires, however, a number of large societies (one thousand or more members) dominated the movement and provided a distinct kind of leadership. These societies had substantial assets in both buildings and capital reserves. They also performed more extensive services for their members; in addition to the normal insurance and social benefits, they provided schools, medical clinics, hospital care, pharmacies, restaurants, and, in some cases, job placement services. Although skilled artisans formed the largest subgroup of members in most Argentine societies, these organizations also included substantial numbers of semi-skilled and white-collar workers. The leaders came almost exclusively from the white-collar members. Furthermore, Italians from all parts of the peninsula joined these societies and rose to positions of leadership within them. Although local ties, politics, and personal rivalries led to some divisions, the large societies were able to develop a relatively united mutualist movement by World War I.[32] The wealthier,

[50] Figures on the number of mutual aid societies and on their membership vary enormously for New York. Edwin Fenton's figures seem the most reasonable to me; *Immigrants and Unions—A Case Study*, 50. Also see "L'Elemento italiano rappresentato nelle associazione di New York, Brooklyn, Hoboken, e Newark, 1884," Archive of the Center for Migration, New York; "Le Società italiane all'estero nel 1908," *Bollettino dell'Emigrazione*, 24 (1908): 1–147; "Le Società italiane negli Stati Uniti dell'America del Nord," *ibid.*, 4 (1912): 19–54; and Baily, "Las Sociedades de ayuda mutua," 491.
[31] Pozzetta, "The Italians of New York City, 1890–1914," 244–65; and Fenton, *Immigrants and Unions—A Case Study*, 49–54.
[32] Baily, "Las Sociedades de ayuda mutua," 487–94.

13

better administered, and more unified mutualist movement in Buenos Aires provided more extensive services for a larger percentage of the Italian population than did the movement in New York.

The Italian-language newspaper was probably the second most important immigrant institution in Buenos Aires and New York. No one joined newspapers, but more Italians read them than there were members of mutual aid societies. Tens of thousands of immigrants scanned their columns in search of job opportunities, notices on the activities of community organizations, tips on how to survive and prosper, guidance in understanding and adjusting to the wider community in which they lived, and information on Italy. Since these papers reached more Italians than any other immigrant organization, they were in the best position to unite the community.

In Buenos Aires, the first Italian newspaper was established in the 1860s. Dozens of others were published in subsequent years, but most had small circulation and did not last very long. *La Patria degli Italiani* had by far the largest circulation and continued publishing longer than any other paper. Founded in 1876 by Italian journalist Basilio Cittadini, it reached a circulation of approximately sixty thousand—or 19 percent of the Italian community—in 1914. *La Patria* was a liberal, anticlerical, and moderately antimonarchist morning daily that attempted to serve the interests of immigrants of all social and income levels within the Italian colony in Buenos Aires. It regularly published information on working and living conditions and explained the grievances of workers involved in labor disputes. Every issue included letters from immigrants, who most frequently described their problems and asked for help. The editors of *La Patria* interpreted Argentine society for the Italian immigrants, defended their various interests, arbitrated some of their disputes, and often spoke for them as a community. In addition, the paper performed several, more unusual functions, particularly in the decade prior to World War I: it ran free medical, legal, and agricultural clinics for its subscribers. These services gave *La Patria* something of the character of a mutual aid society and increased its impact on the community.[33]

The first Italian-language newspaper in New York began publication in 1849, and many others of short duration and small circulation appeared in the following half-century. The largest and most long-lived of these was *Il Progresso Italo-Americano*. Established in 1879 by businessman and labor contractor Carlo Barsotti, the paper reached a circulation of roughly eighty thousand—or 22 percent of the Italian community—by the beginning of World War I. *Il Progresso*, however, made little effort to serve the interests of all of the Italians in New York. It was, most significantly, antilabor, probably because Barsotti was afraid that labor unions might undermine his other businesses. Barsotti frequently used the paper as a vehicle to further his personal interests. "Publishers," as one author explained, "used their journals to advertise their own far-flung enterprises, to praise themselves and their friends, to promote projects in which they were interested, and to

[33] Baily, "The Role of the Press and the Assimilation of Italians in Buenos Aires," 321–40.

attack anyone with whom they disagreed."[34] Although *Il Progresso* provided information on the happenings in the Italian community, defended all Italians against attacks by outsiders, and perhaps helped break down village-based provincialism and foster a larger group awareness, it did little to interpret American society to the immigrants or to strengthen the community as a whole. *Il Progresso* supported the needs of some of the Italians in New York, but it opposed that of the large majority of workers.[35] *La Patria* was more effective in serving the Italian immigrants in Buenos Aires than *Il Progresso* was in New York.

The supporting evidence for some parts of this analysis of the adjustment process of Italians in Buenos Aires and New York is not as complete as it is for others. The evidence on housing conditions, home ownership, residential mobility, economic activity, and community organizations does, nevertheless, all point in the same direction. And, although future studies will certainly provide more information on the Italian immigration experience in both cities, they are not likely to alter substantially the basic conclusion. Italians in Buenos Aires adjusted more rapidly and successfully to their new environment than did those in New York.

THE EARLIER AND GREATER SUCCESS of Italians of Buenos Aires in adjusting to their new environment is clear. The reasons for the discrepancy are somewhat more complex. Were the Italians in Buenos Aires in some way better prepared for the immigration experience than those who went to New York? Did they encounter a more receptive host society? What, if anything, did they do to improve their chances of success? Although a considerable number of interrelated variables explain the different experiences of the Italians in the two cities, they can be divided into three categories: those relating to the character of the immigrant groups when they migrated, to the kind of societies they found, and to the changing nature of the immigrant community over time.

When Italians migrated to New York and Buenos Aires, they brought with them certain attributes that influenced their ability to find jobs and housing and to organize community groups. Among the most important were not only occupational and organizational skills but also expectations regarding the permanency of the move. Unskilled laborers predominated in both groups: 75 percent of those who went to the United States between 1899 and 1910 and perhaps 60 percent of those who went to Argentina were unskilled farm or common workers. Only 25 percent of those who migrated to the United States and 40 percent of those who migrated to Argentina were listed as skilled or white-collar workers. The statistics do not break down the overall figures for those who went specifically to Buenos Aires and New York; but these centers of economic activity undoubtedly attracted at least the same proportions of skilled and white-collar workers, and most likely an even higher percentage of them than the national norm for each country. Italians in

[34] Fenton, *Immigrants and Unions—A Case Study*, 59.
[35] Pozzetta, "The Italians of New York City, 1890–1914," 234–42; Fenton, *Immigrants and Unions—A Case Study*, 58–63; and Robert E. Park, *The Immigrant Press and Its Control* (New York, 1922), 449.

15

Buenos Aires as a group were also more literate than those in New York; some 60 percent were literate in Buenos Aires compared to about 50 percent in New York.[36]

A larger proportion of the Italians who migrated to Buenos Aires were from northern Italy. They were in general not only more skilled and literate than Italians from the south but also more familiar with organizations such as labor unions and mutual aid societies. While 42 percent of those who went to Argentina came from the north, 46 percent from the south, and 12 percent from the center, 80 percent of those who went to the United States were southerners.[37] And not all of their skills were transferable to their new environments. Skills appropriate to rural occupations such as farming were of little use in urban New York and Buenos Aires; those of artisans and white-collar workers for the most part were. With better occupational skills, higher rates of literacy, and greater familiarity with organizations, the Italians in Buenos Aires had an advantage in finding higher status jobs and in developing community institutions to protect their interests.

Expectations regarding the permanency of their emigration differed to some extent between those going to the northern and those to the southern hemisphere. Measuring the Italians' intentions when they left their villages and towns for the New World is, of course, impossible. Nevertheless, data on their respective rates of return and on sex and age composition of the migrants are at least indicative of intent. The percentage of Italians who repatriated for the period 1861–1914 is slightly lower for the Argentine immigrants than it is for the U.S. immigrants (47 percent compared to 52 percent). Those who returned to Italy from both countries were overwhelmingly unskilled males, and New York had a larger proportion of unskilled Italian males than did Buenos Aires. Approximately 30 percent of the immigrants repatriated from Buenos Aires during the decade and a half before World War I, whereas approximately 50 percent repatriated from New York during those same years.[38]

[36] The literacy figures for Buenos Aires refer to all Italians in the city eight years old or more; the U.S. Immigration Commission figures refer to Italians fourteen years old or more entering the United States or to Italian male heads of households in New York. Thus, the actual difference in literacy was probably greater than I have suggested. See Kessner, *The Golden Door*, 33–36; U.S. Immigration Commission, *Reports*, 3: 84, 95–96, 131–38, and 26: 238; Juan A. Alsina, *La Inmigración en el primer siglo de la independencia* (Buenos Aires, 1910), 92–93; Mario Nascimbene, "Inmigración y analfabetismo en Argentina: La Corriente Migratoria italiana entre 1876 y 1925," *Sociológica*, 1 (1978): 121–70; Buenos Aires, *Censo general ..., 1887*, 65; and República Argentina, *Tercer Censo nacional de ... 1914*, 3: 321.

[37] The pre-1919 regions of Italy were as follows: the north included Piemonte, Lombardia, Trentino, Veneto, Emilia, and Liguria; the center included Toscana, Umbria, Marche, and Lazio; and the south included Abruzzi, Puglia, Basilicata, Calabria, Campania, Sicilia, and Sardegna. For a detailed breakdown of the regional origins of the immigrants, see Commissariato Generale dell'Emigrazione, *Annuario Statistico della emigrazione italiana dal 1876 al 1925* (Rome, 1926), 145–51. On organizations in Italy, see Barton, *Peasants and Strangers*, 64–67; and Briggs, *An Italian Passage*, 15–36.

[38] The *golondrinas*—the Italians who went every year to Argentina to harvest the crops—numbered about thirty thousand annually during the decade or so prior to World War I. Because they did not go to Buenos Aires, I have subtracted this number from the total number of returnees to arrive at my estimate. The same cannot, however, be done for the New York Italians. As many temporary migrants went to New York as to other parts of the United States; they apparently remained in the United States for a somewhat longer period than did the temporary migrants to Buenos Aires. Thus, I am using the same figure for New York as for the United States as a whole. See Gould, "European Inter-Continental Emigration—The Road Home," 41–71; Caroli, *Italian Repatriation from the United States*, 25–50; Mark Jefferson, *Peopling the Argentine Pampa* (New York, 1926), 183; Commissariato Generale dell'Emigrazione, *Annuario Statistico*, 830–913; and República Argentina, Dirección de Inmigración, *Resumen estadística del movimiento en la República Argentina, 1857–1924* (Buenos Aires, 1925), 4–5.

16

Demographic distribution of the Italian immigrants in the two cities according to age and sex provides supporting evidence for the relatively greater permanency of the Italian settlement in Buenos Aires. Italians who migrated to both cities were predominantly males between fourteen and forty-four years old. In Buenos Aires, males represented a little less than two-thirds of the Italian population in 1895 (61 percent) and 1914 (62 percent), and two-thirds of all immigrants (65 percent) were between the ages of fourteen and forty-four. The percentage of Italian males and of fourteen- to forty-four-year-old Italian immigrants was higher in New York. During the three decades before 1910 approximately 77 percent of the Italian immigrants to the United States were males, and nearly 80 percent of these were between fourteen and forty-four years of age. There is no reason to assume that the percentages for New York City were any lower. Therefore, while roughly two out of every three Italians who went to Buenos Aires were males between the ages of fourteen and forty-four, approximately four out of every five Italian immigrants in New York were in these age and sex categories.[39]

These figures, significantly, indicate a higher percentage of women, children, and older people in the Italian population of Buenos Aires. This in turn is suggestive of a larger proportion of family units and probably greater permanence for the immigrant community in Buenos Aires. It is, of course, possible that more Italians got married after they arrived in Argentina than they did in the United States, but it is more likely that a greater number of families migrated to the Argentine capital in the first place. To the degree that rates of return and sex and age composition reflect intentions, it seems that more Italians who migrated to Buenos Aires expected to remain and that more who came to the United States were temporary migrants who planned, when they left Italy, to return.

Although the Italians who arrived in New York and Buenos Aires during the forty-four years under consideration here shared to some extent a similar general culture based on a common language, religion, and set of values, they did not have identical group characteristics. Those who migrated to Buenos Aires included more workers with higher levels of skill and of literacy, more individuals with experience in organization, and more people who intended to stay. These differences gave the Italians in Buenos Aires an initial advantage as they sought to find jobs and to develop community institutions to protect their interests. But these differences do not alone account for the vast difference in the two Italian colonies. The receiving environments the immigrants entered also varied dramatically and significantly affected the immigrants' adjustment. The economy, the host society's perception of the Italians, the culture, and the existing foreign-born community in Buenos Aires contrasted sharply with those in New York.

The economies of the two urban societies were strikingly different. In 1869, at the time of the first national census, Argentina was sparsely populated and economically far less developed than Western Europe or the United States. Those

[39] República Argentina, *Segundo Censo nacional de ... 1885*, 15, 28–29, and *Tercer Censo nacional de ... 1914*, 3: 12–13; Massimo Livi-Bacci, *L'Immigrazione e l'assimilazione degli Italiani negli Stati Uniti* (Milan, 1961), 15; U.S. Immigration Commission, *Reports*, 26: 176–77; and Commissariato Generale dell'Emigrazione, *Annuario Statistico*, 187–200.

17

who ruled Argentina during the next forty years were determined to replace the stagnant economic and social structures inherited from Spanish colonial rule with the most dynamic and advanced systems to be found anywhere. They sought to institute such sweeping change by encouraging massive immigration, improving the educational system, introducing new technology, modernizing agriculture and livestock breeding, developing a transportation infrastructure (notably railroads and port facilities), and wooing foreign investment capital. By 1914, the export-oriented, landed elite had succeeded in accomplishing most of its objectives. Argentina had, in a relatively short time, become one of the leading agricultural and livestock-breeding countries in the world. It was a major exporter of grains, the leading supplier of beef to England, and a center of industries to process agricultural and pastoral products for export.[40]

The rapidity of Buenos Aires's economic development, which coincided with the wave of Italian migration, provided opportunities at all levels for the new residents. When Argentine development began, the country had no vital middle class, no significant skilled working class, no other numerically important immigrant groups, and no labor movement or employers' organizations. The traditional native elite continued to confine itself primarily to land and politics, which left commerce, industry, and some of the professions and economic organizations to the immigrants, especially to the large Italian community.

The United States had a much larger population and a more highly developed economy in 1870 than did Argentina. During the next forty-four years, the United States expanded both its heavy and light industry, and by World War I had become a major industrial as well as agricultural and commercial country. The Italians who migrated to New York encountered thriving professional, middle, and skilled working classes composed of native-born Americans and previous immigrants. What the New York economy needed was unskilled construction and industrial workers. There were opportunities for Italians, but opportunities of a kind different from those in Buenos Aires. As a result, the Italians entered the economy at the lower levels and had greater difficulty in achieving upward occupational mobility. More restricted economic opportunity in New York limited the growth of upper-level Italian occupational groups, the resources of the Italian community, and the development of immigrant institutions—all of which made adjustment to the new environment more formidable.[41]

The host society's perceptions of the Italians also influenced adjustment. The Argentine elite viewed the immigrants as a means of "civilizing" the country as well as developing its economy. These leaders believed that the native population of the

[40] James R. Scobie, *Argentina: A City and A Nation* (New York, 1971), 64–135; and Germani, "Mass Immigration and Modernization in Argentina," 289–330.

[41] Klein, "La Integración de inmigrantes," 3–27; Peter S. Shergold, "Relative Skill and Income Levels of Native and Foreign-Born Workers: A Re-Examination," *Explorations in Economic History*, 13 (1976): 451–61; Paul F. McGouldrick and Michael B. Tannen, "Did American Manufacturers Discriminate against Immigrants before 1914?" *Journal of Economic History*, 37 (1977): 723–46; and Gordon W. Kirk, Jr., and Carolyn Tyirin Kirk, "The Immigrant, Economic Opportunity, and Type of Settlement in Nineteenth-Century America," *ibid.*, 38 (1978): 226–34.

interior—symbolized by the *gaucho* ("cowboy") and the *caudillo* ("charismatic leader")—was backward and inferior. European immigrants would, they thought, intermix with the indigenous population and in time help create a biologically superior population. The tiny Argentine elite may have looked down upon Italian immigrants as social inferiors but still saw them as superior to 95 percent of the native population. In this sense, the Italians were bearers of civilization. By the early 1900s, some members of the elite did become concerned about the dominating influence of the immigrants in Argentina. This concern, however, remained limited as long as the economy continued to grow, and it did not translate into significant restrictions either on immigration or on the opportunities for the immigrants until the Depression of the 1930s.[42]

In contrast, Italians who went to New York were viewed in an entirely different way. Many New Yorkers viewed the immigrants—especially the great mass of southern Italians—as an inferior race that threatened to dilute the good Northern European stock and undermine traditional American institutions. The Italians provided the unskilled labor necessary for the growth of the economy, but the native-born elite certainly did not see them as bearers of civilization. The United States had a "superior culture" to which the Italians were expected to adapt if they were to succeed.[43] This negative perception resulted in various types of social and economic discrimination and ultimately in restrictions on Italian immigration. And it reinforced the limitations created by more restricted economic opportunity.

The differences in the cultures of the two receiving societies also had an impact on immigrant adjustment, but these differences were probably of less importance than some scholars have suggested. In Buenos Aires, the Italians entered a Latin culture whose values, language, and religion were similar to their own. Italians in New York, however, confronted a very different culture; there they had problems with the language, were subjected to religious prejudice, and had difficulty understanding some of the values of the host society. As a result, the Italians in Buenos Aires presumably were able to adjust more easily and their success came more rapidly.[44] Although the cultural explanation is of some significance, it has its limitations. Most important, the Italians in Buenos Aires were successful in economic life precisely because they rejected some important Argentine values. Economic opportunity and the host society's perceptions were more significant.

Furthermore, Italians in Buenos Aires inherited a more extensive, wealthier, and more effective organizational network that had been developed by earlier immigrants. When massive migration began in the 1880s, Buenos Aires already had an Italian community of eighty to ninety thousand immigrants. Its established institutions were capable of helping the newcomers adjust to life in the city. In New

[42] Scobie, *Argentina*, 174–91; Germani, "Mass Immigration and Modernization in Argentina," 309–11; and Carl Solberg, *Immigration and Nationalism: Argentina and Chile, 1890–1914* (Austin, 1970), 65–116.

[43] Pozzetta, "The Italians of New York City, 1890–1914," 121–60; and John Higham, *Strangers in the Land: Patterns of American Nativism, 1860–1925* (New York, 1975), 68–194.

[44] Solberg, "Mass Migrations in Argentina," 146–70; Maxine Seller, *To Seek America: A History of Ethnic Life in the United States* (Englewood Cliffs, N.J., 1977), 105–11; and Tomasi and Engel, *The Italian Experience in the United States*, 77–107.

TABLE 1

Foreign-Born Italians in New York City

Year	City's Italian Population	Italian Percentage of City's Total Population	Annual Growth of City's Italian Population during Preceding Decade	New York City's Italians as a Percentage of All Italians in the U.S.
1860	1,464	0.1		12.5
1870	2,794	0.3	9.1	16.3
1880	12,223	1.0	33.7	27.6
1890	39,951	2.6	23.3	21.9
1900	145,433	4.2	26.3	30.0
1910	340,765	7.1	13.4	25.4
1914	370,000 (estimate)			
1920	390,832	7.0		24.3
1930	440,200	6.4		24.6

NOTE: In 1898, New York City—which until that time had comprised only Manhattan and part of the Bronx—incorporated its neighboring counties to assume its current boundaries: Manhattan, Brooklyn (King's County), Queens (Queens County), Richmond (Staten Island), and the Bronx. Thus, the pre- and post-1900 figures refer to different geographical boundaries of the city.

SOURCES: U.S. Censuses, 1860 to 1930.

York, when massive migration began in the 1890s, the Italian community of forty thousand immigrants did not have as developed or effective an organizational infrastructure and was therefore less able to help subsequent immigrants find their way in their new environment.[45] Thus, the differences in the economies, the host societies' perceptions, cultures, and immigrant institutions worked together to make adjustment in Buenos Aires relatively easier and more rapid.

In addition to the skills and attitudes the Italian immigrants brought with them and the characteristics of the receiving environments, the subsequent development of the two Italian communities influenced adjustment. Continuing immigration in the 1890s and early 1900s modified existing conditions within the communities, and the new conditions themselves became important in the relative speed and degree of immigrant adjustment. Among the most important of these new conditions were the pace of immigration, the concentration and numerical strength of the two groups, and the nature of the emerging Italian elites.

The pace of migration to the two cities varied considerably. The flow of individuals to Buenos Aires was spread out more evenly over the four decades following 1870 than it was to New York. In 1870, forty-four thousand Italians lived in Buenos Aires, and less than three thousand lived in New York. The Buenos Aires community grew gradually over the next forty-four years; from 1887 to 1914 the annual increase averaged less than 4.3 percent. The New York community, which started with a much smaller base, grew more rapidly throughout the period. Most significantly, 77 percent of all Italian immigrants who went to the United States between 1860 and 1914 arrived during the fifteen years prior to World War I compared to 50 percent of those who went to Argentina (see Table 3). The larger initial size of the Italian population and the greater effectiveness of immigrant organizations combined with the more even pace of subsequent migration enabled the existing community in Buenos Aires to absorb the newcomers more easily and to help them adjust more readily. But the massive influx of immigrants in a short period of time overwhelmed the less developed and less united existing community in New York and prohibited it from absorbing and guiding the new arrivals.

The consistent relative concentration and numerical strength of the Italians in Buenos Aires further strengthened their position. In 1910 the one and one-third million Italians in the United States represented 1.5 percent of the total population. In Argentina the slightly more than one million Italians in 1914 represented 12.5 percent of the total population. Italians in both countries were concentrated in a relatively few states or provinces and cities, but this concentration, too, was far greater in Argentina. One-third of all of the Italians in Argentina lived in Buenos Aires, and the population of the city was at least 20 percent Italian-born throughout the period. Although approximately one-quarter of all of the Italians in the United States lived in New York, they never accounted for more than 7.1 percent of the city's population (see Table 1). In addition, there were only two major immigrant

[45] Baily, "Las Sociedades de ayuda mutua," 485–514; and Pozzetta, "The Italians of New York City, 1890–1914," 231–66.

21

TABLE 2

Foreign-Born Italians in Buenos Aires

Year	City's Italian Population	Italian Percentage of City's Total Population	Annual Growth of City's Italian Population during Preceding Period	Buenos Aires's Italians as a Percentage of All Italians in Argentina
1856	11,000	12.0		
1869	44,000	23.6	23.0	
1887	138,000	31.8	12.0	
1895	182,000	27.4	3.9	36.9
1904	228,000	24.0	2.8	
1909	277,000	22.5	4.3	
1914	312,000	19.8	2.5	33.6
1936	299,000	12.4		

NOTE: The number of Italians in Buenos Aires has been rounded off to the nearest thousand.

SOURCES: Buenos Aires and Argentine Censuses, 1856 to 1936.

22

TABLE 3
Italian Immigration to Argentina and the United States

Period	Argentina	United States
1861–70	113,554	11,728
1871–80	152,061	55,759
1881–90	493,885	307,309
1891–1900	425,693	651,899
1901–10	796,190	2,104,209
1911–20	347,388	1,165,246
TOTAL IMMIGRANTS, 1860–1914	2,270,525	4,083,000
TOTAL IMMIGRANTS, 1900–1914	1,137,475	3,156,000
IMMIGRANTS 1900–14 AS A PERCENTAGE OF IMMIGRANTS 1860–1914	50	77

SOURCES: República Argentina, Dirección de Inmigración, *Resumen estadística del movimiento migratorio en la República Argentina, 1857–1924* (Buenos Aires, 1925); and U. S. Bureau of the Census, *Historical Statistics of the United States, Colonial Times to 1972* (Washington, 1975).

groups in Argentina compared to at least a half-dozen in the United States: Italians and Spaniards alone made up nearly 80 percent of the total number of immigrants in Buenos Aires before World War I, whereas Russians, Germans, Irish, Austrians, and Italians made up a similar percentage of the total immigrant population of New York in 1900 and 1910.[46] The sheer numerical strength of the Italians in Buenos Aires made them far more difficult to exclude or play off against other nationalities, and their position thus guaranteed them more influence in the local society.

The nature of the emerging Italian elites also influenced adjustment patterns. Only two functioning social classes developed within the Italian community in New York: the *prominenti*, the tiny group of successful businessmen and professionals who remained in the community, and the mass of blue-collar workers. The differences in the interests of these two groups were too great for the *prominenti* to provide effective leadership for the mass of laborers. There was no strong middle class to provide pressure for reform or to link these two groups. The occupational structure in Buenos Aires, however, provided the basis for the growth of a multiclass society within the Italian community. The middle groups—the skilled and white-collar workers—were more influential in the organizations of the

[46] Buenos Aires, *Censo general ..., 1904*, 28; and U.S. Bureau of the Census, *Thirteenth Census of the United States ..., 1910*, 827.

community and, as part of a broader elite, were able to articulate and serve the interests of all Italians.[47]

The differences between the two elites can be seen in a number of areas. The mutualist movement and the leading Italian newspapers in Buenos Aires, unlike those in New York, consistently defended the interests of the blue-collar workers as well as those of the rest of the community. But the differences extended to the degree of cooperation among Italians who originated from different regions. In Buenos Aires both northern and southern Italians joined the same organizations and worked together in ways that they did not in New York. The greater numerical equality of the two groups in Buenos Aires obviously facilitated this cooperation, as did the relative lack of prejudice against southerners in the host society. In New York, the small group of northern Italians sought to escape the negative U.S. stereotype by separating themselves from the southern Italians. But the commitment of the early leaders of major mutual aid societies to a united Italy and the continual reinforcement of this commitment by the leaders of the community were of major importance in the greater ability of Italians from all areas to work together in Buenos Aires. What regional hostility there was never prevented Italians of all origins from working together in the same organizations and from uniting in a community that sought to benefit the interests of all.[48]

In New York the Italians developed two social strata in what was a multiclass society; in Buenos Aires they developed a multilevel social structure in what had been essentially a two-class society. This major difference, along with some of the social, economic, and historical differences, resulted in leadership in Buenos Aires that was more representative, more unified, and better able to develop an effective immigrant institutional structure than that in New York. The interaction among the various social sectors of the two communities was distinct and forms an important part of the explanation of the differing experience.

THE MORE RAPID AND MORE SUCCESSFUL ADJUSTMENT of the Italians in Buenos Aires was dependent upon the skills and attitudes the immigrants brought with them, the characteristics of the receiving societies, and the changing nature of the immigrant communities. All of these variables were interrelated. Although the characteristics of the immigrants and the receiving societies were of primary importance at the time of the immigrants' arrival, these two sets of original variables produced a new set of variables that, once in existence, took on a life of its own. The interrelationship of these three categories of variables is fundamental to an understanding of the process of Italian adjustment.

The labor market in Buenos Aires attracted a relatively more skilled and permanent group of Italians who were perceived by the Argentine elite in more positive terms and who encountered a more developed and effective immigrant

---

[47] Scobie, *Buenos Aires: Plaza to Suburb*, 208–10; Baily, "Las Sociedades de ayuda mutua," 485–514; and Pozzetta, "The Italians of New York City, 1890–1914," 231–44. Also see note 14, page 286, above.

[48] Pozzetta, "The Italians of New York City, 1890–1914," 127–28; and Baily, "Las Sociedades de ayuda mutua," 485–514, and "Italians and Organized Labor" (1967), 55–66.

institutional structure. Thus they had an initial advantage over the Italians in New York as they sought to find jobs and housing, to improve their living conditions, and to organize to protect their collective interests. But once in Buenos Aires the Italians capitalized on their initial advantages to strengthen further the position of the Italian community relative to that in New York. Not only did the Italians in Buenos Aires move into the economy in positions with higher status, but they continued to find better jobs and housing and to develop community organizations. Their efforts were facilitated by the gradual pace of immigration and the concentration and relative numerical strength of the group as a whole. At the same time, the Italian multiclass social structure in Buenos Aires provided the basis for a more representative and effective group of leaders.

I have posited a model of the process of adjustment of Italian immigrants to the Americas based on the important cases of Buenos Aires and New York City. These two cases may well represent the extremes in terms of the speed and success of the process. What we need to do now is to use the model to study other cities and other immigrant groups. Much has, of course, been written on immigrants in cities throughout the world. Unfortunately, few of these studies are comparable. It is my strong conviction that historians of immigration who wish to develop their field successfully must frame their research in such a way as to make the results more readily useful to others. My hope is that the model of the adjustment process developed in this essay will enhance this effort. As the model is systematically applied to other cities and other immigrant groups, we will obtain a sufficient number of comparable cases to be able to understand with greater certainty the fundamental nature of the process itself.

Italians, Jews And Ethnic Conflict

by Ronald H. Bayor*

Ethnic relations based on harmony and cooperation have often not been the norm in the United States. Many studies detail the clashes which have occurred between successive waves of immigrant groups.[1] However, even between outwardly friendly groups, who shared a common immigrant experience, the same disruptive forces are at work. Forever lurking beneath the surface, in all ethnic relationships, are tensions, resentments and frictions associated with living together in a competitive society. An important factor that can escalate these normal attitudes into overt conflict, particularly for immigrant ethnic groups, is the introduction of international issues.[2] This situation occurred during the 1930's when the decisions of foreign rulers began to disturb ethnic relations in New York City. Two ethnic communities affected were the Italians and Jews.

These groups had enjoyed friendly relations since the end of the nineteenth century, the period of first arrival in the United States. There was a feeling of having shared a common immigrant experience that drew them together. For example, in the late 1920's B'nai B'rith and the Sons of Italy discussed a plan for mutual cooperation and assistance. Each organization looked to the other as an ally.[3]

When the Jews rallied in opposition to Nazi Germany in the early 1930's, there were indications of support from Italians. Vito Marcantonio, the Italian congressman from East Harlem, and Mayor Fiorello La Guardia continuously, throughout this period, castigated the Nazis for their treatment of German Jews. Prominent Italians, speaking in defense of the Jews, tended to draw the groups together. The Italian concern with

---

* Ronald H. Bayor, Department of History, St. John's University.
[1] The following list contains a few of the more important studies by historians. Oscar Handlin, *Boston's Immigrants* (Revised ed.; New York: Atheneum, 1968); Donald Kinzer, *An Episode in Anti-Catholicism: The American Protective Association* (Seattle: University of Washington Press, 1964); John Higham, *Strangers in the Land* (New York: Atheneum, 1965); John Higham, "Another Look at Nativism," *Catholic Historical Review,* XLIV (1958) 147-158; Rudolph Vecoli, "Prelates and Peasants: Italian Immigration and the Catholic Church," *Journal of Social History,* II (Spring, 1969), 217-268.
[2] I define conflict as all manisfestations of group hostility which involve a noticeable number of participants of either group. This hostility can include verbal assaults in the ethnic press, group physical attacks or the use of economic or political power as a malicious force.
[3] Copy of interview with Gregario Morabito, Grand Secretary of the New York State Order Sons of Italy in America, by Rev. Silvano Tomasi, New York City, March 28, 1969; Caroline F. Ware, *Greenwich Village, 1920-1930* (Boston: Houghton Mifflin Company, 1935), p. 137.

the Jews in Germany was not widespread in the community, but it was vocal, and Jews could not but be aware of it.[4]

At first, Italian Fascism also provided no problem between the two ethnic communities. Although the majority of Italian-Americans in New York sympathized with Benito Mussolini, this was of no concern to the Jews.[5] In fact the Jewish press constantly compared Italian Fascism favorably to the degenerate German Nazism. "As Mussolini has gained in the respect of the world, the obsessed Fuehrer has won the odium of enlightened mankind," commented one Jewish paper in 1934. Nazism was described as "counterfeit Fascism." The Jews in Italy were pictured as enjoying a renaissance under Mussolini.[6] When Italy's newspapers criticized Hitler's racial dogmas, they were given prominent space in the Jewish press. A full page article in the *Jewish Examiner* described how Mussolini was aiding Jewish refugees from Germany and Jews in Italy.[7]

There were some Jews in New York, of course, who opposed the Italian government on an ideological basis, and therefore found themselves, at times, involved in conflict with Italian-Americans. One incident at the City College of New York serves as an example of this early conflict. In 1934, some Jewish students protested vigorously against a delegation of visiting Italian students because of their Fascist ideology. The Italian visitors received support from Italian-American organizations at the college. As a result, a minor violent clash occurred.[8] This was, however, an isolated event. Italian Fascism did not evoke any hostility or even concern from the majority of the Jewish community in New York.

The Italian-Americans were very pleased not to antagonize the Jews and made a major point of showing the differences between Italian Fas-

[4] Columbian League of Kings County, Inc. to Lehman, March 29, 1933, Herbert H. Lehman Papers (Columbia University Library); Resolution of American Sons of Italy Grand Lodge, December 3, 4, 1938, Box 6, Vito Marcantonio Papers (New York Public Library); A. Palmeri to editor, *Jewish Examiner*, April 14, 1939, p. 4; *New York Times*, June 6, 1933, p. 15; January 31, 1934, p. 4; September 8, 1935, p. 29; March 4, 1937, p. 25; March 16, 1937, p. 1; May 3, 1937, p. 21; November 15, 1938, p. 5; November 19, 1938, p. 4; November 21, 1938, p. 4; November 22, 1938, p. 6; July 5, 1939, p. 13.
[5] Copy of interview with Morabito; Marcantonio to William Feinberg, May 12, 1937, Box 21, Marcantonio Papers; Interview with Leonard Covello, New York City, February 20, 1969; Survey of Italian Fascism in New York, n.d., Box 2675, Fiorello H. La Guardia Papers (Municipal Archives and Records Center, New York City); John P. Diggins, "The Italo-American Anti-Fascist Opposition," *Journal of American History*, LIV (December, 1967), 582.
[6] *American Hebrew and Jewish Tribune*, March 9, 1934, p. 317; September 21, 1934, p. 364.
[7] *Ibid.*, December 1, 1934, p. 101; *Jewish Examiner*, February 2, 1934, p. 1; February 9, 1934, p. 3.
[8] City College, *Final Report of Special Committee of the Associate Alumni of the City College of the College of the City of New York*, 1935, p. 32.

cism and German Nazism. "In Italy everybody is equal: Catholics, Protestants and Jews, all Italians," commented one Italian-American newspaper which was later to become rabidly anti-Semitic.[9]

Yet all was not well in Italian-Jewish relations. Beneath the surface of friendship the usual ethnic tensions and jealousies were beginning slowly to strain the relationship between the two groups. The 1930's represented difficult times. This decade was an era of attacks on Jewry around the world which made Jews in ethnically pluralistic New York sensitive and defensive about any hint of antagonism from another group. It was also an era of economic depression which tended to limit upward occupational mobility and to increase unemployment. This aspect of the depression affected ethnic relations in the city. The Italians, for example, were conscious of the fact, and in some cases exhibited resentment, that the Jews by the 1930's had surged ahead occupationally and politically in New York. The mobility of the Jews seemed to be particularly noticed since they had arrived in the United States at approximately the same time as the Italians.[10]

A number of studies reveal that by the 1930's the Italians were just entering into skilled and semi-skilled occupations while the Jews were heavily represented in the managerial and employer positions. The Welfare Council of New York conducted a study in 1935 of the youth of New York in the 16 to 24 age bracket. On the basis of interviews the usual occupations of the fathers of these youths were determined. Of those fathers born in Russia, whom the survey identified as Jewish, 3.8 per cent were professionals and 31.8 per cent of the 1,657 Russians in the sample were proprietors, managers and officials. The clerical division made up 6.8 per cent, and the skilled and semi-skilled included 52.9 percent of the Jewish sample. Jews in service occupations numbered 2.1 per cent. Only 2.6 per cent of the Jewish fathers were listed as unskilled. In the same study, the Italians had 1.1 per cent of a 1,976 sample as professionals, 17 per cent as proprietors, managers and officials, 2.8 per cent as clerical, 51.1 per cent in skilled and semi-skilled work and 4.6 per cent in the service category. The Italian sample listed 23.4 per cent of the workers as unskilled. It is evident, on the basis of this investigation, that Jews had moved substantially into managerial and proprietary positions while Italians had emerged into skilled and semi-skilled occupations, although still including

---

[9] *Il Grido della Stirpe*, May 15, 1937, p. 3; Generoso Pope to Stephen Wise, July 7, 1937, Stephen Wise Papers (Brandeis University Library).

[10] Interview with Covello; *Il Progresso Italo-Americano*, January 19, 1939, editorial page; D. Spadafora to editor, *Il Progresso Italo-Americano*, July 5, 1938, editorial page; Mary Testa, "Anti-Semitism Among Italian-Americans," *Equality*, I (July, 1939), 27; J.C.M. to editor, *Brooklyn Tablet*, July 23, 1938, p. 6.

a large number of unskilled workers. The same report noted that among Jews and Italians born in the United States and in the 16 to 24 age bracket the extent of unemployment remained less for Jewish youth than for all other non-Jewish gainful workers. The Italians, among all white groups, had the largest proportion of their youth unemployed. Another study, based on the same 1935 figures, stated that "Jews, both male and female, had a greater proportion of employed youth in professional, clerical and managerial work than did non-Jews" in 1935.[11]

The Jewish occupational structure was studied further in 1937 by the Committee on Economic Adjustment of the American Jewish Committee and the Conference on Jewish Relations. This report revealed that 25.4 per cent of the 924,258 Jewish gainful workers in New York City, both immigrant and native-born, were engaged in manufacturing. The other major categories included 25.7 per cent in trade, 10.9 per cent in domestic and personal service, 7.4 per cent in professional work, 5.2 per cent in construction and 13.5 per cent unemployed. Small percentages of Jews were scattered in such categories as finance, transportation, public service, amusements, and public utilities.

These figures become meaningful when it is noted that Jews predominated as employers rather than employees. Of the 34,000 factories in New York City, nearly two-thirds were owned by Jews, but only one-third of the workers were Jewish. In trade, two-thirds of the owners of the 103,854 wholesale and retail establishments were Jews, while only 37.8 per cent of the workers were Jewish. Two-thirds of the proprietors of the 11,000 restaurants and lunch-rooms (classified under domestic and personal service) were Jews, but only 15 per cent of the workers were Jewish. The study concluded that there was a bulking of Jews in employer and semi-employer categories.[12]

Jewish employers, in a number of situations, dominated industries which saw an increasing number of Italian workers. For example, in the Men's Clothing industry, by 1938, the Italians represented the largest single group of workers while in the factories the executives and foremen were predominately Jewish. This situation was also true in other areas of the clothing industry. Many unions which had large numbers of Italian

---

[11] Nettie P. McGill and Ellen N. Matthews, *The Youth of New York City* (New York: MacMillan Company, 1940), Table V, pp. 45, 62; Nettie P. McGill, "Some Characteristics of Jewish Youth in New York City," *Jewish Social Service Quarterly,* XIV (December, 1937), 255, 263-64; Dorothy Helen Goldstein, "The 'Disproportionate' Occupational Distribution of Jews and Their Individual and Organized Reactions" (unpublished Master's dissertation, Dep't of Sociology, Columbia University, 1941), Table VIII.
[12] *New York Jewish News,* February 4, 1938, p. 4; Goldstein, "The 'Disproportionate' Occupational Distribution of Jews" pp. 18-24.

members found their work to be dependent on Jewish contractors and manufacturers. This was true in such unions as the Painters Brotherhood local 874, the International Ladies Garment Workers Union local 89 and the Bedding local 140 of the United Furniture Workers of America. Of course there were also a number of unions and industries dominated mainly by Italians with little dependence on Jews. These would include the Building trades (particularly carpenters, stonemasons, cement finishers, electricians and bricklayers), the Transportation and Communication workers (particularly longshoremen) and the Barbers union. However, the occupational areas in which Italians were dependent on Jews and saw themselves in lower status positions seemed plentiful enough to have caused, what appeared to be, an undercurrent of Italian resentment. This resentment, it seems, was also the product of the widespread unemployment among Italian youth during the depression years.[13]

Politically the Jews also were surging ahead and dominating the major positions. It is quite true that La Guardia was elected Mayor in 1933, and this was considered to be a notable achievement for the Italian community. The election of La Guardia, however, did not satisfy the Italian desire for political advancement and power, nor did it usher in an Italian era in New York City politics. Although La Guardia did appoint Italians to office and made an effort to organize the ethnic community politically, it is significant that one study of the Mayor's political appointees concluded that his choices were 15 per cent Jewish and only 5 per cent Italian. By 1938, 6 out of 19 department commissioners under La Guardia were Jewish. Only two could be identified as Italian. When it can be further noted that from 1923 to 1946 only 7 Italians from New York City served in the State Senate, it is easy to recognize their lack of political power. Ferdinand Pecora, appointed in 1935, was only the third Italian to serve on the Supreme Court of New York. Michael Ditore, appointed in 1930, was the first Italian to serve on the Municipal Court of New York. On the state executive level, Charles Poletti was elected Lieutenant Governor in 1938, but the Governor was Jewish.

---

[13] U.S., Works Progress Administration, Federal Writers Project, *The Italians of New York* (New York: Random House, 1938), pp. 25, 64–66; Joseph W. Anania, "Report on the Interdependence of Italians and Jews living in New York City and the Effects of the Recent Italian Governmental Decrees on Relations between Italians and Jews in New York City," Prepared for the American Jewish Committee, November 25, 1938 (in the files of the Committee); Maurice J. Karpf, "Jewish Community Organization in the United States," *American Jewish Year Book*, XXXIX (September 1937–September 1938), 53, 55–56; Harry S. Linfield, *The Communal Organization of the Jews in the United States, 1927* (New York: American Jewish Committee, 1930), pp. 129–130.

A number of Jews, by this time, had moved into positions of power. In 1934 alone, there were 7 Jews from New York City serving in the State Senate. Among Jewish individuals who had achieved political prominence there was Governor Herbert Lehman (elected in 1932), Congressmen Sol Bloom, Emmanuel Celler and William Sirovich, State Senators Leon Fischel and Joseph Lazarus, Supreme Court Judge Samuel Hofstadter, Municipal Court Judge Edgar Lauer, City Magistrate Arthur Hirsch and such La Guardia appointees as Commissioners Joseph Goodman, Robert Moses, William Herlands and Paul Moss.[14]

The result of this ethnic division was that Italians, throughout the 1930's, called for the election of their own people to office. This would sometimes be followed by a plea that Italians deserved to gain the representation that other groups, particularly Jews, had achieved in politics.[15]

The undercurrent of ethnic rivalry and resentment engendered by another group's occupational and political success is a perfectly normal part of the American ethnic scene. By itself, this ethnic jealously will not lead to conflict. However, the introduction of certain issues, in conjunction with the internal resentment, which clearly and sharply pit the two groups against each other will produce a conflict situation. Mussolini's anti-Semitic decrees in 1938 became such an issue for Italians and Jews in New York.

As Mussolini gradually began to draw closer to Nazi Germany, he introduced racial policies which fit the Nazi model. This shift began slowly. As late as 1936 when German and Italian "volunteers" were aiding Franco in Spain the Italian delegate to the World Jewish Congress could still refer to his country as the "noblest example of perfect equality for

---

[14] La Guardia did, however, appoint more Italians and more Jews than any of his predecessors. See: Theodore J. Lowi, *At The Pleasure of the Mayor* (New York: The Free Press of Glencoe, 1964), pp. 34–39, 41; The information on La Guardia's department commissioners was based on obituary notices and an ethnic study of their names. Any ethnically doubtful names were not counted. For other Jews appointed or elected see: "Appointments and Elections," *American Jewish Year Book,* XXIV-XXXIX (September 1922-September 1938); Giovanni E. Schiavo, *Italian-American History* (New York: The Vigo Press, 1947), I, 572–578, 599; For an excellent study of La Guardia's efforts to organize the Italian community politically before he became Mayor see: Arthur Mann, *La Guardia, a fighter against his times, 1882–1933* (Philadelphia: J.B. Lippincott Company, 1959); For his efforts during the election campaign of 1933 see: Arthur Mann, *La Guardia Comes to Power, 1933* (Philadelphia: J. B. Lippincott Company, 1965).

[15] *Il Progresso Italo-Americano,* November 1, 1934, p. 1; November 2, 1937, editorial page; November 5, 1938, editorial page; November 6, 1938, editorial page; January 13, 1939, p. 1; January 19, 1939, editorial page; August 24, 1939, p. 1; D. Spadafora to editor, *Il Progresso Italo-Americano,* July 5, 1938, editorial page; J.C.M. to editor, *Brooklyn Tablet,* July 23, 1938, p. 6.

Jews." In 1937, the year of the Italian-German anti-Comintern pact, Mussolini's Milan newspaper, *Popolo d'Italia* called on Jews to give wholehearted support to Fascism or leave Italy. The paper stated that any opposition to Nazi ideas would be "irreconcilable with the friendship that binds us to Germany, which has objectives far more vast and fundamental than the Jewish question." The paper noted, however, that Italy had no desire to purge itself of its Jewish population. Mussolini also indicated that a definite policy toward Jews had not been formulated when in July, 1937 he honored an Italian Jewish soldier killed in the Spanish Civil War and refused to accept the resignation of the governing body of Jews in Italy, the council of the Union of Israelitic Communities in Italy.[16]

By 1938, the racial policy had been set. During this year, the world witnessed the German takeover of Austria, the Munich Conference and the Italian effort to conquer Albania. These events brought with them the anti-Semitic decrees. July 14, 1938 marked the starting date. On this day, ten fascist university professors issued a manifesto, under government auspices, accusing the Jews of destroying the qualities that made up the characteristics of the Italian race. By the end of July, Jews were gradually being removed from high office. This action served as the immediate prelude to the actual decrees which initially were promulgated on September 2. The first anti-Semitic order banned Jewish teachers and students from schools. It also ordered all Jews who had emigrated to Italy since the World War to leave within six months. Throughout September, October and November 1938, decrees were passed which restricted marriages between Jews and non-Jews, restricted land and business ownership, Fascist party membership and service in the armed forces or government. Later decrees in 1939 prohibited Jewish professionals from serving anyone but fellow Jews. The simultaneous establishment of a privileged class of Jews who were excluded from the restrictions softened these edicts. This group originally included the families of men who lost their lives in Italian wars or for the Fascist cause, who volunteered in wars or received the military cross and who were members of the Fascist party in the early years of its growth. The privileged category remained until 1943 when the Germans occupied Italy after the overthrow of Mussolini. The Italian public, in contrast to the higher levels of government, did not entirely endorse the anti-Semitic decrees. The result was an effort to soften the provisions through non-enforcement or by placing Jews in the privileged class. However, what was important for Italian-Jewish relations in New York was

---

[16] *New York Times,* August 11, 1936, p. 4; May 26, 1937, p. 1; July 1, 1937, p. 7; February 17, 1938, p. 4.

that the decrees were passed at all, amid a great deal of publicity, and that a number of Jews in Italy were affected by them.[17]

There is an indication that some Jews were aware as early as 1936 that the edicts would be forthcoming in the near future. For example, Rabbi Stephen Wise suggested in 1936 to a number of prominent Italian-Americans that they contact Mussolini "so that he may know of the value of Jewish citizenship to America. If that were done, it might avail to avert that anti-Semitism in Italy which up to this time has not been, but which seems to be foreshadowed by [Roberto] Farinacci's recent attack." There, however, remained in the Jewish community an unwillingness to believe that Italy would really follow Germany's sordid policies. As a result many Jews were unprepared for the events of 1938. One Jewish periodical commented that "Fascist Italy's ruthless campaign against the Jews in Italy came as a shock to many Jews and non-Jews, who somehow associated Jewbaiting with Nazi Germany alone and who thought that Italian Fascism was above the taint of anti-Semitism."[18]

Although the Jewish community as a whole initially expressed shock, the press immediately attempted to calm the situation by urging continued harmony with all Italians. What was evident, however, in the frantic pleas for harmonious relations, particularly with Italian-Americans, was the fear that ethnic relations were already or soon going to be deeply strained. The *New York Jewish News*, for example, commented that "to allow this black poison of hate, imported from abroad, to interfere with the mutual respect the Jews and Italians now feel toward one another would be a grave mistake." The *American Hebrew* pleaded that Jews "should be careful not to be so blinded by fury that they strike at innocent persons who happen to be standing nearby." The editorial continued with the hope that Jews "not transfer our quarrel with the Italian government to this country by undertaking boycotts against Americans of Italian extraction." An article in the *Jewish Examiner* urged Italians and Jews to work together in America in opposition to a repercussion from events in Italy. The newspaper also noted that "Italian sentiment in America is definitely opposed to Mussolini's newly formulated 'Aryan' theory and its implications of anti-Semitism." One writer in the *Jewish Veteran*, perhaps trying to convince himself as well as his readers, stated that "the insane situation

[17] *Ibid.*, July 31, 1938, IV, 5; August 3, 1938, p. 13; September 2, 1938, p. 1; September 11, 1938, IV, 5; October 7, 1938, p. 10; October 8, 1938, p. 7; November 11, 1938, p. 1; January 11, 1939, p. 14; February 28, 1939, p. 6; Raul Hilberg, *The Destruction of the European Jews* (Chicago: Quadrangle Books, 1961), pp. 414–416, 421–432.
[18] Roberto Farinacci was a member of the Fascist Grand Council, former secretary of the party and editor of *Il Regime Fascista*. Wise to Ferdinand Pecora, December 3, 1936, Wise Papers; *Brooklyn Jewish Center Review*, September, 1938, p. 1.

in 'Aryan' Italy will not affect the friendly relationship existing between Jews and Italians in our country."[19]

Besides urging and pleading with Jews not to retaliate against Italian-Americans, there was also a marked proclivity toward mollifying the tensions by exonerating Italians abroad for their actions. In an open letter to Mussolini, the *American Hebrew* stated that "we want to believe - our former admiration and respect urges us to believe - that what you have done in recent days you have not done of your own free will." An article in the *Jewish Examiner* noted that Mussolini and the Italian people were not really in favor of the anti-Semitic campaign.[20]

The leadership of the Italian-American community also exhibited fears that a conflict was imminent and urged harmony. Generoso Pope, the editor of *Il Progresso Italo-Americano*, made repeated efforts in letters and editorials to calm the situation. One letter to Rabbi Wise pointed out that Mussolini intended no harm to the Jews in Italy. An editorial stated that Italy had no desire to imitate Nazi policies. Pope urged that the friendship between Jews and Italians in America not be affected by events abroad. Letters to the newspaper echoed Pope's thoughts. Other Italian-American leaders such as Marcantonio; La Guardia; Poletti; New York Supreme Court Judge Salvatore Cotillo; Philip Bongiorno, former Supreme Master of the Sons of Italy; Santo Modica, Grand Master of the Sons of Italy Grand Lodge (New York State); and Joseph Tigani, president of the Roman American Progressive League, all called for harmony while at the same time fearing repercussions. These leaders were joined by many others when in November, 1938 a number of Italian-American patriotic, civic and religious organizations met in Manhattan to protest against the persecution of Jews in Italy and Germany.[21]

It is evident that the leaders of both ethnic communities wished to avoid conflict. However, what is much more important is what was happening within the ethnic communities. Was there a deterioration in

---

[19] *New York Jewish News*, September 9, 1938, p. 4; *American Hebrew*, September 23, 1938, p. 4; *Jewish Examiner*, July 29, 1938, p. 1; September 2, 1938, p. 1; J. David Delman, "Jewish News and Notes," *Jewish Veteran*, November, 1938, p. 18.

[20] *American Hebrew*, October 14, 1938, p. 3; *Jewish Examiner*, August 12, 1938, p. 1.

[21] Generoso Pope to Wise, July 7, 1937, Wise Papers; *Il Progresso Italo-Americano*, August 1, 1938, p. 6; August 28, 1938, editorial page; September 11, 1938, editorial page; December 25, 1938, editorial page; Dominick Sorrento to editor, *Il Progresso Italo-Americano*, September 2, 1938, editorial page; Marcantonio to Charles Kreindler, December 14, 1938, Box 7, Marcantonio Papers; Marcantonio to Santo Modica, February 22, 1939, Box 6, Marcantonio Papers; *New York Times*, October 8, 1938, p. 7; October 9, 1938, p. 38; November 21, 1938, p. 7; December 10, 1938, p. 1; December 12, 1938, p. 3; Joseph Tigani to Wise, October 9, 1938, Wise Papers; *American Hebrew*, July 29, 1938, p. 10.

Jewish-Italian relations in New York City? Reports from a number of sources indicated an increasing friction between the two groups. Jews began to retaliate against Italians by using their economic power. A study prepared by the American Jewish Committee in 1938 observed that there was a drop of Jewish customers in Italian owned stores due to the decrees. Furthermore, in some instances, there was a decided feeling among Italian workers and union members that work was being denied them due to Jewish discrimination. This was particularly the case in relation to the Painters Brotherhood and the garment industry. For example, the report stated that Italian painters "resent a certain lack of work, although it has not been proven openly that this is a result of Jewish discrimination. They are, however, convinced that such a thing exists." The report continued that several Italian owned garment factories, which depend on Jewish job- bers for their business, had experienced a sharp decline in orders. This drop in orders was felt to be the result of the decrees. There were also reports of Italian doctors losing their Jewish patients due to Italy's ac- tions. The greatest threat of the Jews and the fear most often expressed by the Italians was that of a Jewish boycott of Italian products similar to the anti-Nazi boycott begun against Germany in 1934. Concern was expressed that any boycott would extend to all things Italian. For example, Pope noted that he had heard of a proposed Jewish boycott of Italian goods "which probably would not stop at importations from Italy." Cotillo, in a cable to Mussolini, asked that the decrees be lifted because there is "seri- ous talk of boycotting Italy in our great City of New York where we live in close interdependent relationship. . . . " with the Jews. The Italian government also worried about a boycott particularly after a decline in Italian bonds on the New York market was believed to be the result of the anti-Jewish campaign.[22]

There was a definite awareness in the Italian community of what the Jews were doing and a desire to prevent further discrimination. Pope stated in one editorial that "in my business enterprises I have faithful and loyal workers of many nationalities; I have Jews who hold high positions. . . . It never occurred to me to discriminate against anyone because of race or creed. I hope that Jewish industrialists and businessmen harbor the same sentiments." Concern with this matter eventually reached such a high level that one organization, the Sons of Italy Grand Lodge, found it necessary to set up a Bureau for Good-Will Between Italians and Jews in

---

[22] Anania, "Report on the Interdependence of Italians and Jews," pp. 4–24, 27; *Il Grido della Stirpe*, November 12, 1938, p. 2; *Il Progresso Italo-Americano*, September 11, 1938, editorial page; *New York Times*, October 8, 1938, p. 7; September 8, 1938, p. 4; October 3, 1938, p. 23.

America. One of the main purposes of the bureau was to settle any dispute caused by discriminatory acts. Members were asked to inform the bureau of any complaints of loss of business or employment due to the Italian-Jewish friction.[23]

Simultaneous with the Jewish response, the Italian community reacted with the emergence of anti-Semitism. One study centering on Italian East Harlem indicated that the area was seeing the growth of overt anti-Semitism especially among "Italians who worked in Jewish sweatshops." Another study mentioned a growing anti-Jewish movement among Italians in the Amalgamated Clothing Workers Union and an increasing coolness between Italians and Jews in the Painters Brotherhood. Italian workers were not the only ones involved in this response. Anti-Semitic propaganda from Europe and events in the United States fed the resentments of other Italians.[24]

The emergence of the outwardly anti-Semitic Italian-American newspaper, *Il Grido della Stirpe* (Cry of the Race), published by Dominic Trombetta and such anti-Jewish organizations as the *Associazione Italiano All'Estero* did not help to calm the tensions between the two groups. Trombetta's newspaper and the organizations never gained much support in the Italian community, but they were vocal and persistent. The lack of support was probably related to the lack of respectability of both the newspaper and the organizations and also to the speed with which the organized anti-Jewish attitudes dissipated. Trombetta's newspaper engaged itself in a defense of the Nazis and began to repeat the accusations against Jews found in the German-American Bund (Nazi) newspaper in New York. On one occasion, the newspaper claimed that the Jews were not as poorly treated in Germany as the press tended to relate. Italian-Americans, therefore, were urged not to concern themselves with the Jews and to become more aware of the persecutions directed against Catholics in Mexico and by the anti-Franco forces in Spain. Jews were also described as Communists and anti-Fascists whose goal was to destroy Italian Fascism. A defense of the German-American Bund was offered, and joint meetings were announced between the Bund and the *Associazione Italiano All'Estero. Il Grido della Stirpe* commented that "it is needless to say that the Bund is a patriotic organization determined now more than ever to fight the world's worst parasite, namely Communism." The intent of the

---

[23] *Il Progresso Italo-Americano*, August 28, 1938, editorial page; Circular of American Sons of Italy Grand Lodge to Members, June 1, 1939, Box 6, Marcantonio Papers; *New York Times*, June 13, 1939, p. 9.

[24] Testa, "Anti-Semitism Among Italian-Americans," *Equality*, pp. 27–28; Anania, "Report on the Interdependence of Italians and Jews," p. 4.

newspaper seemed to be to coordinate activities, including propaganda, between Fascists and Nazis in New York City. Trombetta also wished to move the Italian-American community into a position of support for Nazi Germany.[25]

It is difficult to determine the actual effect of this newspaper, but it became evident that the ethnic conflict was spreading. Marcantonio remarked in February, 1939 that "there is existing the danger of the spread of anti-Semitism among our people." He urged that a conference between Italians and Jews be held soon which "will help to destroy once and for all the misunderstanding which is being engendered by dishonest people between Jews and Italians." By June, 1939 a circular sent out by the Sons of Italy Grand Lodge noted that "anti-Semitism in Europe, unfortunately, has had a repercussion in America, particularly in the City and State of New York, causing a spirit of hatred and resentment between Italians and Jews that can only culminate in a daily struggle."[26]

The events indicated that a full scale and lengthy conflict involving street rallies, name-calling and physical attacks was emerging. As a result both the Italian and Jewish community leadership increased their attempts to urge harmony. Apparently this had some effect for the overt tensions soon eased and the conflict evaporated. The reasons for the cooling of the conflict are numerous involving both how Italians and Jews thought of each other and of themselves. The causes for the initial tensions between the groups, Jewish insecurity and Italian resentment of Jewish success, were, oddly enough, involved in the amelioration of relations between the two ethnic groups.[27]

The Italian community was aware of and respected Jewish economic power, and seemingly became concerned that they would suffer in any clash with the Jews. Even the anti-Semitic Il Grido della Stirpe recognized this fact. At the same time that the newspaper was calling Jews Communists, they also noted cases of Jewish economic discrimination against Italians. The result was that the paper asked Jews to continue to live in brotherhood with Italians in America no matter what happened in Italy. "We wish to live in peace with others," the anti-Semitic journal noted.

---

[25] Interview with Covello; Il Mondo, August, 1939, p. 1; Il Grido della Stirpe, July 2, 1938, p. 2; July 9, 1938, p. 2; October 8, 1938, p. 2; November 26, 1938, p. 2; December 10, 1938, p. 2; December 17, 1938, p. 2; Jewish Examiner, April 21, 1939, p. 1.

[26] Circular of American Sons of Italy Grand Lodge to Members, June 1, 1939, Box 6, Marcantonio Papers; Marcantonio to Santo Modica, February 22, 1939, Box 6, Marcantonio Papers.

[27] Santo Modica to Marcantonio, February 20, 1939, Box 6, Marcantonio Papers; Il Progresso Italo-Americano, June 25, 1939, p. 8; Il Mondo, January, 1940, p. 4; Jewish Examiner, June 2, 1939, p. 4; New York Times, July 5, 1939, p. 13.

The Jews, it seems, were not unaware of their power in this respect. The *Jewish Examiner* claimed that the two largest Italian-American newspapers in New York had remained neutral on Mussolini's decrees because three-fourths of their advertising came from Jewish firms. Whether true or not, it indicates that some Jews felt that economic power kept the Italians in New York from supporting the decrees.[28]

This was certainly not the whole explanation. Fascism and anti-Fascism also were factors in the Italian response. There were many Italians, represented by men like Marcantonio, who honestly opposed anti-Semitism for humanitarian reasons. There were also Italian-Americans who were anti-Fascists and attacked everything emanating from Italy during this period. Even for the majority of Italians in New York who were admirers of Mussolini, it was easy to reject the decrees while still expressing esteem for Mussolini and Fascism. Although *Il Duce* attracted the great majority of Italian-Americans, there was very little understanding of what Fascism meant. What was understood was that Mussolini was making Italy a great power, thereby increasing the respect for Italians everywhere. There seemed to be a new dignity in being Italian. Marcantonio remarked that "due to their patriotic feeling, many of them [Italian workers] have become sympathizers of Mussolini. However, if they understood the implications of Fascism, they would join the progressive forces of the City." Therefore, not being ideological Fascists, the Italians of New York were able to spurn the decrees without decreasing their support of Mussolini. This made the rejection of anti-Semitism easier than had the Italian-Americans been committed to all of Mussolini's programs.[29]

Also, enough Italian-American leaders of every political persuasion scorned the decrees to make them unrespectable. If the powers within the Italian community had supported the edicts or remained neutral, the conflict would not have terminated so easily. Community leaders do have a powerful voice in either controlling or spreading these conflicts.

Finally, with the end of the decade and the outbreak of World War II, Italian-Americans faced the prospect of Mussolini's alliance with Nazi Germany against the Western Democracies. It now became very important for Italian-Americans to suppress ethnic hostilities and assert their Americanism. The Italian community was suspect of being too favorable to Fascist Italy; this put them in a decidedly defensive position. "Our Italo-Americans," commented an editorial in *Il Progresso*, "will unani-

---

[28] *Il Grido della Stirpe,* November 12, 1938, p. 2; November 26, 1938, p. 2; *Jewish Examiner,* July 29, 1938, p. 1.

[29] Interview with Covello; Marcantonio to William Feinberg, May 12, 1937, Box 21, Marcantonio Papers.

mously respond to the call to war guided by the sincere wish to be always loyal citizens of this great country." The editorial continued by calling for an end to the wave of suspicions and discriminations being directed against Italian-Americans. One Italian New Yorker offered his opinion that Italian-Americans would be the first to defend their country and this would silence those who question the commitment of Italians to the United States. The Italians found it necessary to note their Americanism in everything they did. "It is very important for us," said Pope, "to vote in order to show the strength of our vote and to show how good American citizens we are." There was no longer a stress on Italian candidates, but rather a plea to let the "interests of the United States be your only guide in choosing among the candidates." In this atmosphere, the Jews and Mussolini's decrees were forgotten and every effort was directed to proving the loyalty of Italians to America. The accompanying result was a cooling of ethnic conflict since these clashes were not considered to be indicative of good Americans.[30]

The Jews also moved away from the conflict situation. This was partly due to the very insecurity which had originally plunged them into difficulties with the Italians. Jews were under attack during the 1930's not only from German Nazism but also from organizations operating in New York such as the German-American Bund and the largely Irish Christian Front. As problems with the Bund and Front increased toward the end of the decade, Jewish leaders began to concentrate on these groups. The much less vocal Italian anti-Semitism faded into the background of Jewish concern. Also it is entirely conceivable that the Jewish community, noting the tensions with the other ethnic groups, did not want to add yet another enemy in New York. This may have been the rationale behind the Jewish effort to suppress any discussion of an anti-Italian boycott and to stress harmony. The aim was to minimize Italian-Jewish differences. The relatively few Jews in Italy and the mildness of Mussolini's anti-Semitism also aided the Jewish effort to suppress conflict. *Il Duce* was never fully identified in the Jewish mind with anti-Semitism. Hitler occupied this position, and the Jews concentrated on him. Finally, the forthright denunciation of the decrees by Italian-American leaders convinced enough Jews eventually that the Italian community was not hostile to them. It was extremely important to have major Italian and Jewish leaders urging harmony.

[30] *Il Progresso Italo-Americano,* June 23, 1940, p. 1; Salvatore Arpino to editor, *Il Progresso Italo-Americano,* November 1, 1940, editorial page; *Il Progresso Italo-Americano,* November 3, 1940, p. 1; F. Beccin to editor, *Il Progresso Italo-Americano,* November 4, 1940, editorial page; Luigi Antonini to La Guardia, June 12, 1940, Box 2675, La Guardia Papers; Louis Franchi to La Guardia, April 30, 1941, Box 2546, La Guardia Papers; Italian Bronx Community House to Lehman, March 18, 1941, Reel 48, Lehman Papers; *New York Times,* October 13, 1940, p. 48; November 30, 1941, p. 64.

In conclusion, the conflict situation between Italians and Jews was based on internal friction plus the introduction of friction over foreign affairs. Both, acting together, were essential for the development of overt conflict. The full maturation of this conflict, however, depended on other forces. The Italians were able to reject and suppress anti-Semitism due to their fear of Jewish economic power, their non-commitment to Fascist ideology, some concern with the plight of Jews and finally their involvement with the problems of Italy's entry into World War II. The Jews became convinced that it would be better to stress harmony rather than clash with still another ethnic group. Also, the Jews eventually felt reassured that Italian-Americans were not supporters of the decrees. In this case the neutralization of the international issue and the suppression of overt internal friction and resentment terminated the conflict situation and led the way to accommodation between the groups.

The ethnic tensions remained, as they do between all ethnic groups, but resentments and hostilities were once more concealed. The two communities again exhibited outward harmony in their relations.

IMMIGRATION, KINSHIP, AND THE RISE OF
WORKING-CLASS REALISM IN INDUSTRIAL AMERICA

Much scholarly disappointment exists over the failure of the American industrial working class to create a meaningful political and revolutionary movement during the half-century after 1890. While some evidence of potential militancy surfaced periodically, modern workers generally engaged in protests which were considerably narrower in their objectives, during periods of crisis such as the 1930's than those of nineteenth century workingmen who fought crusades against social inequality and the "demanding effects of mechanization."[1] Between 1880 and 1920, while an enormous wave of European immigrants entered America, a transformation took place in the objectives of industrial toilers. That the proud, skilled craftsmen of an earlier period gave way to thousands of less-skilled operatives in steel, electrical, and automative plants is rather obvious. Considerably less apparent is why rank and file objectives narrowed and exhibited a growing sense of realism, an inclination to seek practical goals such as job security rather than the loftier ideals which pervaded the protest of earlier times. While a complete resolution of this problem may not be possible here, a beginning will be suggested by probing the work and home life of immigrant workers, a substantial component of the modern industrial workforce. In the interrelationship between work and family, a nexus of concerns which dominated the lives of laborers, clues will be sought to an understanding of the development of worker attitudes in the decades immediately preceding the 1930's and the nature of worker discontent during the Great Depression.

The idealism and larger social objectives of nineteenth century workers have been identified repeatedly in historical studies. Gerald N. Grob, for instance, in his study of the American labor movement between 1865 and 1900, shifted the focus on industrialism's impact away from restricted opportunity to the "dehumanizing" effect mechanization and specialization had on artisans. Because the traditional status of artisans was being eroded, Grob concluded that organizations such as the National Labor Union and the Kinghts of Labor struggled vainly to stem the rush of modernization and retain traditional values.[2]

After analyzing labor reforms in the decade after the Civil War, David Montgomery was impressed by what he saw as attempts to impart human and moral values to a society dominated by commercial ones. Modifying Grob's view of artisans trying to recapture a vanishing past, Montgomery felt labor was pursuing equality with capital, recognition of the dignity of the workingman and trying to impart a "moral order on the market economy." Indeed, Montgomery reached a conclusion similar to the British scholar, E.P. Thompson, who had similiarly found a desire among nineteenth century British workers to "humanize" their environment and temper the drive for production and profit.

Both men saw in the behavior of industrial workers a tendency to oppose the drift toward "acquisitive man."[3] The investigations of Herbert Gutman into late nineteenth century communities also found workers instigating movements of reform and protest which again transcended "bread and butter" issues and sought to achieve human dignity and even racial equality.[4]

Observations of twentieth century workers, however, leave a distinctively different impression. Selig Perlman's *A Theory of the Labor Movement* stressed job consciousness and a desire to regulate access to employment as the overriding preoccupation of the American rank and file. With the growth of industrial America, Perlman felt a psychological shift in worker's concerns took place from one of abundance to one of scarce opportunities. Out of a growing pessimism, he concluded that labor unions such as the AFL emerged with a pure and simple goal: to preserve the limited number of employment opportunities. Perlman assumed, in other words, that union objectives represented the personal aspirations of the rank and file.[5] Montgomery attempted an even further refinement of the Perlman thesis by arguing that in the first two decades of the twentieth century the objectives of American trade unions themselves were actually transformed. Noting the growing militancy of rank and file laborers in large-scale, modern industries, Montgomery argued that labor's demands, while transcending simple "bread and butter" issues, moved into specific areas of work rules, union recognition, discharge of unpopular foremen, and the regulation of layoffs. In other words, workers began to seek greater control of the production process itself. With this bold analysis, Montgomery had now suggested that in both the ideologies of labor spokesmen and the behavior of the rank and file, sobermindedness was replacing larger social objectives of an earlier age.[6]

Despite an abundance of historical research, however, explanations for the rising practicality of worker's goals are not generally agreed upon. Consider the widespread notion that modern American workers increasingly came to accept the dominant values of the middle class. This view of the embourgeoisment of the rank and file stemed originally from the investigations of Robert and Helen Lynd in the 1920's. In their study of Middletown, the Lynds' found that the community's workers were "running for dear life" in the business of making money in order to acquire more and more of their subjective wants. The Lynds' further emphasized that workers pursued education as fervently as a religion in order to obtain upward mobility, while conveniently overlooking their own data which indicated that about one-third of the town's working-class families had no plans for their children's education at all.[7]

The Lynd's view was modified only slightly but essentially retained in the extensive Yankee City series published in the 1940's. W. Lloyd Warner and Leo Srole found some families who encouraged their children to attend college but others who insisted that their progeny find employment as soon as possible. Ultimately, however, the study accepted an assimilationist viewpoint and saw workers and their families acquiring acquisitive, middle-class values of individual carrers and success.[8]

Notions of self-improvement, upward striving and educational fervor have been discovered among working populations elsewhere. E.P. Thompson has shown that the English working-class of the mid-nineteenth century demonstrated a marked desire for self-improvement through literacy, although evidence exists that this drive was withering by the end of the nineteenth century. A proliferation of social mobility studies have sustained the impression that a desire for individual success was a pervasive notion among foreign-born workers.

Accounts of immigrant mobility in New York City, South Bend, Boston, Cleveland, and Chicago have all been based on the assumption that workers diligently pursued social advancement.[9]

Further support for the embourgeoisment thesis emerged from the writings of historian Timothy Smith and his students. Smith's research convinced him that a number of immigrants went into business and nearly all possessed a "commitment to the American dream" and an "indigenous thirst for education."[10]

After examining the backgrounds of Italian immigrants to Kansas City, Utica, and Rochester, John Briggs argued that they were generally intent on individual advancement and proprietorship in America. Briggs' description of Italian attitudes were corroborated by Josef Barton who depicted Italian workers migrating to Cleveland as men ready for improvement and advancement. Even more intent on uplift were Barton's sample of Romanians in the same city; only his study group of Slovaks revealed individuals divergent from the model of a modern day achiever. In a recent dissertation on Hungarians another Smith student, Paula Benkart, has uncovered evidence that Hungarians were leaving for America with "rising expectations" and intending to return to Europe to improve their material condition.[11]

Extensive oral history interviewing with industrial workers and their families in steel and coal districts in Pennsylvania has generated considerable data which suggest a different basis, however, for the narrowing of worker objectives. These interviews have carried the movement toward the microscopic examination of the worker's world into the confines of individual lives themselves and leave an impression that some of the prior assumptions about the American working-class world views are somewhat less than accurate.[12] Life reviews of several immigrants did indicate some tendency on the part of workers to pursue individual success and enter business ventures. John Butrymowicz, a Pittsburgh Pole, left a glass house as a boy to work as a teller in a bank and take banking courses in the evening in order to avoid the fate of thousands of other young Poles who entered local mills. Maria Kresic recalled that her father, an immigrant Slovene, initiated several business establishments and insisted that his son enter college *despite* criticism from fellow Slovenes that the boy should be sent into the mills at Steelton. Italians such as Ray La Marca often learned trades in Italy such as barbering and quickly established these trades in America. One Pittsburgh Pole worked in a factory only long enough to save enough money to open his own tavern. And Louis Smolinski, a steelworker, thought of becoming a salesman soon after entering the Edgar Thompson mill in Braddock. He asked himself, "What the hell am I to do here all my life."[13]

But these examples of rising expectations were rare and most immigrants diverted their energies away from personal advancement to the realities of sustaining their families. The people of industrial Pennsylvania affirmed the view that working-class life allowed little room for risk taking or long-term investments in personal careers. Commonplace was the family whose children left school as soon as possible and entered a wage-earning occupation. While children frequently made the decision to leave school themselves despite parental objections, it was just as likely that the push for an early entry into the job market came from parents eager to increase the income of their household. Joe Rudiak, a second generation Pole, explained that in the company town in which he was raised few adolescents finished high school and most started work after the eighth grade, including a number who left the community for work in the expanding automobile plants of Detroit. Among some Ukrainian-Americans in the 1920's and 1930's early work was "expected." An electrical worker in Erie recalled that if you could leave school and find a job you were considered fortunate.[14]

Additional probes of personal lives have further weakened the generalization that workers were driving feverishly toward success and the acquisition of goods. While the American working class may never have been as impervious to outside ideas as English workers appear to have been in the period 1870-1900,[15] by and large its members revealed rather limited social aspirations and continually sacrificed individual inclinations to family needs. Studies of automobile workers, Italians in Buffalo, and Slovaks in McKeesport confirmed the pre-eminence of familial over personal objectives. Shoe workers in Lynn, Massachusetts actually exhibited a diminishing belief in individual opportunity with the rise of the factory system. Interviews with Amoskeag textile workers in Manchester, New Hampshire revealed a similar emphasis on the present and the family. Mary Cunion, a Scottish weaver at Amoskeag, recounted that, "We just took what came," while Mary Dancause saw employment at the Amoskeag as a means to support her family. In fact, Amoskeag workers found considerable security and contentment in the flexible work routines of the mill and were often unwilling to leave it.[16] Indeed, at the heart of this working-class realism was the ability of industrial workers to remain pragmatic in the face of prevailing American-bourgeois ideology. They were able to recognize all along that the promise of mobility masked the incredible difficulties and risks involved in any attempt to abandon their status of wage laborers. Long before historians discovered the difficulties of achieving middle-class status, most workers recognized that their opportunities were circumscribed and that ways would have to continually be devised to live from paycheck to paycheck.

Familial objectives, then, loom as an alternative force to the lure of social mobility in shaping worker goals. Yet, no reason exists to conclude that family was any less of a concern among immigrant workers of the nineteenth century and in fact, research has shown that familial concerns dominated both preindustrial and industrial eras. In attempting to understand the source of change in worker attitudes it might be instructive to focus on initial contact of "new immigrants" with the American occupational structure and their initial entry into the industrial system. The striking feature of immigrant work patterns in industrial America was the lack of random distribution of workers and the extensive amount of grouping. Clusters were found in the nineteenth century as well. Nearly one-half the Philadelphia Irish in 1850 were in unskilled labor, for instance, while 67 percent of the Germans were artisans. In Buffalo Germans dominated crafts such as masonry, cooperage, and shoemaking while the Irish worked largely as unskilled laborers, domestics, ship carpenters, and teamsters. But this early bunching resulted directly from the possession or lack of premigration skills whereas newer immigrants after 1880, generally with less skills than the Germans, actually intensified the pattern of clustering. By 1911 a study of seven urban areas revealed that nearly one-third of all South Italians were categorized as "general laborers" as contrasted to only 9 percent of the Poles and 7 percent of the Germans. Fully 65 percent of the Poles were in manufacturing and mechanical pursuits compared to only 28.8 percent of the South Italians. Greeks were highly congregated in personal service endeavors while over one-half of all Serbs were in general labor. Groups such as the Swedes, Jews, and Germans were considerably underrepresented in "unspecified labor" positions.[17]

Contemporary scholarship has substantiated the earlier suggestion of initial occupational concentrations. Stephan Thernstrom's massive study of Boston found significant differences in the distribution of immigrants. In 1890, for instance, 65 percent of Boston's Irish labored in low manual callings while about one-half of those from Canada and Germany obtained skilled employment. Thernstrom made an important finding, moreover, when he discovered that clustering continued through two generations. By 1950 Jewish and British newcomers were still overrepresented in managerial and professional classes while the Irish and Italians were heavily lumped in unskilled categories. For second generation Italian and Irish men, overrepresentation continued in unskilled work while Jewish and British males continued to enjoy above normal concentrations of professionals and managers.[18] Recent sociological investigations of upwardly mobile individuals have substantiated the fact that ethnic groups generally followed specific paths in gaining "prominence" since the 1920's.[19]

Studies of individual immigrant waves in various locations sustain the impression of limited dispersion into the occupational structure. In Indiana oil refineries, Croatians held jobs in only three categories: stillman helper, firemen, and still cleaners. In the ready-made clothing industry, Jews predominated in small firms with minimal mechanization and segmentation of labor while Italians concentrated in large factories which tended to require less individual skills. Serbs and Croats in New York City were heavily involved in freight-handling. Italians dominated construction gangs and barber shops in Buffalo, Philadelphia, and Pittsburgh. By 1918 Italians represented 75 percent of the women in the men's and boy's clothing industry and 93 percent of the females doing hand embroidery in New York City. Nearly all of the 3,000 employees in the Peninsular Car Company in Detroit by 1900 were Polish. Polish women dominated restaurant and kitchen jobs in Chicago by 1909, which they preferred to domestic employment. By 1920 one study found an incredible 69 percent of Slovak males in coal-mining and about one-half of all Mexicans working as blast-furnace laborers.[20]

Before rushing to conclude that immigrant clustering was attributable solely to the operation of premigration bonds of kinship or skills brought from Europe, particular attention must be directed toward alterations in the skill levels of American workers between 1880 and 1920. Historian Daniel Nelson has described the factory of the 1880's as a "congeries of craftsmen's shops." Yet a 1906 United States Department of Labor study noted an increase in the division of labor with more operations being sub-divided into minute operations. The report explained that hand trades were rapidly becoming obsolete and labor processes were requiring less overall proficiency. The substitution of unskilled for skilled labor was already widespread in industries such as meat packing, coal mining, and textiles. By 1920 employers had intensified the drive to establish more efficient operations, reduce costs and avoid the burden of extensive worker training programs by reducing skill requirements for incoming laborers. Expansion in child, female and unskilled, foreign labor and the decline of apprenticeship programs and highly proficient operatives underscored the trend.[21] In the early decades of the twentieth century the number of blacksmiths, machinists and glassblowers declined substantially. Apprenticeships among brick and stone masons, and machinists fell from 39, 463 in 1920 to 13,606 a decade later. The number of dressmakers and seamstresses was cut by over 300,000 during the period while that of iron moulders and casters was halved by 1930.

50   journal of social history

Simultaneously the number of laborers in blast furnaces and rolling mills, shirt factories, glass works, electrical manufacturing plants and in the expanding automobile industry increased markedly.[22]

The dilution of crafts and skills accelerated after 1900 and had a negative impact upon the older immigrant stocks from northern and western Europe. Germans in nineteenth century Philadelphia predominated in skilled butchering, tailoring and shoemaking positions. As these occupations declined, Germans were frequently dislocated and found it more difficult to transfer jobs to their sons. A similar pattern among skilled Germans in Poughkeepsie, New York, resulted in a greater number of second generation Germans becoming factory operatives than their parents or concentrating in low paying trades such as barbering or coopering. Indeed, both in Philadelphia and Poughkeepsie less than 9 percent of second generation Germans were lodged in skilled categories; they began to appear in "lower" trades such as cigarmaking which, according to Clyde and Sally Griffen, offered "limited futures."[23]

The blurring of skill distinctions among workers and the implementation of new efficiency schemes were accelerated during the period of the "new immigration." With proletarian protest growing in the late nineteenth century and larger concentrations of workers emerging in urban areas, industrial managers began to impose a bureaucratic structure upon the work force with hierarchical gradations of unskilled and semiskilled operations. This restructuring of work itself resulted in something of a segmentation of the labor market, as some theorists have contended, which created an infinite number of "entry-level" jobs which could only intensify the process of clustering, while making it extremely unlikely that newcomers could implement any previously acquired skills. The promise of industrial America to immigrant workers was not so much that one could rise as that one could gain access at any number of points of entry. Opportunity was not vertical but horizontal, a fact which tended to blunt the rhetoric of social mobility immediately upon arrival.

If skills were no longer crucial to obtaining work in the expanding sectors of the economy, something else would have to take their place. The alternative would be a random entry of thousands of immigrant workers into the industrial complex. But the widespread existence of clusters suggests that a sense of order in joining newcomers and occupations were operative. In even the most cursory survey of immigrant job acquisition, kinship and ethnic ties invariably emerge as the vital link. But the infusion of familial and ethnic ties could not, as Gutman's arguments suggest, solely explain the pattern. To be sure immigrants carried strong kinship bonds to America, although ethnic ties were often nurtured *after* their arrival. Without the diminution of skills, however, these associations could not have been implemented on such a vast scale. Those who would explain immigrant adaptation as a function of premigration culture[25] or argue that immigrants entered occupations which allowed them to implement premigration skills[26] have neglected the structural transformation which characterized expanding industries and the extent to which a match took place between previously acquired behavior and available opportunities in America.

It is true, of course, that even in the period of declining skills, instances of immigrants implementing premigration skills were observed. A group of South Slavs, for instance, from the Dalmatian high country, skilled in butchering and boning, acquired jobs in the meat packing industry. A number of Slovenes in soft coal mining had spent their early years in Austrian mines. Barrel factories in Bayonne, New Jersey employed Slovak coopers as early as the 1880's. Skilled

48

Czechs were making pearl buttons in America in the 1890's. The matching of Jewish tailoring skills with the expanding garment industry in New York City is well known.[27]

Instances of skill implementation were exceptional, however, as immigrants normally relied on ethnic and kinship attachments to establish small beachheads in a given occupation which in turn attracted later arrivals. Although its influence varied from city to city and declined by 1900, the Italian *padrone* system was a well known example of how a cluster could be established. In Philadelphia *padrones* channeled early Italians into railroad construction gangs. But immigrant chains functioned so effectively once established that middlemen and labor agents were inevitably replaced by an informal network of friends and relatives. Theorists who have accepted the "split-labor market theory" and its assumption that ethnic middlemen emerged out of migration streams which possess a "sojourning orientation" overlook the fact that intermediaries usually functioned in the very beginning of immigration and were eventually superceded by ties of ethnicity and kinship.[28]

In the expanding, industrial sectors of Pennsylvania interviews revealed that kinship and ethnicity were particularly effective in distributing the mass of incoming workers, overshadowing skills, labor recruiters, or middlemen. Oral history interviews with Italians and Poles in Pittsburgh reaffirmed the point. Poles established occupation beachheads at the Jones and Laughlin and Oliver's mills on the South Side, Hepponstalls and the Pennsylvania Railroad in Lawrenceville and at the Armstrong Cork Company and the H.J. Heinz plant. Valentine G.* gained his first job in America on the railroad through his brother. Brothers also assisted Peter H. in obtaining employment in a foundry making castings for miners. Ignacy M. left Russian Poland in 1912 and relied on his brother to get him a position piling steel beams. Joseph D. left Prussia for a job in a mill which was procured by his wife's uncle. A cousin found Edward R. work at a machine shop. John S. followed friends from Galicia in 1909 but needed relatives to acquire machinist work for him. Charles W. relied on a friend to transform him from a shepherd in Russian Poland to a moulder at the Crucible Steel Company. And hundreds of Polish women relied on relatives to gain them access to domestic work for Americans and boarding house tasks among the Poles.[29]

Every Italian interviewed in Pittsburgh relied on kin or friends to persuade foremen or other supervisors to hire them. Where a relative had already established a trade or business a position was usually waiting.[30] Kinship networks, in fact, actually narrowed the job search considerably. Thus, both the father and brother of Nicholas R. relied on friends to gain employment on the railroads in 1904. When Nicholas himself arrived in America his father asked the foreman to "give him a break." Nicholas joined his kin in laying tracks. Antonio S. obtained work on the railroad through cousins from the same village. It was not surprising that Leo G. worked for the Pittsburgh Railway Company laying stone base for streetcar tracks. His grandfather, father, brother, and uncle were all employed by the company. Similarly Palfilo C. came to the Bloomfield section of the city in 1900 where his brother-in-law found him employment on a pipe laying gang.[31]

A striking example of the ability of Italians to use kinship in order to thrust themselves into a particular occupational sector was the accomplishment of newcomers to the Bloomfield section from the village of Ateleta in the province of Abruzzi. From the 1890's to the 1930's, repeated instances surfaced of villagers bringing "paesani" to the pipe construction department of the Equitable Gas

*Last names of respondents are abbreviated in instances where anonymity was requested.

Company. One of the earliest to gain employment was Anthony B., a farmer in Italy, who found work with the gas company and informed several friends in Ateleta about job possibilities. Amico L., who initially arrived in 1890, returned to Ateleta three times. Upon each return from Pittsburgh he secured a friend or relative for the pipe-line "gang." Vincent L. came to the city around 1900 and obtained his job laying pipe through an uncle already here. After two more trips to Pittsburgh he returned to Ateleta for good in 1911 but later sent a son who was hired by sewer contractors at the request of friends already working with the firm.[32]

Men were not the only ones to follow kin and ethnic paths into the industrial workplace. Immigrant females as well found such ties convenient. A 1930 study of 2,000 foreign-born women revealed that most had secured their initial jobs through relatives and friends. All had worked in either cigar or textile factories, and less than ten percent had acquired relevent skills for these jobs prior to migrating. Surveys of full-fashioned, hosiery loopers discovered that the majority obtained their positions through acquaintances. One study of hosiery loopers concluded that during the period from 1900 to 1930 younger girls followed relatives into the mill as a "general practice." A 1924 investigation of Italian girls in New York City reported not only that 75 percent acquired their first jobs through friends or relatives but that these women were "ashamed" to seek employment alone and would quit a task if friends or kin left as well. In Buffalo, Italian women assisted each other in obtaining work in canneries while in nearly all cities immigrant women shared information on the availability of domestic work.[33]

What is particularly salient about immigrant clustering is that it was neither short-lived nor totally eradicated in the first American-born generation. The important data compiled by E.P. Hutchinson left provocative evidence of both grouping and the fact that occupations of initial entry profoundly affected subsequent careers of most groups. In a monograph based on special access to the 1950 census data, Hutchinson was able to determine the relative concentration of ethnic groups at mid-century with a proportion of 100 indicating that a group was represented in an occupation in terms equal to their proportion of the population as a whole. Nearly every group revealed several significant concentrations: Greeks as cooks; Italians as tailors, barbers and textile workers; the Irish as cleaners and guards; Germans as bakers, managers and toolmakers; Yugoslavs as dress factory workers, cooks and mine laborers.

Even among immigrant children, who by 1950 would have been well advanced in a career, clustering in entry occupations continued. Greeks were still overrepresented in restaurants, Italians in the apparel industry, the Irish as guards, the Germans as toolmakers, and Yugoslavs as miners and dressmakers. To be sure, intergenerational mobility occurred, but the incidence of grouping is still suggestive of the impact initial occupations had. In fact, among the Irish, Poles and Yugoslavs in the metal industry the relative concentration of their workers actually increased from the first to the second generation.[34]

The attraction of the second generation of industrial workers into the occupational world of their kin and friends, an indication of how newcomers could exploit lowered entrance requirements, was widespread. Studies of mining families in southwestern Pennsylvania and Illinois reveal a pattern of sons being drawn into the mines by their fathers.[35] Between 1920 and 1940 heavy concentrations of Yugoslavs and Poles followed their relatives into South Chicago steel plants. Not surprisingly a scholarly study of immigrant mobility in Cleveland concluded that the overriding influence in the careers of the second generation consisted of the fortunes of immigrant fathers. A 1946 report from a mill town stressed that "father-son" work relationships existed throughout the local plant. Of 61 workers interviewed, one third had brothers in the mill. The National Tube Company in McKeesport, Pennsylvania, was reluctant to move its facilities in 1950 because jobs in seamless-type construction had been "handed down from father to son." Among Philadelphia toolmakers in 1951, one in five explained that the influence of family and friends had attracted them to the work. In a New England textile factory nepotism was found to be so widespread in securing employment that workers with familial connections within the plant were actually held in higher esteem than "unattached" employees who were presumed to be more transient.[36]

Kinship and ethnicity came to function so effectively in distributing workers that industrial managers were frequently not adverse to encouraging the system. Shop foremen, usually too busy to recruit workers, generally relied upon informal contacts with various ethnic groups before and sometimes after the establishment of centralized personnel offices after World War I. At the Pittsburgh Steel Company in Monessen, Pennsylvania, foremen frequented the Croatian Club to obtain not only references for potential workers but twenty dollar bills conveniently left on the bar.[37] Beyond such economic incentives, foremen and managers held definite stereotypes which favored one group over another. Italians were often throught to be better suited for outdoor work while Poles were preferred for factory and mill employment. Such views repeatedly favored immigrant over black workers. At the Illinois Steel Company blacks were overlooked even when the company's own figures showed that they had less turnover and absenteeism than whites. At the Pabst Brewing Company in Milwaukee Germans predominated while Italians moved into the shipping room of International Harvester and Poles were preferred for unskilled labor gangs.[38] Extensive documentation is available to show that at New Hampshire textile mills management relied heavily on the ability of French-Canadians to attract kin and even train them after the creation of a central employment office.[39]

As a consequence of declining skill requirements and emerging kinship-occupational clusters, familial concerns were strongly reinforced. Family objectives now superceded the personal goals of constituent members partially because families were now able to perform crucial functions in the process of job procurement. This ability led to a pattern in immigrant families whereby parents generally dictated the career paths of children and effectively diverted individuals away from personal advancement and even social idealism to objectives of immediate familial concern. Oral data are especially illustrative of this family dominance in working-class life. In order to prepare children for adulthood parents wasted little time in imparting skills which seemed necessary from the perspective of families who labored in mines and mills. Marie S., who was born in a coal town in 1914, aspired to a musical career at age fifteen but her mother asked her to leave school and assist at home in the raising of her brothers and sisters. She was later joined at home by a sister who left school in the ninth grade. Both girls remained at home until marriage, assisting in domestic chores and earning extra income by sewing. They had been well prepared for such tasks for their mother had instructed them in canning, food preparation and sewing since they were eight. Another young Pole, Anna S., said she wanted to study music but her parents thought otherwise. Feeling it was more practical to be a dressmaker, her father bought her a sewing machine and asked her to remain at home to care for her small brother and sew. A Slovene girl wept when forced to leave school by her father after the sixth grade because he felt a girl didn't need schooling "to change diapers."[40]

While girls either remained at home to work on domestic tasks or found employment in silk mills and cigar factories, boys were usually sent to mills or breakers. If girls were introduced to domestic skills at an early age, boys were often told that learning a job skill was preferable to remaining in school. No particular trade or skill seemed favored over another. The point was to acquire some experience which would be useful in gaining steady employment. Usually such training was received on a job which was secured by immigrant fathers. The first job for a Bethlehem steelworkers was learning the operation of a crane from his father at the steel mill. Interviews with Poles in the Lawrenceville section of Pittsburgh revealed that boys were taken during the 1920's and the 1930's to work alongside their fathers at Hepponstalls, Armour Meats and other plants in the area.[41] Where fathers did not provide actual job placement, boys were usually urged to attend trade school to learn carpentry, shoemaking or patternmaking.[42]

This continual imposition of parental wishes was bound to generate intergenerational tensions despite the fact that parents seemed genuinely concerned over their children's welfare in adulthood. Tamara Hareven argues that marriage did not offer an escape from work outside the home because family income depended upon the work of more than one member. But in Pennsylvania coal fields many immigrant girls viewed the situation differently. A number of Polish and Croatian women in Nanticoke and Monessen confessed that they eagerly sought a marriage partner in order to escape their families of origin and the employment burdens they endured. In several instances when a child attempted to defy a parent and remain in school an older brother or sister would object. Consider the case of Stella K. In 1930 she had an opportunity to leave Nanticoke and live with a wealthy family on Long Island. The arrangement was such that she would be allowed simultaneously to perform domestic service and to complete her high school education. The plan was abandoned, however, when her brother bitterly complained because he had been forced to leave high school early and enter the mines.[43]

Even where tensions and discord did surface, the wishes of parents invariably prevailed. George M. was the second of four children in a Croatian family. While his parents wanted him to begin working, he argued that he be allowed to finish high school and enter Carnegie-Mellon University to study electrical engineering. He related, however, that his father opposed the idea. "I was only seventeen," he noted, "I couldn't do anything." Helen M. wanted to study bookkeeping but her parents insisted she help at home. John S., a Braddock Slovak, expressed a desire for the priesthood. His mother's response determined his fate. "Son why don't you go and work," she implored, "school won't make you any money." In 1939 Mary M. wanted to attend a business school in Charleroi with a girl friend. Because her father insisted that she help the family instead, she and an older sister found employment in a glass factory; a brother entered the Pittsburgh Steel Company at Monessen at age seventeen. Mary theorized that her parents "just didn't believe in school."[44] And Rose Popovich concluded:

> In those days children weren't treated the way they are today . . . . It was always work, work of some kind. No matter how young I was they (parents) always found something for me to do.[45]

While internal disagreements over work and school existed, an impression that the were representative would be misleading. More typical in Pennsylvania was the working-class youth who not only abided by parental persuasion but actually initiated the idea for an early termination of schooling himself. Not all parents minimized the potential value of extended schooling. In a small number of homes children were urged to acquire as much education as possible even if tremendous economic sacrifices were required from parents who did without children's earnings. Even in these homes children were likely to display a deep obligation to ease the financial burdens of their parents by leaving school and turning wages over to parents in an almost ritualistic manner. Antoinette W. was one of five children raised in a Polish family. At age fourteen she decided to work in a Wilkes-Barre silk mill. Although her mother was opposed, Antionette explained that she was unable to concentrate on school when money was needed so badly at home. Similarly, her older brother began working on a nearby farm at age eleven and an older sister entered a textile factory at age twelve. A Monessen steelworker left school early and delayed his marriage until age 31 in order to remain at home and assist his parents. Eleanor D. decided to quit after one year of high school. Her immigrant mother recalled, "She was sixteen years old and she just wanted to leave and help in our store." Eleanor's husband left school at age fourteen over parental objections to work with an uncle in a butcher shop. Tom Luketich returned to Cokeburg from Detroit in the 1930's because his father became unemployed and his brother was still too young to work. He revealed that he felt an obligation to support his family. Virginia V. actually felt ambivalent toward marrying and leaving her mother. She was persuaded to do so only because two sisters remained at home to provide support. Joseph G. quit school at age sixteen and entered a coal mine near Daisytown because he felt it would be too great a financial burden for his father if he remained in school.[46] The overall attitude was summarized pointedly by Lillian N. As a young girl she thought of becoming a nurse but decided instead to leave high school after one year and labor in a Nanticoke silk mill. She carefully detailed her reasoning:

"I figured I would leave school in the first year of high school. I couldn't go away to be a nurse because I was needed at home much more than anything else because I helped with the children and all. We had to bathe the children, dress them and put them to sleep. My mother had enough to do with just cooking."[47]

Clearly, family obligations dominated working-class predilections and may have exerted a moderating influence on individual expectations and the formulation of social and economic goals. The assertions of William Goode and Edward Shorter that family member's participation in the industrial labor force led to a growing independence on the part of workers and a diminution in their familial ties and responsibilities weaken considerably in the face of the Pennsylvania data. Shorter, focusing his attention on women, argued that as women worked away from home they were increasingly affected by the mentality of the market place and the pursuit of individual interests.[48] More accurate are the assertions of Elizabeth Pleck who has demonstrated that industrialization did not clearly lead to a separation of work and family interest and that such a separation was more characteristic of the middle class.[49]

Even more striking than the predominance of family interests over personal ones was the realistic assessment of survival displayed by Pennsylvania's laboring families. To be sure some clamored for ideals. John Czelen related how Slavic steelworkers were persuaded by promises of "equality" in Monessen in return for their support during the 1919 strike effort. Misgivings toward an "acquisitive society" were also found woven throughout the consciousness of industrial workers.[50] Certainly a few attempted to leave industrial routines and initiate business ventures of their own. But at the heart of the worker's system of values — his very ethos — stood a fundamental sense of realism. Industrial workers in Pennsylvania coal and steel regions simply confronted the demands and pressures of their world and reacted in ways that were invariably pragmatic. Rose Popovich explained that her family kept boarders in the mill town in Monessen because "that was the only way you could get yourself on your feet" and pay the gas and food bills and the rent. A Bethlehem steelworker claimed that his motivation for working was simply that his family was big and left him no time to be tired. Steve Kika joined an unemployment council in McKeesport in 1932 not to restructure society but because he was looking for ways to find work. The conclusion of an immigrant women caught the essence of working-class realism:

> "I was poor. To live in America is work, work, work. I'm sick and my family was sick. And my husband died so fast and leave me with a mortgage. That was a headache. I didn't sell the home. I go to work and pay my mortgage. I raised the kids. That's enough for me . . ."[51]

This preoccupation with survival strategies and family welfare, however, should not lead quickly to a conclusion that Perlman's stress on pure and simple economic issues was correct all along. To accept such an argument would be to assume economic issues were goals in themselves when, in fact, they were only part of a larger cultural system which focused its energies on the maintenance of the family unit. Perlman and many other labor and economic historians failed to realize that the behavior of individuals in the workplace was an extension of their familial world. Immigrants, blacks, and native-born toilers entered the mines and mills of Pennsylvania prior to 1940 not on their own behalf but because of the needs of their kin. It should not be surprising, therefore, that so many willingly relinquished their paychecks. Personal satisfaction, the control of production, equality and mobility were usually secondary concerns. What Gutman described as a continuation of traditional values in industrial society was not a literal cultural persistence, for changes and adaptations were widespread. What remained constant during the half-century of industrialization after 1890 was the fact that a family-oriented culture continued to serve necessary functions and define the framework of individual lives.[52] Yet few historians have bothered to link this culture with the nature of worker protest, especially during periods of crisis such as the 1930's. If workers agitated for job security more than social equality and demonstrated a realism which disappointed those who would have preferred a greater groundswell of social idealism in America, it was because equality and even mobility were largely personal goals while job security was the key to family sustenance. After all other arguments have been heard, one is still left with a recurring suspicion that for the rank and file in the twentieth century labor issues were essentially family issues.

If the early decades of the "new immigrant's" encounter with industrialized America actually fostered the growth of a family economy which sensibly sought basic economic benefits and muted individual inclinations and idealism in favor of group survival, a framework for labor protest in the 1930's was established before the Great Depression ever began. David Brody, for instance, has argued that the depression experience undermined the prevailing system of labor control. He contends that during the 1920's welfare capitalism raised expectations of economic well-being and security which was exploded by the onset of hard times. Brody believes that the labor activity of the 1930's was generated by a profound sense of betrayal among industrial workers against paternalistic employers.[53] But the recollections of individual lives analyzed here indicate that expectations for well-being were not substantially raised prior to the 1930's and that workers entered the period tied primarily to concerns of kin. In Pennsylvania, expectations seemed somewhat modest and realistic through the pre-depression period as the cadence of industrial life exhibited remarkable continuity. Families generally searched for ways to make ends meet, achieved little savings, sent their children to work early in life and valued steady employment.

Much of the analysis of the rise of unions during the period, moreover, has shifted to the shop-floor experience. Focusing on the pace and process of production and internal activities such as the grievance system, some have suggested that the impetus toward unionization involved above all power and its redistribution, with workers seeking to resist further incursions of scientific managers into the workplace and expand their control over the basic system of production. This view has been supplemented by indications that men in the shop represented a new group, often second generation Americans, who were rational, less intimidated by foremen, calculating, aggressive, and "possessed of an impulse for self-improvement." There is no question that abuses of power angered individual workmen. Frequently statements surfaced in the Pennsylvania interviews regarding the suspicion that some men, more favored by foremen, received slightly higher wages. The interviews also offered considerable information concerning resentment toward arbitrary power exercised outside the workplace in industrial communities, a fact generally overlooked by those focusing exclusively on "shop-floor" experiences. Little expression of resentment over the pace of production — especially during the restricted work week of the 1930s — surfaced at all. Historians such as Montgomery who have described twentieth century worker movements as an "unprecedented quest for social power" and control in reaction to the growing rationalization and dehumanization of work itself may have overlooked somewhat the incredibly powerful need to maintain a family system which emerged from the initial clash of tradition and modern industrial capitalism. Indeed, their focus on skilled operatives more than the lower orders of the rank and file may have blinded them to alternative sources of worker realism. Those who have concentrated their efforts on the workplace, moreover, have generally glimpsed workers at specific points in their lives and have not observed the larger perspective of individuals fabricating lives over time from a complexity of social institutions.[54] Finally, even earlier generations could be calculating and aggressive, but unionism did not take as firm a hold among the ranks at that time.

Some have even discovered in the rank and file militancy of the 1930's an embryonic "revolutionary potential." This theory, advanced primarily in the writings of Staughton Lynd, also emphasizes the importance of shop-level activism. After interviewing working-class organizers from the 1930's, Lynd was impressed with the by now recurring theme of social idealism among working-class spokesmen. He argued that these leaders were attempting to initiate a movement for social democracy. "They believed," he asserted, "that the human right to a job should take precedence over the property right to manage an enterprise as the employer saw fit." Such idealistic objectives were tempered but not wholly discounted in the conclusions reached by Sidney Fine after his study of the 1936-1937 "sit down" strike at Flint, Michigan. Fine sensed that the strikers saw themselves for a time as part of a collective effort to better not just their own condition but the nation as well, viewing the union as a "social and moral force."[55]

Some evidence exists by now to conclude that while a grass-roots movement toward unions did surface in the 1930's — a fact which is substantiated in the interviews discussed here — it was not ultimately revolutionary. While brief flirtations with larger social visions emerged, they were seldom sustained among the rank and file. Robert Zieger, after examining the organization of the converted paper industry in the 1930's, concludes that grass roots militancy played a major role, but it was far from revolutionary and was, in fact, somewhat unpredictable with men frequently neglecting to pay dues or maintain a sound organization. Zieger observed in a later study that the "sporadic militancy" of the 1930's has been somewhat overdrawn given the degree of antiunionism and apathy that existed among workers. Thousands joined unions, Zieger discovered, only after careful calculation of economic interests.[56]

The interviews from Pennsylvania do not specifically refute the assertion of Lynd and others that a tradition of working-class democracy aimed at humanizing the larger society or strains of mobility and self improvement pervaded the industrial working-class. But such conclusions have followed from analysis which concentrated largely on articulate, working-class leaders and intellectuals and have stopped short of penetrating the temper of rank and file objectives. The limits to the groundswell of union activity in the 1930's noted by some observers may have emanated from the scope of family priorities which continued to direct the objectives of most workers. At the same time, a modern account of the 1930's which attributes the lack of American radicalism to a basic acceptance of the "American Dream" on the part of both the employed and unemployed fails to perceive the larger familial context in which men and women went off to work.[57]

Interwoven throughout the discussion of the unionist motives in Pennsylvania was the desire for job security. For all the disagreement over rank and file goals, even historians such as Brody and Peter Friedlander do not seem ready to discount the centrality of this one issue which was not only threatened most by the uncertainty of the 1930's but was the key to family well being and unity. "Sit-down" strikers in Flint were moved to action primarily because of a speedup in production *and* the irregular employment they experienced after 1929. Indeed, the one factor experienced by most industrial workers in the early thirties was the loss or reduction of work, not a quickening of the pace of production. If workers were to stabilize their families' existence they needed an end to the unemployment or shortened work schedules of the Depression.

Some of the disagreement over the motives of steelworkers in the thirties may result from a failure to dissect the course of organization over a period of time. A close reading of Pennsylvania interviews suggests that unemployment and work routines which became suddenly sporadic formed the initial impulse toward doing somthing about the situation. Once men became immersed in the current of organization, however, the question of power — both the companies' abuse of it and their own lack of it — began to crystalize. Consequently men like Dominic D. became enthusiastic when organizers emphasized the potential strength of men united. When workers found the Amalgamated ineffective, they sought, on their own, attachment to more effective organizations. But power never became an ultimate end. It was sought in greater measure in order to attain the original goal of job stability which would bring some regularity to the lives of workers and their kin.

In the life histories analyzed here two points seem clear. Rank and file militancy was a grass roots phenomenon which preceded and even hastened the establishment of the Steel Workers Organizing Committee (SWOC). Secondly, the objectives of the rank and file were not particularly revolutionary, ideological, or as much concerned with production arrangements as they were aimed at gaining secure and stable employment.[58] Dominic D. and Michael Z., for instance, revealed that even before the establishment of the SWOC, steelworkers in Aliquippa concluded that the Amalgamated Association of Iron and Tin Workers was powerless. On their own initiative they sent a delegation to John L. Lewis asking him to begin organizing steel. Louis S. recalled that men in Braddock repudiated the Amalgamated in 1934 and formed their own "Emergency Council," consisting of Slavs in the finishing department. Most rank and file, moreover, could agree with Stanley B., a Braddock steelworker, who exclaimed that he sought a union because after being unemployed he realized that he wanted some form of security and compensation for unemployed men who were married and had children. While Joe R. claimed that unemployment intensified his support for a union, clearly such men also wanted to rectify abuses by foremen and the arbitrary power of companies in local communities where a bank loan was unobtainable unless "you were a fair-haired company boy." But these problems had existed for years and were not exacerbated until the hold on jobs suddenly became extremely tenuous.[59]

Clearly, then, the labor discontent of most immigrants and their children in the 1930's represented a drift away from the social idealism of the nineteenth century and an affirmation of a pragmatic world view which included the valuation of job security and steady wages as a means to family stability. Within these families measures were taken to insure the cooperation of all potential wage earners. This is not to say that workers were unconcerned about power relationships, work routines, occupational advancements or even, on occasion, social transformation. But such objectives were ancillary and tied more to their fate as individuals, while the regularity of employment affected the very foundation of their familial world.

By acknowledging the familial base of labor protest, moreover, the cultural content of the immigrant working class is illuminated. It was a culture, however, which was not simply infused into American society from abroad but was largely generated by the complex process of industrialization itself. In the scholarly preoccupation with class *conflict*, the process of class *formation* has been largely overlooked. Yet, an immigrant working class was created in the decades before the Great Depression with values which represented a departure from an earlier century and which laid the foundation for the pragmatic response of the 1930's.

Pennsylvania Historical and Museum Commission   John Bodnar

FOOTNOTES

1. See Alan Dawley, *Class and Community, The Industrial Revolution in Lynn* (Cambridge, Mass., 1976); Gerald N. Grob, *Workers and Utopia, A Study of Ideological Conflict in the American Labor Movement, 1865-1900* (Evanston, 1961), pp. 197-89; David Montgomery, *Beyond Equality, Labor and the Radical Republicans, 1862-1872* (New York, 1967), pp. 445-47; Melvyn Dubofsky, *Industrialism and the American Worker, 1965-1920* (New York, 1975), p. 41; Staughton Lynd, "The Possibility of Radicalism in the Early 1930's: The Case of Steel," *Radical America*, 6 (Nov.-Dec., 1972); David Brody, "Labor and the Great Depression: The Interpretative Prospects," *Labor History*, 13 (Spring, 1972); Stanley Aronwitz, *False Promises, The Shaping of American Working Class Consciousness* (New York, 1973), pp. 137 ff. Abstract issues such as local power dominated workers in Sedalia, Missouri in the 1880's according to Michael J. Cassity, "Modernization and Social Crisis: The Knights of Labor and a Midwest Community, 1885-1886," *Journal of American History*, 66 (Jan., 1979), 42, 43, 61.

2. Grob, *Workers and Utopia*, pp. 187-89.

3. Montgomery, *Beyond Equality*, pp. 445-47; E.P. Thompson, *The Making of the English Working Class* (New York, 1963), pp. 830-32. See also Dawley, *Class and Community, passim.*

4. Herbert Gutman's work is conveniently collected in *Work, Culture, and Society in Industrializing America* (New York: Vintage Books, 1977). See also Robert H. Zieger, "Workers and Scholars: Recent Trends in American Labor Historiography," *Labor History*, 13 (Spring, 1972), 252-66 for an excellent overview of the development of labor historiography in this area.

5. Selig Perlman, *A Theory of the Labor Movement* (New York, 1928).

6. Montgomery, "The New Unionism and the Transformation of Worker's Consciousness in America, 1909-1922," *Journal of Social History*, 7 (Summer, 1974), 509-23. It should be stressed that Montgomery's study concentrated mostly on native-born workers and did not probe measurably the activities of the mass of immigrant newcomers.

7. Robert S. Lynd and Helen M. Lynd, *Middletown, A Study in American Culture* (New York, 1929), pp. 80, 87, 186-87.

8. W. Lloyd Warner and Leo Srole, *The Social System of American Ethnic Groups* (New Haven, 1945), pp. 79 ff.

9. Thompson, *Making of the English Working-Class*, pp. 719, 728. Gareth Stedman Jones, "Working-Class Culture and Working-Class Politics in London, 1870-1900; Notes on the Remaking of a Working Class," *Journal of Social History*, 7 (Summer, 1974), 464-67; Aronwitz, *False Promises*, p. 400.

10. T.L. Smith, "Immigrant Social Aspirations and American Education, 1880-1930," *American Quarterly*, 21 (Fall, 1969), 522-25; Smith, "Native Blacks and Foreign Whites: Varying Responses to Educational Opportunity in America, 1880-1950," in *Perspectives in American History*, 6 (1972), 311-313. Examples of working-class women seeking a higher status and seeking a divorce to get it are found in Elaine Tyler May, "The Pressure to Provide: Class, Consumerism, and Divorce in Urban America, 1880-1920," *Journal of Social History*, 12 (Winter, 1978), 191. A recent study which claims workers ultimately sought status and success in Daniel Walhowitz, *Worker City, Company Town* (Urbana, Ill., 1978).

11. John W. Briggs, *An Italian Passage, Immigrants to Three American Cities 1890-1930* (New Haven, 1978) pp. 7-10, 68. Barton, *Peasants and Strangers, passim*, Paula Kaye Benkart, "Religion, Family, and Continuity Among Hungarians Migrating to American Cities," (unpublished Ph.D. dissertation, Johns Hopkins University, 1975).

12. John Bodnar, Michael Weber and Roger Simon, "Migration, Kinship, and Urban Adaptation: Blacks and Poles in Pittsburgh, 1900-1930," *Journal of American History*, LXVI (Dec., 1979).

13. See interviews with John B., Pittsburgh, Mar. 3, 1976; Ray L., Pittsburgh, July 11, 1977; Louis S., June 20, 1978, Braddock, Pennsylvania Historical and Museum Commission (PHMC), Harrisburg. All interviews in text are from PHMC Oral History Collection.

14. See interviews in text with Joe R., Pittsburgh, July 21, 1974; Steve K., McKeesport, July 27, 1974; and Thomas Brown, Erie, June 5, 1976. For a more extensive discussion of the subject see Bodnar, "Immigration and Modernization: The Case of Slavic Peasants in Industrial America," *Journal of Social History*, 4 (Fall, 1976), 48-50.

15. Stedman Jones, "Working-Class Culture," 484-85.

16. Eli Chinoy, *Automobile Workers and the American Dream* (Garden City, N.Y., 1955), pp. 110-26; Virginia Yans McLaughlin, *Family and Community: Italian Immigrants in Buffalo, 1880-1930* (Ithaca, 1977); Howard Stein, "An Ethno-Historic Study of Slovak-American Identity, McKeesport, Pennsylvania," (Unpublished Ph.D. dissertation, University of Pittsburgh, 1972), pp. 417-37. A similar deemphasis on social and economic mobility was found among eighteenth century workers in James T. Lemon, *The Best Poor Man's Country: A Geographic Study of Southeastern Pennsylvania* (Baltimore, 1972), pp. 43-85; Dawley, *Class and Community*, pp. 216-17; Hareven and Langenbach, *Amoskeag*, pp. 43-50, 53, 65-66, 113. For evidence that the persistence of familial arrangements could blunt the growth of modernization see Herman Rebel, "Peasant Stem Families in Early Modern Austria: Life, Plans, Status Tactics, and the Grid of Inheritance," *Social Science History*, 2 (Spring, 1978), 285.

17. Theodore Hershberg, "A Tale of Three Cities: Blacks and Immigrants in Philadelphia: 1850-1880, 1930 and 1970," *Annals of the American Academy of Political and Social Sciences*, 441 (Jan., 1979), 68; Clyde and Sally Griffen, *Natives and Newcomers, The Ordering of Opportunity in Mid-Nineteenth Century Poughkeepsie* (Cambridge, 1978), pp. 67-69; Laurence Glasco, "Ethnicity and Occupation in the Mid-Nineteenth Century: Irish, Germans and Native-born Whites in Buffalo, New York," in *Immigrants in Industrial America, 1850-1920*, Richard L. Ehrlich ed., (Charlottesville, Va., 1977), pp. 151-53; 61 Cong., 2nd Sess., S. Doc. 282, *Reports of the Immigration Commission, Occupations of the First and Second Generation of Immigrants in the United States, Fecundity of Immigrant Women* (Washington, 1911), pp. 19-20; 61 Cong., 2nd Sess., S. Doc. 282, *Reports of the Immigration Commission, Immigrants in Cities* (2 vols.; Washington, 1911), I, 130-31; II, 497 ff.

18. Stephan Thernstrom, *The Other Bostonians: Poverty and Progress in the American Metropolis, 1880-1970* (Cambridge, 1973), pp. 125, 131, 139, 141.

19. Stanley Liberson and Donna K. Carter, "Making It in America: Differences Between Eminent Blacks and New Europeans," unpublished paper in author's possession.

20. Edward A. Zivich, "From Zadruga to Oil Refinery: Croatian Immigrants and Croatian-Americans in Whiting, Indiana, 1890-1950," unpublished Ph.D. diss., SUNY at Binghamton, 1977, pp. 37-39; Rosara Lucy Passero, "Ethnicity in the Men's Ready-Made Clothing Industry, 1880-1950: The Italian Experience in Philadelphia," unpublished Ph.D. diss., Univ. of Pennsylvania, 1978; Carolyn Golab, *Immigrant Destinations* (Philadelphia, 1978), pp. 62-63; Yans-McLaughlin, *Family and Community*, p. 46; Bodnar, Weber and Simon, "Migration, Kinship and Urban Adjustment;" Ivan H. Light, *Ethnic Enterprise in American Business and Welfare Among Chinese, Japanese, and Blacks* (Berkeley, 1972), pp. 9-10; John Modell, *The Economics and Politics of Racial Accommodation* (Urbana, 1977), p. 9; Harry H.L. Kitano, *Japanese Americans: The Evolution of a Subculture* (Englewood Cliffs, N.J., 1969), pp. 104-05; Louis C. Odencrantz, *Italian Woman in Industry, A Study of Conditions in New York City* (New York, 1919), pp. 36, 60; Mary Remiga Napolska, "The Polish Immigrant in Detroit to 1914," *Annals of the Polish Roman Catholic Union Archives and Museum*, X (1945-46), 34-35; Joseph John Parot, "The American Faith and the Persistence of Chicago Polonia, 1870-1920," unpublished Ph.D. diss., Northern Illinois University, 1971, *passim*; Niles Carpenter, *Immigrants and Their Children*, (Washington, 1927), p. 297.

21. Walter Weyl and M. Sakolski, "Conditions of Entrance to the Principal Trades," *Bulletin of the Bureau of Labor*, No. 67 (Nov., 1906), 681-690, 714-19; Paul H. Douglass, *American Apprenticeship and Industrial Education* (New York, 1921), pp. 75-81; Douglass, "Is the New Immigration More Unskilled than the Old," *Quarterly Publications of the American Statistical Associations* (June, 1919), 396-97.

22. Daniel Nelson, *Managers and Workers, Origins of the New Factory System in the United States, 1880-1920* (Madison, 1975), p. 4; U.S. Dept. of Commerce, Bureau of the Census, *Sixteenth Census of the United States: 1940: Population, Comparative Occupational Statistics for*

the US, 1970-1940 (Washington, 1943), pp. 104-06. See also George Bancroft, *The American Labor Force: Its Growth and Changing Composition* (New York, 1958), pp. 24-35 and Clarence D. Long, *The Labor Force Under Changing Income and Employment* (Princeton, 1958).

23. Bruce Laurie, Theodore Hershberg and George Alter, "Immigrants and Industry: The Philadelphia Experience, 1850-1880," *Journal of Social History*, II (Winter, 1975), 241-46; Griffen, *Natives and Newcomers*, pp. 183, 281-82. For an account of declining crafts and new demands for unskilled operatives at a particular plant see Howard M. Gitelman, *Workingmen of Waltham, Mobility in American Urban Industrial Development, 1850-1890* (Baltimore, 1974), pp. 54 ff. See also Isaac A. Hourwich, *Immigration and Labor* (New York, 1912), 396-413.

24. See Montgomery, "The New Unionism," 510-24; Montgomery, "Immigrant Workers and Managerial Reform," in *Immigrants in Industrial America*, p. 98; Richard C. Edwards, Michael Reich, and David M. Gordon, eds., *Labor Market Segmentation* (Lexington, Mass., 1973), pp. xi-xiii. Montgomery has argued that the new stress on efficiency and production at the expense of skills caused twentieth century rank and file to forge a "new unionism" which sought to initiate struggles for a greater control of production on the part of workers. He has not, however, mentioned the larger effort to maintain a familial system which was also nurtured by the expansion of unskilled labor.

25. See Gutman, "Work, Culture, and Society;" Kessner, *The Golden Door*, Barton, *Peasants and Strangers*; Yans-McLaughlin, *Family and Community*, p. 36.

26. Golab, *Immigrant Destinations*, pp. 5-6. Jews may be an exception to this premise since they frequently were able to implement premigration skills; see Arcadius Kahan, "Economic Opportunity and Some Pilgrims' Progress: Jewish Immigrants from Eastern Europe in the U.S., 1890-1914," *Journal of Economic History*, XXXVIII (March, 1978), 237-45.

27. Joseph Stipanovich, "'In Unity is Strength': Immigrant Workers and Immigrant Intellectuals in Progressive America: A History of the South Slav Social Democratic Movement, 1900-1918," unpublished Ph.D. diss., Univ. of Minnesota, 1978, p. 128; *American Slav*, 11 (Apr., 1941), 12-13; Joseph Pauco, *75 Rokov Prvej Katolickej Slovenskej Jednoty* (Cleveland, 1965), pp. 6-9; Vera Laska, *The Czechs in America, 1633-1977* (Dobbs Ferry, N.Y., 1978).

28. The "split-labor market" theory originated with Edna Bonacich, "A Theory of Ethnic Antagonisms: The Split Labor Market," *American-Sociological Review*, 37 (1972), 574-79; Bonacich, "A Theory of Middleman Minorities," *American-Sociological Review*, 38 (1973), 583-94. See Hilton, "The Split Labor Market and Chinese Immigration," 101; Modell, *The Economics and Politics of Racial Accommodation*, pp. 94-96; Robert Schoen, "Toward A Theory of the Demographic Implications of Ethnic Stratification," *Social Science Quarterly*, 59 (Dec., 1978), 477-78; William Petersen, "Chinese Americans and Japanese Americans," in *American Ethnic Groups*, ed. by Thomas Sowell (Washington, 1978), pp. 65-92.

29. Interviews in Pittsburgh with Stanley N., Sept. 22, 1976; Joseph B., May 20, 1976; John B., Mar. 3, 1976; Agens G., June 25, 1974; Peter H., June 26, 1974; Ignacy M., July 2, 1974; Joseph D., Sept. 17, 1976; Edward R:, Sept. 10, 1976; John S., Sept. 30, 1976; Charles W., Dec. 10, 1976; Francis P., Jan. 16, 1976.

30. See, for instance, interviews with Dan C., Mar. 31, 1977; Umberto B., March 14, 1977; Amico L., July 28, 1977; Vincent L. June 21, 1977; Lou G., May 11, 1977; Frank A., May 16, 1977; J.S. and L.D. MacDonald, "Urbanization, Ethnic Group and Social Segmentation," *Social Research*, 29 (1962), 433-48.

31. *Ibid.*

32. *Ibid.*

33. Caroline Manning, *The Immigrant Woman and Her Job* (New York, 1970), pp. 106-74; Dorothea De Schweintz, *How Workers Find Jobs, A Study of Four Thousand Hosiery Workers in Philadelphia* (Philadelphia, 1932); George Huganir, "The Hosiery Looper in the Twentieth Century, A Study of Family Occupational Processes and Adaptation to Factory and Community Change, 1900-1950," unpublished Ph.D. diss. (Univ. of Pennsylvania, 1958) pp. 6-8. William Leiserson, *Adjusting Immigrant and Industry* (New York, 1924), p. 31; Louise C. Odencrantz, *Italian Women in Industry, A Study of Conditions in New York City* (New York, 1919), p. 283; Corrine Azen Krause, "Urbanization Without Breakdown, Italian, Jewish, and Slavic Immigrant Women in Pittsburgh, 1900-1945," *Journal of Urban History,* 4 (May, 1978), 296-97.

34. Edward P. Hutchinson, *Immigrants and Their Children* (New York, 1956), pp. 224-238. See Peter M. Blau and Otis Duncan, *The American Occupational Structure* (New York, 1967), pp. 82-89. Additional profiles of immigrant concentrations can be seen in U.S. Dept. of Commerce and Labor, Bureau of the Census, *Special Reports, Occupations at the Twelfth Census* (Washington, 1904), plates 10-12.

35. See Walter Weyl and A.M. Sakolski, "Conditions of Entrance to the Principal Trades," *Bulletin of the Bureau of Labor,* No. 67 (Nov., 1906), p. 690. Bodnar, "Immigration and Modernization," 57; Malcom Brown and John Webb, *Seven Stranded Coal Towns* (Washington, 1941), p. 23; Herman R. Lantz, *People of Coal Town* (New York, 1958), p. 174.

36. William Kornblum, *Blue Collar Community* (Chicago, 1974), p. 55; Barton, *Peasants and Strangers,* pp. 145-46; Charles R. Walker, *Steeltown, An Industrial Case History of the Conflict Between Progress and Security* (New York, 1950), pp. 109, 111, 128, 263-64; Gladys L. Palmer, *et. al., The Reluctant Job Changer* (Philadelphia, 1962), p. 106; John Ellsworth, *Factory Folkways* (New Haven, 1952), pp. 139-40. Classic studies such as Chinoy, *Automobile Workers and the American Dream* (New York, 1955) which suggest that blue-collar workers lacked high aspirations because they lacked knowledge of occupational alternatives do not go far enough in depicting the ease with which kinship could serve as a basis for job procurement. See also Kenneth Kessin, "Social and Psychological Consequences of Intergenerational Occupational Mobility," *American Journal of Sociology,* 77 (July, 1971), 1-17.

37. Nelson, *Managers and Workers,* pp. 79-80; interviews with George Muzar, Monessen, Mar. 22, 1977. Foremen's power is emphasized in Montgomery, "Immigrant Workers," pp. 99-100; Russell L. Greenman, *The Worker, the Foremen and the Wagner Act* (New York, 1939).

38. Yans-McLaughlin, *Family and Community,* p. 43; Bodnar, Weber, and Simon, "Migration, Kinship, and Urban Adaptation;" Robert Ozanne, *A Century of Labor-Management Relations at McCormick and International Harvester* (Madison, 1967), pp. 184-87. Gerd Korman, *Industrialization, Immigrants and Americanizers, The View from Milwaukee, 1866-1921* (Madison, 1967), pp. 66-67; Bodnar, *Immigration and Industrialization* (Pittsburgh, 1977), pp. 35-41. At the Bethlehem Steel Plant in Bethlehem, Pennsylvania, Germans dominated the rolling mill in a similar fashion; see interview with Nick K., July 11, 1974.

39. Hareven, "Family Time and Industrial Time: Family and Work in a Planned Corporation Town, 1900-1924," 365-380; Hareven and Randolph Langenbach, *Amoskeag,* p. 118. See also William Kornblum, *Blue Collar Community* (Chicago, 1974), p. 12 for evidence of recruiting Poles into South Chicago mills.

40. Interviews with Marie S., Nanticoke, Jan. 16, 1978; Anna S., Nanticoke, Oct. 28, 1977; Helen M. Nanticoke, Aug. 20, 1977; Stella K., Benton Township, Aug. 7, 1977; Bodnar, *Immigration and Industrialization,* pp. 129-30.

41. Interviews with Joseph S., Dravosburg, July 2, 1974; Nick K., Bethlehem, July 11, 1974. See Southwestern Pennsylvania Oral History Project, PHMC, reels 110-129. Interviews with Stanley E., Pittsburgh, Sept. 9, 1976; Edward N., Pittsburgh, Oct. 4, 1976; Walter K., Pittsburgh, Sept. 18, 1977; Joseph D., Sept. 17, 1976; Peter L., Pittsburgh, Sept. 17, 1976; Charles W., Pittsburgh, Dec. 10, 1976.

42. Bodnar, "Immigration and Modernization," 57. Interviews with Joseph G., Pittsburgh, April 11, 1977; John B., Monessen, Feb. 22, 1977; George M., Monessen, Mar. 22, 1977.

43. Tamara Hareven, "Family Time and Industrial Time: Family and Work in a Planned Corporation Town, 1900-1924," *Journal of Urban History* I (May, 1975), 377. Interviews with Arlene G., Nanticoke, Dec. 11, 1977; Stella K., Benton Township, Aug. 7, 1977. Winifred Bolin, "The Economies of Middle Income Family Life: Working Women During the Great Depression," *Journal of American History*, 65 (June, 1978), 72-73 suggested that only 15 percent of all married women worked by 1940 because of the cultural stigma against a working wife. It is possible, however, that domesticity seemed a preferable alternative to the drugery working-class women experienced as adolescence in silk mills and cigar factories prior to marriage.

44. Interviews with George M., Monessen, Mar. 22, 1977; Helen M., Nanticoke, Aug. 20, 1977; John S., Pittsburgh, June 7, 1974; Joseph D., Pittsburgh, April 20, 1977, Mary M., Monessen, Mar. 31, 1977.

45. Interview with Rose P., Monessen, Mar. 14, 1977.

46. Interviews with Antionette W., Wilkes-Barre, Sept. 12, 1977; Eleanor O., Nanticoke, Nov. 25, 1977; Mike D., Monessen, Feb. 2, 1977; Thomas L., Cokesburg, June 17, 1975; Virginia V., Nanticoke, Dec. 6, 1977.

47. Interview with Lilian N. Nanticoke, July 13, 1977.

48. William Goode, *World Revolution and Family Patterns* (New York, 1963), pp. 56-57; Edward Shorter, *The Making of the Modern Family* (New York, 1975). A call for much more investigation into kinship roles is found in Tamara Hareven, "Postscript: The Latin American Context of Family History," *Journal of Family History*, 3 (Winter, 1978), 455.

49. Elizabeth H. Pleck, "Two Worlds in One: Work and Family," *Journal of Social History*, 10 (Winter, 1976), pp. 178-83; Hareven, "Family Time and Industrial Time," 366-71. Rosabeth Moss Kanter, *Work and Family in the United States: A Critical Review and Agenda for Research and Policy* (New York, 1976), pp. 20-23; Yans-McLaughlin, *Family and Community*, *passim.*

50. John Bodnar, "Morality and Materialism: Slavic-American Immigrants and Education," *Journal of Ethnic Studies*, 3 (Winter, 1976), 1-20.

51. See interviews below with Steve K., McKeesport, July 27, 1974; and Rose P., Monessen, Mar. 14, 1977.

52. Bodnar, Weber, and Simon, "Migration, Kinship, and Urban Adaptation."

53. David Brody, "Labor and the Great Depression: The Interpretative Prospects," *Labor History*, 13 (Spring, 1972), 243.

54. See David Montgomery, *Workers Control in America: Studies in the History of Work, Technology, and Labor Struggles* (Cambridge, Eng., 1979), 4-5; Brody, "Working Class History in the Great Depression," *Reviews in American History*, 4 (June, 1976), 266; Peter Friedlander, *The Emergence of a UAW Local: A Study in Class and Culture* (Pittsburgh, 1975),

p. 101; James A. Henretta, "Social History as Lived and Written," *American Historical Review*, 84 (Dec., 1979), 1293-1322. For an analysis of how tradition and industrial structures can blend to influence working-class lives see John Bodnar, Michael Weber, and Roger Simon, *Migration and Urbanization: Blacks, Italians, and Poles in Pittsburgh, 1900-1960* (Urbana, Ill.; forthcoming, 1981)

55. Lynd, "The Possibility of Radicalism in the Early 1930's: The Case of Steel," *Radical America*, 6 (Nov.-Dec., 1972); Lynd, "Guerrila History in Gary," *Liberation*, 14 (ct., 1969), 78; Alice and Staughton Lynd, eds., *Rank and File: Personal Histories of Working Class Organizers*, pp. 1-7; Sidney Fine, *Sit-Down, The General Motors Strike of 1936-37* (Ann Arbor, Mich., 1969), p. 340.

56. Robert H. Zieger, "The Limits of Militancy: Organizing Paper Workers, 1933-1935," *Journal of American History*, 63 (Dec., 1976), 640-47; Zieger, *Madison Battery Workers, 1934-1952: A History of Federal Labor Union 19587* (Ithaca, N.Y., 1977), pp. 2-4.

57. Sidney Verba and Kay L. Scholzman, "Unemployment, Class Consciousness, and Radical Politics: What Didn't Happen in the Thirties," *Journal of Politics*, 39 (1977), 322.

58. Brody, "Labor and the Great Depression," 237; Friedlander, *The Emergence of a UAW Local*, pp. 11-12; Fine, *Sit-Down*, p. 60.

59. See interview with Stanley B., Braddock, June 20, 1978. Job security as a fundamental goal among steelworkers in the 1930's is stressed in Roger Simon, "Looking Backwards at Steel," *The Antioch Review*, 36 (Fall, 1978), 451-52. A steelworker in McKeesport stressed that his impulse to join a union was generated primarily by a reduced work schedule between 1930 and 1933; see interview with Rocky D., Port Vue, Aug. 29, 1974.

One Century of foreign Immigration to the United States: 1880 - 1979

BY A. W. CARLSON *

There is no doubt that legal foreign immigration has played an important role in populating the United States. In fact, it accounts for approximately one-quarter or more of this country's annual population growth rate even today. Immigration has become a major factor in the growth of the population once again because of an increasing number of foreigners who immigrate annually and the recent decline in the country's fertility rate. This study is an analysis of American immigration policies which have influenced the sources of immigrants and their characteristics and have had an impact upon the composition of the American people. In addition, immigrants entering a country have had certain positive or negative perceptions, as well as family and other ties which have influenced their decision-making process of where to settle. Between 1900 and 1979, the Immigration and Naturalization Service compiled complete data annually on where foreign immigrants, upon entry, declared their intended permanent residence, by state. A map analysis of these data is included to ascertain their destinations, which have had an impact upon internal population growth, characteristics and distributions.

IMMIGRATION LEGISLATION

For one century after the founding of the United States there was unrestricted immigration, except for those classed as undesirables, in regard to ethnic origins. Incidentally, Negroes brought for the purposes of slavery were not considered as

* Professor, Bowling Green State University, Ohio, U.S.A. Editor of 'Journal of Cultural Geography'.

309

65

immigrants, basically because they did not enter voluntarily. Until the outbreak of the Civil War, nearly all immigrants came from Northern and Western Europe. In fact, in the first federal census of 1790, over 75 per cent of the population was of British origin. This pattern of European immigration continued into the 1880's when nearly 80 per cent of the immigrants were from Northern and Western Europe (Table 1 on page 321). In the 1870's and 1880's, the five leading sources were ranked as follows: Germany, the United Kingdom, Ireland, Canada and China (1870's) and Sweden (1880's). In each decade, these countries contributed over 70 per cent of all the immigrants. It was in the early 1880's that the first significant legislation to restrict ethnic groups was embodied in the Chinese Exclusion Act(1). In the 1890's, Southern and Eastern European countries became the new sources of most immigrants. In this decade, Italy was the leading source followed by Austria/Hungary, Russia, Germany and Ireland. They accounted for over 70 per cent of all immigration. Except for the United Kingdom replacing Ireland in the first decade of the 1900's, the other five leading source countries remained the same, and all five sent more than 75 per cent of all immigrants. Between 1910-1919, Italy, Russia, Canada, Austria and Hungary were the leading sources accounting for nearly two-thirds of the immigrants.

By the outbreak of World War I, immigration had peaked historically at over one million entrants annually for several years and accounted for an estimated 40 per cent of the nation's annual population growth (Fig. 1 on page 324). It must be remembered that only ten million immigrants had entered the country between 1820 and 1880. Immigration declined sharply during World War I, but rose almost as sharply again in the early 1920's, not, however, to its former heights. In the first two decades of the 1900's, arrivals from Southern and Eastern Europe had constituted two-thirds of all immigrants - a dramatic reversal for the origins of immigrants from Europe(2).

Even before the outbreak of World War I, the heavy influx of Southern and Eastern Europeans prompted renewed interest by many Americans in having Congress consider greater restrictions(3). Opposition to unrestricted immigration without numerical ceilings dated back to the Nativist movement of the 1830's and the Know-Nothing political party of the 1850's. Similar sentiments surfaced periodically again after the Civil War, but they did not become a serious matter until the early 1900's, once more to be interrupted by war. Expecting the renewal in the tide of immigration from Southern and Eastern Europe after World War I, Congress passed legislation in 1921 that limited immigration based upon nationality, and included the first numerical ceiling. By using the number of foreign-born residents reported in the 1910 census, quotas of 3 per cent per nationality group were established, which when combined could total no more than 350,000 immigrants per year from the eastern hemisphere. No numerical ceiling and quotas were imposed upon the western hemisphere.

Not only did Congress, reflecting the views of many Americans, believe that the earlier, somewhat unrestricted immigration policies allowed too many immigrants, but also that there was an alarming proportion of immigrants from Southern and Eastern Europe. It was felt that these immigrants, largely Roman Catholic and who spoke non-Germanic derived languages, would displace the dominant resident population which had its roots in Northern and Western Europe and who were Protestant and spoke Germanic languages. Fear had mounted over the potential political and social ramifications that could arise if the character of foreign immigration were to continue without further limitations.

Realizing that the Southern and Eastern European foreign-born populations were already large by 1910 - and therefore the 1921 legislation had little impact, especially upon the character of immigration - Congress passed the second Immigration and Naturalization Act in 1924. This legislation set the quota for each country temporarily at 2 per cent of its foreign-born population resident in the United States, as reported in the 1890 census. It

310

established minimum quotas of 100 immigrants for all qualifying countries. It was an obvious attempt to clearly favour Northern and Western Europeans because they had the largest number of foreign-born residents in 1890. Meanwhile, the methodology for figuring new national origins quotas was to be determined to avoid any perceived future problems. Finalized in 1929, the national origins system allocated quotas to countries based upon one-sixth of 1 per cent of those white nationality (foreign-born and native-born) residents in the United States as recorded in the 1920 census. Again, countries in the western hemisphere were exempted from quotas. This system reduced the total numerical limit of immigrants who could enter annually under quotas to less than 160,000. Moreover, it also allowed Northern and Western European countries to have larger quotas totalling over 80 per cent of the numerical ceiling. The quotas were redetermined periodically, but ranged from 100 to over 50,000 per country. Undoubtedly, a system had been established to reduce immigration from Eastern and Southern Europe. All immigration to the United States declined shortly thereafter, during the world depression of the 1930's, but not before there had been substantial increases in non-quota immigration from Latin America and Canada. More people emigrated from the United States between 1932 and 1935 than immigrated. Five Mexicans left the country for every one who entered during the 1930's.

With the depression followed by World War II, immigration for both the 1930's and the early 1940's declined drastically to the lowest levels so far in this century. During this time, it is interesting to note that several restrictions imposed on Asians and Pacific Islanders during the 1917 'Asiatic Barred Zone' were changed: a small quota was established for Filipinos in 1934, provisions of the Chinese Exclusion Act were repealed and a quota of 105 was initiated in 1943 for Chinese immigrants, and Asiatic Indians were allowed to immigrate to this country beginning in 1946.

As could be expected, immigration to the United States increased substantially after World War II (Fig. 1). Many immigrants came under specially enacted post-war legislation to cope with the humanitarian problems associated with war refugees or displaced persons. The Displaced Persons Act and, to a lesser extent, the War Brides Act, both passed in 1948, had provisions which lifted temporarily the restrictive quotas imposed by the national origins legislation. The new provisions allowed for 'mortgaging' the number of immigrants, up to 50 per cent, against a country's future annual quotas. This again favoured immigrants from Northern and Western Europe. Nearly 350,000 refugees entered under the Displaced Persons Act alone before its expiration in 1952.

Immigration legislation of the 1950's brought minor changes in the national origins quotas for Asian countries, while providing for more refugees to enter the United States. The McCarran-Walter Act or the Immigration and Nationality Act of 1952 retained the national origins quotas, but it established a combined quota of 2,000 immigrants for the countries within the Asia-Pacific triangle. In the following year, another legislative act set minimum quotas of 100 for all countries in the Far East. This was done to improve foreign relations with Asian countries after the Korean War. It was also when immigration had declined by nearly 100,000 upon the expiration of the Displaced Persons Act which had been applicable to Europeans. The Refugee Relief Act of 1953, however, promptly provided for 200,000 European refugees, expellees, and the like, with their families to be admitted as non-quota or exempted immigrants through 1956. This Act was followed by special legislation which allowed for thousands of Hungarian refugees to enter after the 1956 Hungarian uprising, and likewise for Portuguese nationals from the Azores to immigrate after the severe earthquake and flood of 1958(4). In addition, a small number of Dutch nationals displaced from Indonesia were also allowed to enter as immigrants. The

Fair Share Refugee Act of 1960 allowed for the resettlement of refugees, mostly to handle the exodus of people from Cuba.

From the expiration of the Displaced Persons Act in 1952 until 1965, only about one-third of all the immigrants to the United States entered under the national origins quotas established back in the 1920's. The increasing proportion of non-quota immigrants in the form of refugees etc., in addition to immigrants from the western hemisphere, had comprised a larger share of the total immigration. It is true that in the early 1960's, the number of immigrants under national origins quotas increased again to where approximately two-thirds of the quotas were filled: more for some countries and less for others. In 1965, over eighty countries still had the minimum national origins quota of 100 immigrants per year imposed on them. On the other hand, the maximum allocated quotas amounted to over 65,000 for the combined countries of the British Isles, or approximately two-fifths of that year's total allocation of quota immigrants. In 1964, only 103,000 immigrants out of the total quota of nearly 160,000 entered under the national origins quotas. Fewer than 30,000 people, or less than one-half of the allocation for the British Isles, immigrated to the United States. At the same time, non-quota immigration, mainly from the western hemisphere, numbered nearly 190,000.

Bearing in mind that the ethnic and racial preferences established - although somewhat modified - in the national origins quotas were discriminatory, growing concern developed over the partial use of the quotas allocated largely to Northern and Western Europeans and the fact that there were no limitations for the countries of the western hemisphere. This was also during a time of great concern over civil rights in the United States. In 1965, another Nationality and Immigration Act (Amendments) brought significant changes in immigration policies. Firstly, it eliminated the nationality origins quotas and established essentially an open-door first-come, first-served, policy for immigrants. Secondly, a numerical ceiling of 170,000 immigrants annually, with no more than 20,000 immigrants from any one country, was placed upon the eastern hemisphere. Thirdly, the western hemisphere was given a numerical ceiling of 120,000 immigrants annually, but no numerical limitation was placed upon a country. These changes were implemented in July 1968(5).

Immigration to the United States not only continued to increase in the late 1960's after the enactment of the 1965 legislation and in the early 1970's, but it changed dramatically in character. Thousands of people from many countries, which before had very low quotas, became the new wave of immigrants under the open-door policy. In order to provide an even further equitable policy, legislation was passed in 1976 which limited the number of immigrants from any one country in one year to 20,000, regardless of hemisphere. Mexico, for instance, accounted for over 62,000 legal immigrants alone in 1976. This legislation maintained the hemispheric ceilings. They were combined, however, in 1978 legislation which established one world-wide ceiling of 290,000. It continued the provision for numerically unrestricted admission of immediate relatives of United States citizens and others, such as refugees(6).

The last significant piece of legislation enacted was the Refugee Act of 1980. It provided an annual allocation of 50,000 refugees, based upon the admissions of previous years, but it could be changed for humanitarian reasons or national interests by the President in consultation with Congress. Refugees were to be admitted with no geographical or idealogical biases. Previously, Cubans were classed as political refugees and Haitians, for instance, were not because they did not originate from a Communist country. All refugees henceforth were to be considered on an individual basis. The world-wide numerical ceiling was also reduced to 270,000 annually(7).

312

PREFERENCE SYSTEM

Since the immigration legislation of 1924, the United States has imposed a preference system for the admission of immigrants. Those who were considered to be misfits or undesirable to the society continued to be excluded, but a preference system was initiated that favoured certain other types of immigrants. One-half of a country's national origins quota was allocated to the immediate relatives of United States citizens. Another preference was given to skilled agricultural workers. If those preference quotas were not filled in any one year, then other immigrants could be admitted under the non-preference category.

Significant changes in the preference system resulted from the Immigration and Nationality Act of 1952. It established four preference categories and one non-preference category. The first preference was for skilled, technical and professional workers, and the other three preferences were for additional relatives of United States citizens. This time, one-half of a country's national origins quota was assigned the first preference. Other legislation up to the 1965 Nationality and Immigration Amendments reconfirmed, but also realigned the classes of relative preferences.

The 1965 legislation established seven preferences for the eastern hemisphere: four for relatives of citizens and lawful permanent resident aliens of the United States, and special immigrants such as employees of the United States Government; two for designated professional, skilled and unskilled occupations sought by immigrants on a permanent basis in the United States, and one for refugees. Immediate relatives, parents, spouses and children of citizens were not limited numerically. The emphasis continued to be on the reunification of families, but this time admission was not based upon national origins quotas or the place of birth. Occupational preferences were based upon labour certification showing the need for certain skilled, technical and professional and managerial workers. Lastly, the non-preference category was retained for those immigrants who did not qualify for any of the seven preferences. No preference system was established for the western hemisphere.

Immigration legislation passed in the 1970's kept the preferences, but it extended the seven preferences to the countries of the western hemisphere and affected the occupational preferences by imposing stringent labour certification or prearranged employment for entering workers. This was followed by the Refugee Act of 1980 which eliminated the seventh preference for refugees, a group to be admitted under an annual determination by the President and Congress. For instance, the annual allocation was estimated to be 50,000, but many more than that number were admitted in 1981 from Indochina alone. Cubans, who had long been favoured by the refugee preference, were no longer given special admission under this legislation. After one year of residence in the United States, refugees can be granted immigrant status.

In summary, the current United States immigration policy allows for 270,000 immigrants with a ceiling of 20,000 per country, but also allows for immediate relatives and special immigrants to enter without numerical limitations. Other kinship relatives are admitted under one of four preferences and certain skilled or highly trained people enter under the remaining two occupational preferences. When combined, over 500,000 legal immigrants have entered the country each year since 1980.

SOURCES AND CHARACTERISTICS OF RECENT IMMIGRANTS

Legal immigration has once again become a significant factor in both this country's population growth rate and the changing composition of the population from what it was at the turn of the century(8). In the last century, the foreign-born population in 1890 was at a record high of 15 per cent and the low was recorded in 1970 when less than 5 per cent of

313

the country's residents were foreign-born. By 1980, however, the foreign-born population had increased by over four million to 6 per cent. This is attributed not only to the annual increase in immigration - especially since the implementation of the 1965 legislation - but also because of the consistently low crude birth rate which has been 16 per 1,000 population. Considering no immigration or emigration and a crude death rate of 9 per 1,000 population, the natural increase in the population has been less than 1 per cent annually. An estimated one in four new Americans each year has been a legal foreign immigrant. For instance, in 1980, nearly 531,000 legal immigrants were admitted and approximately 80,000 people emigrated from the United States. With the rate of natural increase at .07 per cent, 1.6 million native-born Americans were added to the total population. When this figure is combined with that of net immigration, immigrants constituted approximately one-fourth of the annual growth in population. Immigration is an even greater factor if the annual figures for illegal immigration, which may be larger than for legal immigration, were known and accurately inserted into the country's population growth rate.

Following the present national trend where the population is comprised of 51.4 per cent females and 48.6 per cent males, more females immigrate to the United States than males. In the first decade of this century, males constituted approximately 70 per cent of the immigrants. Many Southern and Eastern Europeans, in particular, arrived singly, whereas earlier Northern and Western Europeans had immigrated largely as family units. By the 1930's, the number of female immigrants comprised a larger share of the total immigration, mainly reunification cases, especially from Southern and Eastern Europe. This trend continued after World War II when many female refugees from Europe, and others largely from Mexico, entered the country. By 1954, there were only 85 male immigrants for every 100 female immigrants, who were on average more than two years younger than the males. Between 1950 and 1979, females constituted over one-half of the total immigration, especially in the age group of 20-29 years (Fig. 2 on page 325). In the late 1970's, three-fifths of the females were of child-bearing age. More females came from the western than from the eastern hemisphere. Overall, immigrants tend to be younger than the population as a whole. For instance, their median age of 26.2 years between 1975 and 1979 was considerably below the country's median age of 30.2 years in 1980 and near the all-time high median age of 30.9 years recorded in 1983.

Over one-half of all the immigrants have entered the United States since 1950 as housewives, children, and others who have no reported occupation. Both the percentage and number of these immigrants have increased by decade (Table 2 on page 322). They entered largely as immediate relatives who were not limited numerically, or they entered under the preferences for other relatives in order to reunite families: many were refugees.

Of the remaining immigrants, most entered under occupational preferences depending upon labour certification, although some of those who came as relatives and refugees also entered the labour force. If only those who came under occupational preferences are considered, they accounted for at least 10 per cent of the annual growth of the labour force. When the refugees and relatives are added, all made up approximately 15 per cent of the annual labour force increase. Conservatively, at least one in every ten new workers, therefore, who enters the labour force each year is an immigrant. Because of stringent labour certification for some occupations, there has been a tendency to permit largely professionals, technical and skilled workers, who can more readily find employment, to enter under occupational preferences. In the 1970's alone, one in every ten immigrants was a professional or technical worker, indicating higher educational attainment (Table 2). Most came from Asia and a much smaller number from Northern and Western European

314

countries. Many of the other workers, mostly unskilled, came from Southern Europe and Latin America. Only a small number of immigrants entered with agricultural occupations, indicating the trends of the American farm scene where there are fewer and fewer farms and increasing mechanization. In order for the immigrants to obtain work, nearly all of them located in urban areas, an ongoing event for the past century.

Until the 1965 Amendments, the majority of immigrants for each decade from 1880 onward originated from Europe (Table 1). This is not surprising because of cultural ties with Europe over the centuries, the immigration legislation which favoured European countries and the outpouring of European refugees and displaced persons, especially after World War II. Only during that war did immigration from Europe decline to an amount slightly over one-half of the total number. The impact of the 1965 legislation, coupled with improved economic conditions in Europe, led to a dramatic decline in European immigrants. At the turn of the century, nearly all of the immigrants were Europeans, but by 1980 only one in five was from Europe.

The removal of the nationality origins quotas and all other barriers opened the door, especially for millions in developing countries to begin the emigration process. In the 1970's, 75 per cent of the legal immigrants were from Asia and Latin America (Table 1). The number of legal immigrants from the Caribbean were, however, larger than all of the countries of South America combined. The numbers from Asia and Latin America can be expected to increase as new residents and naturalized citizens from these regions encourage their relatives to join them here in order to reunify families. For instance, it has been estimated that each Cuban refugee, on average, has been responsible for bringing 1.5 relatives into this country while a resident, and another 1.5 relatives as a naturalized citizen(9).

Of the developing regions, only Africa has not been a major source because American blacks or their descendants are the result largely of involuntary immigration whereby they lost their family identity. Hence, American blacks have the difficulty of ascertaining which Africans could enter under the relative preferences. Furthermore, many black Africans can not comply with the requirements of the occupational preferences. On the whole, Africans in the past did not initiate the emigration process where their numbers would have had to compete with those of the Europeans, and especially the Asians of the eastern hemisphere.

In comparing the total number of immigrants to the United States in the 1950's to that of the 1970's, the number nearly doubled. This increase, coupled with the 1965 Amendments, also led to nearly a doubling in the number of countries which were major sources, as well as a very changed list of major sources (Table 3 on page 322). Except for Mexico, Canada and Cuba, European countries dominated the list of eleven major sources in the 1950's. Only five European countries, Italy, the United Kingdom, Portugal, Greece and Germany, were included in the list of eighteen major sources in the 1970's. By the end of the 1970's more countries had become major sources, but when combined they still contributed 70 per cent of all the immigrants as was the case previously. In the 1950's, the top five major sources accounted for the majority of all immigrants, whereas the top nine accounted for the majority in the 1970's. Despite nearly every country in the world, except for the Communist bloc, having a numerical quota of 20,000, immigrants from certain countries and regions continued to dominate immigration to the United States, as was the case at the turn of the century.

Records on emigrants who were aliens in the country were not kept officially until 1908 and those on departing citizens not until 1910. These records were terminated in 1957. In the period 1908 through 1957, over 4.8 million people left the country; a fairly large number in the 1930's. In comparison, this represents about 30 per cent of the number of immigrants who entered the country during this period. Immigration authorities generally have used the 30 per cent figure in estimating the rate of emigration from 1957 to the present.

DESTINATIONS OF IMMIGRANTS

Data were gathered by the Naturalization and Immigration Service since 1820 on immigrants, but data on the immigrants' intended future permanent residences were not complete until 1892. Upon entering the country, each immigrant was asked where he or she planned to reside. Complete data were published in a table annually for eight decades, through 1979 when the table was discontinued in the Service's annual reports. The tables are the sources for Figures 3-7 on pages 326-330, Table 4 on page 323, and the following review of both the states chosen and avoided by the over thirty million legal immigrants who entered the country after 1900.

Immigrants at the turn of the century were bound largely for America's cities where industrialization was well established(10). In fact, in analyzing the series of decadal maps showing their destinations, most immigrants chose to settle initially in the northern cities of the states in the industrial/manufacturing belt extending from the Atlantic seaboard westward around the lower Great Lakes. This belt included many of the country's largest cities: Boston, New York City, Philadelphia, Pittsburgh, Cleveland, Detroit, Chicago and Milwaukee. New York was from the outset the leading state to be chosen, except in the 1970's when it tied with California, having been selected by over one-quarter of all the immigrants from 1900 onward (Table 4). It was, of course, the major port of entry on the eastern seaboard for immigrants especially from Europe. Many evidently perceived New York to be a place of employment opportunities, or they had relatives and friends there to assist them in their new country. The residential patterns of immigrants who had settled in America before 1900, and for each succeeding generation thereafter, were undoubtedly determinants in the new immigrant's decision-making process on where to settle, at least initially(11). Many immigrants, particularly those from Southern and Eastern Europe, were also too poor to venture far beyond their port of entry.

Besides New York and its neighbouring states, several states on the western and southern peripheries of the country were also early recipients of immigrants, but to a lesser extent and continued to be so through the 1970's. In particular, California has been the destination of significant numbers of new arrivals. It, in fact, emerged as the second leading destination in the 1930's when it received 8 per cent of all immigrants compared to 39 per cent for New York (Table 4). From that time on, California retained its ranking until the 1970's when it became the largest recipient in the country by only a fraction of 1 per cent of all immigrants. This rise in ranking was attributable to an increasing recognition of the state's economic and other opportunities, internal migration of families who sponsored relatives and, most importantly, in the late 1960's and 1970's the dramatic shift to Asian and Latin American sources, including most of the 350,000 Indochinese refugees admitted between 1975 and 1980. California has several ports of entry which have facilitated immigration. Washington was the destination for a much smaller number of immigrants. Seattle is another major port of entry on the Pacific Coast not only for Asian immigrants, but also for nearby Canadians. The metropolitan area's economic opportunities were also perceived favourably.

Texas and Florida on the southern periphery have also been leading destinations for immigrants. In both cases, their rankings can be attributed to heavy immigration from Latin America. In the 1920's, Texas ranked third nationally as a destination. It ranked fourth in the 1950's and 1970's. Mexico has been a major source of immigrants in the 1900's; the leading source in the 1960's and 1970's(12). In the 1970's, Mexican

316

immigration alone nearly equalled that of the next two leading sources, the Philippines and Cuba (Table 3). A large proportion of these Mexican immigrants settled in southern Texas. Many of their relatives followed, resulting in a chain migration similar to that found in earlier European immigration. Both California and Texas have large Hispanic populations today, although on the whole that of Texas is more Mexican in origin despite the fact that Los Angeles has a larger Mexican population than most Mexican cities. California is, however, the destination for many other Latin American immigrants. The state's Anglo-American population now constitutes a minority when compared to the combined numbers of Asians, Latin Americans and blacks.

Cuba has been the major source of Florida's immigrants, especially in the 1960's and 1970's when nearly 800,000 refugees and others fled the island after the establishment of the Castro Government (Fig. 6). The number of Cuban immigrants more than doubled in these two decades from what it was in the 1950's (Table 3), making Cuba the third leading source of all immigrants. As in the case of California and Texas and their Mexican immigrants, Florida's proximity to Cuba and the port of entry at Miami were understandably reasons for Cubans selecting the state(13). Having relatives as residents of Florida and the state's similar climate also helped Cubans in their decision-making process. Nearly two-thirds of all the 800,000 Cubans who immigrated to the United States between 1959 and 1980 resided in Florida in the early 1980's. Dade County's population today is only about two-fifth's Anglo-American. Until the 1960's, Florida had been basically shunned as an initial destination for the hordes of European immigrants, presumedly because of the lack of industry and manufacturing which could provide employment opportunities similar to those found in the industrial/manufacturing corridor extending from the northeastern seaboard to the western Great Lake states. It is interesting to note that the majority of the other immigrants from the West Indies bypassed Florida, except for the very recent Haitian refugees(14). Earlier Haitian immigrants and most immigrants from the Dominican Republic and Jamaica settled in urban centres of the northern industrial/manufacturing belt, especially New York City. Puerto Ricans are citizens of the United States, hence their migration to the United States is not enumerated in the immigration data. They, likewise, headed for the northern industrial/manufacturing centres. Proximity to Florida and its similar climate were evidently not important factors in their decision-making processes.

Undoubtedly, foreign immigration to the United States has had a greater impact upon a few states than the country as a whole. In fact, three-fifths of all immigrants in each decade chose to settle initially within five states. The decadal listing of the five ranking states since 1900 shows a total of only nine different states, reflecting the dominance of certain states in the initial perceptions of this country by immigrants (Table 4). These states remain among the most ethnic and populated states(15). Their ethnic character has been continuously reinforced by immigration.

Correspondingly, many states received very few foreign immigrants since 1900 (Fig. 6). For the most part, these states comprised commonly identifiable regions within the geography of the United States: northern New England, the Upper and Deep South, the Great Plains and the Rocky Mountains-Great Basin. All of them have lacked industries and large metropolitan centres which could have provided more employment opportunities than what could have been filled by rural to urban migration. Most immigrants after 1900 became urbanites in states where manufacturing, industry and services could absorb more people into their labour forces than that produced by both rural to urban migration and resulting from natural increases in the population growth rates. Those immigrants who entered under occupational preferences were largely skilled, technical   and   professional   people   who   could   find   employment   in   the

317

industrial/manufacturing states. Predominantly rural or agricultural states attracted few immigrants, e.g. the South and the Great Plains. Even though the combined populations of the South and the West outnumbered those of the North and the East for the first time in the mid-1970's, very few immigrants sought out much of the Sunbelt, except for Florida, Texas and California. Regions which were not chosen by immigrants, therefore, today have no large dominant populations with a recognized strong ethnic character attributable to recent immigration.

CONCLUSIONS

Legal foreign immigration has once again become a major factor in the population growth rate of the United States, accounting for between 20-25 per cent annually. If illegal immigration is considered, the combined legal and illegal immigrants would probably constitute 40 per cent of the country's annual population growth. The number of legal immigrants is not as great (only about one-half) in recent years as it was at the turn of the century, but the present birth rate is today near the lowest level in the country's history. Legal immigration in the 1970's was the highest for any decade since the period 1910-1919. Consequently, immigrants accounted again for a large share of the population growth rate.

Since the mid-1960's and the passage of non-quota legislation, the sources of immigration have shifted dramatically from the traditional European countries, favoured by earlier nationality origins quotas, to Latin America and Asia. Because economic conditions and other factors were conducive to Northern and Western Europeans not emigrating, many of the countries did not fill their quotas and the nationality origins quotas were themselves considered to be discriminatory in a time of rising national and international consciousness concerning discrimination against ethnic and racial populations. Earlier legislation had sought to manipulate and retain the composition of the United States population. Now, an open-door policy with only certain preferences as limiting factors - but without nationality, ethnicity or racial limitations - has been implemented. Still, only a comparatively few countries dominated immigration through the 1970's, less than twenty being the sources for nearly three-fourths of all immigrants (Table 3). Immigrants have been mainly females, adding to the country's already growing majority of females in the total population. Also, the median age of recent immigrants has been younger than that of the total resident population. This is partially because of the preferences established for family reunion.

Although the United States has gone through significant internal migrations in the early westward movement and in the recent movement to the Sunbelt, immigrants have been very selective in choosing their initial intended permanent residences. Through the century, they have gone largely to the well established northern industrial/manufacturing belt, with exceptions notably in recent decades to Florida, Texas and California. Immigrants settled in the same states where most Americans already resided, contributing to even further growth of these most populated and ethnic states(16). This is reflected moreover in the fact that throughout the decades of this century, three-fifths of all immigrants went to a mere five states. Unlike the population as a whole, it is interesting to note, however, immigrants did not rush to the rest of the Sunbelt. On the other hand, they also did not rush to areas such as the northern Great Plains, which are avoided by most Americans, and basically the interior of the country which is emptying out toward the peripheries. Predictions are that an estimated three-fourths of the American population will live within fifty miles of the national coastlines and shorelines of this country by the year 2000, growing at a rate three times the United States average(17).

318

Partially because of growing concern by many Americans over both the influxes of legal and illegal immigrants, their origins and the lack of employment opportunities, legislation (the *Simpson-Mazzoli* Immigration Reform Bill) has been introduced in Congress to control immigration. Most Americans feel the situation is out of control(18). In particular, the large influx of approximately 125,000 Marielito Cubans, many with undesirable backgrounds, in 1980 tainted the public's perception of immigration policies. The acceptance of nearly 400,000 Indochinese refugees in the 1970's also produced a report by the Joint Economic Committee of Congress that the American government was spending $2 billion annually by 1980 on all refugees. In California alone, reports indicated that over one-half of its 285,000 refugees were on welfare(19).

The economic recession of the early 1980's also raised questions about the employment of immigrants, albeit much of the concern was about the hiring of illegal or undocumented immigrants at low wages. Nearly one million illegal immigrants have been apprehended annually in recent years, while probably another half a million are not caught by immigration authorities. The cost of tracking down illegal immigrants and their deportation have also raised the ire of Americans. Illegal immigrants may be taking jobs from other Americans, such as minorities and particularly blacks who live in the large metropolitan centres. A controversial national identification system is part of the pending legislation. Its intent is to curb the hiring of illegal immigrants and to impose fines on employers who hire them.

When all of the considerations and perceptions are put together, it is not surprising to learn that an ABC News poll on 4 July 1983 revealed that two-thirds of all Americans believed there should be no more immigration, or that at least great limitations be placed upon the number of immigrants who could enter annually.

There is little doubt, however, that today's legal and estimated six to eight million resident illegal immigrants, who would also be given amnesty and eventually citizenship if they were in the country by 1980 or 1982 (Senate vs. House Bill) under the pending Simpson-Mazzoli legislation, will have a significant impact upon both changing the ethnic and non-white composition and reshaping the social, economic and political aspects of the American population. This is especially true within the spatial dynamics and urban ecology of large metropolitan areas of certain states(20). A recent study published by the magazine *American Demographics* revealed '... in 1983 Blacks, Hispanics, Asians and other minorities made up a majority in 25 cities with populations over 100,000. There were only nine such cities in the 1970 census.'(21)

The Senate's version of the pending Simpson-Mazzoli legislation would impose an annual ceiling of 425,000 legal immigrants, including relatives, but not refugees. The House wants to retain the 270,000 ceiling, plus refugees and unlimited numbers of relatives and others. Each country would continue to be allocated 20,000 visas, except Mexico and Canada which would receive 40,000 each(22).

The Select Commission on Immigration and the National Interest suggested the scheme outlined on page 320 for future and manageable annual immigration between the 1980's and the year 2050, based upon present immigration policies and the assumption that illegal immigration can be controlled(23).

Today's new immigrants of about one million legal and illegal arrivals annually will produce large and different nationality groups in the twentieth-first century when the long-established Anglo-American population will find itself declining at a quickening rate in comparison to the rates of past centuries. For the first time, the 1980 United States census included a question on ancestry. In the melting pot for that year, one in every ten Americans spoke a language other than English at home. However, Americans of English lineage still comprised over one-fifth of the total population. In adding the large German and Irish populations and the smaller French, Scottish and Scandinavian populations to the English descendants, people of Northern and Western European ancestry comprised the majority. These populations were, however, located largely in the interior of the country where most of today's immigrants do not settle. Consequently, states on the peripheries have the diverse populations while those states in the interior are experiencing little ethnic change with populations of ancestral origin attributed largely to immigrants of past centuries(24).

The United States has already the seventh largest Hispanic population (over 15 million) in the world and it is being reinforced daily by immigration and by higher than normal birth rates. The Mexican-American population alone nearly doubled in the 1970's and that of the Asians more than doubled from 1.5 million in 1970 to 3.5 million in 1980. These populations are highly concentrated (75 per cent or more) in fewer than ten states which already have considerable political influence.

	Gross Immigration		Rate of Return Emigration
Numerically restricted immigration	350,000	×	30% = 105,000
Unrestricted immigration	170,000	×	30% = 51,000
Undocumented/illegal aliens	50,000	×	30% = 15,000
Refugees (except for 10 of those 70 years when it would be 50,000)	100,000	×	5% = 5,000
Total gross immigration	670,000		176,000
Total emigration	176,000		
Net immigration	494,000		

320

Table 1. Immigrants Admitted by Country or Region of Birth, 1880-1979

Origin	1880-89	1890-99	1900-09	1910-19	1920-29	1930-39	1940-49	1950-59	1960-69	1970-79	1880-1979
Europe	88.3%	96.9%	93.0%	79.7%	60.0%	63.6%	54.3%	62.5%	39.7%	19.5%	71.3%
Asia[a]	1.3	1.7	2.9	3.1	2.6	2.7	3.5	5.4	11.2	34.4	6.9
North America											
1) Canada/Newfoundland[b]	9.4	0.1	1.5	11.2	22.1	23.3	19.2	10.5	9.5	2.7	8.4
2) Middle America	0.6[c]	0.9	1.7	5.1	14.0	8.2	14.3	18.2	31.2	34.5	10.8
South America	---[d]	---	0.2	0.6	1.0	1.4	2.4	2.5	6.8	6.1	1.7
Africa	---	---	0.1	0.1	0.1	0.3	0.8	0.5	1.1	2.0	0.4
Australia, New Zealand and Pacific Islands	0.2	0.1	0.2	0.2	0.2	0.5	2.2	0.3	0.5	0.8	0.3
Other	0.2	0.3	0.4	---	---	---	3.3	0.1	---	---	0.2
Total:	5,248,568	3,694,294	8,202,388	6,347,380	4,295,510	699,375	856,608	2,499,268	3,213,749	4,336,001	39,393,141

[a]Beginning in 1952, the figures for the Philippine Islands were recorded under Asia. Between 1934-1951, they were included in the Pacific Islands. Prior to 1934, they were recorded separately and added to the figures for Asia.

[b]Prior to 1920, this category was given as British North America.

[c]There is no record of immigration from Mexico for 1886-1893.

[d]---denotes less than 0.1%.

Source: Immigration and Naturalization Service.

Table 2. Occupations of All Immigrants Admitted to the United States, 1950-1979

	1950-1959 (2,499,268)	1960-1969 (3,213,749)	1970-1979 (4,336,001)
Professional, technical & kindred workers	7.3%	9.7%	10.2%
Managers, officials, proprietors, administrators, except farm	2.2	2.0	2.9
Clerical, sales & kindred workers	7.6	7.9	4.6
Craftsmen, foremen & kindred workers	7.9	6.2	5.1
Operatives & kindred workers	6.9	4.9	6.0
Private household workers	3.9	3.9	2.1
Service workers, except private households	2.6	3.3	3.7
Farmers & farm managers	2.5	0.8	0.3
Farm laborers & farm foremen	1.7	1.8	1.7
Laborers, except farm & mine	5.0	4.0	3.6
Housewives, children & others with no occupation reported	52.4	55.5	59.8

Source: Immigration and Naturalization Service

Table 3. Major Sources of Immigrants: 1950-1979*

1950-1959		1960-1969		1970-1979	
1. Germany	13.8%	1. Mexico	13.4%	1. Mexico	14.4%
2. Mexico	11.7	2. Canada	9.5	2. Philippines	8.1
3. Canada	10.5	3. Cuba	7.7	3. Cuba	6.4
4. United Kingdom	7.9	4. United Kingdom	7.5	4. Korea	5.7
5. Italy	7.3	5. Germany	6.9	5. China/Taiwan	4.4
6. Poland	6.9	6. Italy	6.1	6. India	3.8
7. Cuba	2.9	7. China/Taiwan	2.7	7. Italy	3.5
8. Yugoslavia	2.6	8. Dominican Republic	2.6	8. Dominican Republic	3.3
9. Ireland	2.5	9. Poland	2.4	9. Jamaica	3.2
10. Hungary	2.5	10. Greece	2.4	10. Vietnam	3.2
11. USSR	2.2	11. Philippines	2.3	11. United Kingdom	2.8
	70.8	12. Portugal	2.3	12. Canada	2.7
		13. Colombia	2.1	13. Portugal	2.5
		14. Jamaica	1.8	14. Greece	2.4
			69.7	15. Colombia	1.7
				16. Germany	1.6
				17. Trinidad/Tobago	1.5
				18. Haiti	1.4
					72.6

* Only countries which were the sources of 50,000 or more immigrants per decade.

Source: Immigration and Naturalization Service

322

Table 4. Destinations of Immigrants, 1900-1979

1900-09

1.	New York	32%
2.	Pennsylvania	19
3.	Illinois	7
4.	Massachusetts	7
5.	New Jersey	7*
		72

1910-19

1.	New York	28%
2.	Pennsylvania	13
3.	Massachusetts	8
4.	Illinois	8
5.	New Jersey	5
		62

1920-29

1.	New York	27%
2.	Massachusetts	8
3.	Texas	8
4.	Michigan	7
5.	Pennsylvania	7
		57

1930-39

1.	New York	39%
2.	California	8
3.	Michigan	7
4.	Massachusetts	6
5.	New Jersey	6
		66

1940-49

1.	New York	33%
2.	California	12
3.	Michigan	6
4.	Illinois	5
5.	Massachusetts	5
		61

1950-59

1.	New York	25%
2.	California	16
3.	Illinois	7
4.	Texas	7
5.	New Jersey	5
		60

1960-69

1.	New York	23%
2.	California	22
3.	Florida	6
4.	Illinois	5
5.	New Jersey	5
		61

1970-79

1.	California	22%
2.	New York	22
3.	New Jersey	6
4.	Texas	6
5.	Florida	6
		62

1900-79

1.	New York	28%
2.	Pennsylvania	10
3.	California	10
4.	Illinois	7
5.	Massachusetts	6
		61

*All numbers are rounded to the next whole number.
Source: Immigration and Naturalization Service.

323

Fig. 1.

Immigration to the United States, 1880-1980.

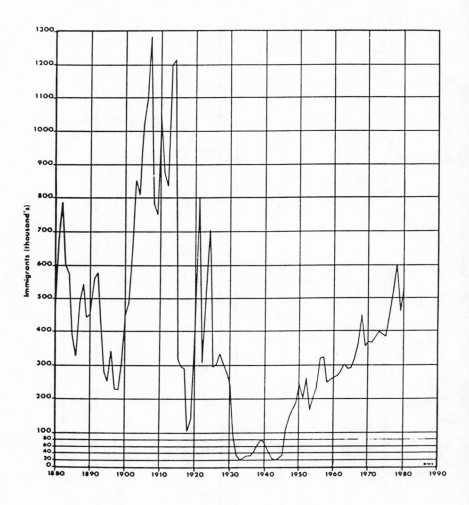

Source: Immigration and Naturalization Service.

324

80

Fig. 2.

Sex/age pyramids of all immigrants admitted to the United States, 1950-1979.

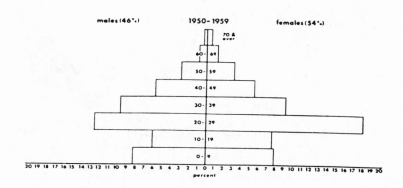

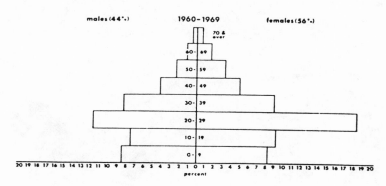

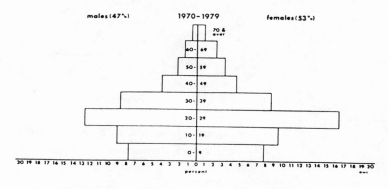

Source: Immigration and Naturalization Service.

325

Fig. 3.

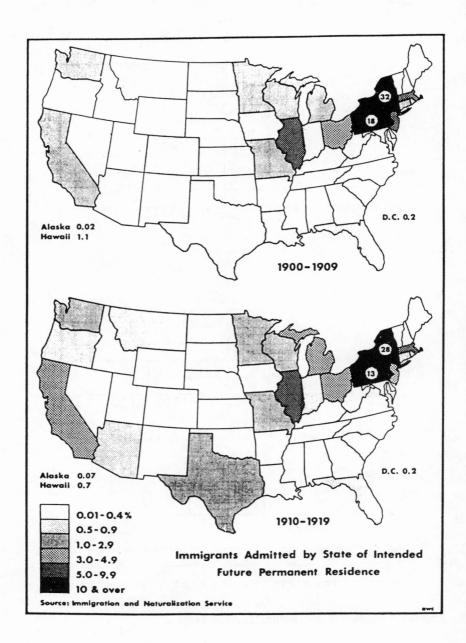

Alaska 0.02
Hawaii 1.1

D.C. 0.2

1900-1909

Alaska 0.07
Hawaii 0.7

	0.01-0.4%
	0.5-0.9
	1.0-2.9
	3.0-4.9
	5.0-9.9
	10 & over

D.C. 0.2

1910-1919

Immigrants Admitted by State of Intended
Future Permanent Residence

Source: Immigration and Naturalization Service

awc

326

Fig. 4.

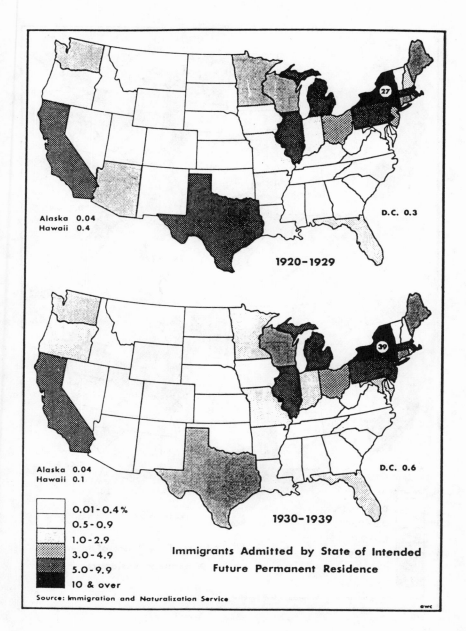

Alaska 0.04
Hawaii 0.4

D.C. 0.3

1920-1929

Alaska 0.04
Hawaii 0.1

D.C. 0.6

1930-1939

0.01-0.4 %
0.5-0.9
1.0-2.9
3.0-4.9
5.0-9.9
10 & over

Immigrants Admitted by State of Intended
Future Permanent Residence

Source: Immigration and Naturalization Service

ewc

327

Fig. 5.

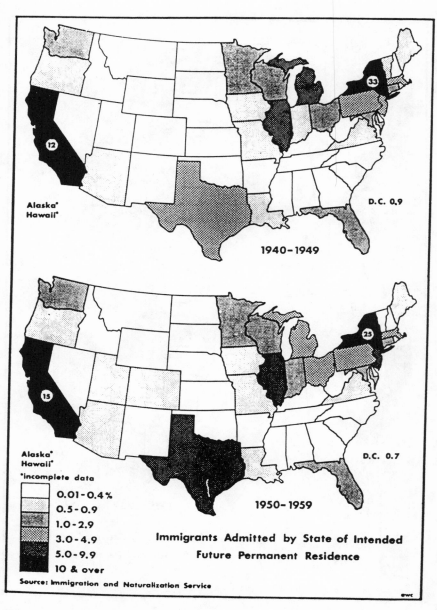

1940-1949

Alaska*
Hawaii*
*incomplete data

0.01-0.4%
0.5-0.9
1.0-2.9
3.0-4.9
5.0-9.9
10 & over

D.C. 0.7

1950-1959

Immigrants Admitted by State of Intended
Future Permanent Residence

Source: Immigration and Naturalization Service

328

Fig. 6.

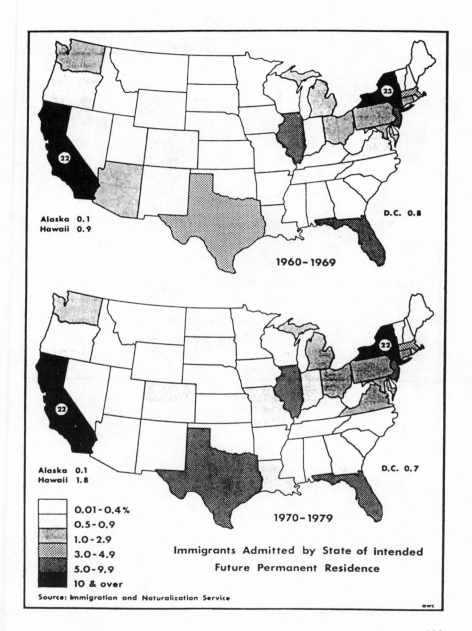

Alaska 0.1
Hawaii 0.9

D.C. 0.8

1960–1969

Alaska 0.1
Hawaii 1.8

D.C. 0.7

1970–1979

0.01-0.4%
0.5-0.9
1.0-2.9
3.0-4.9
5.0-9.9
10 & over

Source: Immigration and Naturalization Service

Immigrants Admitted by State of intended
Future Permanent Residence

329

85

Fig. 7.

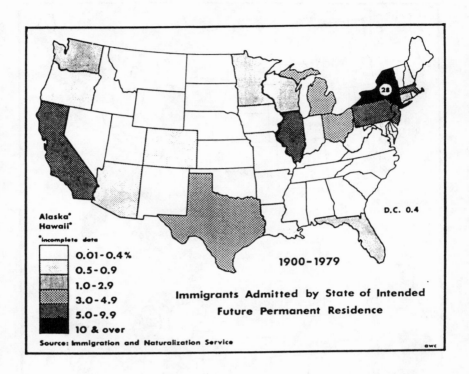

Alaska°
Hawaii°
°incomplete data

	0.01-0.4%
	0.5-0.9
	1.0-2.9
	3.0-4.9
	5.0-9.9
	10 & over

Source: Immigration and Naturalization Service

D.C. 0.4

1900-1979

Immigrants Admitted by State of Intended
Future Permanent Residence

awc

330

FOOTNOTES

1) Stuart C. Miller, *The Unwelcome Immigrant: The American Image of the Chinese, 1785-1882* (Berkeley: University of California Press, 1969).

2) For background information on Eastern and Southern Europeans in the United States, see Irene Portis Winner and Rudolph M. Susel, *The Dynamics of East European Ethnicity Outside of Eastern Europe: With Special Emphasis on the American Case* (Cambridge, Mass.: Schenkman Publishing Company, 1983) and Humbert S. Nelli, *From Immigrants to Ethnics: The Italian Americans* (New York: Oxford University Press, 1983).

3) Henry Cabot Lodge, 'Efforts to Restrict Undesirable Immigration,' *Century Magazine,* 67 (January 1904), pp. 466-469; Frank E. Sargent, 'The Need of Closer Inspection and Greater Restriction of Immigrants', *Century Magazine,* 67 (January 1904), pp. 470-473 and Edith Abbott, *Historical Aspects of the Immigration Problem* (Chicago: University of Chicago Press, 1926), pp. 697-862.

4) Jerry R. Williams, *And Yet They Come: Portuguese Immigration From the Azores to the United States* (New York: Center for Migration Studies, 1982).

5) Ian R.H. Rockett, 'American Immigration Policy and Ethnic Selection: An Historical Overview', *Journal of Ethnic Studies,* 10 (Winter, 1983), pp. 1-26.

6) For literature from 1965 to 1979, see U.S. Department of Justice, Immigration and Naturalization Service, *Immigration Literature: Abstracts of Demographic, Economic, and Policy Studies* (Washington: Government Printing Office, June 1979) and *Selected Readings on U.S. Immigration Policy and Law,* Committee on the Judiciary, United States Senate, Congressional Research Service, Library of Congress, 96th Congress, 2nd Session, October 1980, (Washington: Government Printing Office, 1980).

7) Mary M. Kritz, ed., *U.S. Immigration and Refugee Policy: Global and Domestic Issues* (Lexington, Mass.: D.C. Heath and Company, 1983) and James L. Carlin, 'The Development of U.S. Refugee and Migration Policies: An International Context', *Journal of Refugee Resettlement,* 1 (August 1984), pp. 9-14.

8) James Fallows, 'Immigration: How It's Affecting Us', *The Atlantic Monthly,* 252 (November 1983), pp. 45-106; Brent Ashabranner, *The New Americans: Changing Patterns in U.S. Immigration* (New York: Dodd, Mead and Company, 1983); *Numerical Limits on Immigration to the United States* (Hearing Before the Subcommittee on Immigration and Refugee Policy of the Committee on the Judiciary, United States Senate, 97th Congress, 2nd session, January 25, 1982, Serial J-97-89) (Washington: Government Printing Office, 1982); *U.S. Immigration Policy and the National Interest* (The Final Report and Recommendations of the Select Commission on Immigration and Refugee Policy to the Congress and the President of the United States, March 1, 1981) (Washington: Government Printing Office, 1981); *U.S. Immigration Policy and the National Interest* (Staff Report of the Select Commission on Immigration and Refugee Policy, April 30, 1981) (Washington: Government Printing Office, 1981); 'The New Immigrants: Still the Promised Land', *Time,* 108 (July 5, 1976), pp. 16-21, 23-24; Charles B. Keeley, 'Immigration Composition and Population Policy', *Science,* 185 (August 16, 1974), pp. 587-593; J. Wareing, 'The Changing Pattern of Immigration Into the United States, 1956-75', *Geography,* 63 (July 1978), pp. 220-224; Thomas Kessner and Betty Boyd Caroli, *Today's Immigrants, Their Stories: A New Look at the Newest Americans* (New York: Oxford University Press, 1981) and Tricia Knoll, *Becoming Americans: Asian Sojourners, Immigrants, and Refugees in the Western United States* (Portland, Ore.: Coast to Coast Books, 1982).

9) 'Cuban Refugees May Alter Florida', *Detroit Free Press* (December 3, 1984), p. 4A.

10) *Statistical Review of Immigration, 1820-1910 and Distribution of Immigrants, 1850-1900,* U.S. Senate, 61st Congress, 3rd Session, Document 756 (Washington: Government Printing Office, 1911) and Richard L. Ehrlich, ed., *Immigrants in Industrial America, 1850-1920* (Charlottesville: University Press of Virginia, 1977).

331

87

11) Alvar W. Carlson, 'Recent Immigration, 1961-1970: A Factor in the Growth and Distribution of the United States Population', *Journal of Geography*, 72 (December 1973), pp. 8-18; Lowell E. Gallaway, Richard K. Vedder and Vishwa Shukla, 'The Distribution of the Immigrant Population in the United States: An Economic Analysis', *Explorations in Economic History*, 11 (Spring, 1974), pp. 213-226 and 'America's Melting Pot: Who's In It', *U.S. News and World Report*, 94 (June 13, 1983), p. 11.

12) J. Craig Jenkins, 'Push/Pull in Recent Mexican Migration to the U.S.', *International Migration Review*, 11 (Summer, 1977), pp. 178-189; Thomas D. Boswell and Timothy C. Jones, 'A Regionalization of Mexican Americans in the United States', *Geographical Review*, 70 (January 1980), pp. 88-98; 'Hispanics in the United States', *Interchange*, 12 (October 1983), pp. 1-6; Lourdes Arizpa, 'The Rural Exodus in Mexico and Mexican Migration to the United States', *International Migration Review*, 15 (Winter, 1981), pp. 626-649 and Douglas S. Massey and Kathleen M. Schnabel, 'Recent Trends in Hispanic Immigration to the U.S.', *International Migration Review*, 17 (Summer, 1983), pp. 212-244.

13) For background on the geographical aspects of Cuban immigration to the United States, see Thomas D. Boswell, 'The Migration and Distribution of Cubans and Puerto Ricans Living in the United States', *Journal of Geography*, 83 (March-April, 1984), pp. 65-72; Thomas D. Boswell, Guarione M. Diaz and Lisandro Perez, 'Socioeconomic Context of Cuban Americans', *Journal of Cultural Geography*, 3 (Fall/Winter, 1982), pp. 29-41; Thomas D. Boswell and James R. Curtis, *The Cuban-American Experience* (Totowa, New Jersey: Adams, Littlefield and Company, 1984); Robert S. Bacon, 'Distribution of Cuban Refugees in the United States: National and Urban Scales', *Ohio Geographers*, 4 (1976), pp. 35-44; *Caribbean Migration* (Oversight Hearings Before the Subcommittee on Immigration, Refugees, and International Law of the Committee on the Judiciary, House of Representatives, 96th Congress, 2nd Session), May 13, June 4, 17, 1980, Serial 84 (Washington: Government Printing Office, 1980).

14) Thomas D. Boswell, 'In the Eye of the Storm: The Context of Haitian Migration to Miami, Florida', *Southeastern Geographer*, 23 (November 1983), pp. 57-77; Susan H. Buchanan, 'Language and Identity: Haitians in New York City', *International Migration Review*, 13 (Summer, 1979), pp. 298-313; Antonio Ugalde, Frank D. Bean and Gilbert Cardenas, 'International Migration from the Dominican Republic: Findings from a National Survey', *International Migration Review*, 13 (Summer, 1979), pp. 235-254; Thomas D. Boswell, 'The New Haitian Diaspora: Florida's Most Recent Residents', *Caribbean Review*, 11 (Winter, 1982), pp. 18-21, and James Allman, 'Haitian Migration: 30 Years Assessed', *Migration Today*, 10 (1982), pp. 7-12.

15) 'America's Melting Pot: Who's In It', *U.S. News and World Report*, footnote 11, p. 11.

16) Everett S. Lee and Leon F. Bouvier, 'Endless Movement: America as a Nation of Migrants', *Population Profiles*, No. 6 (1973), pp. 1-8 and 'What Americans Told the Census Takers', *U.S. News and World Report*, 92 (May 3, 1982), p. 12.

17) 'America's Losing Battle to Save Its Beaches', *U.S. News and World Report*, 95 (July 11, 1983), pp. 51-52; '95,000-Mile Battle Line: America's Coasts', *U.S. News and World Report*, 89 (August 4, 1980), pp. 62-63 and Dennis W. Ducsik, *Shoreline for the Public*, (Cambridge, Mass.: MIT Press, 1974).

18) 'Immigration Seen Out of Control', *U.S. News and World Report*, 89 (December 15, 1980), p. 6; 'The Great American Immigration Nightmare', *U.S. News and World Report*, 90 (June 22, 1981), pp. 27-31; 'Crackdown on Illegal Aliens - The Impact', *U.S. News and World Report*, 97 (July 2, 1984), pp. 23-26; Rev. Theodore Hesburgh, 'People Feel the Entire Immigration System is Out of Control', *U.S. News and World Report*, 89 (October 13, 1980), pp. 63-64; 'What Uncle Sam is Doing to Stem the Flood of Illegal Aliens', *U.S. News and World Report*, 97 (November 5, 1984), p. 78; 'Give Me Your Tired, Your Poor ...', *Interchange*, 4 (September 1975), pp. 1-2; Charles B. Keeley, 'Illegal Migration', *Scientific American*, 246 (March 1982), pp. 41-47 and Leonard F. Chapman, Jr., 'Illegal Aliens - A Growing Population', *Immigration and Naturalization Reporter*, 24 (Fall, 1975), pp. 15-18.

332

19) 'More Than Half of 284,000 Refugees in California Are Welfare Recipients', *Daily Sentinel-Tribune* (Bowling Green, Ohio), October 13, 1983, p. 12; 'Immigration Seen Out of Control', *U.S. News and World Report*, footnote 18, p. 6 and Dennis Anderson, 'Illegal Aliens Have Aided Industry in California and Put Burden on Services', *Daily Sentinel-Tribune* (Bowling Green, Ohio), December 12, 1984, p. 6.

20) Alvar W. Carlson, 'A Cartographic Analysis of Latin American Immigrant Groups in the Chicago Metropolitan Area, 1965-76', *Revista Geográfica* No. 96 (Julio-Dic. 1982), pp. 91-106; Alvar W. Carlson, 'The Settling of Asian Immigrant Groups in the Chicago Metropolitan Area, 1965-76', *Philippine Geographical Journal*, 28 (January-June, 1984), pp. 22-40; Alvar W. Carlson, 'Filipino and Indian Immigrants in Detroit and Suburbs, 1961-1974', *Philippine Geographical Journal*, 19 (October, November, December 1975), pp. 199-209; Alvar W. Carlson, 'A Map Analysis of Middle East Immigrants in Detroit and Suburbs, 1961-1974, *International Migration*, 14 (December 1976), pp. 283-298; Alvar W. Carlson, 'The Origins and Characteristics of Foreign Immigrants Settling in Toledo and Northwestern Ohio, 1965-76', *Northwest Ohio Quarterly*, 50 (Winter, 1978), pp. 17-28; Alvar W. Carlson, 'The Mapping of Recent Immigrant Settling in Cleveland and Cuyahoga County Based Upon Petitions for Naturalization', *Ecumene*, 10 (April 1978), pp. 27-34; Alvar W. Carlson, 'Recent European Immigration to the Chicago Metropolitan Area', *International Migration*, 20 (1982), pp. 45-64; Alvar W. Carlson, 'The Settling of Recent Filipino Immigrants in Midwestern Metropolitan Areas', *Crossroads: An Interdisciplinary Journal of Southeast Asian Studies*, 1 (February 1983), pp. 13-19 and 'English Sometimes Spoken Here: Our Big Cities Go Ethnic', *U.S. News and World Report*, 94 (March 21, 1983), pp. 49-53.

21) 'Where Minorities Are a Majority', *U.S. News and World Report*, 97 (November 12, 1984), p. 14.

22) 'Landmark Immigration Bill Clears House By 5 Votes', *Population Today*, 12 (July/August 1984), p. 3.

23) *U.S. Immigration Policy and the National Interest*, Staff Report, April 30, 1981, p. 107.

24) 'America's Melting Pot: Who's In It', *U.S. News and World Report*, footnote 11, p. 11 and 1980 Census of Population, *Ancestry of the Population by State: 1980*, Supplementary Report PC80-S1-10 (Washington: Government Printing Office, April, 1983).

333

CENT ANS D'IMMIGRATION AUX ETAT-UNIS (1880-1979)

L'étude de *A. W. Carlson* est une analyse de la politique américaine d'immigration qui a influencé les origines et les caractéristiques des immigrants, et de son impact sur la composition de la population des Etats-Unis. Il ne fait aucun doute que cette immigration joue un rôle important dans le peuplement des Etats-Unis car elle compte pour environ un quart du taux de croissance annuel et serait probablement égale à 40 pour cent s'il était tenu compte de l'immigration illégale. L'immigration s'est à nouveau révélée comme un facteur majeur de l'augmentation de la population parce qu'un nombre croissant d'étrangers émigrent chaque année vers les Etats-Unis alors que le taux de fertilité de ce pays a récemment décliné.

UN SIGLO DE INMIGRACION EN LOS ESTADOS UNIDOS (1880-1979)

El estudio de *A. W. Carlson* constituye un análisis de las políticas de inmigración estadounidenses, que han influido en la determinación de los lugares de procedencia y de las características de los inmigrantes y que han tenido a la vez un importante efecto en la composición demográfica del país. Es también indudable en el presente que la inmigración viene todavía determinando en gran medida el perfil de la población de los Estados Unidos, pues a ella corresponde aproximadamente la cuarta parte del incremento demográfico anual y quizás hasta el 40 por ciento si se toma en cuenta la inmigración ilegal. El elemento inmigratorio ha vuelto a convertirse en un factor principal del crecimiento de la población estadounidense, dado el número cada vez mayor de extranjeros que ingresan año tras año en el país, paralelamente con la actual declinación de la tasa de fertilidad.

334

Chinese and Japanese in North America: The Canadian and American Experiences Compared

Roger Daniels

This essay examines two streams of migrants to North America: one from China and one from Japan. While this conflation may outrage some nationalistic historians on both sides of the border, it is certainly justified from the point of view of the migrants who, for a long time, largely ignored the international boundary. It was notorious for decades in the Pacific Northwest that the four chief Chinese communities near the border—Port Townsend and Port Angeles in Washington State and Victoria and Vancouver in British Columbia—did a thriving business in goods and persons with little regard to the law that made the southern and northern shores of Juan de Fuca Strait parts of separate nations. Moreover, if the strait itself or the docks and piers on either side of it were too heavily patroled, there was always the convenient chain of San Juan Islands or, on the mainland, miles of unguarded common frontier.[1] For Japanese migrants, too, the border was not a great inconvenience. The reminiscences of one Japanese pioneer illustrate the point nicely. Kihachi Hirakawa, a twenty-six year old bachelor, took advantage of an 1890 rate war between Yokohama ticket agencies which cut fares from fifty to twenty-five yen, to come to "America." He found out about the opportunity just three days before the ship's departure, which was not enough time to get a passport. A ship's officer told him: "A passport was not necessary, and if I paid my fare I would be accepted. Then I asked if I could land without a passport at Vancouver, B.C., and the officer replied, 'Maybe...but I am not sure.'"

Canadian Review of American Studies, Volume 17, Number 2, Summer 1986, 173-187

Hirakawa, gambling that he could get in, borrowed forty yen, bought the ticket and a second-hand suit, and changed his remaining ten yen into $8.90 (U.S.). After a fifteen-day journey, during which he was so seasick that he could eat only on the first two days, his ship, the British steamer *Abyssinia* (3,250 tons), arrived in Vancouver. Still concerned about the lack of a passport and so sick that he had to be helped down the gangplank, he encountered no problems in entering Canada. After resting two days in a hotel, he nervously began the last leg of his trip to Seattle on 11 August 1890: "A few customs house officials boarded our boat from a small boat to examine our baggage. Again I was concerned about the lack of a passport [but] they merely made a brief inspection....The next morning our boat docked at the port of Seattle. Thus I easily entered the United States."[2] Hirakawa, whose migratory experience was not atypical, would make four more trans-Pacific voyages before settling, for good, on Bainbridge Island, just off Seattle.

There was even some confusion about the border of "America" to the far south. I have read one life history of a Japanese immigrant to Mexico which describes, with some chagrin, his arrival in 1907 armed with a Japanese-English dictionary that was all but useless, and how it took him six months to procure a Japanese-Spanish dictionary from Tokyo.[3] The cultures of the United States and Mexico were so different, however, that each immigrant group quickly learned to differentiate them. Most Chinese and Japanese migrants in Mexico would have preferred to be north of the Rio Grande: traffic, legal and illegal, was largely one-way. Between the United States and Canada there was—and continues to be—two-way traffic. The two countries remain almost equally desirable goals for migrants from Asia: given equal opportunity the choice may well be idiosyncratic. One French-educated Chinese physician who had such a choice in 1949 chose New York over Montreal because he feared that immigration to Canada would somehow involve taking an oath of allegiance to a descendant of Queen Victoria, something abhorrent to him because Victoria had forced opium on China a century before and the drug had been ruinous to some members of his gentry family.[4]

Hirakawa and Dr. Li were not typical migrants. To understand the broader aspects of migration from Asia it is first necessary to talk about purposes, numbers, economic niches: that is, why and when the migrants came, how many there were, and what roles they played in their new homes. Since Chinese migrants preceded Japanese, I will speak of them first. Much ink, far too much ink, has been spilled over the question of whether or not the Chinese migrants to North America were immigrants or "sojourners," that is persons who did not really intend to stay. Gunther Barth, in fact, has made this central to his study of the early decades of Chinese migration to the United States. As far as this paper is concerned, all persons who crossed the Pacific to work in North America will be called migrants, immigrants, Chinese Canadians or Chinese Americans, regardless of what their original intention might have been and regardless of what they actually did. This should be standard practice for immigration historians: as Dino Cinel put it recently in his study of the Italians of San Francisco, the work of the immigration historian is to deal "with change and continuity in the lives of [those] who immigrated...whether permanently or temporarily."[5]

Chinese, and particularly those from South China, had been migrating to the area they call Nanyang or "South Seas," what we call Southeast Asia, for centuries before significant migration outside of Asia began in the middle of the nineteenth century. At that time, two new and distinct kinds of Chinese migration began to occur: free immigration, chiefly to the United States, Canada and Australia, and the coolie trade, of largely unfree and/or unwilling migrants to such places as Peru and Cuba. Hugh Tinker has taught us that Chinese were not the first unfree Asians to be imported by plantation economies: before large numbers of Chinese were involved in the coolie trade, tens of thousands of Indians were involved in an indenture system that Tinker calls *A New System of Slavery*, in which laborers, both Hindu and Muslim, were taken to toil on plantations in such places as Mauritius and Fiji in the old world, and Trinidad and Guiana in the new.[6] The Chinese branch of this trade, as Persia Campbell Crawford demonstrated long ago, was simply horrendous. The trade in Indians was at least inhibited by the government of India; the Chinese government was not only largely impotent in the nineteenth century, but for a long time was not even interested in the welfare of its subjects who went overseas.[7] As one Chinese viceroy put it to an American diplomat: "The Emperor's wealth is beyond computation; why should he care for those of his subjects who have left their home, or for the sands that they have scraped together."

Despite the fact that anti-Asian agitators in both the United States and Canada categorized Chinese immigrants as "coolies"—and that generations of unsympathetic historians have emulated them—the coolie trade could not exist in either North America or the Antipodes. To be sure, there were exploitations and social control of these immigrants by both the brokers who often financed their passage and the labor contractors who arranged for their employment—often these were the same person or agency—but these immigrants were largely able to change jobs and, eventually, have some control over their own employment. As early as the mid-1850s, an American consul in Hong Kong reported that one of the ways in which Chinese were tricked onto the coolie ships bound for Peru or Cuba was that they were told that they were going to America or Australia. The tendency of historians and others who write of Chinese immigrants to treat them as, somehow, different from other immigrants, has its roots in perceptions and misperceptions of this coolie trade and in the essentially racist notions that even "liberal" nineteenth-century westerners entertained about Asians generally and Chinese in particular. This tendency to treat Chinese as, somehow, special and different from other immigrant groups continues to the present: many contemporary scholars—and the government in Beijing—continue to speak of "Overseas Chinese" to describe persons of Chinese ancestry regardless of how many generations they have lived abroad. Nevertheless, as Craig A. Lockard noted some years ago: "The Chinese are no longer really 'overseas' Chinese, anymore than American Jews are 'overseas' Jews, Argentinians of Italian extraction, 'overseas' Italians, or Arab Shariffs in Malaya are 'overseas' Arabs. The diaspora has claimed the emigrant Chinese and their descendants: it will probably not return them to their ancestral home."[8]

Although there were Chinese seamen reported on the east coast of North America as early as 1785, the earliest Chinese who can be called immigrants to North America arrived in San Francisco in 1848, just before the Gold Rush began. That rush brought large numbers of Chinese to California, and when, in the 1850s, gold was discovered in Australia and in the Fraser Valley of British Columbia, Chinese from California were in the vanguard of the immigrants who went to those places. Initially, like so many newcomers of other nationalities in the North American West, the Chinese were drawn by gold. The hostility of white miners often drove them from the gold fields, but the Chinese quickly filled other economic niches, both as domestics performing what was largely regarded as "women's work," and as laborers who performed key roles in the construction and maintenance of trans-continental and other railroads in each country. From mid-century to the mid-1880s, when each nation enacted restrictive legislation, more than 300,000 Chinese are recorded as entering North America. Well over 90% of these were adult males. The censuses of 1890/91, however, enumerated fewer than 120,000, more than 100,000 of whom were in the United States (see appended table). Clearly, many of the immigrants had returned to China, some of them with enough money to buy land, but our concern is with those who stayed. In each nation at that time Chinese were heavily concentrated in the Far West: 98% of Canada's Chinese were in British Columbia, while in the United States 79% were on the Pacific Coast and 90% in the eleven westernmost states and territories.

The restrictive legislation passed in the United States—the Chinese Exclusion Act of 1882 which, in one form or another, was to remain in effect until late 1943—was effective enough to put a cap on the Chinese population in the U.S. For almost half a century—from 1882 until sometime in the 1920s—the Chinese American population steadily decreased. The 1920 census found only 60,000, just 57% of the 1890 total. Since there was almost certainly an intercensal high of perhaps 125,000 Chinese in the U.S. in 1882, this was a reduction of more than half of the population. Canada's restrictive legislation took the form of a head tax: first levied in 1886 at $50 per capita, it was raised in stages to $500 by 1904. Yet, such was the perceived advantage of migration to Canada that the still overwhelmingly male Chinese Canadian population continued to grow until sometime in the 1930s, hitting a censal peak of 46,500 in 1931, a more than fivefold increase in forty years. The Chinese Canadian population, which had been less than a tenth of the Chinese American population in 1890/91, was more than three-fifths of it in the 1920s and 1930s. Similarly, the incidence of Chinese in the U.S. population fell from a high of two-tenths of one percent (.002) in 1890 to six one-hundredths of one percent (.0006) in 1940, while the incidence of Chinese in the Canadian population rose from about the same level—one-tenth of one percent (.001) in 1881—to almost one-half of one percent (.0045) in 1921 and 1931, falling to three-tenths of one percent (.003) in 1941.

Despite these opposite population trends, there is no reason to believe that there was any appreciable difference between the anti-Asian prejudices of Canadians and Americans: all of the evidence that I have seen leads me to conclude that there was a basic attitude of white supremacy in each country. The difference in behavior—that one nation put an effective cap on the Chinese population and the other did not—was due, rather, to the very different political systems in each nation, and to the fact that Western American voters had more direct leverage than did the voters of Western Canada. Or, to put it another and somewhat paradoxical way, the more directly democratic political system in the United States allowed the anti-democratic impulses of its electorate to be registered more directly and efficiently than did the less populistic political system of Canada. Had the groups whom Alexander Hamilton once characterized as "the rich, the good and the wise" been fully in control in either country, many more Chinese and other Asian laborers would have been admitted.

It seems clear to me that although there are certain differences in the ways that one would periodize Chinese American and Chinese Canadian history, there is a distinct similarity in the overall pattern. In both countries there is a clear break, as we shall see, in the era of the second World War, but in the U.S. an earlier break comes in 1882, with the Chinese Exclusion Act, while the equivalent Canadian statute comes only with the 1923 Chinese Immigration Act, an act that was tantamount to exclusion and which the Chinese community characterized as "the forty-three harsh regulations." In the 1880s, as we have seen, Chinese immigration to Canada was quite small; the mid-twenties were, as John Higham and Howard Palmer have noted, times of extreme nativism in each country and perhaps denote its high water mark in both.[9]

Despite this difference—and it is an important one—when the geographical and economic distribution of the North American Chinese is examined, a common pattern emerges. In each country the original concentration is almost wholly in the Far West: in 1880/81, for example, 99% of all Chinese Canadians were British Columbians, while 96.1% of all American Chinese were in the eleven far western states and territories. From then until the era of World War II that concentration was steadily diluted until by 1940/41 only 54% of Chinese Canadians were in British Columbia and 60.4% of Chinese Americans were in the Far West. (I must here note that the data in the recent volume, *From China to Canada*, edited by Edgar Wickberg, that suggest geographic stability between 1921 and 1941, are simply miscomputed and that, sadly, the statistical tables are not to be relied upon. In one table of thirty-four computations, I found three to be erroneous.)[10] In addition, in each country, Chinese became more urbanized with almost every census: the chief urban area in all of Chinese North America was, of course, its metropolis, San Francisco, whose real importance cannot be judged by numbers alone, although the numbers are impressive. Between 1880 and 1920 its congested Chinatown contained between one-fifth and one-eighth of the total Chinese American population; after 1920, as births began to swell that population again, it reached a peak of almost 23% in 1940. In Canada, the concentration was even more pronounced. The British Columbia centers of Victoria and Vancouver, between them, had a stable fourth of the Chinese Canadian population between 1911 and 1921; this rose to more than one-third in 1931, and dropped to just under 30% in 1940.

Urban concentration was not limited to the three largest cities of Chinese North America. In the U.S. the Chinese became, like many other immigrant groups, not only urban, but large city urban. Unlike most other urban-centered ethnic groups, however, the Chinese moved to large cities after first having been largely rural and small town, working on railroads, in mines and agriculture. In 1880, for example, only about one-fifth of Chinese Americans lived in cities of over 100,000. This percentage increased with every census so that by 1910 almost half of Chinese Americans lived in such places, and by 1940 the figure had risen to almost three-quarters. The Canadian pattern was not dissimilar: the percentage of Chinese living in a handful of cities grew from almost 40% in 1911 to more than half in 1931, dropping to just under half in 1941.

The North American Chinese, even more than most immigrant groups, lived in distinct ethnic enclaves. While it is customary today to write off such enclaves as "ghettos"—and Chinatowns on both sides of the border certainly had many of the worst characteristics of urban slums—there was for many of the immigrants and their successors a positive aspect to these Chinatowns. As one Chicagoan remarked of his Chinatown in the mid-1920s: "Most of us can live a warmer, freer and a more human life among our relatives and friends than among strangers....Chinese relations with the population outside of Chinatown are likely to be cold, formal and commercial. It is only in Chinatown that a Chinese immigrant has society, friends and relatives who share his dreams and hopes, his hardships and adventures. Here he can tell a joke and make everybody laugh with him; here he may hear folktales told which create the illusion that Chinatown is really China."[11]

Chinese employment in each nation shifted from railroads and mining to petty urban employments, largely those providing certain services, like laundry and cooking, to both the general population and to the Chinatowns. In Canada, for example, in 1931 only three-tenths of one percent (.003) of all employed Chinese were in the professions; 14.7% were shopkeepers and small business-men, and 4.2% were farmers and gardeners. Just under a fifth of the population were entrepreneurial, i.e., 19.2%. Very few — 3.7% — were left in the occupations that once employed most of them — mining, railroad work, lumbering and canning. The largest two occupational groups — each of which comprised just over one-fifth of all workers — were cooks and waiters on the one hand and laborers on the other. Almost one-seventh worked in laundries, about 5% were servants or janitors, while 6.5% were scattered in miscellaneous employments, and almost 2% were retail employees.

In each country the small but growing number of educated, native-born Chinese faced a dilemma. As one told an interviewer years later: "Among the Canadian-born Chinese, there were a few of us who went to university. Some of them, like my two brothers, got their degrees at UBC. But none of them was able to find work. One of my brothers was a civil engineer, who graduated in 1933. He wasn't able to get anything, so he had to go to Quebec....My other brother got a degree in dairying. He wasn't able to find anything, so he went back to China around 1935...."[12]

Going to China — and for native-born Asian North Americans it was not really going back — was not an isolated phenomenon, and it indicates well the orientations of both the Chinese and Japanese communities of North America before the war: each ethnic community to a very large degree had its face turned toward Asia, not toward North America. The finest memoirist of Chinese America, Jane Snow Wong, explained that her family felt that an American-born Chinese could realize his full potential only in China: "Father and son agreed that the study of medicine in China would prepare Older Brother for his career. Knowing the Chinese language, he could establish himself where medical personnel was [sic] greatly needed, and he could strengthen his ancestral ties by visits to Daddy's native village and relatives."[13]

In many ways the Chinatowns of Canada and the U.S. were similar to other ethnic enclaves, the Little Italies or the Greektowns. The extreme sex and age disparities between Chinese North Americans and most other contem-porary ethnic groups, however, are two of the factors that make their history unique. From the time of French settlements in Upper Canada and British settlements in Virginia and Massachusetts until the era of World War II, most immigration to North America had been male, with that sex accounting for perhaps two-thirds of all entries. The sex ratios among Chinese immigrants to North America — and later among some other Asian groups — were much higher. These ratios were similar in each country. In the U.S., for example, in 1860 there were more than eighteen Chinese men for every Chinese woman. By 1940, this had shrunk to "only" 2.9 to one. For the foreign-born Chinese, the adult males, however, the available partners were, for decades, much scarcer than the general sex ratios would indicate. In 1900, for example.

when the community sex ratio was almost nineteen to one, the sex ratio for foreign-born Chinese was nearly twice that, more than thirty-six to one. Since the overwhelming majority of citizen females were small children, the larger figure is the more meaningful one as a largely "bachelor" society developed. For 1920, when we have age specific data, one can be more precise. The median age of the male Chinese American population that year was forty-two; for females, the median age was nineteen. If we subtract all Chinese, male and female, under ten that year, we find that for Chinese ten years of age and older, there were almost ten males for every female, as opposed to an overall ratio of seven to one for the whole community. Broken down another way, among foreign-born Chinese Americans the sex ratio was sixteen to one; among native-born it was 2.6 to one.[14] Non-age specific sex ratios for Canadian centers of Chinese population in 1921 range from six to one in Victoria, to ten to one in Vancouver and seventeen to one in Toronto. In a smaller center like Regina there were 246 male Chinese and four females, while in places like Kingston and St. John there were ninety-six and eighty-three Chinese males and no females at all. Many of the "bachelors" in each country were actually married, however, i.e., the husbands were in North America and the wives in China. Peter S. Li has estimated that in 1941 there were 1,177 "intact conjugal" families of Chinese Canadians, 1,459 "broken families" in which one or both partners were widowed or divorced, and 20,141 "separated" families in which the wife was outside Canada. Thus almost nine out of ten married Chinese men in Canada were separated from their wives in 1941.[15]

If one were trying to create a population model that would be likely to resist acculturation, one could do a lot worse than to use the reality of Chinese North America. Add to that demographic model a heavily male-dominated culture, a history of brutal discrimination, extreme residential segregation and a high degree of cultural differentiation between Chinese and most other North Americans, and one can begin to understand why acculturation took so relatively long for the bulk of the Chinese communities in North America.

*   *   *

Superficially, at least, the migration of Japanese to North America resembles that of the Chinese, and throughout the twentieth century writers in both Canada and the U.S. have referred to the common problems of "Oriental immigration." There have, however, been fundamental differences in the histories of the two groups, differences which help to explain the quite divergent patterns of community life and acculturation which came to prevail.

The first Japanese immigrants came to the U.S. in 1868 and to Canada in 1877. They, and those who began to follow them in significant numbers after about 1890, did come to the same region—the Far West—and performed, initially, the same kinds of labor that had occupied the Chinese. No one was more acutely aware of the superficial similarities than were certain officials of the Imperial Japanese government. Before either North American government had taken a single step to regulate or discriminate against Japanese immigration and immigrants, the government in Tokyo had showed its concern. In 1891, for example, Nagamoto Okabe, Japanese Vice Minister of Foreign Affairs, instructed Japanese consuls in both San Francisco and Vancouver to cooperate with police and immigration officials in curbing Japanese prostitutes because of the "scandalous publicity" which was interfering with "Japan's honor and dignity."[16] Japan's "honor and dignity," of course, did not call for it to try to stamp out either prostitution at home or the extensive industry in Japanese prostitutes throughout East and Southeast Asia.[17] The Japanese government feared— quite presciently—that the discrimination directed at Chinese immigrants would also be directed at immigrants from Japan. The thought of the international humiliation that would come with a "Japanese Exclusion Act" weighed heavily on the Japanese. Exclusion, of course, eventually came to the U.S. in 1924 in a different form, but so strong was the phobia about a "Japanese Exclusion Act" that Kodansha, the publishers of the recent multi-volume English-language *Encyclopedia of Japan*, tried to commission me to write an article about it! Japan, as we know, eventually executed "gentlemen's agreements" with both North American democracies under which it would limit immigration—much as it today limits auto exports— and also spent a great deal of time and energy exhorting its nationals in North America to acculturate. To that end it sponsored organizations, called "Japanese Associations," in each country to serve both as immigrant protective agencies and to exercise kinds of social control.[18]

For their part, both North American governments had to be more careful in dealing with Japan than with China; Japan, after all, was an emerging power and, after 1902, actually allied with Britain and thus with Canada. Most white westerners wanted the same kinds of legislative treatment meted out to the Japanese as had been inflicted on the Chinese, but their wishes were either thwarted or delayed by the politicians in Ottawa and Washington. Japanese exclusion was accomplished only in 1924 in the U.S. and, in Canada, only after the Pacific War broke out in 1941. Certainly, had it not been for international pressures, the U.S. would have cut off Japanese immigration in the first decade of this century and Canada would probably not have been far behind.

From the 1860s to the era of World War II fewer than 350,000 Japanese immigrated to North America: some 275,000 to the U.S., some 40,000 to Canada. As with the figures for the Chinese, these numbers significantly overstate the number of Japanese involved. Many made more than one trip and entered more than one country—our gambling immigrant, Hirakawa, may have been counted as many as six times. The census figures give a clear picture of the demographic impact of Japanese immigration. At the turn of the century there were fewer than 30,000 Japanese in North America; by the early 1920s there were 125,000 and, on the eve of the great Pacific War, there were just over 150,000. In none of these years did the incidence of the Japanese in the population of North America exceed one-tenth of one percent (.001), and the figure for each country was about the same. The concentration of Japanese in the Far West was even more pronounced than that of the Chinese: in 1901, 97% of all Japanese Canadians lived in B.C.; by 1941, 95.5% still lived there. The incidence of Japanese in B.C. was higher than in any American state: B.C.'s Nikkei comprised 3.2% of the population in 1931; the highest comparable figure in the U.S. was reached in 1921 when Japanese Californians were 2.1% of the Golden State's total.

Japanese residential patterns also differed from those of the Chinese. While many in each country were concentrated in a few urban areas originally— particularly Vancouver, Seattle and San Francisco—the Japanese quickly became one of the most rural of twentieth-century minority groups, specializing in vegetables and other truck crops in the U.S. and in pomiculture in Canada. In addition, large numbers were fishermen, particularly in B.C.

Perhaps the most striking demographic difference between Japanese North Americans and their predecessors from China was in the sex ratios among the immigrants and the patterns of family life. Significant numbers of Japanese women immigrated, particularly after 1908, so that family life in both countries was closer to "normal"; i.e., the "separated" family that characterized Chinese North American demography did not predominate in Japanese communities. In 1940/41 the sex ratios in B.C. and the U.S. were almost identical: females comprised 48.3 and 43.3% of the ethnic Japanese populations. Similarly, in each country native-born ethnic Japanese already outnumbered the immigrant generation: 59.1% of the Japanese Canadian community were native born, as were 62.7% of the Japanese American community. In each country, in 1940/41, the majority of Chinese were still foreign born. Since the Chinese had been in North America a good half-century longer, this says a great deal about relative rates of acculturation. One who merely looked at the 1940/41 data would have "predicted" a much smoother course for the Japanese than for the Chinese in North America.

*   *   *

The war in the Pacific, of course, changed all that, at least for a time.[19] The Japanese became the enemy and the Chinese became, after a fashion, allies. As long as the war was confined to Europe, the U.S. government treated its citizen Japanese as it treated other citizens: they were subject to the draft, accepted for military service, given reserve commissions, etc. In Canada, despite many evidences of loyalty, the Japanese were not generally accepted for military service. In the spring and summer of 1941 all persons of Japanese origin over sixteen were required to undergo a special registration and to carry their registration cards at all times. These cards were color-coded: native-born Canadians got white ones, naturalized citizens got salmon-pink ones, and aliens got yellow ones. In the U.S. in 1940, all aliens had been required to register and carry what amounted to an internal passport. The Japanese attacks of 7/8 December 1941 expanded the war for Canada and brought the U.S. formally into it. Although there had been some desultory preliminary discussions about coordinating Canadian-American actions against ethnic Japanese in case of war, the two nations arrived individually at strikingly similar decisions.[20] In each country the action was ethnic and geographical. No distinction was made between alien and citizen in Canada, or between native and foreign born in the U.S. If one lived east of the Pacific Coast—as very few Japanese did—one might remain in nervous liberty in either country. The 130,000 ethnic Japanese who lived on the Pacific Slope suffered a common fate. In executive instruments of the national governments dated less than a week apart—U.S. Executive Order 9066 was dated 19 February 1942, and Canadian Order in Council P.C. 1486 was dated 24 February 1942—each country ordered the uprooting of almost the entire west coast populations, separated them from most of their real property, and incarcerated them. The actions and procedures were very much alike, only the government agencies were different. In Canada it was strictly a civilian operation, performed by the R.C.M.P. under the auspices of Minister of Justice Louis St. Laurent. In the U.S. the Attorney General, Francis Biddle, had some scruples about the constitutional rights of citizens—even those of Japanese ancestry—so the United States Army herded the west coast Japanese into camps. In each nation special agencies were created to manage the incarcerated people: in Canada, the federal British Columbia Security Commission; in the U.S., the War Relocation Authority. The U.S. used a traditional —and expensive—form of confinement. Ten camps were built—largely in deserts—surrounded with barbed wire and guarded by soldiers. Canada, using a technique devised by Czarist Russia, exiled the Japanese to isolated ghost towns and special camps in the mountain vastnesses of B.C., letting the terrain do most of the guarding. Both nations incarcerated men, women and children. The more frugal Canadian government spent much less per capita on various social services. In each country persons deemed to be dangerous were interned with enemy aliens, as were those regarded as "bad actors."

Also similar were the post-war plans for the Japanese North Americans. Both Franklin Roosevelt and Mackenzie King wanted to break up the pre-war concentrations of ethnic Japanese. The Prime Minister told Parliament that it would be "unwise and undesirable...to allow Japanese population to be concentrated in [B.C.] after the war." FDR stressed the importance, in a press conference, of spreading Japanese Americans more evenly throughout the country.

There were nevertheless important differences: Japanese Americans, but not Japanese Canadians, were allowed to perform significant military service.

Moreover, in the U.S. the Supreme Court, although it did not significantly inhibit the incarceration of Japanese Americans, did, at the end of 1944, significantly speed up their release. In Canada, the Japanese were not allowed to return to the west coast until 1 April 1949, and a much larger percentage of the population was shipped to Japan, largely under duress.

While Japanese North Americans were being degraded, the Chinese in both countries saw an improvement in their condition and status. In each country Chinese were accepted for military service and, in the U.S., embarrassment over the blatant discrimination shown toward an ally caused the repeal of the Chinese Exclusion Act at the end of 1943, the granting of an annual immigration quota of 105 a year for China and, even more important, the Chinese were removed from the "aliens ineligible to citizenship" category and allowed to become naturalized on the same terms as other aliens. In retrospect this 1943 statute can be seen as the hinge upon which all American immigration and naturalization policy eventually turned. Statutory improvement in the position of Chinese Canadians had to wait for the end of the war. In 1947, a predominantly Caucasian group, the Committee for the Repeal of the Chinese Immigration Act—seemingly patterned after an American pressure group headed by Pearl Buck—waged a successful campaign for the repeal of the 1923 act. There quickly followed the granting of the franchise to the Chinese in elections at all levels.

In the final analysis, however, the war years were a turning point for both groups in each country. Although the post-war years are beyond the scope of this essay, I would like briefly to indicate some of the factors which have transformed both North American immigration policy and the position of persons of Chinese and Japanese ethnicity in North American life:

1. The war itself. Fighting a war against fascism, against an official, despicable racism, threw into bold relief the undemocratic aspects of the democracies' immigration policy.

2. The Cold War era. In the Cold War ideology became more and more important, race less and less. There were good and bad Chinese—politically speaking—as there would later be good and bad Koreans.

3. There was, in both countries, a change in the perception of which groups were, and which groups were not, acceptable, and both Chinese and Japanese came to be seen as much more acceptable than many of the ethnic groups desiring admission.

These factors—combined with factors in Asia which are beyond the scope of this essay—have produced tremendous changes in the populations, changes which no knowledgeable person would have thought possible just four decades ago.[21] While the ethnic Chinese populations of each country increased in a similar fashion—multiplying 8.3 times in Canada between 1941 and 1981, and 10.4 times in the U.S. between 1940 and 1980—ethnic Japanese populations grew much differently. Reflecting the much harsher conditions for Canadian Japanese, their population did not even double in the period 1941-81, while the Japanese American population multiplied 5.5 times between 1940 and 1980. The censuses which began the 1980s showed a distinctly higher incidence of Chinese in Canada and of Japanese in the U.S. Chinese were 1.1% of Canada's total population and .3 of 1% of the U.S.'s, while Japanese were .3 of 1% of the U.S. population and .2 of 1% of Canada's. In addition to mere numerical growth, the class, status and prestige of each group have improved startlingly, so startlingly that persons of Asian ethnicity are often held up as exemplars for emulation.

None of the foregoing is to suggest that the post-war democratization of North American immigration policies is necessarily permanent. There are now nativist movements afoot on both sides of the 49th parallel. What this essay does suggest, however, is that there have been extraordinary changes in the condition of both Chinese and Japanese North Americans in the past century and that, despite all kinds of national differences, many of them not even alluded to here, these changes have followed essentially the same course in each country. There is no reason to believe that such similarities exist only in ethnic history. This suggests, to me at least, that the comparative history of Canada and the United States ought to be explored systematically by scholars from several disciplines and sub-disciplines and with a variety of points of view.

A Century of Chinese and Japanese Population in North America,
1880/81-1980/81

	Canada		United States	
	Chinese	Japanese	Chinese	Japanese
1880/81	4,383	—	105,465	148
1890/91	9,129	—	107,488	2,039
1900/01	17,321a	4,738	89,863	24,326
1910/11	27,774	9,021	71,531	72,157
1920/21	39,587	15,868	61,639	111,010
1930/31	46,519	23,342	74,954	138,834
1940/41	34,627	23,149	77,504	126,947
1950/51	32,528	21,663	117,629	141,768
1960/61	58,197	29,157	236,084b	473,170b
1970/71	118,815	37,260	435,062	591,020
1980/81	289,245	40,995	806,027	700,747

Source: Censuses of the United States and Canada, passim.

a. As adjusted by 1911 Census.

b. After the admission of Hawaii as the 50th state in 1959, U.S. population figures include Hawaii. In 1960 Hawaii contained 207,230 Japanese and 39,152 Chinese.

Notes

1 I have benefited greatly from reading an unpublished manuscript on the Chinese communities of Northern Puget Sound by Margaret Willson and Jeffrey L. Macdonald, as well as from constructive criticism by Cornelius Jaenen and Pat Roy. For census data, 1880/81-1980/81, see the appended Table.

2 Kihachi Hirakawa, typescript autobiography, University of Washington archives.

3 C. Watanabe, "The Japanese in Mexico," unpublished M.A. thesis, California State University, Los Angeles, 1983, Appendix One.

4 T.G. Li, untitled memoir, in my possession.

5 See, for example, Anthony Chan, " 'Orientalism' and Image Making: The Sojourners in Canadian History," *Journal of Ethnic Studies*, 9/3 (1981-82), 37-46; Gunther Barth, *Bitter Strength* (Cambridge, Mass., 1963); Dino Cinel, *From Italy to San Francisco* (Stanford, 1983), p. 3. Hans van Amersfoort has astutely observed that "many theories about immigrants are based on a distinction between *stayers* and *returnees* without making clear that the distinction between the two groups is very fluid. Anyone with [even] limited knowledge of immigrant communities knows that one cannot predict whether a given immigrant will return or not." Hans van Amersfoort, *Immigration and the Formation of Minority Groups: The Dutch Experience, 1945-1975* (Cambridge, 1982), p. 8. See also Jin Tan, "Letter," *The Asianadian*, 5/4 (1984), 30-31.

6 Hugh Tinker, *A New System of Slavery* (Oxford, 1974).

7 Persia Campbell Crawford, *Chinese Coolie Emigration to Countries within the British Empire* (London, 1923). See also Robert L. Irick, *Ch'ing Policy toward the Coolie Trade* (San Francisco, 1977), and Denise Helly, *Ideologie et ethnicité: les chinois Macao à Cuba (1847-1966)* (Montreal, 1977).

8 Craig A. Lockard, "Some Recent Writings on the Overseas Chinese in Southeast Asia and Beyond," *Jernal Sejarah* (Kuala Lumpur), 15 (1977-78), 154-62.

9 John Higham, *Strangers in the Land* (New Brunswick, N.J., 1955). Howard Palmer, *Patterns of Prejudice* (Toronto, 1982). Many Canadian scholars, while not denying the existence of "prejudice," argue that "nativism," as defined by Higham, is strictly an American phenomenon. The commentator on this paper, Cornelius Jaenen, suggested that perhaps "nativism" was more appropriate for Western Canada than for the entire nation. Despite my respect for Jaenen's sensitivity to every aspect of ethnic studies in Canada, and perhaps mesmerized by my attempts at a "continental vision," I continue to assume that "nativism"—as defined by Higham but without his qualifying adjective of nationality—is a bi-national occurrence.

10 Harry Con, Ronald Con, Edgar Wickberg, William Willmot, ed. Edgar Wickberg, *From China to Canada* (Toronto, 1982), Table 5, pp. 300-01; Table 7, p. 303. Also cf. Table 10, p. 306. The first gives the 1921 Chinese population of Vancouver as 6,484. The second states that in 1921, 5,790 of Vancouver's Chinese were male and 585 female, for a total of 6,375. For a recent brief survey, see Jim Tan and Patricia E. Roy, *The Chinese in Canada* (Ottawa, 1985).

11 Ching-chao Wu, "Chinatowns: A Study in Symbiosis and Assimilation," unpublished Ph.D. dissertation, University of Chicago, 1928, p. 158. After writing this I came across the following, written by an exchange student in journalism from the People's Republic, describing aspects of ethnic life in contemporary Toronto's Chinatown: "For older generation Chinese who have established themselves, life in the city can be rich.... They can shop at Chinese stores, eat at Chinese restaurants, buy traditional medicines and read any one of six Chinese daily newspapers....They can play mah jong all night long...watch stage shows in Chinese theatres, see Chinese films or get together at clubs and community centres." Li Na Xie, "Culture Shock, Chinese Style," Toronto *Globe and Mail*, 19 July 1984.

12 Peter S. Li, "Chinese Immigrants on the Canadian Prairie, 1910-47," *Canadian Review of Sociology and Anthropology*, 19 (1982), 533.

13 Jade Snow Wong, *Fifth Chinese Daughter* (New York, 1950), p. 103.

14 Many of the "native-born" Chinese Americans of this era were the so-called "paper sons": China-born males who successfully claimed that status from fathers who had—often fraudulently—established U.S. citizenship. Their alien mothers were not admissible and few, if any, attempts were made to bring in "paper daughters." For details, see Victor and Brett de Bary Nee, *Longtime Californ'* (New York, 1973).

[15] Peter S. Li, "Immigration Laws and Family Patterns: Some Demographic Changes Among Chinese Families in Canada, 1855-1971," *Canadian Ethnic Studies*, 12 (1980), 58-73. Li also shows that by 1971 the pattern was nearly reversed: 24,350 Chinese Canadian families were "intact," 6,435 "broken," and 1,558 "separated."

[16] This and other Japanese diplomatic documents were translated by Mr. Yasuo Sakata for Robert Wilson of UCLA. I am indebted to both for permission to use their research. Copies of the originals are on file in the Japanese American Research Project, UCLA. In an informative and useful article, Masako Iino claims that "emigrants to Canada were not numerous enough to attract the attention of the Japanese government until early in the twentieth century." See "Japan's Reaction to the Vancouver Riot of 1907," *B.C. Studies*, 60 (1983/84), 46.

[17] For an informed discussion of organized overseas Japanese prostitution, see D.C.S. Sissons, "Karayuki-san: Japanese Prostitutes in Australia, 1887-1916," *Historical Studies*, 17 (1977), 323-41, 474-88.

[18] For a fuller discussion see my "The Japanese," in John Higham, ed., *Ethnic Leadership in America* (Baltimore, 1978), pp. 36-63.

[19] Comparative material on the Japanese is largely a summary of what I have said previously in "The Japanese Experience in North America: An Essay in Comparative Racism," *Canadian Ethnic Studies*, 9 (1977), 91-100, and in "Japanese Relocation and Redress in North America: A Comparative View," *The Pacific Historian*, 26 (1982), 2-13 and the works there cited.

[20] Roger Daniels, "The Decisions to Relocate the North American Japanese: Another Look," *Pacific Historical Review*, 51 (1982), 71-77.

[21] Jaenen, in his comments, wondered what effect the impending reunification of Hong Kong with China might have on Chinese immigration here. It would seem to me probable that in the period before reunification the migration of *both* Chinese persons and capital to North America is likely to be accelerated. One can anticipate the possibility of special "Hong Kong refugee" acts and administrative decisions.

OSCAR HANDLIN

Historical Perspectives on the American Ethnic Group

IT IS A COMMONPLACE of both scholarly and popular comment that American society is pluralistic in its organization. The immense size of the country, its marked regional differences and diversity of antecedents have sustained complex patterns of association and behavior and have inhibited tendencies toward uniformity. Social action in the United States, therefore, is presumed to come not within large unitary forms but within a mosaic of autonomous groupings, reflecting the underlying dissimilarities in the population.

Yet it is significant that serious attention to the operations of these groups has focused primarily upon the pathology of their relations with one another. Discrimination and prejudice, tension and conflict have provided students with their primary subject matter, perhaps because these produced the problems of greatest contemporary urgency, perhaps because they produced the most visible and most dramatic manifestations. For whatever reason, the normal functioning of American pluralism has been relatively neglected.

The result has been a serious deficiency in the understanding of the past development and present structure of American society. Viewed only at the points of breakdown, its healthy operations have remained shadowy and obscure; and without a clear comprehension of how the system worked, it has been difficult to explain the causes of its occasional failures.

This paper deals with one important type of American group, that in which membership tended to be transmitted by birth from generation to generation. An individual generally identified himself as an Odd Fellow or a Californian, as a member of the American Medical Association of the United Mine Workers, through decisions he made in the course of his own lifetime. He was usually, although not always, a Jew or a Negro, a Yankee or an Irish-American, through forces which existed from the moment of his birth and over

220

which he had relatively little control. Ethnic ties frequently influenced the broader range of associations in which any given person participated, but they form a discreet subject of investigation which had peculiar importance in the United States. The analysis which follows aims at providing an account of the historic reasons why that was so.

It was the conscious desire of those who planted the colonies that would later become the United States to reproduce the social order they had left in Europe, entire or in an improved form. Once it became clear that these were not simply to be provisional trading stations but permanent settlements, the residents attempted to re-create the unitary communities they had known at home. That effort would be repeated in the eighteenth and nineteenth centuries by each succeeding group of arrivals.

In each case it failed. The communities the emigrants left had been whole and integrated, and had comprehended the total life of their members. There was one church, as there was one state, one hierarchy of occupations and status, a fixed pattern of roles and expectations, and the individual was therefore located in a precise place that defined the whole range of his associations.

Cracks in the solidarity and homogeneity of these communities had already begun to appear in seventeenth-century Europe. They would widen and deepen as time went on. Moreover, the men and women who went to America were peculiarly those least fixed in their places—religious dissenters, servants with no masters, uprooted peasants, captives by force of arms, and the victims of economic disaster. Their intentions remained attached to the norms of the society that had cast them out, but their lives were unsettled from the moment of their departure, and could rarely be restored to the old grooves after the shattering experiences of migration.

Moreover, all the conditions of the New World were uncongenial to the reestablishment of the old community. Even as coherent a group as the Massachusetts Bay Puritans found it difficult to exclude the disruptive influences of the unfamiliar environment. The terms of life of the wilderness, the dispersal of settlements over great distances, the inability to maintain discipline or to create distinct lines of authority—all these vitiated every effort to restore the traditional whole community. These hostile elements were even more powerful to the southward of New England, where settlement was less purposefully directed and where it lacked the leadership of an elite inspired by religious zeal and armed with sacerdotal sanctions.

221

107

The American setting remained unfriendly to efforts to unify communal life in succeeding centuries. In the eighteenth and nineteenth centuries, uninterrupted territorial expansion was the most consequential element in the situation. The constant penetration of one frontier after another, each with its own challenge of an altered physical environment, was repeatedly unsettling to the men who advanced into them and to the societies they abandoned. Almost everywhere the concomitant was a spatial and social mobility that exerted a continued strain upon existing organizations and habitual modes of behavior. And, before the effects of that form of expansion had played themselves out, industrialization and urbanization created new sources of communal disorder. The results were unqualifiedly destructive of every effort to reconstitute whole communities that bore some resemblance to the transplanted or inherited images derived from European antecedents.

These tendencies received additional force from the heterogeneity of the American population, already notable in the seventeenth century and destined to be immensely increased thereafter. Diversity of sources ruled out the possibility that some myth of common origin might supply a basis for creating communal order; it juxtaposed different and sometimes contradictory ideals of what that order should be like; and it left prominently embedded in society conflicting interests and values. Furthermore, since the various elements stood in no clearly delineated relation of superiority and inferiority to one another, except in so far as slavery depressed the Negro, none could impose its own conceptions upon the rest. In a country in which Quakers and Presbyterians, Anglicans and Catholics, Jews and Baptists all coexisted and all had access to power, it was impossible to think of one state, one church. In towns where Yankees and Germans, Irishmen and Italians lived together, no single set of institutions could serve the social and cultural needs of the entire body of residents. Given these differences, American communities could only be fragmented rather than whole, partial rather than inclusive.

The looseness of political institutions furthered the same results. Not through design but through the unanticipated circumstances of colonial settlement, authority was long only tentatively exercised and the state was long too weak to serve fully the functions expected of it. The resultant vacuum nurtured habits of spontaneous, voluntary action on the part of the citizens. Through disuse, some powers of government atrophied, and the spheres in which they had been applied came to be occupied by associations which operated, not with political sanctions, but with the unconstrained support of their

222

108

members. A pervasive ideology that interpreted every relation between the individual and the larger groups to which he belonged as contractual and dependent upon his free acquiescence set these practices within a context of respected rights that were not readily to be violated. The end result was hostility toward large overarching organizations remote from their membership, and the encouragement of smaller bodies deriving their competence to act from the consent of their participants.

The fluidity of American society, the diversity of its population, and the looseness of its institutional forms interacted upon and stimulated one another. The results therefore were cumulative in the extent to which they inhibited the appearance of a unitary community, the various arms of which were organically articulated with one another. Despite frequent conscious efforts to guide developments in that direction, the people of the United States did not become homogeneous, nor were their modes of action integrated into common over-all forms.

The only exceptions appeared in pockets of population which, for one reason or another, became isolated from the dominant currents of American life. Relatively small groups—the Pennsylvania Amish, the Southern mountaineers, the farmers of Northern New England, for example—were able to achieve a solidarity and continuity of experience that elicited the admiration of romantic observers who set a high premium upon stability and tradition. But the price was social stagnation and detachment from the forces which shaped the rest of the nation. Indeed, the contrast offered by these aberrations is a measure of the extent to which the main lines of social organization led away from the unitary community.

The result was neither anarchy nor the casting adrift of the individual left to his own resources. Rather, the failure to create a single integrated community led to the appearance of numerous smaller bodies which operated within fragmented sectors of society. Their character can best be understood in terms of the forces that brought them into being.

Men no longer embraced within the sheltering fold of a whole community felt the pressure of two types of needs they could not satisfy alone. Important functions in their lives could only be executed in groups; and, in addition, deep-rooted emotional desires for personal association also called for common action.

The American who had left or had never been part of a community that by tradition and habit satisfied all his needs quickly became sensitive to his inability to deal with problems that extended

223

109

beyond his own person. The round of ritual and the patterns of reaffirmed beliefs of which the church had been custodian lost their potency when performed or held in isolation. It was essential to create the communion that would make them effective even without the aid of the state and at no matter what cost.

The crises of death, disease, and poverty produced a dependency that was intolerable in isolation. The necessities of these situations were twofold, bearing both upon the victim and the witness of man's helplessness. The dread of improper burial after death, of wasting illness, and of want troubled everyone conscious that he might himself be stricken down; and the worry haunted Americans more than it did other peoples who could anticipate such crises as expected incidents within a familiar setting. Equally as important, the obligation to dispose of the corpse, to succor the ill and to aid the indigent (all of which often bore a religious connotation) troubled everyone who could foresee such challenges to his conscience. It was imperative therefore that these functions should be performed in a group and with a propriety that would console both the victim and the witness. Again, in the absence of a community that did so, it was necessary to bring into being the organized means for performing these functions.

An analogous need arose out of the disruption of communications that was a consequence of the breakdown of the old community. The culture which expressed men's attitudes and which provided them with emotional and esthetic satisfaction had been wrenched away from its traditional media. The threatened deprivation of a heritage that gave life meaning hastened Americans toward contriving new forms through which they could speak and listen to one another.

Yet in the process of creating the vast array of churches, philanthropic societies, and cultural institutions that became characteristic of the United States, the participants were moved not only by the importance of the functions to be served. They were influenced also by the personal need to belong to a group, whatever function it served. As individuals, they sought a sense of anchorage through identification with some larger entity, hoping thus to offset the effects of the unsettling elements of life in and on the way to America. The achievement of such an identification would provide some compensation, furthermore, for the psychological loss of the unitary community.

The distinctive qualities of family life in the United States made the need for anchorage to a group particularly acute there. Whether

224

in the seventeenth century or the nineteenth, the extended family quickly shrank after immigration to the conjugal pair and its offspring. Detached from the community and often physically and socially isolated, the American family was thrown back upon its own resources; and uncertainty as to the roles of its members frequently produced severe internal tensions. Such conditions increased the desire for identification with a group that would provide the family with roots in the past, locate it in the larger society, and supply it both with a pattern of approved standards of behavior and with the moral sanctions to aid in maintaining internal discipline.

The wish to belong for the sake of identification and the wish to belong out of the need for some functional service coincided most nearly when it came to subjects about which men had inherited firmly implanted beliefs and attitudes. In satisfying the need for religious worship and ritual and in arming themselves against the contingencies of dependency, they were likely to use forms that would draw together people of a common heritage and thus also satisfy the need for a sense of belonging.

Within the complex pattern of American associational life, therefore, clusters of organizations which served discreet ends but which were linked by derivation from a common pool of membership appeared. That pool constituted the ethnic group. A shared heritage, presumed or actual, formed the matrix within which the group organized its communal life. That heritage, in the United States, was sometimes associated with descent from common national or regional origins, sometimes with color, and sometimes with religion. Some groups were already aware of their identity at arrival, as were the Jews of the seventeenth and eighteenth centuries; others, like the nineteenth-century Italians, only developed theirs through the experience of life in the New World. In either case, these were not monolithic entities but aggregates of individuals, often internally divided and sometimes unclear about the boundaries to which their membership extended.

The ethnic group by no means preempted the total social experience of Americans. Other associations drew their participants from sources only slightly delimited by considerations of antecedents. But ethnic groups were peculiarly important by virtue of their durability, which extended them across the generations, and by virtue also of the critical segments of personal life that they organized.

Not every individual, of course, fitted neatly into one ethnic box or another. Many, particularly in the large cities of the nineteenth and twentieth centuries, remained unaffiliated and unattached and

225

111

drifted into the disorganization resulting from their lack of a fixed place. Others were torn by multiple identifications, which were the product either of mixed antecedents or of the incompatibility of individual interests and intentions with the norms of the group. Still others permitted themselves only a limited and partial affiliation, participating in some activities on some occasions and refraining from taking a part in others. But it was precisely in such flexibility that the strength of the ethnic group lay. By permitting men to organize their lives on their own terms, without compulsion and with a wide latitude of choice, the ethnic group provided them with the means of acting cooperatively in those sectors of life in which they felt the need to do so, and yet it refrained from imposing irksome restraints upon them. It thus supplanted the totally organized, integrated community with a fluid pattern of association, that left the individual as unconfined as he wished to be.

The American ethnic groups maintained their fluidity through a delicate balance between the forces that detached and those that connected their members to the society outside their boundaries. They were able to preserve their identity without becoming segregated or isolated enclaves in the total society. Functioning effectively over long periods, they nevertheless were inhibited from acquiring attributes that would have permanently and decisively set apart the individuals affiliated with them. That balance left room for wide areas of personal choice on the part of the members, to whose interests and ideas the group was necessarily sensitive.

The internal dynamics of many groups led them, at the same time, to seek to preserve their own identity and yet to reach out to influence and even absorb outsiders. These contradictory impulses were particularly characteristic, although by no means confined to groups of English descent, who felt a special compulsion to make their limits coextensive with the whole nation.

By the eighteenth century, a missionary spirit had dissolved the earlier exclusive sense of election that had formerly separated one element from another. The desire to bar outsiders gave way to an urge to assimilate them; and a variety of groups came to consider themselves in competition for new adherents. The rivalry for the loyalty of new members was stimulated thereafter by the constant appearance of new religious sects which conducted unremitting raids upon the unaffiliated or the loosely affiliated.

Yet the ability to make converts, either in the religious or social sense, demanded some accommodation to the tastes, interests, and ideas of those who were to be persuaded. No group could attract

226

outsiders by stressing the unique qualities of its own antecedents. A subtle process of adjustment, therefore, found each drifting away from the particularities of its heritage and reaching out toward a more general view of itself that would confirm and strengthen its place in the whole society. Through the eighteenth and nineteenth centuries a gradual softening of exclusionary doctrines and practices and a general accommodation to a shared pattern of beliefs and behavior that might be termed "American" were manifestations of this process.

The desire to assimilate outsiders altered many ethnic organizations as these widened the scope of their endeavors. Quaker efforts at benevolence, for instance, originally directed within the group, acquired a universal character when the group recognized its obligations to the whole society. Institutions like those for higher education, which were established to serve a specific ethnic group, also changed as they expanded their appeal. The early sectarian colleges were thus driven toward a steady broadening of their social bases. The whole process of extending the boundaries of the group tended to dilute its ethnic character.

The competition for the loyalty of their members also affected those groups which had no clear missionary intentions. The Jews and Italians of 1900, for instance, aimed not at drawing other Americans within their folds, but simply at preserving their hold over their own adherents. But to do so, they had to offset the attractions of potential rivals by establishing their own images as fully American and by emphasizing the depth of their own roots in the country. That involved a sacrifice of their own particularity. To the extent that they celebrated Haym Solomon or Christopher Columbus, they drew attention to elements that made them similar to rather than different from other Americans. They could develop a capacity for resisting the incursions of other groups only by diminishing the range of differences that set them apart. The necessities of a situation in which a multitude of ethnic groups coexisted in an open society prevented any one of them from erecting walls about itself unless it wished to become completely isolated.

The situation remained open because some contact among the members of various groups was inescapable in important sectors of social action. The organization of American economic, political, and cultural life compelled individuals often to disregard ethnic lines.

There were significant degrees of concentration in the distribution of occupations by ethnic groups. That situation was in part a product of their members' common experience and common prepa-

227

ration for the job market. Irishmen who came to New York City in
1850 lacked the skill or capital for anything but unskilled labor;
Yankee newcomers to the same city had the education and resources
to go into trade or take places as clerks. Furthermore, ties of kinship,
country of origin, and religion sometimes significantly affected the
conduct of business and the access to opportunity. It was advantageous to be a Scotsman in mid-nineteenth-century Pittsburgh, as
Andrew Carnegie discovered. Conversely, prejudice and discrimination barred the way to desirable situations. Young women who were
colored or foreign in appearance were not likely to become secre-
taries to executives, no matter how competent they were.

Nevertheless, the American productive system did not tolerate
the development of caste-like groupings. Individuals always found
it possible to move upward. In the swiftly expanding, competitive
order of American enterprise, in which success held a preeminent
value and in which the dangers of catastrophic failure were always
imminent, men could not afford to subordinate the calculations of
the market place to noneconomic considerations. The entrepreneur,
aware of his own interests, hired the most efficient hand, bought
from the cheapest seller, sold to the highest bidder, or suffered in
consequence. That course built into the economic system the necessity for cooperation across ethnic lines, and this grew steadily more
compelling as business became less personal and more closely oriented to considerations of price and cost. Business, professional, and
labor organizations, which often had a distinct ethnic character to
begin with, felt a steady pressure, therefore, to make room for qualified outsiders.

So too, ethnic groups often formed significant voting blocs. Party
allegiances, thus engaged, enjoyed considerable continuity over time
and occasionally outweighed other considerations in determining the
outcome of political contests. But no group formed a majority secure
enough to hold power, except on a very local level; those who sought
office or advantages through politics quickly recognized the necessity for developing alliances that transcended ethnic divisions. The
machines of Boston and New York in 1910 were Irish, but they depended upon working arrangements with Germans, Jews, and Italians. As in the economy, the imperatives of politics in an open
society prevented any group from maintaining exclusiveness for very
long.

Out of the conditions of these and other contacts there grew a
vast array of media for general communication. The newspapers, the
public schools, television—all addressed individuals rather than the

228

members of groups. Even when they began with a specific ethnic orientation, the advantages of reaching out for the largest possible audience transformed those which survived and expanded. In the long run, the more general the medium, the more powerful it became. Its influence, therefore, tended to break down group exclusiveness.

As a result, a given American at any moment located himself in society by a complex of reference points. He was a German, but also a Lutheran, a Republican, a farmer, a Midwesterner, a reader of the *Volkszeitung* and the *Tribune*, a Mason, and a member of the Turnverein. Not all these affiliations were purely ethnic, although there was an ethnic element in most of them; and not all had equal weight in his existence. Which were salient and which subordinate depended upon the particular configuration that established the individual's identity. The ethnic factor was important by virtue of its connections with the past, with the family, and with the most impressionable years in the development of the personality. But it receded in importance if it were isolated, if the man's German affiliations appeared only on infrequent occasions, while his primary associations as a citizen, a resident, and a producer had other contexts.

The fluidity of the social system increased the necessities for contact and added to the variety of individual configurations. A rough correlation was always discernible between social status and ethnic membership. While the pattern was certainly not consistent at every time and place, social and ethnic groupings tended to coincide. Recent immigrants generally entered the labor market at the bottom, a place commensurate with their want of skill, capital, and prestige. That circumstance established the low social character of the group. Italian peasants who migrated to the United States at the end of the nineteenth century were prepared only for unskilled labor; Italians therefore were identified as among the lowest social groups. But in turn, by association, any kind of work that Italians did was imputed to be inferior. In actuality, the group's experience and the reputation it acquired thus reinforced one another.

Nevertheless, the actuality was never as restrictive as the reputation. Occasionally individuals did succeed in rising in the social and occupational hierarchy; Giannini and Bellanca were not permanently held down by their antecedents. Social mobility was a genuine, although as yet unmeasured, feature of American life.

Some men who moved up passed out of the group of their origin and entered another more compatible with their new positions; social and religious conversion remained significant throughout American

229

history. But whether such individuals altered their identification or not, social mobility opened important avenues of contact with other groups. The exceptional men who remained within the group of their birth played a significant mediating role. Their rise in status brought with it the eminence of outside recognition and of leadership within the group, and it also broadened their contacts with the rest of society, which treated them as spokesmen for the group. They were thus marginal, influenced by a variety of contacts, and subject to a multiplicity of expectations.

Within the groups that were the product of immigration, the rate of upward mobility seems certainly to have increased in the second and subsequent generations. The children of those who had moved were even more marginal than their parents; born within a group, they passed significant parts of their youth and adolescence outside it. They too became channels for contacts across ethnic lines that occurred with increasing frequency and intensity, for the group could survive only by adjusting to their changing interests.

Conversely, the range of contacts narrowed when a group was excluded permanently or temporarily from the opportunities of American society. The prejudice that depressed the Negroes, the discrimination that sometimes held back Jews and Catholics, not only turned these people defensively inward but also reduced the possibilities for mediation and for mutual interaction between them and others. The abatement of prejudice and discrimination therefore was almost an essential precondition for opening the group to the influence of the broader society.

Underlying all these relationships and further militating against the solidarity of the group was a spirit for which no better term is available than individualism. In the eighteenth century, and even more intensely in the nineteenth, the assumption had formed that every man was to be judged and treated as an individual, without consideration of his group affiliations. His place in society, by the American creed, was to be the product of his own efforts, independent of antecedents or inheritance or identification. There were certainly great deviations in actuality from this ideal, but it nevertheless remained a vital element in American thought.

Above all, this assumption implied that group interests were invariably to be subordinated to individual ones. The consequences were nowhere more clearly illustrated than in relationship to intermarriage. The defined posture of every ethnic group was a hostility to marriages that crossed its own lines; only through endogamy could the group perpetuate itself across the generations and secure

230

its survival. Yet, while the statistics are notoriously inaccurate, there is no doubt that unions across group lines were frequent, barred neither by legal impediments nor by social disapproval except where color was involved.

Marriage in America was not a means of securing the continuity of the group but of satisfying the desire of the individual for fulfillment as a personality, apart from any social considerations. The theme of romantic love grew steadily in importance; and it emphasized the capacity of the individual to surmount the barriers of ethnic difference, as also those of class. It was symptomatic of the conviction that the values associated with the individual invariably took precedence over those of the group. It existed to serve him, not he, it.

Thus, the very provisions of American society that permitted the ethnic group to exist freely also permitted its members to adjust their identification to the needs of their own personalities. The strength of these groups, derived from the voluntary accession of their participants, could not be used to isolate or segregate them.

It is against this background that one can best understand the points of breakdown at which conflicts among ethnic groups have appeared. A variety of such groups coexisted without difficulty so long as a fluid social order maximized their members' freedom of association. That is why the periods of greatest immigration and greatest expansion were usually free of tension.

Conflicts appeared rather as the result of efforts to introduce rigidity into the system, most often when one group sought to assert its own preeminence and to impose its own standards upon the others. Nativism, for example, was not simply a battle of "Americans" against immigrants. It was, rather, the effort of particular ethnic groups, whose position was challenged by events over which they had little control, to maintain their earlier dominance under cover of a fixed conception of Americanism.

The extreme of conflict appeared when the terms of ethnic affiliation were so defined as to eliminate all fluidity and to separate unalterably one group from another. The racist ideology of the latter half of the nineteenth century thus categorized individuals by heredity and treated their identifications as genetically fixed. It threatened therefore to eliminate the possibilities for contact and free movement that had theretofore been the essential conditions of group life in the United States. The Negro, who was most clearly identified, most decisively isolated, and burdened with the imputa-

231

117

tion of inferiority from his past as a slave, was the most seriously threatened by these views. But the danger to other groups—like the Jews and the Italians —was also serious, only slightly less so than that to the Negroes.

In the last two decades, the dissolution of racist ideas has ended that threat to the fluid social order of the United States, at least for groups not stigmatized by color. And there is the promise that the extension of the same degree of equality to Negroes will relax the most important tensions in their relations with other Americans and provide them with the basis for a sound group life of their own.

From time to time, efforts at voluntary segregation have also posed a threat to the free functioning of the ethnic group in American society. It is certainly possible such tendencies may gain force in the coming years. The spread of suburban life, which reduces the anonymity of the individual, the desire for stability and security in personal relationships, the drive for conformity in patterns of behavior, and the pressure to belong to some group—no matter which—are all evidence of developments in this direction. Whether they will be able to counteract the forces that continue to encourage mobility and fluidity remains to be seen.

In any case, the ultimate measure of their effect upon the ethnic group will be the latitude left to the individual in choosing the associations within which he conducts his life. In a period in which the isolated individual must confront the immense powers of the state and of the other massive organizations of the naked society, mediating institutions, such as those provided by the ethnic group, can still serve important functions. They can provide him with legitimate means, by which he can assert his distinctive individuality if he wishes to do so. On the other hand, if these groups become rigid and fall into place among the other instruments by which the individual is controlled and regulated, then they become assimilated to the other massive organizations that crush rather than liberate him.

THE HISTORY OF AMERICAN IMMIGRATION AS
A FIELD FOR RESEARCH

THE fact that the American Historical Association's Committee on Research has listed the history of immigration among the topics that stand in need of investigation makes unnecessary any discussion of its importance. The addition to our population between 1815 and 1914 of more than thirty million Europeans, and their services in the national development of that century, constitute an era in colonial history no less significant to our future than the two centuries that preceded. In time the change in sovereignty that occurred in 1776 will be regarded as an unnatural dividing line, and settlement will be viewed as a continuous process from the beginnings in 1607 to the close in 1914. The term " immigration ", however, is in usage generally restricted to the period since the Revolution or more specifically to the more modern period characterized by individual as distinguished from group migration. Earlier the settler came in a company bringing with it all the instruments of community life; later a social atom detached itself from one society and attached itself to another the framework of which was already constructed.

The pioneers of the seventeenth and eighteenth centuries looked upon themselves as exiles, driven from their native land by an intolerant government or a hopeless material condition. Their successors were never quite clear as to motives. Sometimes they considered themselves exiles; at other times they were fortune-hunters. Whether they left Europe because they could no longer live in it or because they could live so much better in America, they never quite decided. But the distinction is fundamental. In the one case the causes are to be found in Europe; in the other in America. Either the immigrants were expelled or they were attracted.

A study of the various waves which have marked high points in the westward tide reveals a limited geographical origin for each. " Old " and " new " are the adjectives used to describe the shift from Northern and Western Europe to the South and East in the course of the century. But this general movement is no more significant than the changes within the two areas. At any given time the phenomenon of emigration appears not in a nation as a whole, but in a comparatively restricted part of that nation; and when it again makes its appearance, though the emigrants may still be listed as Germans or Italians, their origin is distinct. In every case the exodus is accompa-

(500)

nied in that district by a social and economic reorganization usually indicating an adjustment to modern life. Such reorganizations have taken place without emigration to America. But they are always accompanied by changes in population—sometimes a drift to the cities, sometimes a movement to hitherto waste lands or to other parts of Europe. On occasion they have resulted in a congestion of population which has produced great social unrest. To the United States their members have gone only when American industry was prospering, and each wave of migration coincides with an era of unusual business activity. During the century, therefore, it may be said that America was a huge magnet of varying intensity drawing to itself the people of Europe from those regions where conditions made them mobile and from which transportation provided a path. American conditions determined the duration and height of the waves; European the particular source.

Accordingly, both Europe and America are the field for research. Because students of nineteenth-century Europe have concentrated so prevailingly upon the political developments, the student of American immigration will be forced to do much pioneer work which at first glance seems to have little bearing on his topic. How extensive these researches must be may be understood from the suggestion that emigration has been connected with as many phases of European life as immigration has of American life. Freedom to move, desire to move, and means to move summarize these phases. But each is a wide field. Freedom to move involves the process by which the remaining feudal bands were loosened and the systems of land tenure revolutionized; in short, that break-up of the solidarity of the community which, in making the individual mobile, forced him to shift for himself. Desire to move concerns political and economic, social and psychological motives, and its roots may be found now in one, now in the other of the great movements of the century. How the emigrant obtained the means to move is a part of the history of the transfer of property and of the development of land and sea transportation.[1]

Until a cheap, safe, and individual crossing of the Atlantic was provided, any mass emigration was impossible. A description of

[1] The student will be led into a consideration of topics such as these: the legal development of the right of emigration; military obligations affecting emigration; marriage laws, standards of living, birth and death rates in relation to the growth of population in any given region; migration to cities; division of the common lands; formation of a class of mobile agricultural laborers; laws of tenancy; decline of household industry; changes in systems of land culture—arable or grazing; religious movements and ecclesiastical policy; social results of the revolutions of 1848; transport policies of European railroads; effects of competition with American agriculture; effect of crop failures and years of scarcity; popular knowledge of America.

the transport difficulties of the eighteenth century would be a fitting introduction to an appreciation of this factor in the nineteenth. A study of the emigrant trade from the days when the captain made a winter journey inland to solicit passengers for his annual spring voyage to the time when no village was without its agency and not a day passed without a speedy emigrant ship leaving some European port would be a contribution to the history of both migration and commerce. But much preliminary work must be done, as the subject is bound up with technical progress, sanitary regulations, and the economics of return cargoes.[2]

When upon the high seas the emigrant was in the hands of some shipping company and its policies constituted a vital factor in his movements. After the Civil War the rivalries of the lines were often the dominant factor, as would be shown by a study of the competition of the German and English companies for the control of the Scandinavian trade, or the more general struggle to capture that of the Mediterranean. There were rate wars waged upon the North Atlantic which determined the extent and character of American immigration in certain years; and the treaties of peace which closed these wars had more influence upon the movement in succeeding years than any contemporary American legislation. Every port of embarkation has its history, concerned on the one hand with the development of its interior net of communication and on the other with the nature of its Atlantic commerce. Thus the tobacco trade of Bremen, the cotton trade of Havre, and the timber trade of Liverpool have dictated the American terminus of the voyage and thereby determined the racial complexion of certain sections. Were the archives of shipping companies opened we could see the agents in operation, and how, when one reservoir of mankind was becoming exhausted, steps were already being taken to educate another in the advantages of emigration.

Though the American tariff policy has long been a subject of historical research, the development of the legal conditions under which the most valuable of all our imports has entered is entirely neglected. The state laws of immigration and settlement are usually characterized as dead letters, but neither the shippers nor the immigrants thought of them as such. The assumption of regulation by the federal government was the culmination of a long agitation which

[2] Some definite subjects will indicate the wide range of interests involved: reasons for the domination of Americans in the trade from 1820 to 1850; effects of the repeal of the British Navigation Laws in 1849; transfer of shipping to other activities in bringing about a sudden decline, as in 1855; transition, in the carriage of emigrants, from sailing vessels to steamships (1860–1870) in relation to price and in relation to the disappearance of the American flag from the seas.

concerned the Supreme Court, the transportation companies, the labor unions, and the farmers. A cross-section of all these influences could be obtained by studying the Immigration Convention which met in Cincinnati in 1870. The progress of the movement for restriction, leading up to the present-day legislation, involves much social and political history but there is need of a concise presentation. Castle Garden and Ellis Island are each worthy of a volume; and the administration of laws, the labor bureaus, and the welfare activities at Boston, Philadelphia, Baltimore, Charleston, and New Orleans should not be neglected.

In the history of immigration no subject is more important than that of the process of distribution. Not only did it determine the permanent location of races, but its methods have been agents of Americanization and its phases have marked eras in national development. It is unfortunate that statisticians have not been located at Buffalo and Pittsburgh and at the bridges across the Mississippi to record the migrations westward. Their figures would show the rise and fall of the movements, indicating waves not unlike the waves of immigration. The years and extent of the flow, however, have been obtained from other sources. They may be related to the waves of immigration and at once a significant fact is revealed. They do not coincide. Immigration and distribution are two distinct movements, chronologically related; and the periods of small immigration are periods of continental dispersion.

This is the more remarkable because the old immigration is recognized as being one of land-seekers. But the majority did not reach the land directly. To do so, either they would be obliged to settle upon the frontier, or they must be possessed of sufficient means to offer a price which would induce the established farmer to sell. As frontiersmen they were not successful. Neither by training nor by temperament were they fitted. As purchasers their resources were usually limited. Accordingly they reached the land through the medium of industry—an intermediate stage—becoming farmers when their finances improved or industry failed them.

Immigration and dispersion were part of the same cycle. A period of industrial activity created optimism and American capital looked to the future. Railroads, canals, and highways were built, and cities were improved with business blocks and more pretentious homes. Coal and iron mines were opened, furnaces put into blast, and rolling-mills into operation. There was apparently a limitless demand for labor, and every immigrant who could handle a spade filled his pockets with gold. Many who arrived to seek land, lured by the high wages, postponed their intentions. The farmer was prosperous with an ever expanding home market, and he called for hands to increase his production. But it was overdone. Capital employed in transportation was put into a fixed form, unremunerative until surrounding lands were settled and local trade stimulated. The weight of obligations exceeded the earning capacity, and collapse ensued. Unemployment faced millions; there was no prospect of revival; and the farmer, who had usually mortgaged his estate to buy more lands or to make improvements, was ruined.

So to save himself he went west. The railroads offered him their lands and he began anew in the wilderness. The immigrant of a few months' or years' residence was without his job, but if he could not earn wages he could at least raise his own bread; and with his savings he bought the semi-improved farm that the American deserted. Others lacked the courage for even this mid-frontier venture and they returned to Europe, forming that eastward migration so noticeable in all periods of depression. Bringing gloomy reports they helped to stem the tide that had already been checked by the arrival of discouraging letters and the decline in the number of prepaid passages. A period of immigration had ceased and one of dispersion commenced.

Thereupon new states began to appear in the West. Millions of acres were homesteaded; the railroads strengthened their position by the sale of lands. Vast areas were put under cultivation, and fertility so cheapened production that new markets were captured. Soon the settler could afford to buy more than necessaries. Activities at the stores in the new villages began to increase, and their orders influenced the cities. The little tricklings of exchange began to roll together into a great current of prosperity. Optimism returned. The furnaces were relighted, factory wheels moved, and the instruments of expansion reached westward into new fields. Again there was a call for labor. But the immigrant farmer would not leave his soil and if his son responded it was to serve in the higher ranks. Then through millions of human channels it became known in Europe that things in America had changed, that employment was abundant and wages good, and a new migration was in motion.

It is through some such hypothesis that the history of immigrant distribution should be approached. The immediate destination of immigrants during each of the eras of prosperity should be studied and their participation in the landward movements following the crises in 1819, 1837, 1842, 1857, 1873 determined. The return European migrations after 1893 and 1907, when it was easier for the immigrant to obtain land in Italy than in America, should receive special attention. Not until much detailed work has been done can a theory of distribution be stated; but the investigation of many of its single aspects will be valuable contributions towards such a theory.

Before the days of the railroads the immigrants considered the journey from the seaport to the interior as difficult a stage of their migration as crossing the Atlantic. Often it was, in fact, as expensive and lasted as long. The immigrant trade on the great natural highways—the Hudson River, the Mississippi, the Ohio, and the Great Lakes—should be studied in the same way as that of the Atlantic, in relation to the commerce. Pittsburgh and Buffalo, Chicago and St. Louis should be investigated as immigrant distributing centres. Local ordinances and police regulations will reveal how the hotels, land offices, and labor exchanges were regulated. The reasons for the popularity of certain states or regions at certain times, as Pennsylvania and Illinois in the 'twenties, Missouri and Ohio in the 'thirties, Wisconsin in the 'forties, and Iowa and Michigan in the 'fifties, will be profitable studies in both transportation and publicity.

With the era of internal improvements a new factor in distribution appears. The census of 1850, the first providing statistics of foreign-born by counties, reveals all lines of communication bordered with heavy alien percentages. These represent in part accessibility and in part the residue left by the construction gangs. An analysis should be made of the labor policy of canals and railroads—the hierarchy of contractors and subcontractors, the recruiting of men, labor conditions, and the preservation of order. The history of a "shanty town" may be as rich in primitive self-government as any mining gulch in California and marks the first participation of its inhabitants in American democracy.

These alien fringes were sometimes caused by the labor being stranded by the absconding of the contractor, but more often they represent the permanent staff necessary for the up-keep of every mile of the canal or railroad, those who judiciously chose uncleared lands or snapped up an opportunity in improved farms, and those who were drawn in by the stimulated industrial activity. A study of biographies, in local histories or obituary notices, will reveal how often the nucleus of a later extended foreign settlement was formed by such pioneers. When the railroads and canals possessed lands themselves, their land policy will explain much settlement. That the great Western railroads rank with the colonial trading companies as American colonizers is becoming recognized, but the influence of the railroads in the older sections should not be overlooked. The opening of the Erie Railroad, for instance, brought thousands of newly arrived immigrants into southern New York and northern Pennsylvania.

Access to a market was demanded by the foreigner who settled upon the land, whereas the native American was more self-sufficing.

When the railroad net was completed to the Mississippi the carriage of immigrants became an important feature, sought by the rail-roads not only for the immediate revenue or disposal of their lands, but for the more permanent income to be derived from settlement. Hence tickets were sold in the interior villages of Europe, alliances were formed with steamship lines, competition was bitter in the ports, and rates were reduced to ridiculous figures, as in the railroad war of 1885 when for a time the flat rate from New York to Chicago was only a dollar. The varying policies of individual roads, the relation of rates to settlement in any area, the agreements with certain industries for the supply of labor, as well as the history of the immigrant train itself as an institution, are all topics concerning this third and final stage of migration worthy of investigation. Nor should the " home seekers " excursions be forgotten which in times of industrial depression drew away from congested centres those who had settled in the cities.

Land companies and individual landowners supplemented the activities of the railroads. The rise of the great land fortunes of America, the creation of these estates of hundreds of thousands and even millions of acres, is a phase of American settlement as yet obscure. But the dissolution of these estates will be found to be intimately connected with the immigration of foreigners, as the advertisements in the German and English agricultural journals of the 'seventies and 'eighties unmistakably reveal. Agents of such estates may also be found operating in the European villages, sticking their posters in the public houses, lecturing to the improvement clubs, and, allied with the railroad and state representatives, smoothing all the difficulties of migration. Though it was in the last quarter of the century that this mode of settlement is most noticeable, the same influence operated from the very beginning and often was instrumental in determining the permanent character of a given region. Thus it was probably the opening of the Astor lands at an opportune moment that turned the tide of Germans to Wisconsin.

There were other factors exerting a positive influence upon the process of distribution. Religious ties, which must be interpreted as including language and social customs as well as spiritual needs, determined the location of many; and those church statesmen who had at heart the future of their faith used this sentiment for the benefit of both the settler and his organization. The early history of many rural parishes will show how the minister or priest turned solicitor and by working quietly year after year changed his feeble missionary charge into a vigorous church. Ecclesiastical administrators undertook comprehensive plans, the Catholic Church producing a group of colonizing bishops, Fenwick of Boston, Ireland of St. Paul, and Byrne of Little Rock, the activities of each of whom will repay study. The Irish Colonization Convention which met at Buffalo in February, 1856, upon the suggestion of D'Arcy McGee, proved a failure; but an analysis of the plans there promulgated will prove an interesting indication of racial consciousness, and their final wreck due to the opposition of Bishop Hughes of New York will provide an enlightening picture of rival racial ambitions. Many congregations, especially of Germans and Scandinavians, migrated as a group; but although almost any county history of the Middle West will mention the arrival of some such body, the economic history of one of these enterprises has never been written.

By the operation of these factors of distribution the immigrant became attached more or less permanently to some economic activity in country, village, or city. In each of these he has had an historical development which has left him on quite a different plane and has in turn influenced the American evolution of those activities.

The economic history of foreign farming communities has varied with the local conditions existing upon their arrival and their financial resources.[3] Many immigrants were left, as it were, stranded in the small towns and villages. Here they served as carpenters, masons, blacksmiths, and casual laborers. Some obtained a footing in commercial life and their children have become merchants and bankers. Professional men of foreign parentage have been recruited almost exclusively from this class, so their influence as leaders of the second generation has been far greater than their numerical proportion would warrant. Others of this group, however, have been the ne'er-do-wells that have contributed so much to the flavor of Main Street literature. The part that industry has played in the transitional stages of distribution has been emphasized above. The principles will be clarified when approached from a different angle and when the labor history of a coal mine, a factory, or the construction of a railroad is written. The racial evolution of a purely manufacturing city, such as Lowell, Massachusetts, will provide additional illustrations, with the Irish displacing, or at least taking the place of, the

[3] Suggestive fields for investigation are: the immigrant as an outright purchaser; the rise of the hired man to ownership; the immigrant as renter or mortgaged debtor; occupation of abandoned farms by any race; the different racial customs in providing for the second generation; the immigrant as a market gardener, cotton planter, or tobacco grower, as a fruitman, rancher, or ordinary prairie mixed-farmer; employment of farm hands and older sons in lumbering, ice-cutting, and other seasonal labor; attitude towards improvements and scientific farming.

Yankees; the French Canadians succeeding the Irish; and they in turn followed by the Greeks and Slavs.[4]

When the process of distribution had been completed and some definite economic status achieved, social life appeared. If the immigrant's lot was cast in a purely American environment, he soon lost his characteristics or became a social hermit. More often he was surrounded by hundreds of the same life-history, and in company with them he built up a society, neither European nor American. At present there exist probably a score of types (which ought to be classified). Upon their vitality the future complexion of American life in large measure depends. An understanding of the evolution of these types is a necessary preliminary to any policy of Americanization.

Research should begin with the reaction upon the individual. How did it affect his health? When did he discard his old clothing and when and why did he become ashamed of being " different "? What changes occurred in his principles and morals and why did he become more ambitious? What new interests did he most naturally adopt and which of the old most naturally disappeared? The determination of how immigrant reaction has varied with time, place, and nationality may seem to present insuperable difficulties. But it is not impossible. Biographies, reminiscences, and letters exist by the thousand; acute observations were made by travellers; and the missionary reports teem with comments because the attitude of the individual towards his old religion was usually an index of his whole mental outlook.

The social history of the family will provide a clue to much community development. What variations in internal administration and authority resulted from the migration? The persistence of family traditions, customs, and even names, the training of children in the years before going to school, the family pastimes and mutual obligations are pertinent topics. In time the second generation became a disturbing element. Unnumbered household revolutions occurred, the rebels demanding modernization of furniture, food, and dress, and often a change of religion. When they became successful in securing

[4] Other topics are: immigration in relation to the construction of street railroads, factories, dams, and canals, and the dispersion of the workers when completed; the influences which led certain races into certain occupations; the acquisition of city property; rise in the standard of living; levers by which a group raised itself to a higher plane of industry; efforts to retain control of a particular industry against the inroads of later comers; the circumstances that culminated in the Anti-Contract Labor Law; attitude of the immigrants to the unions, their radicalism, their conservatism, their leadership, their utilization as strike-breakers, and their influence in the formation of the immigrant restriction laws.

control of the family the strongest bulwark of hyphenism was carried. The success or failure of such movements should be related to nationality, location, religion, and community type.

Finally, community activities demand research. Every-day life in Boston and Milwaukee and a score of other foreign " capitals " should be described. The sociology of the hundred-and-sixty-acre farm is as worthy of investigation as that of the ante-bellum plantation. What amusements, festivals, commercial and social habits prevailed? How was an aristocracy of its own created and was it an expression of European or American standards? What was the opinion upon intermarriage with other groups and what was the social effect of such alliances? Did each race manifest a characteristic attitude towards social problems such as temperance and Sunday observance? At what stage and why did native prejudice express itself and did it cause an intensification of peculiarities? What traits persisted after the first generation had passed, and was a constant influx necessary to maintain racial individuality?

As long as any group retained its own language any amalgamation with American social life was impossible. From the first their leaders complained of the eagerness with which immigrants discarded their mother tongue. Its retention became the corner-stone of all efforts to maintain racial solidarity. Historically, therefore, the problem has two aspects: first, the varying circumstances that led to the adoption of English; and secondly, the positive language-policy of the leaders.

The matter being so personal, the materials for the study of the first are very scant. But the second generation, now so widely represented in the colleges, might be subjected to a questionnaire, for it was in the inner life of the bilingual families that the transition took place. For the second point the materials are abundant. Sooner or later in every denomination the language question arose, and the proceedings of church conventions and the columns of their official organs are filled with debates and resolutions. Even more abundant are the materials for a history of the teaching of foreign languages in the public schools. Every state board of education was subjected to tremendous pressure and in many states every ward and school district witnessed similar political propaganda. The language legislation during the war, interesting as a manifestation of war psychology, can be more clearly understood as a reaction from these former concessions.

The language question is but one phase of the much broader subject of the migration of institutions. How these institutions were set up, how they throve in the American atmosphere, and how they competed with the native institutions is part of the history of immigration. The process of their transplantation is obscure, though a few years after settlement we can see them in full bloom, churches, parochial schools, academies, fraternal organizations. There are Portuguese bands, Welsh eisteddfods, German turnvereins, Bohemian sokols, Polish " falcons ", and Greek " communities ".[5] Each nationality at every period demands study of its own. What applies to the Irish differs from what applies to the Hungarians; and the situation among the Germans in 1840 is quite different from that in 1880. It varied with the intensity of the national feeling in the European countries, with the amount of support given by organizations at home, with the internal politics of any race in America, and the amount of opposition which native institutions exhibited.

It was the American churches and their missionary activities that offered the strongest resistance. They met the invaders on their own ground and fought them with their own language. With their seminaries on American soil they had an advantage which the European training schools could not duplicate and their success was the despair of the early missionaries from the churches of Europe. Psychologically the years of migration provided a fertile field for the propagation of new faiths, and the result was the division of the nationalities, especially the old immigrants, among sects and the break-up of migrating denominations into many branches. Much as these divisions were to be deplored from the point of view of effective religious service, they did act as agents of Americanization by breaking the ties with European hierarchies and placing administration in the hands of those who were directed by American organizations.[6]

[5] In connection with their origin many questions arise: Did the immigrants create these institutions because there were none to serve them or because they were content only with their own? Did these institutions arise spontaneously or were they due to the activity of some enterprising individuals? Was assistance in finance or leadership received from any society in the home country, and, if so, what were the motives of this society? There were other parts of the world to which emigrating Europeans brought their institutions. As many Irish settled in England in the years after the famine as entered America; Italians by the hundreds of thousands have colonized the Argentine, and there are flourishing German settlements in Brazil. By comparing the institutional history of the races in these differing environments the problems and significance of their development in the United States may be the more clearly understood.

[6] The problem of the organization of immigrants may be approached most successfully through biography. A few among the hundreds of such pioneers are, the Catholics, Rev. James Fitton and Rev. Henry Lemcke; the Lutherans, Rev. C. F. W. Walther and Rev. L. P. Esbjørn; the Methodist, Rev. Wilhelm Nast; and the two Protestant Episcopal bishops, Philander Chase and Jackson Kemper.

This mingling of social systems raises the natural question, what has immigration as a whole or any group as a race contributed to American culture? Many of the intellectuals among the newcomers thought of themselves as being the bearers of a higher civilization and their descendants have been assiduous in pressing their claims, so that to-day the racial origin of every man who has achieved distinction has been duly acclaimed. We have lists of statesmen, soldiers, poets, novelists, engineers, and educators presenting a formidable array.

It is submitted, however, that this method does not reach the heart of the problem. It is in the township, the village, or the city ward that the leaven in the lump can be detected. There the investigator will find the German singing society which gradually took into its ranks non-Germans, stimulated the formation of other societies, and provided a winter's concert course. There he will find the immigrant music teacher who passed on the training of his old-world masters to hundreds of the offspring of a dozen nations. He will see a reading circle develop into a library indelibly characterized by the particular bent of its originators, thereby determining the literary character of the community. He will see the immigrant schoolmaster expressing his own education and producing among his pupils an unusually large proportion of scientists, philosophers, or farmers. When a few hundred such studies have been made and compared, then we can more confidently say what each race has contributed to the cultural possessions of American society.

In certain centres the mingling of racial contributions may be analyzed. There are the universities, many members of whose faculties have been drawn from the European institutions and whose training can be traced in the organization and scope of the curriculum as well as in the class-room. Hundreds of each nationality have sat in Congress and in the state legislatures. Have they been especially active in producing legislation that will foster the development of arts and sciences? In the cities there have existed theatres promoted by almost every national group. When they disappeared did they leave any trace of their influence upon the American stage? At what times and for what reasons have European classics become popular either in the original or in translation? What scientific, literary, artistic, or musical causes have been championed by the national societies? What literature did the immigrants produce and what characteristic traits of contemporary American literature may be traced to this origin? [7]

---

[7] The immigrants produced many novelists whose work will never live as fiction. But as reactions to American environment these attempts repay study. Characters and plots are drawn from the community life with which the authors were acquainted.

131

These questions can be answered only by access to sources that depict the inner life of a group. Such a source is found in the foreign-language press. Fortunately it was most numerous. To peruse the pages gives a vivid cross-section of community activities. Their advertisements show the food, clothing, books; their news columns express their own doings as well as those of their American neighbors. To the foreigner who had church, school, club, and society the newspaper told of the larger American world in which he lived, and assisted materially in the transition from the old to the new.[8]

But it is as political exponents or political instructors that the foreign press will always command the greatest attention; and throughout the nineteenth century, with the increasing percentage of naturalized voters, its relation to each of the succeeding political crises becomes of greater significance. In these matters, however, it is a question whether it merely reflected group opinion or made it. In another and increasingly important field it became the guide—foreign affairs. Not until the World War does the foreign press appear as a great public influence. But that influence was not of sudden growth. Whatever may be said of the course of the American press generally in respect to European news before the war, the foreign-language press was not ignorant and did not slight such topics. Each of the diplomatic crises that mark off the advance to August, 1914, forms the basis of news and editorial comment that reflected the prevailing opinion in the country of origin. Consequently these people in America were almost as prepared for war, psychologically, as any in Europe; and when the conflict did come the whole battery of the press was turned upon the American policy of neutrality, thus creating many of the internal problems of the troubled years from 1914 to 1917. The historian who will attempt to unravel the political skein of that period must first trace the development of the international state of mind of the groups with which he deals.

Mrs. Mary Sadlier and Paul Peppergrass (Rev. John Boyce) write of the Irish, J. R. Psenka of the Czechs, and Abraham Cahan of the Jews. Among the Scandinavian writers are the well-known Knut Hamsun and Johan Bojer. But less prominent authors such as Waldemar Ager should not be overlooked.

[8] In addition to a study of certain important papers which may well be called the mouthpieces of respective groups, it would be enlightening to investigate the careers of some of the leading journalists. Among them are: Oswald Ottendorfer of the New York *Staats-Zeitung*; Hermann Raster of the *Illinois Staats-Zeitung*; William Doenzer of the *Anzeiger des Westens*; John Anderson of *Skandinaven*; Byrnild Anundsen of *Decorah Posten*; Patrick Donahoe and John B. O'Reilly of the Boston *Pilot*; Patrick Ford of the *Irish World*; James A. McMaster of the New York *Freeman's Journal*; Col. Hans Mattson of the *Svenska Amerikaner*; and Solon J. Vlastos of the Greek paper *Atlantis*.

In the formation of this state of mind the press was by 1914 receiving the assistance of powerful allies. The foreign national elements were becoming more conscious of their origin. Immigrants of forty years' residence were becoming reflective. An unusually large number of reminiscences appeared; histories were being written; and alliances, foundations, and leagues were being organized. Though very largely cultural in their ambitions, these national societies could not exclude politics in times of crisis, and in 1914 they played the rôle in national politics that for practically a century local societies had enacted in their own neighborhoods.

It is in these local circles that the student of the influence of racial groups in American politics will make his start. There are perhaps a hundred of such clubs that demand an historian. He will investigate the circumstances attending the organization of each, trace the political allegiance of the moving spirits in the venture, analyze its programmes, ferret out the speakers, and interpret the toasts at the annual banquets. Soon he will find its leaders becoming aldermen and its more prosperous members being favored with city and state contracts. Governors and mayors appear on the programmes. The advantages of naturalization are urged and committees are appointed to welcome the immigrants and train them up in the political way in which they should go. These features, be it emphasized, are not necessarily the most important activities of the society. Charity and good fellowship may be more pronounced as prestige and wealth grow with numbers. But this approach to the problem is the direct path into the maze of local politics where new and bewildered voters are captured for this or that party, and in turn the party is influenced in its attitude towards even national issues.

The immigrant came with many preconceived attitudes which were the basis of his reaction to American life. One of them relates that for ten years before his departure he read every printed word he could find on the United States; he read all the letters which reached the village from those who had already migrated; and when he heard that here or there within the range of a dozen miles someone had returned to visit relatives or friends he called on foot to catechize him more particularly. From such reminiscences, in newspapers and magazines, books and lectures, an attempt should be made to deduce the prevailing attitude towards American problems at various periods, in order to estimate the background of political reactions. Important among such sources will be the addresses and writings of the many successful immigrants who were later returned to their native country to serve as ministers and consuls and who looked upon themselves as interpreters of America to their former compatriots.

The political machines found the foreigners susceptible. The issues that were emphasized, the attentions paid to visiting foreign notables, the injection of religious controversies were all means to an end. The fire, police, and street departments of every city have a racial history. Naturalization clubs flourished in all communities, some of them bona-fide efforts to train immigrants into the status of citizens, others the creatures of the machine. Their activities should be related to the nature of the impending political struggles. As early as the decade of the 'thirties, efforts to secure the German or Irish vote may be recognized locally. The spread of such tactics from city government to state government and thence on into national politics should be traced.

In the rural regions, either the foreigners in one township were so few that they did not count, or so many that they had entire control. A township of the latter type will provide an enlightening laboratory. Here is a community governed by men who have had no training in democracy, and with only the barest outlines of the structure provided by a higher authority. Under such circumstances what type of man came forward? Was political service looked upon as a burden? Now that they were in the land of freedom did they hasten to govern themselves? Did they merely imitate their neighbors or were they more progressive or more conservative? To which did they pay the more attention, schools or roads? Were the German immigrants after 1848 more politically-minded than their predecessors, and did any change occur after 1871? It is questions such as these that the student who has before him the records of a North Dakota or a Wisconsin township can answer.

With these matters disposed of, it will be more possible to generalize as to whether the immigrants have contributed anything to American political ideals. Perhaps they have retarded the progress of democracy by burdening it with a mass of citizens lacking the qualities necessary for self-government. It may be that their European attitude has led to more social legislation and has fostered the movement towards centralization. On occasion they have forgotten that they were in America and have been more interested in fighting the battles of the old country than in participating in those of the new; but in so doing they have inadvertently complicated the existing American issues and created many entirely new.[9] Irish, German, Hungarian, Polish, and Italian patriotic movements operated from

---

[9] This is especially true of the Irish, who for almost a century championed the cause of their island through a series of movements: the Repeal agitation of the 'forties, the Fenianism of the 'sixties, the Land League of the 'eighties, and the Sinn Fein movement of our own time. Each of these will be found closely connected with the social as well as the political issues of the time.

an American base about the middle of the last century; and research will probably reveal that the emergence of the new nations of Eastern and Central Europe in consequence of the war was possible only because there had existed in America, for a generation or two, active colonies of those nationalities, which had kept alive the ideal of independence and which could offer financial support and political pressure when the time for reconstruction had arrived. All such activities, which to the natives have seemed so alien to American life, have prepared the way for the anti-foreigner movements from the time of the Know-nothings down to the era of No-entanglements and the new immigration act.[10]

Countries of origin were never blind to their loss when they saw their ports thronged with the sturdiest of their peasantry. Efforts to stem the movement were attempted. To the student these efforts will by contrast indicate the strength of the forces that attracted to America, and reveal the local conditions that urged departure. Special attention should be directed to the societies which in the Scandinavian countries agitated against emigration, and the relation of empire settlement to the variations in the flow of the British current. The positive policy of Italy in securing economic advantages from the movement will be found an essential factor in the development of the characteristics of the new immigration.

European governments, moreover, realized that their political as well as their economic life was involved. Experience with a few returned radicals revealed a new threat to their institutions. Consequently all who had been in America were looked upon with suspicion and if necessary their freedom in action and speech was limited. At times newspapers and periodicals, books, and even personal letters were subjected to the censor. But it was evidently all in vain. And here is a rich field for those who would trace the development of nineteenth-century democracy. What influence American political theory had upon the minds of those who were the leaders; how the framework of the American republic was the model for projected European republics; and how the peasant who had neither political theories nor visionary governments in mind vaguely began to feel that things could be better because they were better across the Atlantic— these circumstances require investigation. It is not unlikely that the

---

[10] Political biography offers a great array of governors and members of Congress. They should be studied more from the point of view of their relations to the group from which they came. Though Carl Schurz has often been written of as an American statesman, his career as a German-American is even more significant. Governor John A. Johnson, Senators Knute Nelson and James Shields, and the Bohemian Charles Jonas, who had a varied career at home and abroad, should be approached from this point of view.

results of such researches will compel a revaluation of factors and the " leaven of the French Revolution ", which has so long stood first in the list, will be displaced by the influence of America, gradually becoming known to Europeans as a practical example of democracy, conducted by men among whom were those who had once been their neighbors.

The above topics indicate the type of source-material from which the history of immigration can be drawn. Not until the movement was clearly defined were bureaus for its supervision created by the European governments. Long before their reports appear, however, pertinent official documents are available. There are ponderous investigations of land tenure, feudal services, taxation, marriage laws, poverty, and military affairs, that contribute to an understanding. Petitions to legislatures provoked debates in which members added their testimony and suggested remedies. Consuls residing abroad reported on the fate of fellow-countrymen who had settled in their districts. There were charitable organizations that investigated the feasibility of obtaining relief by systematic emigration and in doing so laid bare the social maladjustments that were stimulating departure and the actual conditions under which emigration was already taking place. Farmers discussed the problems of rural labor at their annual meetings, and local correspondents of agricultural journals, in reporting from month to month on weather conditions and harvest prospects, commented on the changes in population that were effecting a revolution in local society.

In the countries of Northwest Europe, emigration produced a literature of its own. Before commerce undertook the task of watching over the voyager from his native village to his new home, emigrants travelled " by the book ". A comparative study of these guides reveals the changes that took place from decade to decade in the routes, difficulties, costs, and even motives of emigration. But books could not keep up with the ever changing conditions of the new world, and emigrants' periodicals began to appear with the first great wave of the movement. Their files present a rich opportunity, with advertisements of land and transportation companies, news items, letters from settlers, notes on labor conditions, and descriptive poetry and fiction.[11]

[11] The following list of German and Swiss emigrant papers is probably not complete, but it indicates their nature: *Der Nordamerikaner* (St. Gall, 1833–1834); *Allgemeine Auswanderungs-Zeitung* (Rudolstadt, 1846–1871); *Der Deutsche Auswanderer* (Darmstadt, 1847–1850); *Germania, Archiv zur Kenntniss des Deutschen Elements in allen Ländern der Erde* (Frankfurt am Main, 1847–1850); *Der Sächsische Auswanderer* (Leipzig, 1848–1851); *Der Auswanderer am Niederrhein* (Meurs, 1848–1849), a series of pamphlets; *Deutsche Auswanderer-Zeitung*

In time, catering to the needs of the emigrants became the principal business for several months of the year at the ports of embarkation. Their newspapers and commercial journals, and the official city and port documents record the almost daily variation in the flow, as well as the general trade conditions influencing transportation. City information bureaus were established, protective societies formed, and religious organizations were not slow in undertaking missionary work. All of these left their documents. The actual transatlantic journey is depicted in the works of travellers, all of whom made excursions through the steerage. The less picturesque aspects of the business may be discovered in the annual reports of shipping companies, the columns of commercial periodicals, and official investigations of the passenger trade.

In America all sources of pioneer history can make a contribution. But there are two which bear directly on the foreign element in the process. The one is the immigrant press discussed above, the other the great mass of literature connected with the religious condition of the immigrants. Bishops and missionaries on their travels could not overlook the material situation of their flocks, and in their reports this interest was reflected. How much lies buried in church archives

(Bremen, 1852–1875); *Hansa, Central Organ für Deutsche Auswanderung* (Hamburg, 1852–1857); *Hamburger Zeitung für Deutsche Auswanderungs- und Kolonisations-Angelegenheiten* (Hamburg, 1852–1858); *Das Westland: Magasin zur Kunde Amerikanischer Verhältnisse* (Bremen, 1851–1852); *Atlantis: Zeitschrift für Leben und Literatur in England und Amerika* (Dessau, 1853–1854); *Neuestes über Auswanderung und von Ausgewanderten* (1850–1853), an annual review edited by August Schultze; *Anschauungen und Erfahrungen in Nordamerika, eine Monatschrift* (Zurich, 1853–1855); *Schilderungen aus Amerika, eine Monatschrift* (Zurich, 1859–1860); *Taschen-Bibliothek der Reise-, Zeit-, und Lebensbilder* (Rudolstadt, 1854–1857), including an annual emigrants' calendar; *Der Tollense-Bote, Blätter zur Unterhaltung und Belehrung, Auswanderungs-Zeitung und Anzeiger für Mecklenburg* (Neubrandenburg, 1855–1856); *Der Emigrant* (Bremen, 1868); *Der Auswanderer* (Zurich, 1872–1873); *Der Pfadfinder* (Gotha, 1872–1873); *Weltpost: Blätter für Deutsche Auswanderung, Kolonisation, und Weltverkehr* (Leipzig, 1881–1885); *Neue Auswanderungs-Zeitung* (Leipzig, 1880–1881), continued as *Deutsch-Amerikanische Zeitung* (1882); *Amerikanische Nachrichten* (Berlin, 1883–1884), continued as *Deutsche Weltpost* (1885–1886). In addition to these, volume III. of *Der Kolonist* (Bern) appeared in 1854, and volume VIII. of the *Schweizerische Auswanderungszeitung* (Bern), in 1873; but I have not yet been able to locate complete files of these two papers.

For British emigrants the following papers, all published in London, appeared: *The Emigration Gazette* (1841–1843); *The Emigrant and Colonial Gazette* (1848–1849); *Sidney's Emigrant's Journal* (1848–1849); *The Universal Emigration and Colonial Messenger* (1850–1851); *The Emigration Record and Colonial Journal* (1856–1858); *Land and Emigration* (1871–1873); *The American Settler* (1872–1874 and 1880–1892). *The Anglo-American Times* (1865–1896), though not primarily an emigrant journal, contains a great deal of information about land, the process of settlement, and the industrial situation.

can only be imagined. The great amount that found its way into print has hardly been touched.[12] In Europe societies were formed to promote the spiritual welfare of the diaspora, and their publications are even more informative.[13]

Very often the history of a parish is the history of an immigrant community and the local press should be searched for commemorative addresses on anniversary occasions and for biographical sketches of the clergy.

But such materials can be found in very few libraries to which students have ready access. A long and semi-blind search for their location is necessary before the investigator can attack his problems. Especially one who studies a common phase of all emigrations is confronted by an almost hopeless task. Accordingly it is suggested that as the first step in opening up the field a survey be made to locate the raw materials. Such a survey would extend beyond the libraries of universities and the great public libraries. It would explore the riches of the theological institutions and the archives of church headquarters. It would reveal unexpected treasures on the shelves of local historical societies and in the libraries of immigrant communities. It would discover under what conditions the files of an immigrant newspaper may be consulted or, if defunct, into whose hands they have passed. Such a comprehensive investigation would do more than shorten the labors of the student. It would be the best guaranty that the history of American immigration be written on the broad and impartial lines that its place in national development deserves.

MARCUS L. HANSEN.

[12] How extensive this literature is may be realized by referring to the article "Periodical Literature" in *The Catholic Encyclopedia*, vol. XI., pp. 692–696; and to the list of Lutheran papers in John G. Morris's *Bibliotheca Lutherana* (Philadelphia, 1876), pp. 131–139.

[13] The most important of these publications are: *Annales de l'Association de la Propagation de la Foi* (Lyons, 1827–); *Berichte der Leopoldinen-Stiftung im Kaiserthum Oesterreich* (Vienna, 1832–); *Das Missionsblatt* (Barmen, 1826–); *Allgemeine Zeitung des Judenthums* (Leipzig, 1837–); *Kirchliche Mitteilungen aus und über Nordamerika* (Berlin, 1843–); *Missionsblatt der Brüdergemeinde* (Hamburg, 1837–); and *Fliegende Blätter aus dem Rauhen Hauses zu Horn* (Hamburg, 1844–).

R. F. HARNEY

The Commerce of Migration

Between national unification in 1870 and World War I, millions of Italians migrated to the Americas. In Italy that emigration became part of a national polemic on the need for colonies and the problem of the South. As immigration, the migration became a sub-theme in American urban and ethnic historiography. The differences in perspective and concern of those who view the migration as emigration and those who see it as immigration obscure the continuities in the migrant society. This paper is about an aspect of that continuum, the mediating and exploiting role of the middle classes in Italy and America.

American observers saw misery and hunger driving South Italians overseas. J. F. Carr wrote in *Outlook* that "through whole districts in this overcrowded land Italians have to choose between emigration and starvation."[1] Some Italian advocates of emigration like Senator Nobili-Vitelleschi felt that without mass migration "the land would strangle in its own excess population 'soffocare nella sua pletora,' and everyone would have to eat one another to survive . . ."[2] On both sides of the Atlantic, stereotypes and self-images colluded to make Italian emigration seem natural. The South of Italy was poor, over-populated, and mis-governed. America was a land rich and underpopulated, ergo migration. In such a natural human flood, differentiation of classes and roles, distinctions between natural and artificial uprooting appeared insignificant. It was assumed that misery drove men from Italy and *La Miserià* was so total that the perils of migration, the hostility of "Anglosaxons," and the difficult struggles ahead could not deter the peasant.[3] The prefects of Southern Italy, overwhelmingly attributed migration to misery.[4]

Unfortunately, misery was exactly what North American historians saw as Europe's peasant condition, the misery of potato famine and the hungry '40's, the misery of the Russian Pale and pogroms. The plight of Southern Italy seemed to be of the same order. In *The Uprooted,* Oscar Handlin confidently generalized about the European situation. "Year by year, there were fewer alternatives until the critical day when only a single choice remained — to emigrate or to die."[5] But misery in Italy did not really mean to "emigrate or to die." In 1906, about 435,000 left Italy for America; in the same year, 158,000 returned to Italy. Some came back for good, others, like the *golondrine* (swallows), were simply commuting from harvest to harvest, from Autumn in Piedmont to Spring in Argen-

140

tina.[6] There is no way to compare return rate with that of the Irish and Germans of the hungry '40's or the Jews of the Pale, but the answer, even accepting changes in transport, is self-evident. R. F. Foerster observed of the Italian emigrants in 1919 that though "the notion of flight is rudimentary . . . Rarely if ever does it alone govern the man's conduct." Most Southerners, had a "notion, however vague, of a tangible positive gain to be secured, a notion that generally depends upon the evidence of other's success."[7]

Interpretations of Italian emigration stressing the volition of the migrants and the role of a secondary group of caretakers, exploiters, and agents have taken a number of forms. Emphasis on agents and sub-agents has often been a conservative device in Italy used to deny or obscure the real plight of the South or to justify the policing of emigration in the interest of the land owning classes.[8] South Italian radicals condemned the legislation of the 1880's that sought to regulate the activity of South American state recruiters, control steamship companies, and reduce the numbers of official subagents. Since such critics of the government saw the roots of the problem in the backwardness and suppression of the South, analogies to the negro slave trade, phrases such as *commercio di carne umana* (trade in human flesh) or *i negrieri* (slave traders) and *merce/uomo* (men as goods) came easily to their tongues. Legislation against agents, they felt, was either a conservative ruse or the product of a naive devil theory.[9] Grazia Dore, in her *La Democrazia italiana e l'emigrazione in America,* (1964) remarked that the term *agenti* was employed by the government both as a perjorative and to imply the artificial nature of emigration. She added that some of the Southern bourgeoisie, seeing easy profit in the emigration trade, served as subagents for steamship companies, labour contractors, and South America 'white settler agents.'[10] Unfortunately, Dore's concern was political history; she ignored the natural role of the middle classes as mediators between the literate and illiterate, between countryside and city, between the individual migrant and alien government.

In North America, following the lead of the Congressional Commission of 1911 (referred to henceforth as the Dillingham Commission), historians have uncovered two "unnatural" stimuli in Italian migration, the steamship agents and the *padroni,* or contract labour boss. In its most pernicious form — peasants seduced by a labour contract from their European villages and virtually in thrall to a boss in North America — the *padrone* system had a brief if lurid career. With the growth of little Italy communities, exploitation began to take more subtle forms.[11] In 1888, the Italian vice-consul reported that there were no longer *padroni* in New York City.[12] A recent historian of the Chicago Italians, even claims that the bulk of prepaid passages were probably paid for by relatives rather than labour contractors.[13] However, the Dillingham Commission, sensing the limits of its definitions and investigation, was not naive enough to count the *padroni* out completely. The Commission noted that immigrant bankers' offices (often travel agencies as well) had a way of serving as hiring halls and labour bureaux.[14]

Other villains in the piece were obviously the big steamship companies who encouraged uprooting, winked at the illegal practices of their subagents, and were pleased when the emigrant failed because it assured them of an eastbound cargo in the lucrative Mediterranean trade.[15] One line, the Inman Steamship Company, in 1892, was reputed to have 3500 agents in Europe.[16] Drumming up steerage trade was "a business which can be almost indefinitely expanded by vigorous pushing. A skillful agent can induce any number of simple and credulous peasants of a backward European country to emigrate, who had scarcely had such an idea in their heads before."[18] The Fagin-like qualities of men who ran strings of bootblacks from the Basilicata, the *padrone* as *negriere,* and the callous approach of the steamship companies in filling their steerage quotas were all real but they turned a socio-economic situation into a morality plan. The study of the role of intermediaries remains too political in Italy and too moral and too fragmentary in North America.

The new interpretation of Italian emigration, identifying the role of chain migration, ethnic receiving neighbourhoods, and continuity of kinship ties from Italy to the receiving country improves upon the devil theories about *padroni* and agents. The Australian demographer, J. D. Macdonald presents a model for emigration "in which prospective migrants learn of opportunities, are provided with transportation, and have initial accommodation and employment arranged by means of primary social relationships wtih previous migrants."[17] The "chain migration" interpretation has an easy answer to the charge that South Italians are "amoral familists" who distrust everyone beyond their nuclear family. Emigration itself brought more extended kinship and friendship systems out of desuetude because they were needed. This is the contention of an excellent study of Buffalo Italians by V. Y. McLaughlin. Stress on family ties and the anthropological approach have advantages but one obvious drawback is the tendency to observe the strength of the immigrant family and to see ethnic neighbourhoods as primitive idylls, where money, class, and terror — all realities of the Italian countryside — do not penetrate. McLaughlin, for example, discusses the number of boarding houses in Buffalo and remarks that many boarders were *paesani* of the homeowners. There is no mention of the possibility of their paying rent, let alone of their being gouged or exploited.[18]

The process of migration was not as familial and *"paesano"* as "chain migration" theory implies or as episodic and rapacious as the literature about *padroni* would suggest. Often ignored is the impact of class structure in Southern Italy, in the migration itself, and in the Little Italy receiving depots. "Middle class brokers" served and preyed upon their countrymen from Calabrian village, along the railways, to Naples, and finally in New York, Buenos Aires, and Toronto. Neither in Italy nor in America was this so-called *borghesia mediatrice* (middle class go-between) class a caste. Just as people known as *generetti* (little big people) or *mercanti di campagna* (merchants of the countryside) emerged in the South of Italy after unity, so too the business of emigration made other emigrants rich or richer in America. In that world of preindustrial social groups petty transactions and literacy as "white magic," the role of the middle classes is ill-defined. If one accepts the view of Antonio Gramsci that "the South was reduced to a semi-colonized market of the North,"[19] it is possible to see that a natural product of such an economy is men. The 'slavetraders' may have been a few *padroni* in America or the subagents and agents of large steamship companies in the Italian South but all the middle classes gained from the commerce of migration.[20]

Money and socio-economic structure were at the heart of emigration. To understand the role of middle-class intermediaries, we must enlarge our definition of agents, and look for all the parts of the process of migration where services were rendered and money exchanged. The agents were all those who stood between the parochial, rural lower classes and the large society, those who mediated between feudalism and modernity.

The steamship, as the intrusion of modern technology into the South, allowed the middle classes a role in migration to North America and in the process of urbanization itself. They responded to the enlarged economy with their only product, men. When, for example, the government in the 1900's, tried to reduce the number of official subagents to one for each district with more for those areas recognized as remote, almost 2000 communes petitioned to be classified as remote areas.[21] Men obviously encouraged emigration for the *senseria* (steamship company bounty) alone, and in towns like those that petitioned, most of the non-peasant structure saw profit in emigration. Prime Minister Crispi defined agents inclusively in his 1888 legislation.[22] Article Six of Crispi's Law promised jail and a fine for any unlicensed person "who, for financial gain, counselled or excited the peasants of the nation to emigrate, who furnished and procured ships passage for the emigrants, intervened as mediators between the emigrant and the steamship lines, or who transported them to the port of embarkation, or to the place of destination, or in any way, personally, or by means of others, with verbal, written or printed information set out to promote emigration."

Sensing perhaps, the blurred line between cash transactions, favour and patronage in such a setting, Article 7 added a fine of 1000 lire for clergy, mayors, and communal officials who, using written or verbal exhortation promoted emigration *"anche senza fine di lucre,"* (even without a profit motive). In fact, the problem faced was a simple one and endemic in the South. The government intended to use the wolves as shepherds for the flock. In the various legislative efforts to regulate emigration and to mitigate the harsh conditions of emigration, the people made responsible were those for whom migration had become a lucrative trade. An Italian Senator, supporting legislation that made local committees of notables responsible for the emigrant's well-being saw the problem. "And when one speaks of local authority, we mean to speak of all; from mayor to pharmacist, from tax collector and doctor to field guard — all must treat the peasant differently." Yet any addition to the rules increased the power of go-betweens.[23] Bureaucrat or businessman, the middle-class brokers, stood between the less literate and the newly enlarged state and economy.

A case in point is the Royal Decree of 1901 requiring the prospective emigrant to apply in writing or orally to the mayor of the commune for a passport.[24] The latter would investigate and, if he approved, forward a *nulla osta* (no obstacle) to the prefect who would judge the case. To receive the *nulla osta,* the emigrant had to guarantee that he was leaving no dependents; that he was not under age; that he was not an ex-convict, and that he was not enmeshed in Italy's military conscription and reserve system. If all went well, the emigrant would receive his passport for 2 or 3 lire. With the problem of illiteracy and the peasant's assumptions about government corruption in mind, let us examine the possibilities of this minor and well-intentioned piece of legislation.

It is here one should question the concept of "amoral familialism" and "chain migration" in the *Mezzogiorno*. How will the emigrant move through the maze of unknown regulations; can he do it through emigration-wise relatives? Perhaps. The "war of all against all" has in the South of Italy as in any capitalist society a logical extension. What cannot be done through the family, can be done with money. Money insures that services rendered are in the self-interest of both parties. A little *"bustarella"* (a small envelope full of lire) for the mayor, even if he is an honest man, some votive candles bought for the Church when the priest writes a letter to a brother in Boston. Social and economic interaction in a South Italian village does not end at the borders of the family. Somewhere near those borders money could produce truces and allies in the war of all against all, and it made one man's family interest another man's family interest. In fact, what is pathetic about the South Italian conversion to a money nexus is that the peasant's understanding of it causes him to force money on those honest brokers, "caretakers," and state officials whom he need not pay. "Chain migration" and travel-wise veterans could only provide the map of whom to pay and how much to pay. If, as Macdonald claims — familialism and patronage were "the motor driving the chains which took so many emigrants from this part of Italy . . ." then money was the grease on the chains, and the migrants knew it.[25]

Our emigrant, then assuming that government is a thing of 'foreign thieves' must take the first steps toward the American shore through a maze of papers, extortion, and hostility. Let us see how many ways he can spend his money. He might perhaps hire a notary to write up the petition to the mayor for a *nulla osta;* his own illiteracy, the fact that the notary is the mayor's cousin, and the tendency of the genteel classes to treat him as a beast of burden make that a wise precaution. Now what if he had dependents or had been convicted of a felony, might he not pass the line of legality and, *bustarella* in hand, sally forth to buy the necessary approval. If he were too young, he could pay a notary or lawyer for signed statements that he was of age, and if there were complications in his military status, he could expect to spend both legal and illegal money. Then he waited for his passport, fearing, as only the illiterate can, the places he had marked his name, and the papers he had seen passed. In the very act of leaving, he may have tied himself down. "The sale of his cottage or farm hut, the mortgaging of a few goods to procure money for the trip" or the outright deal with a loan shark were not things that freed him from his *paese* but tied him to the local "middle class brokers."[26] The man called a *mercante di campagna* in one source may simply be a loan shark in another, and if a Verga novel can be trusted, he may often be an uncle as well. Money borrowed against property ran as high as 60%. Tribute to the middle class and its full scale commitment to profit as intermediaries is the fact that by 1913 interest on mortgages and loans was down from 50% to 3 or 4%, and the day was gone, according to one source, when "a single agent in a single year in not too big a town, could make 25,000 lire."[27] The ship's bounty, even at 50 lire, was but the beginning; it was only the most obvious transfer of money in the migrant process. The *via dolorosa* of Oscar Handlin's uprooted peasant of the 1840's was by the 1890's an organized and mechanized *via commerciale* for South Italians.

"The inevitable decorations at every train station [were] the placards of sailing and steamship companies," and in the harbour area of Naples more banners, agencies with confusing names, and men with as much chance of being fleeced as of embarking. "The region around the harbour [was] thronged with steamship ticket offices, often flying the American flag and with emigration agencies, and the line between the two [was] frequently very difficult to draw."[28] The importance of "chain migration" lay in the fact that they "had folk knowledge of the obstacles and pitfalls ahead." For example, peasants from a certain village in Basilicata could resist the gaudy advertising for Lloyd Sabaudo or the German steamships because they had been told by a veteran migrant that "on English ships, one always eats more civilly.[29] Even though forewarned, the migrants travelling from village to town to Naples were subject, before they reached the port, to such a camorra of sensali, incettatore, viaticali, grande, piccoli, minuti commercianti, — all names for go-betweens — that one can describe the trade as having primary and secondary benefits. Naples, a somnolent port, grew rapidly and that growth was based on the trade in men. In 1900, the port of Naples represented only 8% of the total port activity of Italy but was first in third class passengers.[30] The port too was embarkation point for wine, olive oil, garlic, cheese, macaroni and other products for growing Italian colonies overseas. Returning migrants — the successful *Americani* travelling first class, the failed *cafoni* in steerage — remittances, ship provisioning, kept the port expanding. After humans, the coal for the new railways was the most important cargo coming in. Narrow gauge track networks spread out from Naples.[31] No one has studied their development and relationship to emigration, but the small coaches and the routes chosen suggest that they were an integral part of the commercial network of migration.

Only local area studies will fully explain the ramifications of emigration. For every account of fields left fallow and gentry left without peasants, references exist about refurbished villages along the railway right-of-way. A Sicilian mayor claimed that only American remittances kept most small holders from losing their property for non-payment of taxes.[32]   Still, it is clear that bureaucrat, notary, lawyer, innkeeper, loan shark, *mercante di campagna,* runners in the harbour city, agents, even train conductors depended on the emigration trade.   On the other side of the ocean the scale of remittances, uninterrupted traffic of emigrant and repatriate, all the auxiliary food trades, (seasonal migrants) and the net-work of financial and commercial exchange justify treating Southern Italy and Italy overseas as one society and one informal economy, and parallels to the rural/urban migration become more trenchant.   No Italian city, least of all Naples, provided enough urban employment for the Southern masses, but when New York, Chicago and Pittsburgh are treated as part of a whole, then a useful picture emerges.   Replace agents in Italy, *padroni* in America, not just with "chain migration and ethnic neighbourhood," but wtih the thought that the same social relations and class structures (allowing ecological variants) existed on both sides of the Atlantic.   The expansion of employment for peasants in the industrial world outside of Italy meant expanding opportunity for the pre-industrial middle class in Southern Italy.   According to Isaacs, "at all times a relatively large number of capitalist immigrants has soon joined the ranks of the destitute while others, after starting without any means, become highly successful within a relatively short time."   As one old emigrant put it: "The big fish always follow the minnows that they feed on."[33]

Paeans to American opportunity such as one finds in Nelli's study of Italians in Chicago — "Over the years newcomers and their children moved up the eco-nomic ladder, progressing from unskilled labour into commercial, trade, and pro-fessional lines, "— obscure the social structure and economy of emigration.   In an earlier riposte to *The Uprooted,* Vecoli observed that most immigrants came from or near a "rural city" not "simple communities of agriculturists . . . their social structure included the gentry and middle class as well as the peasants."[34]   Even if more new men were apparent in a Little Italy's elite, they had 'arrived' in the same way as the middle-class *generetti* in Southern Italy.   The trade that made them successful was a trade in men and in handling the problems of less literate country-men.   Let me give, before I go on, some impression of the magnitude and the intercontinental nature of that trade.[35]

Most contemporaries noted the steamship companies' preference for the South European passenger trade because of the high rate of returnees.[36]   The flow of people in a peak year like 1907 — about 250,000 returnees and 300,000 outward bound — provides a sense of the scale and the unity of the emigrant business. Money went and came with the migrants.   The Dillingham Commission estimated that 85 million dollars was sent to Italy in 1907; $52 million of that was processed by immigrant bankers.   The Cashiers Office at Ellis Island as a depository of alien funds held as much as $500,000 monthly.   An "Immigrant Clearing House" of the Trunk Line Railroad Association on Ellis Island often handled $40,000 a day in cash ticket sales.[37]

Remittances were made to relatives for the support of the young or the old, for sisters' dowries, as bride prices, or as passage money in cash or in the form of pre-paid tickets.   Money was also sent home to pay mortgages contracted to make the original trip or to invest in new land.[39]   All such transactions passed through the sticky hands of brokers on both sides of the ocean.   Profit ranged from the staid and honest 2 or 3% on every transaction taken in by the subagents of the Banca di Napoli to that of "shrewd speculators acquiring vacant land parcels at low prices, in anticipation of the return of emigrants, then breaking them into cultivable units, and selling them in advance."[39]   The process of departing and the process of re-mitting served the long-range purposes of those who since the Risorgimento had seen the land as a commodity and not a patrimony.   The mortgaging and selling and the rebuying of small-holds, the consolidation of arable property, beyond providing endless opportunity for notary, lawyer, banker, pawnbroker, and local bureaucrat, continued a process begun against the impecunious nobility by the *mercante di campagna*. In Italy overseas, ethnic realtor, "immigrant banker," broker, and travel agent waited to perform similar functions. The continuum was noticed by an Italian Senator writing in 1905.⁴⁰ He observed that, though the crops and employment situation in the South were no better or worse in 1904 than other years, there was a decline in migration, new mortgages, and land sales. He reasoned that the decline had to be the result of a crisis of confidence, engendered by the presidential campaign in the U.S. and the bloody strikes with Italian involvement in Colorado and Pennsylvania. One economic pulse beat for the Italian South and for Italo-America.

Earlier, the short life of the real *padrone* structure was mentioned. The term itself, conjuring up both too much *padrono* and too much ward healer has not died. Although disinclined to see the role of brokers and the money economy in the 'family' process of emigration, "chain migration" theorists have not completely given up the *padrone*. Macdonald, for example, includes under that heading "employment agents, sweatshops, subcontractors, bankers, landlords, foreman, scribes, interpreters, legal advisers or ward bosses."⁴¹ Two American historians have provided an interesting study of a man whom they label a *"padrone."*⁴² His career included the following occupational sequence: 1888 — foreman, saloon owner, 1890 — emigrant banker and court interpreter, 1891 — grocery business, notary public, and steamship agency, 1893 — general contractor and ultimately political notable. The progression in this *padrone's* career suggests that he was a general go-between, a *mediatore,* that he began as a labour boss simply reflected the mediation needs of the first migrants. His later career grew from serving as broker in the variety of encounters that immigrants had with the Old and New World governments and economies. In other words, he provided the same services as his middle class counterparts in the Italian South. In the same way, his pretensions to power in the Republican Party ran parallel to the *generetti's* attempt to join the older *signori* of the South.⁴³ All in all, it would be better to drop the attenuated term *padrone* and recognize the ethnic middle classes.

Using the less equivocal term, "immigrant banker" the Dillingham Commission tried to explain the intermediary role of the immigrant middle-class in turn-of-the century New York. The need for intermediaries in North America was as great or greater than in Italy. Instead of a Tuscan bureaucrat or Piedmontese *carabiniere,* one might have to face an Irish 'cop' or Yankee customs officer. High illiteracy rates created an equally high dependence on scribes, notaries, and interpreters. Now the neologisms that bred in the strange new world of migration increased dependence upon the 'middle class' *paesano* who spoke English, Italian, dialect, and the new Italo-American language of *setaiola* (city-hall) and *grosseria* (store).⁴⁴ The handling of money, bureaucratic problems, and minor legal questions, some loan sharking, and problems of transport were the main business of the go-between on both sides of the ocean. On both sides, dependence on a literate *paesano* was the lesser evil in the face of officials assumed to be thieves and known to be outsiders. Familialism and patronage in simple anthropological terms are just not compatible with the number of notaries and quasi-lawyers in the South Italian global village.

Of 47 Italian immigrant bankers investigated by Dillingham's Commission, all served as agents or subagents for steamship companies: 34 carried on other business as well.⁴⁵ 20 were notaries; 6 realtors; 8 employment agents; 9 postal substations; and 7 grocery stores.

Imagine the immigrant broker's storefront and look at a contemporary Toronto ethnic travel agency: "all available space is filled with steamship posters, money-changing notices, and many coloured placards, alluring always in the inducements they present." There above the door, it says *Banco Italiano-Notario-publico—agente marittimo*. The affairs that go on inside the door affect the economy of two continents. The notarized papers, prepaid tickets and mortgage agreements have their counterpart in Avellino, Benevento, Campobasso, all the cities of the South. The banker takes 3% on your remittance, but he speaks your dialect. He buys your lire at 5% discount and sells at 3%, but even the *Banco di Napoli* agent cannot understand your problem, fails to stay open in the evening, and he does not know where your home town is. Your remittance may change the cadastral structure of your village, make your sister marriageable, or fix your mother's cottage roof, but a percentage of it at both ends falls in myriad and wonderful ways to the middle-class brokers. Why should the ethnic neighbourhood be different from the home town, and why not continue to accept the evil one knows over the unknown evils of American or Piedmontese bureaucracy?

Although there are obvious changes in the *ambiente* and ecology of migration, the idea of a 'commerce of migration' and of a *'borghesia mediatrice'* can be pursued in contemporary Toronto.[46] The most important changes are probably, 1/ the aeroplane, 2/ the increased consciousness of Italian nationality and increased literacy in the post-Fascist period, and 3/ the presence in the Canadian-Italian migration of more Northern Italians and more urban people. Despite these changes, the 'commerce of migration' in Canada, it seems to me, provides better comparisons for research with the old migration than does the contemporary United States where two generations of nostalgia have softened the image of exploiters, relatives, and *paesani*. Most groups of Italo-Americans now unconsciously or pridefully overemphasize the extended family and its patriarchal strength. Healthy family structure is, after all, one of the criterions that they use to distinguish themselves from more recent Latin and Black migrants.[47]

The Italian community of greater Toronto numbers almost half a million people. The continuity between this Italo-Canada and Italy is less tentative than in the earlier migration. The technical acceleration of communications; the competition between CP and Alitalia for the airborne version of steerage, is obvious. The new immigrant, more literate and attuned to a mass consumption economy, is followed to Canada by more than the cheese, oil, and occasional musical maestri that came after the Umbertine peasants who migrated to the United States. Phonograph records, clothing styles, packaged foods, Fiats, follow and create or being a merchant class to profit from and distribute them. Even a construction worker who winters on unemployment cheques among the mandarin oranges and prickly pears of their *paese* do his part for the social and economic continuity.

Despite higher literacy and the benign welfare state, the emigrant still seems to need a "middle class go-between." Mistakes at airports, before government agents, and in banks can be just as costly as they were in Naples in 1895 or New York in 1910. Signing the wrong papers can bring anything from unwanted aluminum siding to deportation. It was estimated in 1961 that 25% of the Italians in Toronto spoke no English at all. Many others were surely functionally illiterate in English; most are more comfortable in dialect than in Italian itself. In his book, *Non Dateci Lenticchie,* O. Bressan, a 'leader' in Italo-Toronto, notes that his countrymen have "a pessimistic concept of public officials in general and of state and parastatal officials in particular."[48] The same structure of illiteracy and distrust of government agencies that characterized life in the south of Italy exists in contemporary Toronto. Naturally then, intermediaries emerge or follow the migration. "Caretakers" and "intellectuals" dedicated to serving the migrants also proliferate. Toronto has political groups, religious and educational institutions, and philanthropic organizations for the immigrant community.[49] To the extent that the middle classes — those who are *civile e gentile* in the eyes of the migrant — dominate these institutions, they are little different from commercial intermediaries like banks and travel agencies. "The claim of any person or institution to be inspired by zeal for public rather than private advantage will be regarded as a fraud."[50] In observing this, Banfield mistakenly considered peasant distrust of the middle class as an aspect of amoral familialism's "war of all against all." However, distrust is the heritage of how expensive dependence on one's "betters" in Italy has been, especially since the advent of the cash economy. Can you really trust a man who offers to translate for you at an immigration hearing, or to make out your tax returns without charge? What is his game? Since the end of feudalism, or at least of the Risorgimento, the common people have paid in cash and deference for their inferior social and educational status, and they are used to it.

There is in Italo-Toronto, dependence on middle-class "brokers" ranging from ethnic driver education schools and realtors to consulting only doctors from one's *paese*. The most typical broker in the community is probably the travel agent. The Italo-Canadian Commercial Directory for 1971 lists about fifty travel agents in Toronto, although the number would be far greater if it included formal and informal subagents.[51] Toronto agencies often have business or familial ties with subagents in Italy, and some also tend to serve a specific *paese*: e.g., the Trinacria agency for Sicilians, the Venezia agency for people from the northeast of Italy. The pattern follows that of the "immigrant banks" of New York in the 1900's. The agent serves as go-between for his immigrant client in almost all conceivable encounters with the outside world.

A travel agency advertisement in the Italo-Canadian Commercial Directory almost duplicates the immigrant banker's advertisements addended to the Dillingham Commission reports of 1911. After mentioning the travel part of the business, the agency offers *"servizio Contabilita,* Bookkeeping service, Income Tax, *procure* [proxies], *atti notarili, cambio valuto,* servizio per il publico [sic] fino alle ore 9:00 pm." Another travel agent offers *"prenotazioni e biglietti per ogni destinazione"* but also *"pratiche di ogni genere, rimesse di denaro . . ."*[52] The following in order of frequency are the services that first generation Toronto Italians expected a travel agent to render: 1/ Tickets, prepaid tickets for relatives in Italy and other travel arrangements, 2/ Arrangement of passports, 3/ "going to Immigration," 4/ Remittances, 5/ Helping with unemployment insurance, 6/ Making out Income Tax forms, 7/ Dealing with the Workmen's Compensation Board, OHSIP, Old Age Pensions, and 8/ Dissolving partnerships and other notarial work.[53]

After doctors and lawyers, travel agents ranked highest among Italo-Canadian professionals and semi-professionals in the minds of those interviewed. Some people, in fact, expected to pay a fee for visiting a travel agent just as they would for visiting a doctor or lawyer. The most common remark about these agents was that they "know the right people." Although the phrase smacks of mystery and criminality, it is simpler than that. According to one immigrant, his travel agent was his "voice to the outside." That is what the intermediaries always were. Because of their assimilation to *italianità,* the money economy, and the Piedmontese conquest, the South Italian middle classes stood between local society and the larger polity. The "immigrant bankers" of the American East Coast dominated their countrymen because they were already bourgeois or Italo-American while the newcomers were still greenhorns and peasants. In Toronto, the intermediaries are also men between cultures. They may support ethnic radio stations and Italo-Canadian newspapers; they promote local Italian culture, but their role in the community comes as much from their assimilation to Canadian life as from their higher levels of literacy and sophistication.

Their humbler countrymen pay the intermediaries for the use of their literacy and assimilation. For example, it is estimated that, before the introduction of the current points system, 80% of the migrants to Toronto from Italy were "sponsored." Sponsorship constitutes the most obvious form of chain migration. Yet 60% of the people interviewed had consulted travel agents about sponsoring relatives, and some had depended upon agents to find them sponsors. All had paid for the services rendered over and above the price of prepaid tickets. When asked why he had consulted an agent about sponsorship, a veteran migrant showed the resignation and skepticism of those who depend upon intermediaries. "You may not need a travel agent to get to Canada," he said, "then again, you may not need a priest to get to heaven."

All this is not intended to suggest the existence of a criminal bourgeoisie or to justify the 'waspish' response of those who have always dismissed immigrant problems as the exploitation of one "dirty foreigner" by another. It does maintain that coherent class analysis can cross oceans in a way that the random and episodic study of separate kinds of exploitation cannot. And, now that it is not fashionable to see the immigrant as an up-rooted and disoriented countryman, the alternative view should not simply be an anthropological idyll where smiling people use their sense of kinship to cope with modernity. Modernity existed in migration in the form of lire, denari, soldi, and dollar bills. A semi-professional, commercial, and bureaucratic bourgeoisie was and is as much a part of an Italian ethnic neighbourhood or of a Neapolitan village as are religious festivals, grandmothers in black, and godfathers.

FOOTNOTES

1. John Foster Carr. "The Coming of the Italian" *Outlook* LXXXII (1906) p. 421.
2. Sen. F. Nobili-Vitelleschi. "Espansione coloniale de emigrazione" *Nuova Antologia* (May 1902) 183:107.
3. F. S. Nitti "L'Emigrazione italiana e suoi avversari (1888)" *Scritti sulla questione meriodionale* (Bari, 1959) 11:327.
4. Nitti. "L'Emigrazione." II:333-334 for a breakdown of the prefectoral reports. G. Dore. *La Democrazia italiana e l'emigrazione in America.* (Brescia, 1964) p. 45 suggests that the phrasing of the questionnaire sent to the prefects encouraged miserià as an answer.
5. O. Handlin. *The Uprooted.* (New York, 1951) p. 37.
6. F. Thistlethwaite. "Migration from Overseas in the Nineteenth and Twentieth Centuries" in H. Moller. *Population Movements in Modern European History* (New York, 1964) p. 77. *La golondrina* left Italy in November and went to Latin America for the summer there. In 1904, 10% of Italian migrants entering the United States had been there before. The aeroplane has made such seasonal migration from Italy to the Americas even more common.
7. Robert F. Forester. *The Italian Emigration of Our Times.* (Cambridge, Harvard, 1919) p. 416.
8. The best account of the politics and legislation of emigration is F. Manzotti, *La Polemica sull'emigrazione nell'Italia unita.* (Milano, 1969).
9. F. Nitti. "L'Emigrazione." pp. 305-307; Manzotti. *La Polemica*, pp. 69-76.
10. Dore. *La Democrazia italiana*, pp. 38-42.
11. *Reports and Abstracts of the Immigration Commission,* 41 volumes, Document No. 747 61st Congress: 3rd Session (Washington, 1911). Cited henceforth as the *Dillingham Commission.* The padrone system and the legislation directed against it are discussed in Volume II of the Abstracts, pp. 375-408. The Commission apparently felt that the system was so moribund by 1910 that it did not deserve a separate report. For a warning against the uncritical use of the Commission's Reports see O. Handlin. *Race and Nationality in American life,* N.Y., 1957.
12. C. Erickson. *American Industry and the European Immigrant, 1860-1885.* (Cambridge, Harvard, 1957) pp. 85-86.

13. H. Nelli. *Italians in Chicago, 1880-1930. A study in Ethnic Mobility.* (New York, 1970) pp. 55-87.

14. *Dillingham Commission.* II:419.

15. *Dillingham Commission.* I:26.

16. H. P. Fairchild. *Immigration.* (New York, 1913) pp. 148-149.

17. J. S. Macdonald. "Chain Migration, Ethnic Neighbourhood ⚬Formation and Social Network." *Millbank Memorial Fund Quarterly.* XLII (Jan. 1964) p. 82.

18. E. Banfield. *The Moral Bases of a Backward Society.* (New York, 1958). V. Y. McLaughlin. "Working Class Immigrant Families: First Generation Italians in Buffalo, New York". Paper delivered at Organization of American Historians (April, 1971) pp. 6-7 and 11-13.

19. A. Gramsci. *Sul Risorgimento.* (Roma, 1967) p. 103.

20. The term *negriere* (slave trader) was used by F. Nitti. "La Nuova Fase della emigrazione d'Italia" (1896) in *Scritti sulla questione meridionale* II:387. A Mosso. *Vita moderna degli italiani.* (Milan, 1906) uses the phrase "commercio di carne umana" p. 76.

21. Mosso. *Vita moderna,* pp. 77-78.

22. Quoted in Nitti. "L'Emigrazione" pp. 304-305.

23. See V. di Somma. "L'Emigrazione nel Mezzogiorno" *Nuova Antologia* (May, 1970) CXXIX:517.

24. Royal Decree of 1901 in *Dillingham Commission,* IV:211. On illiteracy rate see *Annuario Statistico* analysed in *Dillingham Commission* IV:186-187. The chief migrating areas of the Italian South - Abruzzi, Campania, Apulia, Basilicata, and Calabria) had about 60% male illiteracy and 80% female illiteracy. Illiteracy in Sicily was probably higher. Since emigrants came usually from the more rural parts of these areas, the rate of illiteracy among them was probably even higher.
V. di Somma. "L'Emigrazione" p. 514. "In 1905, in a commune of about 2000 people, of 22 inscribed for military service, only 2 presented themselves, all the others had emigrated."

25. J. S. Macdonald and L. Macdonald. "Italian Migration to Australia. Manifest Function of Bureaucracy versus Latent Function of Informal Networks." *Journal of Social History* (Spring 1967) p. 254.

26. A. di San Giuliano. "L'Emigrazione italiana negli Stati Uniti d'America" *Nuova Antologia* (July, 195?) CXVIII:89-91. See G. Verga. *I Malavoglia.*

27. Amy Bernardy. *Italia Randagia attraverso gli Stati Uniti.* (Torino, 1913) p. 313. However, H. P. Fairchild, *Greek Immigration in the United States* (New Haven, 1911) p. 222 suggests that the weight of remittances lowers the mortgage rate. In either case, the middle class receives its share.

28. Bernardy. *Italia Randagia,* p. 311; Fairchild. *Immigration,* p. 151.

29. Bernardy. *Italia Randagia,* p. 312.

30. G. Aliberti. "Profilo del Economia napoletana dell 'Unita al Fascismo" *Storia di Napoli* X. L. Fontana-Russo, "La Marina mercantile e l'emigrazione" *Rivista coloniale* (May-June, 1908). Foerster. *Italian Immigration.* pp. 467-468.

31. F. Benedetti. "Ia Strade ferrate della Basilicata e della Calabria" *Nuova Antologia* (June 1902) 183:500-512. This article describes the railroad development but sees no connexion with migration.

32. Mosso. *Vita moderna,* p. 114, and L. Bodio. "Del l'emigrazione italiana e della legge 31 gennaio 1901 per la tutela degli emigranti" *Nuova Antologia* (June, 1902) 183:533.

33. J. Isaac. *Economics of Migration* (London, 1947). p. 232.

34. Nelli. *Italians in Chicago.* p. 20. R. Vecoli. "Contadini in Chicago: A Critique of the Uprooted" *Journal of American History* (Dec. 1964) LI:3, pp. 408-409.

35. Foerster. *Italian Immigration,* p. 15 on emigrants; pp. 19-20 on repatriation. Isaac. *Economics of Migration,* p. 63 estimates a 40% return rate. Foerster points out the limits of the statistics which were based on passports issued and emigration from Italian ports plus LeHavre. Since passports were good for three years, three seasonal migrations as well as any illegal (draft-dodging) migration could go undetected. See also F. P. Cerase. "Nostalgia or Disenchantment: Considerations on Return Migration" in S. Tomasi and M. Engel (eds.) *The Italian Experience in the United States.* (Staten Island, 1970). See Ph.D. thesis on Italian repatriation and remittances written for NYU by Betty Boyd Caroli.

36. Mosso. *Vita moderna.* pp. 72-74; *Dillingham Commission,* I:26.

37. *Dillingham Commission.* II:427. Vol. 37, Chapter V of the Commission reports had a detailed analysis of Italian remittances and the practices of immigrant bankers. See esp. pp. 271-285. For Ellis Island statistics, the memoirs of the Commissioner E. Corsi. *In The Shadow of Liberty. The Chronicle of Ellis Island.* (New York, 1935), pp. 123-126.

38. Isaac. *Economics of Migration,* pp. 244-245; Bernardy. *Italia Randagia.* p. 314, and Mosso. *Vita moderna,* p. 114.

39. Foerster. *Italian Immigration,* p. 451.

40. A. di San Giuliano. "L'Emigrazione italiana", p. 91.

41. J. Macdonald and L. Macdonald. "Italian Migration to Australia, p. 257.

42. L. Iorizzo and S. Mondello. *The Italian Americans.* (New York, 1971) p. 143. The career is that of Thomas Marnell of Syracuse. The authors describe him as "a classic example of the small Italian businessman's struggle for economic and political power for himself and his people."

43. The mayor in G. di Lampedusa. *The Leopard* is an excellent example of a Sicilian *generetto.*

44. Bernardy. *Italia Randagia,* pp. 89-93, on new dialects.

45. *Dillingham Commission,* 37:211 and 311; on immigrant banks generally pp. 197-350.

46. The impressions of Toronto's Italian community in this part of the paper are drawn mainly from two sources. For eight years, students in my Italian history course at the University of Toronto have written one of their two term papers on "anonymous immigrant history" subjects. Palmacchio Di Iulio, pre-Law Student and Immigration Receiving Counselor at the Malton Airport, and Joseph Cornacchia, Law Student, helped in the interviewing of over a hundred first generation Toronto Italians.

47. For a scholarly example of this emphasis, see L. Tomasi. *The Italian American Family* (New York), 1972) p. 8.

48. O. Bressan. *Non Dateci Lenticchie. Esperieni, Commenti, Prospettive di Vita Italo-Canadase.* (Toronto, 1958) p. 26.

49. For the use of the term "caretakers" as dogooders see H. Gans. *The Urban Villagers. Group and Class in the life of Italian-Americans.* (New York, 1962) pp. 142-162. There is a list of Associazioni assistenziali e culturali in *Italo-Canadian Commercial Directory, 1971 (Metro Toronto)* (Toronto, 1971) p. 8.

50. Banfield. *The Moral Bases of a Backward Society,* p. 98.

51. *Italo-Canadian Commercial Directory,* pp. 50-51.

52. *Italo-Canadian Commercial Directory,* pp. 51 and 52: Compare these advertisement with the examples in *Dillingham Commission.* 37:340. Appendix VI.

53. Of a hundred people interviewed, 90% expected services 2 and 3 from a travel agent; about 70% expected service 4, and 40 to 60% expected the other services.
    To the migrant, the phrase "going to immigration" meant that the agent solved a problem or "arranged" a difficult case. The agents seemed to protect their role as mediators by affecting an air of mystery about the nature of such transactions.

AHR Forum

Social History as Lived and Written

JAMES A. HENRETTA

THERE ARE MANY PRACTITIONERS of the "new social history" in the United States, but few theorists or philosophers. No manifesto marked its advent, and no single handbook or work of scholarship decisively shaped its development. A few prescient observers—William O. Aydelotte, Lee Benson, Jesse Lemisch, and Robert F. Berkhofer, Jr., among others—have provided the new movement with some form and direction, but theoretical writings have been less important than substantive works of historical analysis.[1] Instruction has been by example, not by precept. Between 1961 and 1965 a number of European and American scholars published seminal works of social history, and graduate students and established academics in the United States quickly utilized the new insights and innovations in their own research.[2] The results are diverse and uneven, in part because of the decentralized institutional structure of American historical scholarship. Two trends are, however, readily apparent: (1) causal precision in the methods of quantitative research and (2) analytic expertise in the theories of the social sciences.

Earlier drafts of this paper were presented at a Newberry Library Conference sponsored by the Mathematical Scoocial Science Board of the National Science Foundation and at Livingston College, Rutgers University. The author wishes to thank members of those conferences and of graduate research seminars at Boston University and the University of California, Los Angeles, for their suggestions, and the following individuals for their written comments: John Gillis, Rhŷs Isaac, Peter Loewenberg, Daniel Scott Smith, Geoffrey Symcox, Richard Weiss, and especially Michael Merrill and Patricia Wilson.

[1] Aydelotte, "Quantification in History," *AHR*, 71 (1965–66): 803–25; Benson, *Toward the Scientific Study of History: Selected Essays of Lee Benson* (Philadelphia, 1972); Berkhofer, *A Behavioral Approach to Historical Analysis* (New York, 1969); and Lemisch, "The American Revolution Seen from the Bottom Up," in Barton J. Bernstein, ed., *Towards a New Past: Dissenting Essays in American History* (New York, 1968), 3–45.

[2] Philippe Ariès, *Centuries of Childhood: A Social History of Family Life*, trans. Robert Baldick (London, 1962); Lee Benson, *The Concept of Jacksonian Democracy: New York as a Test Case* (Princeton, 1961); Alfred H. Conrad and John R. Meyer, *The Economics of Slavery and Other Studies in Econometric History* (Chicago, 1964); Eric H. Erikson, *Childhood and Society* (2d ed., rev., New York, 1963); Robert W. Fogel, *Railroads and American Growth* (Baltimore, 1964); David V. Glass and D. E. C. Eversley, eds., *Population in History: Essays in Historical Demography* (Chicago, 1965); Peter Laslett, *The World We Have Lost: England before the Industrial Age* (New York, 1965); George Rudé, *The Crowd in History: A Study of Popular Disturbances in France and England, 1730–1848* (New York, 1964); Lawrence Stone, *The Crisis of the Aristocracy, 1558–1641* (Oxford, 1965); Stephan Thernstrom, *Poverty and Progress: Social Mobility in a Nineteenth-Century City* (Cambridge, Mass., 1964); E. P. Thompson, *The Making of the English Working Class* (London, 1964); and Charles Tilly, *The Vendée* (Cambridge, Mass., 1964). For a work published earlier, which became very influential during this period, see Stanley Elkins, *Slavery: A Problem in American Institutional and Intellectual Life* (Chicago, 1959).

1293

Precision and expertise for what? What is the "new social history"? The use of statistics? The adoption of concepts and the modes of argument of the social sciences? Are either of these approaches compatible with the traditional chronological emphasis of the discipline and with its venerable rhetorical mode of presentation? Beginning in the eighteenth century, Leo Braudy has suggested, "both novelists and historians sought to form time, to discover plot, and to give compelling and convincing narrative shape to the facts of human life." This admiration for a chronological form of presentation and a literary prose style and close attention to the values and motives of individual actors have come to constitute the dominant historiographical tradition in the United States. Most treatments of the American past, according to C. Vann Woodward, are "narrative, largely nonanalytical" accounts that are judged by the profession "according to old fashioned canons and values: thoroughness of research, objectivity of view, and clarity of logic, together with the lucidity and grace of the writing."[3]

Few of the new social historians have categorically rejected these standards, but their own work represents a fundamental reorientation of many of the traditional concerns of the discipline. Those historians with mathematical or logical skills—the "cliometricians"—have defined counterfactual propositions or hypotheses that can be tested and have then subjected historical data to elaborate statistical analyses. The research of these social science historians has thrown new light on patterns of congressional voting, the social correlates of political identity, and many aspects of economic development.[4] Other scholars have eschewed quantitative methods and have instead embraced the analytic approaches of contemporary social theorists. This interdisciplinary emphasis has been equally enlightening. Historians of the family have greatly expanded the dimensions and importance of their subject by exploiting theories derived from anthropology, demography, psychology, rural sociology, and labor economics. Scholars of urban history have likewise benefited from sociological approaches to stratification, geographical perspectives on building patterns, and architectural conceptions of urban esthetics.[5] While receptive to these statistical and theoretical techniques, another group of social historians has pursued a different goal: the resuscitation of the critical democratic scholarship of the Progressive era. By focusing on the lives of the vast majority of the American people, these authors have viewed the discipline "from the bottom up," exploring—indeed, in

[3] Braudy, *Narrative Form in History and Fiction* (Princeton, 1970), 3; and Woodward, "History and the Third Culture," *Journal of Contemporary History*, 3 (1968): 24, as quoted in David S. Landes and Charles Tilly, eds., *History as Social Science* (Englewood Cliffs, N.J., 1971), 35. Also see Gilbert Shapiro, "Prospects for a Scientific Social History," *Journal of Social History*, 10 (1976): 196–204.
[4] For a survey of some of this literature, see Van Beck Hall, "A Fond Farewell to Henry Adams: Ideas on Relating Political History to Social Change during the Early National Period," in James Kirby Martin, ed., *The Human Dimensions of Nation Making: Essays on Colonial and Revolutionary America* (Madison, Wisc., 1976), 323–71. For continuing discussions of method by these historians, see the *Historical Methods Newsletter* (1968–) and *Social Science History* (1976–).
[5] See, in particular, the articles and reviews published in the *Journal of Interdisciplinary History* (1970–). For some examples of this approach, see Tamara K. Hareven, ed., *Family and Kin in Urban Communities, 1700–1930* (New York, 1977); Thomas Bender, *Toward an Urban Vision: Ideas and Institutions in Nineteenth-Century America* (Lexington, Ky., 1975); and David Ward, *Cities and Immigrants: A Geography of Change in Nineteenth-Century America* (New York, 1971).

many cases, discovering—the historical behavior and consciousness of immigrant workers, blacks, Native Americans, and women.[6]

The multiplicity of aims and methods is clearly evident. The "new social history" in the United States does not resemble a coherent subdiscipline but rather a congeries of groups—cliometricians, interdisciplinary social theorists, and critically minded social democrats—with often complementary and sometimes contradictory approaches to historical scholarship. The diversity of substantive interests is less striking than the sharp lines of methodological cleavage. Is a historical statement "true" only if it meets the test of rigorous statistical proof? Can the determination of individual motivation be attempted without an explicitly stated and internally consistent psychological theory? Does the behavior of a social group that has left no written documents provide adequate evidence of its values and goals? These questions have profound interpretive significance, for they address the legitimacy of various modes of argument and the admissibility of different types of evidence. Many of the new social historians begin from contradictory epistemological premises, accept divergent standards of proof, and argue creatively only with those who share their assumptions—as the confused controversy over the character of black consciousness under slavery amply demonstrates. The alternative is not an agreed-upon epistemological prolegomenon (for that is a chimera) but rather an ongoing debate among American social historians that confronts these issues in a direct manner and a search for a philosophy of historical analysis that combines methodology, social theory, and political ideology.

This essay addresses these issues in four ways. First, an explication of two modes of European scholarship—the French *Annalistes* and the English Marxists—demonstrates the feasibility of coherent intellectual systems of historical inquiry. Second, this two-part discussion begins the task of defining the prime features of social history and sets the stage for the third section of the paper: an investigation of the epistemological assumptions of most historians born in the United States. The weaknesses of the American tradition of pragmatic analysis are stressed in some detail, but the emphasis falls finally upon the great strength of this approach—a phenomenological perspective that depicts the historical experience "as it was actually lived" by men and women in the past. Fourth, the argument concludes with a discussion of various modes of historical discourse and the presentation of an "action model," a rhetorical strategy and methodological synthesis designed to reconcile the divergent social scientific, interdisciplinary, and ideological tendencies of the "new social history" written in the United States during the past two decades.

"SOCIAL HISTORY IS NOT A PART OF HISTORY," the British scholar Harold J. Perkin has argued, but "all history from the social point of view." Eric J. Hobsbawm

[6] Lemisch, "The American Revolution Seen from the Bottom Up," 3–45; and Alfred F. Young, ed., *Dissent: Explorations in the History of American Radicalism* (DeKalb, Ill., 1968), and *The American Revolution: Explorations in the History of American Radicalism* (DeKalb, Ill., 1976). Also see the increasingly influential *Radical History Review* (1973–).

has concurred; because the "societal aspects of man's being cannot be separated, from other aspects of his being," social history consists of the holistic analysis of "specific units of people living together and definable in sociological terms." These definitions are instructive but limited, at least when viewed from across the English Channel. They focus, according to Richard T. Vann, on human aggregations, "churches, sects, social classes, village communities, and . . . the family" rather than on the geographic or environmental regions that form the "central subjects" of the *Annales* school of French historians.[7] Consider, for example, Fernand Braudel's minute attention to the seasonal rhythms of the Mediterranean world of the sixteenth century. All of the peace treaties dated from the winter months; conversely, "with summer's coming, war sprang to life in all its forms: land warfare, galley warfare, pirate attacks at sea, and brigand raids in the countryside." These regularities were clearly understood by contemporaries and often figured prominently in people's behavior. "The banks of Naples," Braudel pointed out, "regularly in winter months invested their clients' money in government bonds whereas in summer they used it to buy up the many agricultural products of the kingdom, a profitable speculation."[8] Such patterns of existence were pervasive; they impinged, however unequally, upon all of the social groups in the region.

This stress on the prime structural features of social, technological, and cultural life within a specific geographic environment defines the approach of Braudel and of other *Annalistes*. Indeed, their geographic and structuralist approach represents a distinct intellectual system, a conception of history that is at once a method, a subject matter, and an interpretation. "What is the philosophy of the *Annales* school?" Hugh R. Trevor-Roper asked in 1972. He isolated three interrelated elements. First, there was the use of quantification, "to reduce the area of incomprehension by rigorous statistical analyses." Second, the *Annalistes* sought "to grasp the totality" and "the vital cohesion of any historical period" by delineating all of its structures. Finally, these French historians inclined toward a "social determinism," a belief that "history is at least partially determined by forces which are external to men." As Braudel himself noted, the structures of history ("chains of small facts indefinitely repeated") live on "for so long that they become stable elements for an indefinite number of generations; they incumber history, they impede and thus control its flow."[9]

This intricate web of method, theory, and philosophy gives intellectual coherence to French social history, and a distinctive interpretive position emerges as a result of the definitions given to three terms: quantification, totality, and struc-

[7] Perkin, "Social History," in Fritz Stern, ed., *The Varieties of History: From Voltaire to the Present* (2d ed., New York, 1973), 433; Hobsbawm, "From Social History to the History of Society," in T. C. Smout and M. L. Flinn, eds., *Essays in Social History* (London, 1974), 5; and Vann, "The Rhetoric of Social History," *Journal of Social History*, 10 (1976): 222.

[8] Braudel, *The Mediterranean and the Mediterranean World in the Age of Philip II*, trans. Siân Reynolds, 2 vols. (New York, 1975), 1: 257, 266.

[9] Trevor-Roper, "Fernand Braudel, the *Annales*, and the *Mediterranean*," *Journal of Modern History*, 44 (1972): 466–71; and Braudel, *Capitalism and Material Life, 1400–1800*, trans. Miriam Kochan (New York, 1975), 442, and "History and the Social Sciences," in Peter Burke, ed., *Economy and Society in Early Modern Europe: Essays from* Annales (New York, 1972), 13, 17–18.

ture. The use of statistical methods by the *Annales* historians, Georg G. Iggers has suggested, proceeds from their attempt to comprehend the past in causal terms. This positivist approach reflects the influence of Emile Durkheim on Marc Bloch, one of the founders of the *Annales* school. Following the great social theorist, Bloch assumed that "society manifested itself in concrete forms which could be observed from the outside very much like the phenomena of nature."[10] Because of Bloch's profoundly historical orientation, however, this social scientific premise did not result in a search for statistical regularities or general historical laws. The prime concern of the early *Annalistes* was the unique character of past civilizations, and during the 1930s and 1940s most of the historians influenced by Bloch—and by Lucien Febvre—concentrated on a close examination of literary documents. Their goal was the discovery of the intellectual and psychological climate of an age, the *mentalité* of individuals and social groups. Only in the 1950s did quantification and heavy reliance on economic documents begin to take precedence, and by then the emphasis on traditional types of historical questions was well established. As a result, statistical expertise did not become an end in itself, the technical fetish that has distorted the focus of the work of some American cliometricians. Rather, the *Annalistes* subordinated the quantitative mode to their historical perspective, examining various aspects of the past in their own terms: the trade of Seville in the sixteenth century, the cycles of life, death, and subsistence in Beauvais between 1600 and 1730, the movement of agricultural prices on the eve of the French Revolution.[11]

If the later *Annalistes* successfully integrated chronology and quantification, they were unable to solve the problem of focus. The research of the early French social historians—of Bloch, Febvre, and their contemporaries—was innovative in its choice of subjects and wide in analytic scope. As J. H. Hexter has suggested, much of their scholarship fell under the rubric of *histoire problèm*. It demonstrated the "integral relationships among all facets of human existence" but did so within the comprehensible boundaries of a traditional monograph; the broad approach was balanced by a precise focus. Then, with the publication of Braudel's monumental treatise on *The Mediterranean and the Mediterranean World in the Age of Philip II* in 1949, both the scale of the analysis and its philosophical underpinnings changed dramatically. Braudel's appetite for the past (in "its largest lineaments and its most intimate details") was Gargantuan. And he translated this personal vision into a method, "a new kind of history, total history."[12] All aspects of life—from climate to topography to architecture, from popular culture to capitalist values to high art—were sketched in to create a comprehensive multidimensional Cubist portrait of the society. The superfluity of detail and the multiplicity of perspectives inhibit easy interpretation. The inherent diffuseness of *histoire totale* is apparent even to its advocates. "The more

[10] Iggers, *New Directions in European Historiography* (Middletown, Conn., 1975), 50, chap. 2 *passim*.
[11] Pierre Chaunu and Huguette Chaunu, *Seville et l'Atlantique: Partie Statistique*, 8 vols. (Paris, 1955–57), and *Seville et l'Atlantique: Partie Interpretive*, 4 vols. (Paris, 1959–60); Pierre Goubert, *Beauvais et le Beauvaisis de 1600 à 1730: Contribution à l'histoire sociale de la France du XVII* siècle* (Paris, 1960); and Ernest Labrousse, *La crise de l'economie française à la veille de la Révolution* (Paris, 1944).
[12] Hexter, "Fernand Braudel and the *Monde Braudellien* . . . ," *Journal of Modern History*, 44 (1972): 523, 537–38.

aspects you study," Theodore Zeldin has observed with respect to his own massive history of modern France, "the more specialization there is, and the more
life becomes a mass of 'factors' and 'influences' with no unifying theme."
Method shades imperceptibly into philosophy. The past consists of a chaotic
mass of facts and details, Zeldin concluded, "a vast number of permutations, the
divisions between men cutting across each other."[13]

Braudel did not embrace this stark empiricist position but instead sought pattern and meaning in the historical record itself. The positivist heritage of the
early *Annalistes* was undoubtedly an important reason for this choice but so, too,
was the growing importance of structuralist modes of analysis in French intellectual life. Ferdinand de Saussure, the influential early twentieth-century
philologist, demonstrated the crucial difference between *langue*, the basic system
of grammatical rules and conventions, and *parole*, the ordinary act of speech that
unconsciously (but unfailingly) embodies these norms. Subsequently, the eminent anthropologist Claude Lévi-Strauss proposed a similar analytic distinction
between "social relations," the data of the empirical reality of human life, and
"social structure," the "models which are built up after it." For de Saussure and
Lévi-Strauss the task of the scholar was to decode reality, to penetrate beneath
the complex surface of human existence to its basic structures.[14] Braudel proceeded to apply this analytic framework to the history of the vast Mediterranean world. Amid the diversity and sheer human chaos of his massive subject
the new dean of the *Annales* school isolated three distinct structures or "conceptions of time." The first and most basic was geographic or environmental time,
"those local, permanent, unchanging and much repeated features which are the
'constants' of Mediterranean history." These enduring patterns of settlement,
subsistence, and social relations were overlaid during the early modern period
by a "long duration" of specific institutions. Some of these formal organizations
and patterns (tax systems, technology, the incidence of disease and famine)
"barely moved in any significant way, from the fifteenth to the eighteenth century"; but there were also a number of medium-term trends or cycles in economic and social life, "conjunctures" such as the price inflation of the sixteenth
century and fluctuations in the rate of demographic change. Finally, Braudel
turned to the conception of time that gave prime attention to "the short term,
the individual, and the event," the political acts and diplomatic maneuvers that
were the subjects of traditional history. The last third of *The Mediterranean and the
Mediterranean World in the Age of Philip II* renders in great detail the political
struggles, dynastic wars, and personalities that dominated the historical surface
of the era. By delineating these three different structures of human life and activity, the great French historian hoped to make manifest their relationships: "to

---

[13] Zeldin, "Social History and Total History," *Journal of Social History*, 10 (1976): 243–44, 244.
[14] Lévi-Strauss, *Structural Anthropology*, trans. Claire Jacobson and Brook Grundfest Schoepf, 1 (New York,
1963): 279, chap. 15 *passim*. Also see de Saussure, *Course in General Linguistics*, ed. Charles Bally and Albert
Sechehaye, trans. Wade Baskin (New York, 1959); and Howard Gardner, *The Quest for Mind: Piaget, Lévi-
Strauss, and the Structuralist Movement* (New York, 1972).

acquaint the reader with their coexistence, the conflicts, and contradictions, and the richness of experience they hold."[15]

This impressive intellectual scheme contains two significant flaws. Although the concept of time-related structures assists historians in ordering the disparate data of social life, the simple three-fold classification is reductive. The categories cannot encompass the diversity and complexity of reality. As Braudel himself has now acknowledged, there are "many measures of time, . . . each of them attached to a particular history." If this revision obviates one major criticism and significantly increases the analytic precision of the structuralist approach, it also accentuates the second major methodological weakness. *The Mediterranean and the Mediterranean World in the Age of Philip II* does not demonstrate how the historian might link the various levels of reality, to tie "the durable phenemona of history with those that involve rapid change." The long chapter on the battle of Lepanto, for instance, takes the form of a traditional political and military narrative; Braudel has not directly specified how its causes or outcome were affected by the social and economic patterns minutely examined in the preceding four hundred pages. The three dimensions of existence—geographic, social, and political—are not interrelated but simply stand one beside the other, "each . . . itself an essay in general explanation."[16]

This failure to specify causal relationships is neither accidental nor peculiar to Braudel's scholarship; rather, it proceeds directly from the method. To interpret the world in structuralist terms is to contest the philosophical primacy of nineteenth-century notions of unilineal causation. The understanding of an event depends less on a comprehension of its antecedents than on an understanding of its position or function within an existing system. Structuralists adopt a "holistic" perspective, stressing the internal relationships among elements of a self-contained institution or world view. Thus, the controversial French intellectual Michel Foucault has rejected a "history" of ideas—in Arthur O. Lovejoy's sense of chronological transmission and essential continuity—in favor of an "archeology" of knowledge. For Foucault the past consists of separate strata or "epistemes," each with its own internally consistent paradigmatic vision. Certain concepts may be inherited from the past, but their significance is radically transformed by the new context of meaning; the study of antecedents gives way to an analysis of relationships. Although Foucault's dismissal of the intrinsic value of the discipline of history is extreme, it reveals the tension between a structuralist form of presentation and a chronological depiction of a causal sequence.[17] A graphic illustration of the implications of the structuralist approach appears in the organization of Robert Mandrou's stimulating *Introduction to Modern France,*

[15] Braudel, *The Mediterranean and the Mediterranean World in the Age of Philip II*, 2: 892–900, 1238–39, 1244, and *Capitalism and Material Life, 1400–1800*, x.

[16] Braudel, *The Mediterranean and the Mediterranean World in the Age of Philip II*, 2: 1238; and Hexter, "Fernand Braudel and the *Monde Braudellien*," 534.

[17] Foucault, *The Archeology of Knowledge*, trans. A. M. Sheridan Smith (New York, 1972), and *The Birth of the Clinic: An Archeology of Medical Perception*, trans. A. M. Sheridan Smith (New York, 1973). For an incisive explication and critique, see Hayden V. White, "Foucault Decoded: Notes from Underground," *History and Theory*, 12 (1973): 23–54.

1500–1640. Although Mandrou conceded that "the precariousness of material life or chronic malnutrition cannot be understood without reference to techniques of agricultural production, or to the system by which land revenues were distributed" and admitted "the great degree of artificiality" in relegating these topics to different parts of his book, he ultimately chooses to present his material in this causally unrelated manner. Like many other *Annalistes* Mandrou is primarily interested in the pattern of existence.[18] Seen in this context, Braudel's failure to link "event, conjuncture, and structure" is less an interpretive weakness than a distinctive feature of a national mode of intellectual discourse.

The structuralist method accounts as well for the sense of "determinism" that Trevor-Roper has detected in *Annales* history. Long-term patterns of stable relationships under the *Ancien Régime* are described by the French social historians both as empirical regularities and as reified constraints on human choice and action. "Man's whole life is restricted by an upper limit," Braudel declared at one point, a boundary which is "always difficult to reach and still more difficult to cross." This profoundly tragic view of man as "trapped in his former achievements for generations on end" has deeply influenced the outlook of other scholars. Pierre Goubert has written of the eternal cycle of famine and death in the pre-industrial world, while Emmanuel Le Roy Ladurie has emphasized both the limiting effects of climate on agricultural production and the prevalence of backward *mentalités,* the "invisible spiritual frontiers which constrained economic growth." The decisive role of consciousness has been fully developed by Mandrou, who has presented the history of France between 1500 and 1640 in terms of the "basic forces for solidarity," the constraining intellectual and institutional environment that "closely circumscribed everyday human activities within a web of tradition." Whether geographic, biological, or cultural, the structures of the *Annalistes* imprison the individual "within a destiny in which he himself has little hand." History reveals a record of forced accommodations, for every choice is made within the terms inherited from the past. As Braudel has concluded, "All efforts against the prevailing tide of history . . . are doomed to failure."[19]

The various French aspects of *histoire totale*—its tragic sense of existence, its emphasis on stability and continuity, and its diffuse structuralist treatment of causality—restrict its appeal and its range. The scholarly weight of the *Annalistes* remains anchored in the realities of the pre-industrial world, in the lives of human beings who "move within the strict confines of a physical space, obey impulses, and submit to barely visible forces of tradition." By contrast, many Anglo-American social historians are concerned with processes of change and conflict, with the political and economic revolutions of the post-1750 era. As

---

[18] Mandrou, *Introduction to Modern France, 1500–1640: An Essay in Historical Psychology,* trans. R. E. Hallmark (Paris, 1961, 1974; New York, 1976), 72, *passim.*

[19] Braudel, *Capitalism and Material Life, 1400–1800,* 25, ix; Le Roy Ladurie, *The Peasants of Languedoc,* trans. John Day (Urbana, Ill., 1974), 269; Mandrou, *Introduction to Modern France, 1500–1640,* 78; and Braudel, *The Mediterranean and the Mediterranean World in the Age of Philip II,* 2: 1244. Also see Goubert, *Beauvais et le Beauvaisis de 1600 à 1730;* and Le Roy Ladurie, *Times of Feast, Times of Famine: A History of Climate since the Year 1000,* trans. Barbara Bray (Garden City, N.Y., 1971).

Richard Mowery Andrews has astutely pointed out, the dominant philosophical assumptions of English Marxists and American liberals alike "have been vóluntarist—postulated on the notion that human will, moral and pragmatic, determines social and political realities."[20] Yet to stress regularity and structure is not necessarily to endorse a predictive determinism or to negate the existence of variation, contradiction, and conflict. Any "total" view of society will demonstrate the multiplicity of relationships and the diversity of cultural patterns. Choice takes place in the interstices of this social matrix, in a fashion suggested by the English structural anthropologist Frederick George Bailey. He has regarded the "structure" of the social environment "not so much as made up of relationships which are obligatory upon the various actors, but rather as imposing some kind of limit on possible action, while leaving within these limits an area of discretion and choice, which the actors can manipulate in order to achieve their ends."[21] Whatever the philosophic force of this apologia, the pessimistic bias of the *Annales* school cannot be ignored. Men and women act out their lives within the confines of a rigid system, and these structures of existence are often the real subjects of analysis—statistically plotted and totally explicated in a distinctly French rationalist tradition.

CONTEMPORARY MARXIST SCHOLARSHIP, like that of the French structuralists, begins from a positivist premise. "The subject matter of history," declared the French Marxist Pierre Vilar, "is structured and accessible to thought, is scientifically penetrable like any other sort of reality." As for the *Annalistes*, this epistemological position represents merely a single facet of a complex intellectual system. To adopt a Marxist perspective toward history is to acknowledge the essential validity of Marx's critique of the development of capitalism. This entails four propositions. The first analytic principle states that the productive system is of crucial importance in the life of a society, and the second asserts that the social relations of production are manifest in class divisions. The third Marxist axiom posits change and contradiction as fundamental features of social reality and explains historical change in terms of the dialectical process first specified by Hegel. The final proposition insists that capitalist social relations alienate men and women from both their labor and their inherent selves. This moral supposition justifies the methodology and defines its task. The Marxist scholar

---

[20] Andrews, "The Mediterranean," *New York Times*, May 18, 1975, sec. 7, p. 1. For a supplementary analysis, see Iggers, *New Directions in European Historiography*, 65–79. The work of the *Annales* school has been most influential among scholars of the pre-1750 period of American history. These historians have emphasized historical change to a greater extent than their French counterparts but have placed these alterations *within* the established structures of the world of pre-industrial agriculture. See Kenneth A. Lockridge, "Land, Population, and the Evolution of New England Society, 1630–1790," *Past & Present*, no. 39 (1968): 62–80, and *A New England Town: The First Hundred Years—Dedham, Massachusetts, 1636–1736* (New York, 1970); and Philip J. Greven, Jr., *Four Generations: Population, Land, and Family in Colonial Andover, Massachusetts* (Ithaca, N.Y., 1970).

[21] Bailey, *Tribe, Caste, and Nation: A Study of Political Activity and Political Change in Highland Orissa* (Manchester, 1960), 11–12. As H. Stuart Hughes has suggested, "Some such conviction of the inevitable limitations on human freedom—whether by physical circumstances or through emotional conditioning—has become the unstated major premise of contemporary social science"; Hughes, *Consciousness and Society: The Reorientation of European Social Thought, 1890–1930* (New York, 1958), 4.

must achieve a critical, theoretical understanding of the historical development of productive systems, class divisions, and the process of change so that the present social order can be comprehended and then transformed.[22]

Many American social historians categorically reject a Marxist theoretical approach while finding much to praise in the writings of such leading Marxists as Eugene D. Genovese, Christopher Hill, Eric J. Hobsbawm, and Edward P. Thompson. This paradox stems in part from the mistaken identification of Marxism with doctrinaire scholarship and a "vulgar materialist" approach to historical interpretation. Yet these Marxist authors differ significantly with respect to analytic emphasis and causal explanation. And, as their American readers have clearly recognized, the arguments of these scholars are not reductive in the least; their interpretations are based on a mass of empirical evidence and demonstrate a mastery of the extant primary documents.[23] Indeed, with respect to the charge of economic determinism, the antagonists have switched sides. Contemporary Marxists have accused the "new economic historians"—liberal American academics whose quantitative methods and causal reasoning have often assumed the primacy of economic motivation and market forces—of reductive scholarship, a criticism echoed by many non-Marxist writers.[24] Given this blurring of old ideological lines, it is necessary to explore the dimensions of recent Marxist historiography and to comprehend its approach to the historical process.

In an interesting explication of "Base and Superstructure" in Marxist theory, Raymond Williams has re-examined the traditional categories of Marxist analysis. He began by pointing out the limiting effects of "the language of determination and even more of determinism" that Marx inherited from theological arguments regarding free will. This heritage, Williams has suggested, accounts for the notions of "prefiguration, prediction, or control" in some of Marx's writings. Williams then advanced a concept of causal explanation derived from social experience rather than from religious or philosophical ratiocination, of forces or institutions "setting limits, exerting pressures" on human action.[25] He has also reassessed other terms. To speak of a cultural or ideational superstructure that "reflects" an economic or material base is to succumb to the anachronistic philosophic concepts and linguistic usages of the nineteenth century. "What is wrong with all questions about the relation of 'subjectivity' to the world," the Polish-born philosopher Leslek Kolakowski has argued in a related discussion of the etiology of knowledge, "is that we are not able to express them or answer

---

[22] Vilar, "Marxist History, a History in the Making: Towards a Dialogue with Althusser," *New Left Review*, 80 (1973): 66, as quoted in Iggers, *New Dimensions in European Historiography*, 144. For a concise statement of Marxist analytic principles, see E. J. Hobsbawm, "Karl Marx's Contribution to Historiography," in Robin Blackburn, ed., *Ideology in Social Science* (Bungay, 1972), 265–83.

[23] See, for example, Genovese, *Roll, Jordan, Roll: The World the Slaves Made* (New York, 1973); Hill, *The World Turned Upside Down: Radical Ideas during the English Revolution* (New York, 1972); Hobsbawm, *Primitive Rebels: Studies in Archaic Forms of Social Movement in the 19th and 20th Centuries* (New York, 1959); and Thompson, *The Making of the English Working Class*.

[24] Iggers, *New Dimensions in European Historiography*, 139, 165; and Michelle Perrot, "The Strengths and Weaknesses of French Social History," *Journal of Social History*, 10 (1976): 174.

[25] Williams, "Base and Superstructure in Marxist Cultural Theory," *New Left Review*, 82 (1973): 3–16.

them except with the help of spatial symbols, while we know that what matters are not topological relations." "Expressions like 'in the consciousness' . . .," Kolakowski concluded, "hinge necessarily on this spatial language, and they cannot get at the literal form."[26]

Recognizing these conceptual difficulties, Williams has proposed two solutions. The first alternative (and, in a philosophic sense, the more radical) renounces nineteenth-century notions of unilineal causality because of their inherent tendency to depict ideas as epiphenomena of social reality and substitutes a "theory of social totality." This holistic approach replaces the "formula of base and superstructure" with the "more active idea of a field of mutually if also unevenly determining forces." Thus, Williams has argued that

we have to revalue "determination" toward the setting of limits and the exertion of pressure, and away from a predicted, prefigured and controlled content. We have to revalue "superstructure" toward a related range of cultural practices, and away from a reflected, reproduced or specifically dependent content. And, crucially, we have to revalue "the base" away from the notion of a fixed economic or technological abstraction, and toward the specific activities of men in real social and economic relationships, containing fundamental contradictions and variations and therefore always in a state of dynamic process.[27]

This theoretical position has been elaborated, in various forms, by other Marxists. Antonio Gramsci has proposed "the notion of 'historic bloc,' in which the material forces are the content and ideologies the form—merely an analytical distinction since material forces would be historically inconceivable without form. . . ." As Martin Jay has explained with great precision, similar "analogical" solutions to the problem of the sociology of knowledge were devised by non-Marxists such as Karl Mannheim and the neo-Hegelian Marxists of the early Frankfurt School. This "totalistic view of cognition" implicitly underlies Williams's second, and more specific, alternative. The historian can retain the concepts of base and superstructure but focus on the point at which they intersect in people's lives. Through the process of "mediation," historical actors give cultural significance to their material existence; their condition constantly forces them to resolve the inherent contradictions between present circumstances and received wisdom.[28]

Ironically enough in view of its widespread identification with economic determinism, Marxist historiography invariably addresses this complex relationship between life and thought—the cognitive aspects of social action. Marxist scholars have stressed the "role of consciousness as an active factor in social

---

[26] Kolakowski, *Husserl and the Search for Certitude* (New Haven, 1975), 80–81. Following Henri Bergson, Kolakowski has argued that these difficulties constitute "a lasting feature of language itself"; *ibid.*, 81. For a similar analysis of Durkheim's conceptual and linguistic problems, see Hughes, *Consciousness and Society*, 283.

[27] Williams, "Base and Superstructure in Marxist Cultural Theory," 5–6. Williams has explored other implications of his position in the Introduction to Lucien Goldmann, *Racine*, trans. Alastair Hamilton (Cambridge, 1972), iii–xxii.

[28] Gramsci, *Il materialismo storico e la filosofia di Benedetto Croce: Opere*, 2 (Turin, 1949): 49, as quoted in Eugene D. Genovese, "Marxian Interpretations of the Slave South," in Bernstein, *Towards a New Past*, 98; Williams, "Base and Superstructure in Marxist Cultural Theory," 7, 10–11; and Jay, "The Frankfurt School's Critique of Karl Mannheim and the Sociology of Knowledge," *Telos*, 20 (1974): 72–89.

change" and have been in the forefront of the broader movement that Lawrence Stone described as "a new, more sophisticated, and subtle attempt to link
intellectual history with a social matrix." The distinct Marxist contribution to
this literature consists in the exploration of the values and political consciousness
of various oppressed social groups: black slaves in the United States, primitive
rebels in marginal economic regions of modern Europe, merchant seamen during the American War for Independence, millennial revolutionaries in seventeenth-century England, and the pre-industrial European crowd.[29]

This new methodological and interpretive perspective has transformed our
understanding of the process of social conflict during the transition to capitalism
in early modern Europe and America. To take one prominent example, E. P.
Thompson has demonstrated the existence of a definite set of social values
among many participants in the food riots that swept across eighteenth-century
England, a conception of a "moral economy" that informed their actions.
"Being hungry," Thompson has asked, "what do people do? How is their behavior modified by custom, culture, and reason?" His careful examination of
"the complexities of motive, behavior, and function" prompted him to reject a
narrow materialist interpretation of these uprisings as "a direct, spasmodic, irra-
tional response to hunger." Instead, he has argued that these actions of the
crowd were purposeful attempts to preserve the traditional notion of a "just
price" in an age of agricultural transition; bakers and grain merchants were often forced by public pressure to sell their goods at the "usual" price, rather than
at a level determined by the market forces of supply and demand. If a Marxist
perspective informs Thompson's account and enables him to see that these riots
represented a conflict between long-standing social values and the imperatives
of a new system of political economy, the interpretation is very much his own.
The struggle between the landless working classes and the capitalists who controlled the supply of food, he suggested, was fought out partially in cultural
terms, as a conflict between opposed conceptions of the ideal social order. "To
say that it was 'cultural' is not to say that it was immaterial, too fragile for analysis, insubstantial," Thompson argued, conducting an implicit dialogue with
more materialist-oriented Marxist scholars like Louis Althusser on the one hand
and with idealist symbolic anthropologists on the other. Rather, to say that the
conflict was "cultural" is to analyze the different modes of production in terms
of the consciousness of the historical actors themselves—as "images of power
and authority, the popular mentalities" of hegemony and resistance.[30]

[29] Iggers, *New Directions in European Historiography*, 152; and Stone, as recorded in "Dialogues: New Trends in
History," *Daedalus*, 98 (1969): 957. Also see Rudé, *The Crowd in History*; Jesse Lemisch, "Jack Tar in the Streets:
Merchant Seamen in the Politics of Revolutionary America," *William and Mary Quarterly*, 3d ser., 25
(1968): 371–407; and the works cited in note 23, above.

[30] Thompson, "The Moral Economy of the Crowd in Eighteenth-Century England," *Past & Present*, no. 50
(1971): 77–79, 135–36, and "Patrician Society, Plebian Culture," *Journal of Social History*, 7 (1974): 387. To ascertain the distinctiveness of Thompson's position, it is necessary only to compare the formulation of the
French Marxist Louis Althusser—"in its religious, ethical, legal, and political forms, etc., ideology is an objective reality; the ideological struggle is an organic part of the class struggle"—with that of Antonio Gramsci—
"revolutionary thought does not see time as a factor of progress. . . . To pass through one stage and advance to
another, it is enough that the first stage be realized in thought." Yet Gramsci's position is less Idealist than the
semiotic definition of culture advanced by the American symbolic anthropologist Clifford Geertz: "man is an

Manifest in Thompson's superb treatment of the behavior and values of the eighteenth-century English crowd is a distinct and coherent intellectual position. His theoretical understanding constantly informs his analysis and prompts him to examine certain types of social relationships: property, class, and power. Yet, like other contemporary Marxist scholars, Thompson has accepted the historical integrity of his data; they need not conform to a simple schema. "The general theory of historical materialism," Eric Hobsbawm has indicated, "requires only that there should be a succession of modes of production, though not necessarily any particular modes, and perhaps not in any particular predetermined order." Such formulations admit the complexity of a given historical situation while advancing two interpretive principles. The first proposition states that "the analytic base of any historical inquiry . . . must be the process of social production."[31] This position should not be confused with narrow materialism. "There is no excuse for identifying the economic origins of a social class with the developing nature of that class," Eugene Genovese has explained, for "every social class . . . [is] the product of a configuration of economic interests, a semi-autonomous culture, and a particular world outlook." All aspects of life form parts of a Marxist approach, but the disparate patterns of existence are subordinated to the basic configuration, "the way the given society maintains and transforms itself—its manner of social reproduction."[32]

An investigation of the modes of production necessarily involves a second major analytic concern: the isolation of the dominant system of relations within the society. There are many structures of belief and behavior, as the *Annalistes* correctly insist, but some are more important than others. "Historians," Hobsbawm declared, "will be tempted—and in my view rightly—to pick on one particular relation or relational complex . . . , and to group the rest of the treatment around it—for example Bloch's 'relations of interdependence' in his *Feudal Society*." As Hobsbawm's choice of illustration suggests, the quest for a central relational complex does not constitute a distinctively Marxist perspective but becomes so only when combined with an emphasis on the process of social production, the hierarchical arrangement of the structures of life and the distribution of authority within the society, and "the existence of internal contradictions within systems, of which class conflict is merely a special case."[33]

This concern with power and change clearly differentiates the Marxist analytic framework from that of the later *Annalistes*, with its static assumptions,

animal suspended in webs of significance he himself has spun." See Althusser, *For Marx*, trans. Ben Brewster (New York, 1969), 11–12; Gramsci, as quoted in Eugene D. Genovese, *In Red and Black: Marxian Explorations in Southern and Afro-American History* (New York, 1971), 393; and Geertz, *The Interpretation of Cultures* (New York, 1974), 5. Also see Iggers, *New Dimensions in European Historiography*, 165–71.

[31] Hobsbawm, "From Social History to the History of Society," 10, and *Pre-Capitalist Economic Foundations* (New York, 1965), 19–20, as quoted in Iggers, *New Dimensions in European Historiography*, 205 n. 35.

[32] Genovese, "Marxian Interpretations of the Slave South," 97, 98; and Lisa Vogel, "Rummaging through the Primitive Past: A Note on Family, Industrialization, and Capitalism," *Newberry Papers in Family and Community History*, no. 76-2 (1976): 1–2.

[33] Hobsbawm, "From Social History to the History of Society," 10–11, and "Karl Marx's Contribution to Historiography," 273–74. For a similar formulation, see Perry Anderson, *The Lineages of the Absolutist State* (London, 1974), 423.

causal diffuseness, and apolitical stance. Marxists not only specify economic and cultural structures but also relate them to one another and demonstrate patterns of confrontation among them. Most Marxists also restrict the scope of their research to an issue with a defined focus (the device of *histoire problème*), in part because they wish to emphasize the personal dimensions of historical experience. Many Marxist scholars approach their material with a moral perspective derived from the Romantic critique of capitalism and from the early, "humanistic" writings of Marx. This social philosophy portrays men and women as alienated from their inherent natures by forces that they cannot always control and depicts them as struggling valiantly, if often unsuccessfully, against the impact of historical developments that threaten their autonomy and their traditional way of life. However sober and realistic the analysis, the ideological message is optimistic: the world can be transformed by purposeful action. This precept applies to the present as well as the past, and imposes a duty upon the historian. Marxist scholarship seeks to transcend the often sterile limits of scientific "objectivity," to infuse historical writing itself with values, and to discuss the morality as well as the actuality of past events. As Thompson has argued, the historian must first determine the "values *actually held* by those who lived" through an epoch of the past and then must make "some judgment of value upon the whole process."[34] Manifest in Thompson's work and in that of many other Marxist scholars is a critical methodology and a moral purpose that American social historians might well emulate.

THE RELUCTANCE OF HISTORIANS born and trained in the United States to accept the analytic systems formulated by Marxists, *Annalistes*, and other European social theorists proceeds in part from the very different historical experiences of the various groups of intellectuals. "Braudel's post-voluntarist and post-imperial vision," Richard Andrews has pointed out, reflects the influence of "a culture that has finally assimilated the failure of its imperial ambitions and its positivistic optimisms." Whatever the nagging political doubts and philosophical uncertainties characteristic of American academe, this profound sense of the restricted limits of human endeavor is largely absent; as C. Vann Woodward has indicated, only southern-born Americans have personally participated in the common European experience of decades of intractable social conflicts and of crushing military defeat. If the relative national success of the United States inhibits its intellectuals from adopting the tragic vision of the *Annalistes*, then the absence of a viable working-class socialist movement has discouraged the development of a strong Marxist historiographic tradition. The predominance of bourgeois parties and values in twentieth-century American politics, Eugene Genovese has

---

[34] Thompson, *The Making of the English Working Class*, 444. John Higham has likewise urged historians to take a critical stance, "to assume an active responsibility both to a phase of the past and to a contemporary public, and to engage one with the other"; Higham, "Beyond Consensus: The Historian as Moral Critic," *AHR*, 67 (1961–62): 609–25. Also see Perkin, "Social History," 441; and E. P. Thompson's "Postscript: 1976" to his *William Morris: Romantic to Revolutionary* (1955; New York, 1977), esp. 790–807.

suggested, encouraged politically minded academics to neglect "class forces and the process of capitalist development in favor of . . . the glorification of the Jefferson-Jackson-Roosevelt liberal tradition. . . ."[35]

These political realities found expression in intense ideological debates, especially during the period of the Cold War. The military confrontation between the socialist states and the capitalist nations produced an analogous conflict within the American historical profession. The validity of Marxism as an intellectual system was the crucial point at issue in this academic debate. "The way social change in fact took place is something we may find out by *using* our framework," J. H. Hexter proclaimed some two decades ago in a candid polemical attack on Marxist historiography; "it is not and *ought not be* something to be found *in* the framework."[36] Whatever its political motivation, Hexter's argument effectively rebutted reductionist scholarship in general and a "vulgar materialist" economic approach in particular; but contemporary Marxism is largely immune from such intellectual shortcomings. Of greater importance here is the legitimacy of Hexter's implied "empiricist" alternative to the Marxist framework. Serious epistemological questions immediately arise. Most American-born historians have silently imbibed a pragmatic philosophical perspective from their culture. They accept the primacy of sense perception and attempt to establish the "facts" in a "spirit of neutral, passive detachment." Their approach assumes a correspondence theory of truth; the relations among the empirical data are thought to be as real and as immediately apparent to the historian as the facts themselves. These are dubious propositions. As the philosopher of science Carl Hempel has pointed out, broad agreement exists among mid-twentieth-century philosophers that even "scientific hypotheses and theories are not derived from observed facts, but invented to account for them."[37] Thus, there is no ontological certainty that the external world corresponds to the models created by the scientist—or by the historian. Hexter's empiricist framework is, therefore, just as much of an intellectual invention as that proposed by a Marxist or, for that matter, the structuralist frames of reference preferred by de Saussure, Lévi-Strauss, and Braudel or the paradigmatic formulas of Michel Foucault and Thomas Kuhn. Any model that is "used" has certain assumptions about the nature of reality embodied "in" it.

Yet important differences do exist between the pragmatic empiricist position endorsed by Hexter and the epistemological assumptions underlying the European intellectual traditions of Marxism and structuralism. The latter are rationalist philosophies; they elevate the power of human reason and exalt its critical

[35] Andrews, "The Mediterranean," 44–45; Woodward, "The Irony of Southern History," in his *The Burden of Southern History* (Baton Rouge, 1960), 167–91; and Genovese, "Marxian Interpretations of the Slave South," 91.
[36] Hexter, "A New Framework for Social History," in his *Reappraisals in History: New Views on History and Society in Early Modern Europe* (London, 1961), 16.
[37] Cushing Strout, *The Pragmatic Revolt in American History: Carl Becker and Charles Beard* (New Haven, 1958), 8; and Hempel, *The Philosophy of the Natural Sciences* (Englewood Cliffs, N.J., 1966), 15, as quoted in Iggers, *New Dimensions in European Historiography*, 6. Also see Hughes, *Consciousness and Society*, 183–87; Harriet Gilliam, "The Dialectics of Realism and Idealism in Modern Historiographic Theory," *History and Theory*, 15 (1976): 231–56; and Thomas S. Kuhn, *The Structure of Scientific Revolutions* (Chicago, 1970), 111–35, 167–70.

function, while contesting the primacy of mere facts. Hence, Lévi-Strauss has attacked the "empirical and naturalistic" procedures of the eminent English anthropologist A. R. Radcliffe-Brown and has disputed his ability to understand the "social structure" of a community from an examination of its pattern of social relationships. "The term 'social structure,'" Lévi-Strauss asserted, "has nothing to do with empirical reality but with models which are built up after it." Similar rationalist postulates form the philosophical foundations of Marxism. As Stuart Hall has pointed out, Marx rejected a correspondence theory of truth; for, "if things were synonymous with their surface appearances, there would be no need for science."[38] Thus, when American-born historians raise the "facts" to a position of ultimate authority, they assume a distinct epistemological postion—an empiricist approach based on three interrelated propositions: that human reason has limited power to understand the world; that models or frameworks can comprehend only the immediate data to which they apply; and that there are no fundamental patterns or structures of human life. These premises lead directly to the conclusion that each historical case has to be treated on its own, as a unique constellation of specific conditions or events. The most general result that can be obtained is an "hypothesis," but this must be "tested" with respect to each new case. The "facts" remain supreme.

This inbred pragmatic American approach to historical reality is gradually being eroded by the subtle pressures exerted by various theoretical systems. The "functionalist" social theory of Talcott Parsons, for example, has deeply influenced the thinking of many social historians in the United States. Parsons' scholarship embodies an anti-empiricist bias, for it assumes the existence of systematic relations in the world of social reality. The social systems specified by Parsons possess three general properties and propensities: "the interdependence of parts or variables . . . , *order* in the relationship among the components . . . [, and] a tendency to self-maintenance, which is generally expressed in the concept of equilibrium." The psychoanalytic principles originally elaborated by Sigmund Freud and increasingly employed by American academics likewise stress the importance of fundamental patterns in human life and the ability of the disciplined mind to comprehend them. There are many schools of psychoanalytic thought, but each posits a relationship between childhood experience and adult action that is not immediately apparent from naive empirical observation. The trained psychoanalyst maintains the validity of the general theoretical system—while attempting to understand its unique manifestation in the particular case—even in the face of the patient's explicit denial of the suggested linkages between present behavior and the emotional trials of early childhood. The *Annalistes* and the Marxists use their social theories in a similar fashion—to probe behind the surface of events to achieve a more convincing explanation of reality than that afforded by an empiricist approach. In the end, each mode of analysis stands or falls by the degree to which it meets the test of the "reality rule," a more con-

---

[38] Lévi-Strauss, *Structural Anthropology*, 279; and Hall, "Marxism and Culture," *Radical History Review*, 18 (1978): 12.

vincing Hexter guideline: "the best and most likely story that can be sustained by the relevant extrinsic evidence."[39] This criterion cannot be satisfied simply by ascertaining the "facts," for the point at issue is the explanatory scheme that penetrates to the heart of their reality. This problem demands discussion and debate; it cannot be resolved by the a priori exclusion of Marxism or any other rationalist social theory.

Although the pragmatic tradition has narrowed the critical scope and interpretive range of American historical analysis, it has produced a number of significant methodological approaches to the study of the past. In particular, this empiricist perspective has encouraged the careful examination of the personal experiences of historical actors—their values, goals, and behavior. This focus on the details of existence and people's perception of them constitutes a crucial aspect of the discipline of social history, for it is within the inchoate world of everyday life—the matrix of half-seen and imperfectly grasped objective structures—that men and women seek to interpret reality and to affect it. How do historical actors comprehend the flux of daily existence? How can the observer reconstruct their subjective world-views? These questions move us on to new terrain. The shape of the objective contours of the cultural landscape—its structures, productive modes, and hierarchies of power—diminish in importance. The subjective dimensions of human experience take precedence. Given the complexity of the social world, how do individuals formulate and then seek to attain their goals?

"Most men are philosophers," the Italian Marxist Antonio Gramsci once suggested, " in as much as they operate on the practical level and in their practice (in the controlling pattern of their conduct) have a conception of the world, a philosophy that is implicit." This perceptive remark to the contrary, the systematic examination of the significance of the ordinary behavior of individuals has its strongest theoretical roots not in Marxism but in American pragmatic philosophy. "The meaning of an intellectual conception," Charles S. Peirce insisted, resides in the "practical consequences [that] might conceivably result by necessity from the truth of that conception." The pragmatism of Peirce and of William James embodied a phenomenological theory of human knowledge; as subsequently developed by the German philosopher Edmund Husserl, this epistemology takes as its point of departure the "pure phenomena" of the individual's act of "perceiving, judging, experiencing, and willing." This cognitive approach to human reality finds contemporary expression in the ethnographic methods and goals of many American anthropologists. Two of the central tasks of anthropology, Clifford Geertz has asserted, are the comprehension of the "subjective" mental worlds of the members of a social group and the elucidation of the "system of ideas ... immanent in every overt process of human action."[40] A similar phenome-

[39] Parsons, *Social System* (New York, 1951), as cited in Berkhofer, *A Behavioral Approach to Historical Analysis*, 183–85; and J. H. Hexter, "The Rhetoric of History," *History and Theory*, 6 (1967): 5, reprinted in his *Doing History* (Bloomington, Ind., 1971), 19.
[40] Gramsci, *Il materialismo storico e la filosofia di Benedetto Croce*, 96, as quoted in Gwynn A. Williams, "Gramsci's Concept of Egemonia," *Journal of the History of Ideas*, 21 (1960): 590, 586–99; Peirce, *Collected Papers of*

nological perspective informs the historical scholarship of Herbert G. Gutman. Gutman's perceptive and sympathetic studies of American workers and of Afro-Americans are presented, in nearly overwhelming detail, through first-person accounts. Quotations from a myriad of documentary sources—diaries, letters, songs, sermons, speeches, and newspapers—tell the story from the inside, from the perspective of the historical actors. Although he provides a coherent picture of the objective realities of class positions and social authority, Gutman's primary concern is not with structures of power but with the inherent value of the lives of the people who inhabit them. His main goal remains the depiction of the traditions, experiences, and struggles of those who inhabited the past—their own conception of the world in which they lived.[41]

The study of "collective mentality" by the important French social historian Robert Mandrou reflects somewhat similar analytic principles. Mandrou's methodology involves both a close examination of written documents that reflect the actors' conceptions of reality and a careful assessment of the cultural and psychological impact of the objective structures of existence: What states of mind and of feeling, for instance, might appear in a society with a high rate of mortality and a low level of agricultural production? How might these be molded or distorted by the theological doctrines propagated by the dominant religious institutions of the culture? Mandrou's hypotheses are stimulating, in part because of their precise formulation, for he has separated "the elements prevailing throughout French society" during the sixteenth century (hypersensitivity of temperament, social aggressiveness, and a feeling of impotence in relation to the natural world) from the "differential mental structures" of distinct groups; "each social class—as also each profession or even religious group—had its characteristic outlook."[42]

These attempts by cognitive anthropologists and phenomenologically inclined historians to comprehend the consciousness of individuals and social groups are replete with difficulty. One French critic points to the "disconcerting ease" with which historians of *mentalité* move from an analysis of social behavior to the depiction of the ideas or the mental states that behavior is alleged to indicate. These problems are particularly acute with respect to those nonelite members of the population who left few written records. Even the availability of first-hand accounts does not resolve the problem of interpretation, for the historian (unlike the anthropologist) cannot verify a hypothesis by talking to living informants. The "thick description" of a culturally significant episode—the intensive method of presentation that Geertz prescribed for anthropologists and that Gutman intuitively employed—obviates some of these criticisms. Still, im-

---

Charles Sanders Peirce, ed. Charles Hartshorne and Paul Weiss, 5 (Cambridge, Mass., 1935): 6; Kolakowski, *Husserl and the Search for Certitude*, 37, 69; and Geertz, *The Social History of an Indonesian Town* (Cambridge, Mass., 1965), 141. Also see William James, *Pragmatism and Other Essays*, ed. Joseph L. Blau (New York, 1963), 23–24, 92–93; and Raymond Williams's Introduction to Goldmann, *Racine*, xvi–xviii.

[41] Gutman, *Work, Culture, and Society in Industrializing America: Essays in American Working-Class and Social History* (New York, 1976), and *The Black Family in Slavery and Freedom, 1750–1925* (New York, 1976).

[42] Mandrou, *Introduction to Modern France, 1500–1640*, 236–42.

portant conceptual problems confront the historian who wishes to present a phenomenological portrait of a complex nontribal society. Nonlocal or specialized institutions (such as a banking system) often cannot be depicted subjectively, because their scope extends beyond the experience of most individuals in a society.[43] This deficiency can be offset, at least in part, by the anthropological technique of using different informants or documentary sources to construct a comprehensive picture of the social world. No individual or group sees the cultural landscape as a whole, but a mosaiclike tableau can be pieced together from the various perspectives.

The innovative scholarship of Clifford Geertz is instructive in this regard. In his *Social History of an Indonesian Town* Geertz constructed a "cultural paradigm," a symbolic structure that encompasses "the main conceptual categories in terms of which the inhabitants of the Modjokuto of 1952–1954 themselves perceived their society—of the principles of social grouping they used, the manner in which they regarded those principles to be interrelated, and the qualitative characteristics in terms of which they assigned concrete individuals to particular groupings." According to Geertz, his description represented a "realistic classification of the primary blocks of the regional social system" and embodied Javanese perceptions. The symbolic model was "phenomenologically real . . . despite the fact that no single Modjokutan could present it . . . as a system."[44] Such cultural paradigms, though created by the anthropologist, are recognized as substantially correct by various members of the society—at least insofar as these models accord with their own experience. By clarifying the prime features of a complex reality, these symbolic syntheses broaden the interpretive scope of a phenomenological approach. The distanced, composite conceptions of the social analyst are very different from those of any single actor, but the vantage point is much the same. The society is presented from the inside, as subjective experience.

Geertz devised a cultural paradigm that was "phenomenologically real" to more than a single individual to avoid the dangers inherent in phenomenology: its subjective emphasis and idealist assumptions. In a less symbolic manner Pierre Bourdieu resolved similar epistemological problems in a fine study of the marriage strategies of the peasants of Béarn, a remote area of the Pyrenees. On the basis of careful documentary research and extensive questioning, the French anthropologist argued that these land-owning families have always acted purposefully "to safeguard the essential at all times" and that their main goals were culturally defined as the maintenance of the family line on an economically viable landed estate. Like the concept of "moral economy" held by the eigh-

---

[43] Perrot, "The Strengths and Weaknesses of French Social History," 171; Geertz, *The Interpretation of Cultures*, chap. 1; Julian H. Steward, *Theory of Cultural Change: The Methodology of Multilinear Evolution* (Urbana, Ill., 1955), 46–55; and Hobsbawm, "From Social History to the History of Society," 16.

[44] Geertz, *The Social History of an Indonesian Town*, 121, 141, 119–50 in general. For a philosophical explication and defense of this approach, see Peter L. Berger and Thomas Luckmann, *The Social Construction of Reality: A Treatise in the Sociology of Knowledge* (New York, 1966). And, for two attempts to relate these theoretical premises to historical study, see Richard R. Beeman, "Community in Colonial America," *American Quarterly*, 29 (1977): 422–43; and Harry S. Stout, "Culture, Structure, and the 'New' History: A Critique and an Agenda," *Computers and the Humanities*, 9 (1975): 216–29.

teenth-century English laborers whom Thompson studied, these commitments to the lineage and the patrimony reflected long-standing values, "the whole sys* tem of predispositions inculcated by the material circumstances of life and by family upbringing." Parents undertook a "concerted effort at indoctrination and cultural reproduction" so that the children might understand that "the land belongs to the eldest son and that the eldest son belongs to the land."[45] To those born into this rural culture, the principle of primogeniture was experienced as an orally transmitted value and as a visually perceived occurrence. By precept and by example each adult generation taught its successor that the land inherits its heir.

If the objectives were clear, the process by which they were realized was not. Each peasant family was locked in a situation that it could affect but not control. Parents confronted the vagaries of fertility and mortality; they could not ensure that the first- or second-born child would be male, would survive the diseases of childhood, or would have the requisite physical strength and financial cunning to manage the property. Nor could they determine the level of prices for their agricultural products or the regional demand for wage labor. Most important of all, the parents could not affect the availability of suitable marriage partners for their children. Yet all of these factors (as well as their own health) influenced their ability to achieve their goals. Because reality was so complex and unpredictable, these peasants had no recourse to fixed or immutable rules of conduct—to a blind implementation of legal rules or cultural norms governing the inheritance of property. Were they therefore completely at the mercy of the accidents of fertility and translocal historical forces? Were their lives bereft of personal control and cultural direction?

The implications of Bourdieu's answers to these questions transcend the substantive points at issue, for his analysis demonstrates the existence of purposeful action within the bounds of rigid cultural structures. The decisions made by the peasants of Béarn, Bourdieu has suggested, indicate that they had a "system of schemes" for achieving their goals amid the contingencies of the world. Their marriage priorities were crucial in this respect. Their strategies were not explicitly or coherently articulated, but they can be seen upon close inspection to have been "rooted in a small number of implicit principles": the primacy, most importantly, of men over women and of the eldest over all younger siblings. Thus, younger sons were often discouraged from marrying so that their labor could be utilized on the family holding. A family overburdened with daughters usually attempted to marry them off to less affluent partners, in order to minimize the amount of the dowry (*adot*). Conversely, parents contemplated a socially "upward" marriage for the eldest son but consummated it only under certain circumstances—the arrival of a high-status bride sometimes threatened the "principle of male pre-eminence" within the household and endangered the standing

---

[45] Bourdieu, "Marriage Strategies as Strategies of Social Reproduction," in Robert Forster and Orest Ranum, eds., *Family and Society: Selections from* Annales (Baltimore, 1975), 119, 118, 129–30. For the explication of a philosophical position very similar to that underlying Bourdieu's analysis, see James Miller, "Merleau-Ponty's Marxism: Between Phenomenology and the Hegelian Absolute," *History and Theory*, 15 (1976): 109–31.

of the male lineage in the community. The advantageous marriage of a son also increased the risk of subsequent disaster, since the dowry had to be repaid in full if the husband died before an heir was born. Given the wide variety of circumstances and considerations, it is impossible for the outside observer to predict how a given family would act on a particular occasion. Yet the decisions of these rural cultivators had an internal logic when seen in relation to "the entire *matrimonial history* of the family." Seen from the inside—from a phenomenological perspective—their strategies were "the product of *habitus*, meaning the practical mastery of a small number of implicit principles that have spawned an infinite number of practices."[46]

This conceptualization constitutes an important contribution to the definition of the process of social persistence and social change. For Bourdieu, *habitus* means an action-oriented world-view that furnishes "the basis for the casuistic thinking required to safeguard the essential at all times." It comprises both the productive mode of this French rural culture and the flexible and contradiction-ridden process by which it has been perpetuated and altered. Since the peasant's *mentalité* has been "the product of the very structures" it has tended to reproduce, it has embodied elements of stasis and tradition. A dynamic, creative aspect has also been present, for the hard-pressed cultivator has continually had to resolve the tensions created by changing social and economic circumstances.[47] Like the young, nineteenth-century rural women studied by Louise A. Tilly and Joan Scott (girls who took jobs in urban and industrial settings in order to continue to contribute to the traditional "family economy"), Bourdieu's peasants were neither prisoners of the past nor masters of the contemporary environment. Rather, they have behaved as active agents seeking by one means or another to cope with an emergent reality. Their goals have been at least partially manifested in their rules of behavior, their pragmatic "system of schemes." This matrix of strategies has constituted their "implicit philosophy" in Gramsci's sense of the term. The peasants' world-view has been at once their conception of life and the system of social and productive relationships that have sustained it, a *Weltanschauung* anchored in reality and phenomenologically real to the actors.[48]

For American social historians, Bourdieu's conceptualization of human agency and social process represents an attractive synthesis of the dominant pragmatic and voluntarist tradition of their native culture and the rationalist European intellectual systems of structuralism and Marxism. The limiting structures of the inherited past—its settled institutions, habitual practices, and constricting ideologies—form an integral part of the analytic framework, but these structures do not predominate. Equal importance is accorded to the con-

[46] Bourdieu, "Marriage Strategies as Strategies of Social Reproduction," 119, 134, 136, 141, *passim.*

[47] *Ibid.,* 119, 141. Compare Bourdieu's argument with that advanced by the intellectual historian J. G. A. Pocock: "Every society possesses a philosophy of history—a set of ideas about what happens, what can be known and done . . . which is intimately a part of its consciousness and functioning. . . . The concepts which we form from, and feed back into, tradition have the capacity to modify the content and character of the tradition conceptualized . . ."; Pocock, *Politics, Language, and Time: Essays on Political Thought and History* (New York, 1971), 233, 235.

[48] Tilly and Scott, "Women's Life and Work in Nineteenth-Century Europe," *Comparative Studies in Society and History,* 17 (1975): 36–64.

flicts inherent in the modes of social reproduction and the dialectical process by which they are resolved. Finally, these objective structures and conflicts are subordinated to the subjective experiences of the historical actors; their "lifeworlds" stand in the foreground. Bourdieu's phenomenological approach demonstrates the ability of men and women to shape their own lives, however narrow and restrictive the bounds of the cultural environment. This stress on human agency among modest tillers of the soil should have an especial appeal to historians in the United States. In a society formally committed to the democratic ideals of liberty and equality, the ultimate test of a historical method must be its capacity to depict the experiences of all members of the culture and to comprehend the ability of all individuals in the culture to make their own history.[49]

WHAT TYPE OF LITERARY PRESENTATION is implied by a methodology that seeks to determine the objective structures of existence, to define the hierarchical relations among them, and to depict the experiences of historical actors from a phenomenological perspective? Both the mode of argument in a work of history and its prose style affect the substantive content and thereby influence its intellectual or emotional impression on the reader. Carl Schorske has called attention to "the impact of a book's mental structure . . . , its grammar—the way it gives plausibility to the empirical materials and the tightness of its articulation." Like any other form of written endeavor, a social history must attain the appropriate synthesis of substance, argument, and style. The rhetoric of a work of scholarship, for example, often reflects the methodological preferences of the author. "A social structure can be described without any reference whatsoever to particular individuals and without the use of specific cases," F. G. Bailey has noted in this regard, and "a description of this kind, if well done, makes a strong appeal to the intellect; it is elegant, sparing in detail, rounded and complete, and has a sharp, tidy, thoroughly 'scientific' exactness." Bailey's objection to this "work of logic" proceeds less from esthetic than from interpretive principles; such neat and self-contained models of social equilibrium cannot easily explain "the dynamic aspects of social life: growth, conflict and transformation."[50] An equally serious criticism relates to the reductive features of such an account. By systematically excluding the ambiguities of individual existence, it fails to convey the full emotional complexity of the historical situation. What is the value of a social history that primarily demonstrates the conceptual skills of the author and eliminates the contradictions inherent in the lives of the actors—many of which can be depicted only by a more biographical form of presentation?

This question raises important issues of method and is best approached

---

[49] In following Jesse Lemisch's admonition to "study the conduct and ideology of the people on the bottom" of society and thus to "make the inarticulate speak," it is also crucial to heed his advice to "continue to examine the elite" in order to assess its critical role in the historical process; "The American Revolution Seen from the Bottom Up," 6.

[50] Schorske, as quoted in "New Trends in History," 955; and Bailey, *Tribe, Caste, and Nation*, 14.

through a consideration of the epistemological categories devised by Louis O. Mink. Mink has distinguished three "modes of comprehension" by which the human mind orders and assimilates the "data of sensation, memory, and imagination": the theoretical, the categoreal, and the configurational.[51] These abstract terms, which Mink derived from the disciplines of mathematics, philosophy, and literature, refer in effect to three distinct approaches to the writing of social history. These divisions are similar to, but not identical with, the three paths taken by the practitioners of the "new social history" in the United States. Some authors employ quantitative techniques, seeking—in Mink's terms—a theoretical understanding of human reality. Others instinctively conceptualize their data, creating categories of social groups and types of historical behavior. Finally, still other historians rely on a narrative framework as a prime analytic device, assuming that meaning will emerge from a close description of the chronological process. Each of these modes of understanding—quantitative, conceptual, and narrative—has certain strengths and weaknesses that, upon examination, reveal the necessity of a composite rhetorical mode of presentation, an "action model," that offers one means of reconciling the competing organizational priorities of chronology and analysis. This "action model" also addresses the relationship between the rhetoric of a work of history and its interpretive assumptions. In a manner similar to Bourdieu's concept of *habitus*, the "action model" focuses attention on the importance of human agency even as it depicts the limiting forms, structures, and geographies of the historical context.

Quantification holds great appeal for many historians working in the American pragmatic tradition because of its resemblance to the empiricism of nineteenth-century science. The analysis of empirical data with statistical methods supposedly produces results that are precise and value free. Neither assumption is completely warranted. Quantification achieves incontestable interpretive conclusions only in restricted areas of research—those dealing with established institutional systems, clearly defined rules of behavior, or a small number of discrete variables. Legislative voting has been analyzed with considerable success because of its narrow context, while broader studies of the socioeconomic correlates of membership in a political party have been much less convincing. A second methodological shortcoming is equally important. Despite its apparently scientific character, quantification does not necessarily yield an objective view of human reality. Consider the study of "social mobility," an area of intense research in the United States during the past fifteen years.[52] The quest for home ownership by working-class immigrant families has not been interpreted, for the most part, in "traditionalist" terms—as the parents' attempt to provide security for themselves during old age or to root the old lineage firmly in the soil of the

---

[51] Mink, "History and Fiction as Modes of Comprehension," *New Literary History*, 1 (1969–70): 547–49, *passim.* The following argument relies heavily on the categories and reasoning expounded in this fine article..

[52] See, for example, Jackson T. Main, *The Social Structure of Revolutionary America* (Princeton, 1965); Stephan Thernstrom, *The Other Bostonians: Poverty and Progress in the American Metropolis, 1880–1970* (Cambridge, Mass., 1973), and *Poverty and Progress: Social Mobility in a Nineteenth-Century City*; and Edward Pessen, *Riches, Class, and Power before the Civil War* (Lexington, Mass., 1973), and Pessen, ed., *Three Centuries of Social Mobility in America* (Lexington, Mass., 1974).

New World. Rather, the purchase of a house has usually been viewed from a "liberal" perspective, as the achievement of the individual male laborer in his effort to "get ahead." Since both interpretations are consistent with much of the quantitative evidence, the perspective of the author has determined the thrust of the argument, not the evidentiary base.

The inherent demands of the statistical method for numerically comparable data has also distorted the immigrant experience. Quantitative historians have measured "success" according to performance on a uniform scale of economic achievement and not in terms of the cultural values and social priorities of specific ethnic groups. Many Irish laborers, for example, did not "want" to invest their hard-earned dollars in small businesses, the extensive education of their children, or the acquisition of new occupational skills. They "preferred" to support the Roman Catholic Church and to achieve the security of home ownership. A mere statistical comparison of their occupational or economic success with that of the members of other ethnic groups (with different priorities) distorts the significance of their lives. The very features that make the quantitative mode of understanding such a powerful analytic tool—its empiricism, narrow focus, and statistical precision—serve to conceal the phenomenological essence of the life-worlds of European, Asian, and Afro-American migrants to the industrial cities of the United States.[53]

Aware of these limitations, other American social historians organize their research in a conceptual manner and thus exemplify the second of Mink's formulations. For purposes of presentation, these scholars simplify reality by placing individuals and events that have similar features into a distinct category. This approach encourages a holistic, contextual analysis of social groups. Thus, many historians of colonial American communities study families in generational cohorts. Their investigations admit diversity within a given chronological period but stress the crucial importance of a common historical experience. The range of family behavior (with respect to age at marriage, number of children, and pattern of inheritance) within the same generation appears to be less significant than the differences between successive groups of parents.[54] A similar analytic principle underlies Peter Loewenberg's innovative study of the emotional and nutritive deprivations produced by World War I on a generation of German infants, the cohort of young men and women who subsequently came of age during Adolph Hitler's rise to power. Loewenberg's conceptual approach provides great interpretive leverage. Viewing the decisions of young people to support the authoritarian government of the Third Reich from a generational perspective,

---

[53] James A. Henretta, "The Study of Social Mobility: Ideological Assumptions and Conceptual Bias," *Labor History*, 18 (1977): 166–78; Daniel D. Luria, "Wealth, Capital, and Power: The Social Meaning of Home Ownership," *Journal of Interdisciplinary History*, 7 (1976): 262–82; and William H. Sewell, Jr., "Social Mobility in a Nineteenth-Century European City: Some Findings and Implications," *ibid.*, 217–33.

[54] See, for example, Greven, *Four Generations: Population, Land, and Family in Colonial Andover, Massachusetts*; Daniel Scott Smith, "The Demographic History of Colonial New England," *Journal of Economic History*, 32 (1972): 165–83; Robert V. Wells, "Family Size and Fertility Control in Eighteenth-Century America: A Study of Quaker Families," *Population Studies*, 25 (1971): 73–82; Nancy Osterud and John Fulton, "Family Limitation and the Age at Marriage: Fertility Decline in Sturbridge, Massachusetts, 1730–1850," *ibid.*, 30 (1976): 481–94; and Kenneth A. Lockridge and Alan Krieder, "The Evolution of Massachusetts Town Government, 1640 to 1740," *William and Mary Quarterly*, 3d ser., 23 (1968): 549–74.

he has suggested that these choices had a common psychological origin in the experiences of children during the wartime years. Like the historians of *mentalité*, Loewenberg constructed a conceptual model that attempted to demonstrate a collective psychobiographical pattern where others had seen only accident and variety.[55]

Although this conceptual form of presentation is ideal for the depiction of the composite "mind" of the elite of an age (as the impressive synthetic creations of Perry Miller in *The New England Mind* and Henry Nash Smith in *Virgin Land* attest), it does not permit the specification of precise causal relationships or the delineation of unique historical events.[56] These deficiencies proceed directly from the method, for individual cases are subsumed within or subordinated to a controlling conceptual scheme. The historian creates a coherent mosaic from disparate materials, a pointillist technique applicable to social as well as intellectual history. E. P. Thompson's articles on food riots, work-discipline, and plebian culture in eighteenth-century England are cases in point. Thompson has presented a great quantity of evidence drawn from primary documents that suggests the consciousness of the historical actors, but his conceptual approach makes it difficult to trace an actual series of events in a specific locality. Examples of the social conflicts generated by the transition from the traditional system of food distribution to the new political economy of agricultural capitalism are drawn from widely separated regions and from different decades. Thompson has juxtaposed a food riot in Norwich in 1740 with one in Gloucestershire in 1766; the "just price" demanded by a hungry crowd in the Isle of Ely receives articulate justification in an edict propounded by a paternalistic magistrate in Middlesex and an anonymous "Clergyman in the Countryside"; and a passage from *The Wealth of Nations* defends the proposition that the calculus of the market distributes grain in the most socially efficient manner. Thompson has used a conceptual mode of presentation to isolate the historic groups, economic forces, and cultural values present in England during the extended transition to capitalism, and he has then set them in conflict with one another—collapsing chronological time and ignoring geographical distance for purposes of drama and argument.[57] This adept organization overcomes the inherent limitations of the conceptual mode of comprehension with respect to specificity and causality, but only by a deft sleight of hand. The exact process of capitalist transformation—as it actually occurred in a circumscribed social context, with

[55] Loewenberg, "The Psychohistorical Origins of the Nazi Youth Cohort," *AHR*, 76 (1971): 1457–1502. For a good general survey of the literature, see Alan B. Spitzer, "The Historical Problem of Generations," *ibid.*, 78 (1973): 1353–85.

[56] Miller's first volume was published in 1939 and was based on the writings of only sixty colonial authors, six of whom accounted for 56 percent of Miller's documentation; Miller, *The New England Mind: The Seventeenth Century* (New York, 1939); and George Selement, "Perry Miller: A Note on His Sources in *The New England Mind: The Seventeenth Century,*" *William and Mary Quarterly*, 3d ser., 31 (1974): 453–64. The later work of Smith has a more symbolic approach but is also restricted to the literary elite; Smith, *Virgin Land: The American West as Symbol and Myth* (Cambridge, Mass., 1950); and Rush Welter, "The History of Ideas in America: An Essay in Redefinition," *Journal of American History*, 51 (1965): 599–614.

[57] Thompson, "The Moral Economy of the Crowd in Eighteenth-Century England," 89–91, 97, 110–11, 133, *passim*. Also see Thompson, "Time, Work-Discipline, and Industrial Capitalism," *Past & Present*, no. 38 (1967): 56–97, and "Patrician Society, Plebian Culture," 382–405.

177

the causal links palpably manifest (and thus "verified") in individual lives—escapes confirmation.

Yet this type of historical account, the presentation of identifiable actors in a distinct spatial-temporal setting, constitutes the most familiar form of historical writing. This narrative tradition falls within Mink's third mode of understanding: the configurational method of "grasping together in a single mental act" various diverse events; and Mink has attempted to demonstrate its explanatory power and its utility in historical analysis. Narratives, he has maintained, "are not imperfect substitutes for more sophisticated forms of explanation and understanding, ... the unreflective first steps along the road which leads toward the goal of scientific or philosophical knowledge." The comprehension at which narratives aim represents "a primary act of mind," he has argued; both from history and from fiction "we learn how to tell and to understand complex stories" and "how it is that stories answer questions." For example, great difficulties attend the analysis of the exact "combination of motives, pressures, promises and principles which explain a Senator's vote." To apprehend "the tableau of objects in their concrete particularity as well as in their manifold relations" requires a complex act of mind; all of the diverse contexts and sequences of action must be connected in a convincing manner "by a network of overlapping descriptions."[58] Most events—as psychohistorians often point out—are "over-determined," the product of the convergence of a multiplicity of personal and circumstantial causes; thus, it requires sharp analytic and synthetic skills to construct a convincing "story." To compose a coherent and compelling narrative is to engage in a high-order intellectual activity with stringent standards of excellence.

Nonetheless, many social historians remain skeptical of the interpretive range and power of the narrative mode of presentation. Traditional chronological accounts are often restricted in scope to public affairs and to the lives of the elite. Moreover, narrative history is often impressionistic in its use of evidence, theoretically diffuse, and—because of its dependence on literary documents—ill-equipped to grapple with the wide variety of important historical problems amenable to quantitative or conceptual types of analysis. The validity of these criticisms may be readily granted without negating the very real utility of the narrative mode in the writing of social history. This approach directly addresses questions of time, change, and sequence; such chronological concerns, as the scholarship of Marxists and the early *Annalistes* acknowledge, form crucial aspects of the discipline of history. Narratives also embody a phenomenological perspective, and for that reason have been widely adopted by historians working in the pragmatic tradition. By placing as much (or more) emphasis upon the subjective perceptions of the actors as upon the objective circumstances of existence, narratives underscore the importance of human agency.[59] Finally, histo-

---

[58] Mink, "History and Fiction as Modes of Comprehension," 547, 556–58. For a stimulating defense of the narrative tradition, see Vann, "The Rhetoric of Social History," 221–36.

[59] Although some degree of artifice enters into the construction of a narrative—in that the author already knows the outcome of the story and therefore provides a false sense of open-endedness–artifice alone does not

rians who adopt a chronological framework establish a basic congruence between the lives of their subjects and those of their audience. Most readers view the past in the same manner that they comprehend their own existence—not in quantitative or conceptual terms but in terms of a series of overlapping and interwoven narrative life-stories. Narrative history holds great appeal for the lay reader not primarily because of the absence of "jargon" but because its mode of cognition approximates the reality of everyday life.

The task is clear. If American social historians are to reach a wide audience, then they must fashion a rhetorical mode of presentation that reconciles narration and analysis. Impressive advances have already been made in two grandly conceived studies of Afro-American society during the nineteenth century. In *The Black Family in Slavery and Freedom* Herbert Gutman has demonstrated the evocative power of a phenomenological depiction of the Afro-American experience and, through the pragmatic application of anthropological methods, has interpreted this experience in terms of a wider theoretical framework. Different analytic priorities inform the scholarship of Eugene Genovese. While his *Roll, Jordan, Roll: The World the Slaves Made* also describes the world-views of various groups within the black population, Genovese has subsumed these subjective perspectives within a Marxist structural analysis of southern slave society and a dialectical model of the development of black (and white) consciousness. His rationalist and structural approach stands in marked contrast to the pragmatic and phenomenological assumptions underlying Gutman's work.[60]

For a synthesis of these contrasting modes of analysis and their integration with a chronological narrative, less sweeping examples of historical scholarship are more instructive. The fine book by Paul Boyer and Stephen Nissenbaum, *Salem Possessed: The Social Origins of Witchcraft*, serves as a fine example. *Salem Possessed* begins with a short narrative account of "What Happened in 1692," the judicially sanctioned murder of thirteen women and six men for the practice of witchcraft. This moment in American history remains compelling, and the authors have consciously exploited its hold on the public imagination. Like many writers of fiction, they employed the device of the "symbolic moment," using the "interaction of the two—the 'ordinary' history and the extraordinary moment—to understand the epoch which produced them both."[61] Michael Katz has utilized a similar strategy (with respect to less familiar and less dramatic materials) in his stimulating examination of early school reform in nineteenth-century Massachusetts. "This study," Katz explained, "focuses on small, concrete situations, which it tries to examine thoroughly." Intuitively adopting the technique of "thick description" advocated by Geertz, Katz isolated key paradigmatic events—such as the rejection, by working-class voters in Beverly, Massachusetts, of a plan for a publicly supported high school—and assessed their wider social

---

constitute a major objection. For the reader's imperfect knowledge approximates that of the historical actor; neither knows for certain how events will turn out.

[60] For a statement of these differences in a strident form, see Elizabeth Fox-Genovese and Eugene D. Genovese, "The Political Crisis of Social History: A Marxian Perspective," *Journal of Social History*, 10 (1976): 210–17.

[61] Boyer and Nissenbaum, *Salem Possessed: The Social Origins of Witchcraft* (Cambridge, Mass., 1974), xii.

importance. His technique was "to start with the concrete and through careful analysis to work outward to conclusions of broad cultural significance."[62]

These dramatic devices have important methodological implications. In scholarly terms, the authors of both works have defined a *histoire problème*, a small but crucial event that manifests many of the major social forces and intellectual currents extant in the larger society. The successful emotional depiction and analytical resolution of this limited but nonetheless complex causal puzzle provides an elegant answer to the organizational problem defined by Braudel—a method that would integrate "event, conjuncture, and structure."[63] This conceptual approach can be widely utilized; even those scholars addressing broad, open-ended processes of cultural change can focus parts of their account around particularly instructive episodes.

Salem Possessed offers another rhetorical strategy of considerable utility to social historians, for it demonstrates how quantitative data and conceptual models can be presented as a series of interrelated problems or arguments within a chronological and narrative framework. Early in their account Boyer and Nissenbaum posed the question of the geographical relationship between the alleged witches and their accusers. According to the maps drawn by the authors, the houses of the two groups were not distributed in a random fashion across the landscape. Rather, the locations of their residences conformed to a wider sectional and religious division within the community. The alleged witches were tied by propinquity and financial interest to Salem Town, a diversifying commercial-seaport, while their accusers lived predominantly in the agricultural region known as Salem Village. As important as the substance of this argument are the explicit terms in which it is made. Throughout *Salem Possessed* Boyer and Nissenbaum have addressed methodological questions in the text itself. The narrative that opens the study is gradually transformed into an intricate exploration of empirical evidence and analytic methods, thus expanding the cognitive skills of the readers while deepening their understanding of the historical context. Although the organization remains chronological in form, based on interwoven stories relating to specific lives and events, a "Collective Profile" illuminates the common features in the lives of the condemned witches and statistical tables chart the correlations among the variables of wealth, church membership, and factional alignment.[64] Yet these structural and statistical analyses (as well as psychobiographies of the leading protagonists and a textual exegesis of the minister's sermons) are consistently subordinated to the two main narrative themes: the transition from subsistence to commercial production in Salem during the late seventeenth century and the chains of causation linking the individuals caught in this economic transformation to the tragic events of 1692.

This astute resolution of the problems involved in combining Mink's three modes of comprehension represents a significant achievement. When Clifford

---

[62] Katz, *The Irony of Early School Reform: Educational Innovation in Mid-Nineteenth-Century Massachusetts* (Cambridge, Mass., 1968), 14–15.

[63] Hexter, "Fernand Braudel and the *Monde Braudellien*," 537–38.

[64] For the geographical analysis, see Boyer and Nissenbaum, *Salem Possessed: The Social Origins of Witchcraft*, 33–35, and, for the "Collective Profile," see *ibid.*, 190–201. The book contains seven maps and six tables.

Geertz published his *Social History of an Indonesian Town* in 1965, he suggested that narration and analysis were contradictory rather than complementary. His book, therefore, constituted "an attempt not so much to re-create the past as to discover its sociological character." As Geertz took pains to point out, his account is "not a story and so has neither moral nor plot"; rather, "it is a theoretically controlled analysis of certain processes of social change and contains instead an argument."[65] Both Boyer and Nissenbaum's *Salem Possessed* and Katz's *The Irony of Early School Reform* transcend this formulation; for they illustrate the possibility of simultaneously introducing characters, chronology, and a matrix of action on the one hand and diverse analytic methods on the other. In the case of *Salem Possessed*, argument and plot converge—literally and symbolically—in Boyer and Nissenbaum's contention that the witchcraft hangings can ultimately be traced back to a conflict between religious factions "in which a subsistence, peasant-based economy was being subverted by mercantile capitalism."[66] Although the authors fail to demonstrate their argument in a completely convincing fashion (minimizing the autonomy of religious world-views and neglecting to prove that the members of the two church factions employed different modes of production), they have fashioned a powerful organizational method. Their synthesis, like the epistemological formulation by Pierre Bourdieu, represents an important contribution to the theory of the "new social history."

INDEED, WHEN TAKEN TOGETHER, the methodological innovations of Bourdieu and of Boyer and Nissembaum suggest a composite analytic and rhetorical strategy, an "action model" designed to discover and depict history as it was lived by men and women in the past. The implementation of this model demands, in the first place, the definition of a *histoire problème*, a focused paradigmatic episode, the resolution of which speaks to the validity of a social theory or to an important question of historical interpretation or cultural significance. The direct specification in the text of moral and methodological problems constitutes a second aspect of this approach, for an avowed goal is the development of the critical and cognitive consciousness of the audience. As Paul Hernadi has argued, the contemporary historian should not pretend "to *mirror* what really happened" but should "freely admit that he mediates." The responsibility of the scholar is, in fact, "to make us see the past from within and from without at the same time—as evolving drama and as the fixed target of distanced retrospection."[67] A method for achieving this dual objective makes up the third characteristic of the "action model." The quantitative techniques and structural approaches of *Annalistes*, Marxists, and social scientific historians are used to delineate the objective character of the society and to determine its hierarchial systems.

---

[65] Geertz, *The Social History of an Indonesian Town*, 2.
[66] Boyer and Nissenbaum, *Salem Possessed: The Social Origins of Witchcraft*, 178, xii.
[67] Hernadi, "Re-Presenting the Past: A Note on Narrative Historiography and Historical Drama," *History and Theory*, 15 (1976): 45, 47.

1322   AHR Forum

Simultaneously, a narrative, chronological framework of organization facili-tates the presentation of the world-views of the actors themselves, a phenome-nological perspective drawn from American pragmatic philosophy and cultural anthropology. The "actions" of individuals—their emotions, their values, and their behavior—remain the ultimate point of reference and give the "model" its name. A social history written in terms of these three postulates focuses narrowly but interprets broadly, critically surveys the past with reference to the present, and, most important of all, records the paradoxical and even tragic history of human agency—of "people acting yet acted upon by the structures of their own history."[68]

[68] The quotation is from an essay on American social history written by Michael Frisch; it will appear shortly in *History and Theory*.

Hanging Together:
Divergent Unities in American History

JOHN HIGHAM

F OR about a decade American historical writing has been characterized by a repudiation of consensus and an invocation of community. Present-day historians seem substantially agreed that many of their predecessors overemphasized unities in American history and society. Yet perhaps never before have so much interest and effort gone into a search for those times and places in which a high degree of solidarity obtained. On first notice, we have here a curious contradiction. The repudiation of consensus was supposed to permit a rediscovery of profound conflicts in our past. It has done so only to a very limited degree. The exciting advances in contemporary scholarship have more to do with understanding cohesive structures: the New England town, the family, the ethnic subculture, the professional and trade associations, the political machines.

A moment's reflection dispels the paradox. Historians who are interested in the issues of consensus and community are actually trying to distinguish between true and false communities, between the social arrangements that sustain participants and those that coerce or scatter them. The term "consensus" is commonly applied to a factitious conformity, arising from manipulation and acquiescence. When we speak of "community" we refer to a more authentic, more truly shared bond. To look at American historiography in this light suggests that for some time historians of quite different persuasions have been asking the same questions, though giving different answers. The so-called consensus historians who came to the fore in the 1950s—Richard Hofstadter, David Potter, Louis Hartz, and Daniel Boorstin—created the conceptual universe their present-day critics and successors inhabit. Both groups have been studying the possibilities and the limits of social solidarity in our peculiarly amorphous country.

A striking feature of this grand enterprise is the high proportion of negative conclusions it has so far produced. At first many historians described

This essay was delivered as the presidential address of the Organization of American Historians at Denver, Colorado, April 18, 1974. John Higham is professor of history in Johns Hopkins University.

5

an all-embracing community, shaped by a common national character.[1] Before long this kind of community began to seem too thin, even illusory, to have much significance. Interest in national character has survived only to the extent that it can be treated—as Michael Kammen does—as a bundle of contradictions: six characters, so to speak, in search of a historian.[2] The locus of community has shifted to smaller, presumably more homogeneous entities. The closer these are examined, however, the more they reveal their own fissures and stultifications. A remarkable number of recent studies focus on the points at which or the ways in which American communities have failed. A small army of historians has been trying to determine how and when the early New England towns came apart. Some say it was during the era of the Great Awakening; but Michael H. Frisch argues that Springfield, Massachusetts, kept its organic wholeness until the middle of the nineteenth century. Michael Zuckerman, on the other hand, insists that the cohesiveness of the New England towns was always contrived, that it rested on an intolerance of differences, and that it has never broken down but rather has spread throughout American group life. Survival of "the massive coercion of the monolithic community," Zuckerman sternly remarks, "belies the belief that we are a liberal society." Taking a different tack but reaching an equally gloomy verdict, Sam Bass Warner, Jr., portrays the entire span of American urban history as a story of "endless failures . . . to build and maintain humane cities."[3] With some important exceptions[4] the

[1] John Higham, with Leonard Krieger and Felix Gilbert, *History* (Englewood Cliffs, N.J., 1965), 221-26. For a more general *post mortem* see Thomas L. Hartshorne, *The Distorted Image: Changing Conceptions of the American Character since Turner* (Cleveland, 1968).

[2] Michael Kammen, *People of Paradox: An Inquiry Concerning the Origins of American Civilization* (New York, 1972).

[3] Sam Bass Warner, Jr., *The Urban Wilderness: A History of the American City* (New York, 1972), 3; Michael H. Frisch, *Town Into City: Springfield, Massachusetts, and the Meaning of Community, 1840-1880* (Cambridge, Mass., 1972); Michael Zuckerman, *Peaceable Kingdoms: New England Towns in the Eighteenth Century* (New York, 1970), 257. See also Darrett B. Rutman, *Winthrop's Boston: Portrait of a Puritan Town 1630-1649* (Chapel Hill, 1965); Richard L. Bushman, *From Puritan to Yankee: Character and the Social Order in Connecticut, 1690-1765* (Cambridge, Mass., 1967); Kenneth Lockridge, *A New England Town, The First Hundred Years: Dedham, Massachusetts, 1636-1736* (New York, 1970). The vicissitudes of other collectivities are treated in: Richard Sennett, *Families against the City: Middle Class Homes of Industrial Chicago 1872-1890* (Cambridge, Mass., 1970); Wilson Carey McWilliams, *The Idea of Fraternity in America* (Berkeley, 1973); Laurence Veysey, *The Communal Experience: Anarchist and Mystical Counter-Cultures in America* (New York, 1973); R. Jackson Wilson, *In Quest of Community: Social Philosophy in the United States, 1860-1920* (New York, 1968).

[4] Most impressively, Anthony F. C. Wallace, *The Death and Rebirth of the Seneca* (New York, 1969). But see also Herbert G. Gutman, "Work, Culture, and Society in Industrializing America, 1815-1919," *American Historical Review*, 78 (June 1973), 531-88.

search for community has led American historians either to a rediscovery of consensus or to a scene of alienation and disorder.

Bemused with so much failure, a reader must wonder what kind of social integration, what experience of unity, might qualify as successful. By what criteria do our historians distribute praise and blame among different kinds of communities? May we call one parochial because it is small and self-sustaining and another weak because it is large and non-exclusive? Under what conditions should we expect a unifying force to bind people more closely together, or to respect their partial autonomy, or release them completely? I ask these questions to suggest that the quality and nature of social cohesion pose fundamental dilemmas for Americans. A historian can not resolve the dilemmas, but he can ask the past to clarify their shape and duration.

America has exhibited not only an enormous variety of communities but also some underlying differences in the forms of unity our peoples have sought. Much of the confusion in current scholarship seems to arise from a propensity to judge one pattern of social integration by criteria derived from another, and thus to demean the first at the expense of the second. American history has been in considerable measure a struggle between rival ways of getting together. In actual experience the alternatives have overlapped very greatly. Instead of facing a clear choice between commensurate loyalties, Americans have commonly been enmeshed in divergent systems of integration. That is not a condition peculiar to America. It is intrinsic to modern life. This essay sketches in barest outline three adhesive forces that have pulled people in different directions wherever the process of modernization has occurred. I intend to point up, not the uniqueness of American experience, but rather the special salience here of disparities every modernizing society seems to confront. I shall concentrate on the sequential unfolding of three forms of unity, which American historians have studied only in fragmentary ways. Obviously I shall not take account of all cohesive structures. In particular I leave aside the working of sheer political or economic domination, in order to concentrate on types of integration that function through consent, whether tacit or explicit.

At the most elementary level, the peoples of America have participated in what Clifford Geertz has called "primordial" unity: a corporate feeling of oneness that infuses a particular, concrete, unquestioned set of inherited relationships. The primordial tie is so much taken for granted that it may be nameless. It binds one to kinsmen, to neighbors, to memories of a distinct place, and to the symbols and rites and customs associated with that heritage. It is therefore localized, specific, yet undefinable. Primordial consciousness differs in its intimacy and unbounded concreteness from what we ordinarily describe as ethnic feeling. The modern ethnic group is a federation of primordial collectivities. It depends on a conceptual simplification and extension of primordial sentiments. It comes about through encounters with outsiders and reflects in part their perceptions.[5]

Primordial ties vary enormously, in character and strength, between groups and over time. In American history the primordial bond has probably been most intense, enduring, and pervasive within the separate Indian tribes. Among Indians primordial unity permeated every dimension of life. As a result, the development of a wider ethnic consciousness—a pan-Indian identity—came very slowly;[6] and when primordial solidarity has given way under pressure from the dominant white society the psychological consequences have often been unbearably painful and demoralizing.

Primordial attachments flourished also among those immigrants who arrived in America with little if any sense of nationality, who knew themselves as the people of a particular Norwegian valley, the sons of a certain Calabrian village, the members of an eastern European *shtetl*, the countrymen of one small district on the Chinese coast. So far as their circumstances permitted, immigrants recreated those local solidarities in the New World. Chinese clustered under the shelter of their warring district companies. Eastern European Jews ordinarily limited their synagogues, their mutual aid societies, and often their workshops to "landmen," so that the whole round of daily life could occur within a circle of fellow townsmen. Italian peasants grouped themselves by village or province on the streets of New York. Often the people from a particular locality would maintain a conspicuous conformity in dress and avoid competing with one another in business.[7]

It would be a mistake to suppose that primordial identities have originated

[5] Clifford Geertz, "The Integrative Revolution: Primordial Sentiments and Civil Politics in the New States," Clifford Geertz, ed., *Old Societies and New States: The Quest for Modernity in Asia and Africa* (New York, 1963), 105-57; Joshua A. Fishman, and others, *Language Loyalty in the United States: The Maintenance and Perpetuation of Non-English Mother Tongues by American Ethnic and Religious Groups* (The Hague, 1966).
[6] Hazel W. Hertzberg, *The Search for an American Indian Identity: Modern Pan-Indian Movements* (Syracuse, 1971).
[7] Gunther Barth, *Bitter Strength: A History of the Chinese in the United States, 1850-1870* (Cambridge, Mass., 1964), 77-101; Theodore C. Blegen, *Norwegian Migration to America: The American Transition* (2 vols., Northfield, Minn., 1931-1940), II, 582-84; Arthur A. Goren, *New York Jews and the Quest for Community: The Kehillah Experiment, 1908-1922* (New York, 1970), 20-21; Robert E. Park and Herbert A. Miller, *Old World Traits Transplanted* (New York, 1921), 145-51.

only outside native white American society and have lingered only on its fringes. Solidarities of this kind emerge wherever people live together long enough to enclose their daily experience in a skein of common memories. Perhaps the most tenacious primordial attachments among American whites developed in the eastern counties of the South in the late seventeenth and eighteenth centuries and spread into the lower Mississippi Valley in the nineteenth century. There alone the archaic Elizabethan term "kinsfolk" survived, slightly Americanized into "kinfolks."[8] It was a constant reminder that complex networks of personal relations extend far beyond the household. No sharp line separates antecedents from neighbors, kin from community. In the world of kinfolks, vestiges of a folk society and a folk memory endured. Here is the root of that concrete sense of place and belonging which Thornton Wilder and C. Vann Woodward have described as one of the hallmarks of a southerner. Whereas most Americans sought their identity in abstractions, southerners resisted the abstract in clinging to "the blessing of being located—contained."[9]

Other Americans, abstract and dislocated, have sometimes greatly envied that attachment to past and to place and have contributed enthusiastically to the celebration of it. American yearnings for a lost primordial world shaped the image of the South in the nineteenth century and invested it with immense nostalgia. It was an Ohio-born minstrel who composed what became the war song of the Confederacy and a polyglot New York audience that first popularized it:

> I wish I was in de land ob cotton,
> Old times dar am not forgotten;
> Look away, look away . . .[10]

In adverting to southerners and to the land of cotton, we are indeed looking away. We are looking away from New York; but we are also looking beyond the primordial matrix. We have entered a larger universe, where primordial experience is transmuted into a collective image that can focus the allegiance of people with roughly similar linguistic and geographical origins. The creation of group identities grounded in primordial life has

[8] Harold Wentworth, *American Dialect Dictionary* (New York, 1944), 341; *Oxford English Dictionary* (13 vols., Oxford, 1933), V, 710.

[9] C. Vann Woodward, *The Burden of Southern History* (New York, 1961), 23-24. The quotation is from Eudora Welty. See also David M. Potter, "The Enigma of the South," *Yale Review*, LI (Autumn 1961), 150-51.

[10] *The Annals of America* (18 vols., Chicago, 1968), IX, 146. See also William R. Taylor, *Cavalier and Yankee: The Old South and the American National Character* (New York, 1961).

continued to be a significant industry in American popular culture: it has given us the Down-Easter, the Hoosier, and the cowboy, to name but a few; and our own time has brought forth new species, such as the hippie, which have not yet acquired a stable geographic base. But the multiplication of ethnic and regional groups can not disguise a long-term tendency for primordial ties to come apart. The peopling of America required at the very outset a profound rupture in primordial solidarity, and the enormous mobility that has churned American society ever since has given special importance to other integrative mechanisms. The most powerful of these in the eighteenth and nineteenth centuries was ideological.

Since I propose to talk at some length about the importance of ideology in American history, I must say at the outset how I am using that elusive term. I do not, like many of the critics of ideology, restrict it to rigid, totalistic outlooks; nor do I limit it to secular political creeds. On the other hand, I wish to avoid also the looser usage that describes any rationale for a social loyalty as an ideology. A culture or a group may or may not have an ideology, depending on the degree to which its goals are explicitly formulated and also endowed with transcendent significance. Ideology is therefore a variable in history; perhaps it may even give us a measure of the importance of ideas in motivating and directing a society. American historians, defending their particular bailiwicks and points of view, have characteristically argued over the causal force of ideas in history without sufficiently appreciating that ideas may be enormously more significant in one era or society than in another. We have therefore overlooked one of the great systemic changes in American history.

To come more directly to the matter of definition, I wish to designate as ideologies those explicit systems of general beliefs that give large bodies of people a common identity and purpose, a common program of action, and a standard for self-criticism. Being relatively formalized and explicit, ideology contrasts with a wider, older, more ambiguous fund of myth and tradition. It includes doctrines or theories on the one hand and policies or prescriptions on the other. Accordingly, it links social action with fundamental beliefs, collective identity with the course of history. This combination of generality with directional thrust has enabled ideology to function as an important unifying force. Arising in the course of modernization when an unreflective culture fractures, ideology provides a new basis for solidarity.[11]

---

[11] See Clifford Geertz, "Ideology as a Cultural System," David E. Apter, ed., *Ideology and Discontent* (New York, 1964), 47-76; and Willard A. Mullins, "On the Concept of Ideology in Political Science," *American Political Science Review*, LXVI (June 1972),

Ideological unity assumed its special importance in America at the outset. One large part of early American society was founded upon an ideology. Elsewhere ideologies arose out of dissatisfaction with the existing social order. In the Old World this was the case with Puritanism. It constituted the first great ideological movement in English history. As a revolutionary force, it cut through established institutions and relations like a laser beam.[12] Yet Puritanism ultimately failed in England, and after its shattering defeat in 1660 ideology never again provided the primary basis for social integration. America, on the other hand, had no preexisting structure for Puritans to overthrow. Here ideology arrived not as a subversive or divisive force but as a bedrock of order, purpose, and cohesion.

If ideological unity was from the outset fundamental in New England, primordial unity was correspondingly weak. The researches of Sumner Chilton Powell suggest that the early settlers of New England towns could not rely very much on the local familiarities and affinities of primordial experience. Sudbury's first settlers came from widely scattered parts of England; they melded together a surprising variety of customs and practices.[13] In addition to a common English culture, however, they possessed an ideology that put a heavy stress on mutuality and discipline. It bound them with written covenants, taught them formal creeds, and commanded them to subordinate all private concerns to one collective end. Since the New England colonies adopted a loose, decentralized government in both church and state, they entrusted to ideology much of the regulative function that elsewhere belonged in the hands of constituted rulers. In place of hierarchical authority, the Puritans substituted a voluntary mobilization of belief. In doing so, they originated a peculiarly American combination: institutional decentralization and ideological uniformity.

Although Puritanism was never overthrown, its pristine vitality ebbed toward the end of the seventeenth century. The remarkable social cohesion of the preceding decades in New England diminished.[14] During the next

498-510. I have resisted the special constructions the term has been given by Marxists and their successors, as Ben Halpern, " 'Myth' and 'Ideology' in Modern Usage," *History and Theory,* I (No. II, 1961), 129-49, and by conservatives, as in Edward Shils, The Intellectuals and the Powers *and Other Essays* (Chicago, 1972), 23-41; but I have tried to avoid the sweep and elevation ideology loses in the strictly functionalist definition employed in Talcott Parsons, *The Social System* (New York, 1951), 331-32, 348-58.

[12] Michael Walzer, *The Revolution of the Saints: A Study in the Origins of Radical Politics* (Cambridge, Mass., 1965).

[13] Sumner Chilton Powell, *Puritan Village: The Formation of a New England Town* (Middletown, Conn., 1963).

[14] Timothy H. Breen and Stephen Foster, "The Puritans' Greatest Achievement: A Study of Social Cohesion in Seventeenth-Century Massachusetts," *Journal of American History,*

half century a rising consciousness of the common English heritage uniting all parts of the British Empire helped to stabilize colonial life.[15] But the programmatic fervor of ideology subsided. About this first decline of ideology in American history we know very little, except that it proved short-lived. American Christianity recovered in the eighteenth century an ideological thrust that sustained it into the early twentieth. With the dispersion of population from the clustered settlements of the seventeenth century, the original Puritan reliance on ideological mobilization revived and intensified.

The Puritans had needed the discipline of ideology to hold their ranks, to stave off fragmentation. Their descendants had to cope with a society already fragmented. To encompass a people rushing away from one another —a people straining the last ligaments of a common life in their pursuit of land and freedom—Americans put their ideological inheritance to expanded uses. What had been a discipline became also an incitement. Exploding churches turned the full power of the Word outward to reach the unconverted and to penetrate a culture no single group could dominate. This produced, of course, enormous conflicts. It split congregations and multiplied competing sects. Like any other integrative mechanism, ideology divides as well as unites. Nevertheless, the point remains: the Great Awakening marks the moment in American history when ideology undertook the task of forging a new solidarity among individuals who had lost through migration and competition any corporate identity.[16]

The new solidarity was very difficult to achieve and not fully worked out until the Second Great Awakening in the early nineteenth century. Gradually, however, the impulse toward union broke through the theological and ecclesiastical fences that had separated Protestant bodies in the past. Whereas the Puritans had generally insisted that a single comprehensive faith should enclose a tightly knit society, eighteenth-century Christians developed an intellectual framework that accommodated unprecedented diversities. What I shall call the Protestant ideology had as its working principle a distinction between two levels of belief. Specific creeds and confessions adorned the more formal, visible level. They served as identifying marks for particular segments of the population and as concrete symbols of

LX (June 1973), 5-22. See also Stephen Foster, *Their Solitary Way: The Puritan Social Ethic in the First Century of Settlement in New England* (New Haven, 1971).

[15] Jack P. Greene, "Search for Identity: An Interpretation of the Meaning of Selected Patterns of Social Response in Eighteenth-Century America," *Journal of Social History*, 3 (Spring 1970), 189-220.

[16] Bushman, *From Puritan to Yankee*, 183-95; Alan Heimert, *Religion and the American Mind from the Great Awakening to the Revolution* (Cambridge, Mass., 1966), 95-158.

a pervasive freedom of choice. At a deeper level, unaffected by the clash of creeds, dwelled the inclusive truths, which required neither debate nor strict definition. Thus the Protestant ideology accepted conflict between "denominations" as permanent, legitimate, and inspiriting; for the conflict could be seen to rest on and to demonstrate the worth of certain unifying ideals.[17] As time passed, theological doctrines acquired a largely honorific, ceremonial status in America's pantheon of religions. The basic ideology stood guard, and one could question its tenets only at the risk of heresy.

This dynamic relation between ideals shared by the great majority of people and distinct creeds that attracted only limited followings helps to explain an anomaly puzzling to European observers of nineteenth-century America. How could intense religious activity proceed unobstructed in a setting that seemed largely secular? In actuality secular life was suffused with a pan-Protestant ideology that claimed to be civic and universal. Pledged to leave private beliefs undisturbed, it was vague enough so that increasing numbers of Jews and Catholics could embrace it. But it infused a generalized piety in school textbooks and civic oratory.[18] At the same time the Protestant ideology gave a special focus and initiative to the Protestant churches. It offered them a unifying purpose. It encouraged their members to feel a praetorian responsibility for the whole society.[19]

Necessarily, the tenets of the Protestant ideology were few and simple. First among them was the conviction that no compulsion should rule the choice of faith. Genuine religious commitment is a private and voluntary act. While it remains so, a pure religion and a sturdy morality will undergird American institutions. The great diversity of churches guarantees that no one of them can corrupt this truth or reduce an energetic people to apathy.

Secondly, the Protestant ideology offered Americans a collective task and a sustaining hope. Aiming at nothing less than the redemption of mankind, it held that God had assigned to America the leading role in the enterprise.

[17] Guy Howard Miller, "A Contracting Community: American Presbyterians, Social Conflict, and Higher Education, 1730-1820" (doctoral dissertation, University of Michigan, 1970) ; Sidney E. Mead, *The Lively Experiment: The Shaping of Christianity in America* (New York, 1963).

[18] Ruth Miller Elson, *Guardians of Tradition: American Schoolbooks of the Nineteenth Century* (Lincoln, Neb., 1964), 46-55, 58; *McGuffey's Fifth Eclectic Reader* (New York, 1962, reprint of 1879 edition), 296-97. See also Philip Schaff, *America: A Sketch of Its Political, Social, and Religious Character*, Perry Miller, ed. (Cambridge, Mass., 1961), 72-95.

[19] James Fulton Maclear, " 'The True American Union' of Church and State: The Reconstruction of the Theocratic Tradition," *Church History*, XXVIII (March 1959), 41-62; Lois W. Banner, "Religious Benevolence as Social Control: A Critique of an Interpretation," *Journal of American History*, LX (June 1973), 35-41.

America's history and destiny assumed a sacred character, which the great
historian George Bancroft captured in making providential guidance the
grand theme of his ten-volume epic.[20] In origin, this sense of divine mission
flowed straight from the millennialism of seventeenth-century Puritans;
nothing more clearly revealed the continuity of the Protestant ideology with
the Puritanism from which it sprang. All Calvinists looked forward to the
coming of a new order. Those who emigrated to New England identified
themselves as a people especially chosen to advance it. The Scriptures
promised an ultimate reign of holiness, peace, and happiness, and the New
England Puritans knew they were summoned to do some special work
toward that end—perhaps to build, in Edward Johnson's ringing words,
"a new Heaven, and a new Earth in, new Churches, and a new Commonwealth together. . . ."[21] In the seventeenth century, however, the millennial
promise held as much terror as hope. An oppressive sense of the insufficiency of their own efforts made the Puritans particularly sensitive to signs
of failure and to prophecies of premillennial doom. Beginning with the
Great Awakening, Alan Heimert tells us, the millennial idea lost for many
people its cataclysmic implications. The awakening that was already under
way was securely building Christ's Kingdom on earth. America began to be
seen as the spiritual center of Christendom.[22] Thus the Protestant ideology,
instead of enshrining a single creed, exalted a sacred place.

We ordinarily think of ideologies as jealous masters, contending with
one another for exclusive possession of a society. Yet American history offers
a striking exception. The two ideologies that exercised the widest influence
eventually overlapped and reinforced one another to the point almost of
complete convergence. By giving the millennium a temporal and secular
character, the Protestant clergy identified the Kingdom of God with the
American Republic; and the Protestant ideology thereupon attached itself
to American nationalism. In principle and in origin the two were different.
The national ideology was primarily political and secondarily social. It was
born in the struggle for, and dedicated to the defense of, an independent
Republic. It drew heavily on non-Christian sources, notably the Enlighten-

[20] George Bancroft, *A History of the United States, from the Discovery of the American Continent* (10 vols., Boston, 1834-1874).
[21] [Edward Johnson], *Johnson's Wonder-Working Providence 1628-1651*, J. Franklin Jameson, ed. (New York, 1910), 25. The importance and scope of the millennial idea are brought to the fore in Ernest Lee Tuveson, *Redeemer Nation: The Idea of America's Millennial Role* (Chicago, 1968); David D. Hall, "Understanding the Puritans," Herbert J. Bass, ed., *The State of American History* (Chicago, 1970), 336-41; and Sacvan Bercovitch, "Typology in Puritan New England: The Williams-Cotton Controversy Reassessed," *American Quarterly*, XIX (Summer 1957), 179-91.
[22] Heimert, *Religion and the American Mind*, 59, 94-96.

ment and the tradition of classical humanism.[23] The Protestant ideology, for all of its entanglement with American culture, was supranational. It subordinated all political structures and all territorial communities to the will of God. Still, each came to supplement the other. Together, they forged the strongest bonds that united the American people during the nineteenth century.

Collaboration pivoted on a mutual commitment to an American destiny. Both systems of belief posited a national mission to realize the hopes of mankind. Like the patriotic clergy of the Revolutionary era, secular leaders construed America's character and promise in universalistic terms. On a secular plane, the Founding Fathers grounded their independence in the laws of nature. They ransacked historical experience in framing institutions suitable to the universal tendencies of human nature; and they conceived of their enterprise as a new beginning for mankind. Quoting Virgil, the Continental Congress in 1782 designed the Great Seal of the Republic which proclaimed "Novus Ordo Seclorum"—A New Order for the Ages.[24] From both points of view—Protestant and classical-republican—Americans defined themselves as a people who had broken out of a traditional mold in order to fulfill certain general truths. The significance of the American people, therefore, belonged more to the future than to the past. Their very identity inhered in their abstractions.

The interlacing of American nationalism and American Protestantism extended far beyond their common invocation of an ideological mission. It may be observed also in the symmetry of other major tenets. Where Protestantism endorsed a diversity of denominations and confessions, the national ideology asserted the importance of a multiplicity of political bodies and social interests. Profoundly distrustful of centralized authority, Americans relied on a separation and division of powers in the political sphere,

[23] The most thoughtful effort to date to define an "American ideology" is Yehoshua Arieli, *Individualism and Nationalism in American Ideology* (Cambridge, Mass., 1964), but it needs to be corrected in the light of recent scholarship on republicanism, notably Gordon S. Wood, *The Creation of the American Republic, 1776-1787* (Chapel Hill, 1969); and Gerald Stourzh, *Alexander Hamilton and the Idea of Republican Government* (Stanford, Cal., 1970). I have also profited from: J. G. A. Pocock, "Virtue and Commerce in the Eighteenth Century," *Journal of Interdisciplinary History*, III (Summer 1972), 119-34; Edmund S. Morgan, "The Puritan Ethic and the American Revolution," *William and Mary Quarterly*, XXIV (Jan. 1967), 3-43; Perry Miller, *Nature's Nation* (Cambridge, Mass., 1967), 90-120; Max Savelle, "Nationalism and Other Loyalties in the American Revolution," *American Historical Review*, LXVII (July 1962), 901-23; Eric Foner, *Free Soil, Free Labor, Free Men: The Ideology of the Republican Party before the Civil War* (New York, 1970). Another formulation, different from mine, is presented in H. Mark Roelofs, "The Adequacy of America's Dominant Liberal Ideology," *Bucknell Review*, XVIII (Fall 1970), 3-15.
[24] Gaillard Hunt, *The History of the Seal of the United States* (Washington, 1909).

just as they relied on a wide distribution of ecclesiastical power in the religious sphere. "The security for civil rights," James Madison wrote in the *Federalist*, "must be the same as that for religious rights. It consists in the one case in the multiplicity of interests, and in the other in the multiplicity of sects. The degree of security in both cases will depend on the number of interests and sects. . . ."[25] Variety became fundamental to the dominant American ideal of unity: E Pluribus Unum.

No less fundamental was a shared passion for individual liberty. If the theoretical goal of American ideology was to exemplify and disseminate universal truths, and if the chief structural principle was a dispersion of power, surely the animating idea was a belief in the equal rights of individuals in the interest of maximum personal autonomy. The Protestant stress on unfettered personal choice as the key to true religion had its corollary in the American stress on the free individual as the source of energy and the seat of value in the good society.[26] The adherents of the American ideology could thus feel united by their common possession of equal rights and their common opposition to artificial inequalities.

The three beliefs I have touched on—a collective mission, a dispersal of power, an individual locus of opportunity—made for a large, loose faith. It could not easily become an orthodoxy. It explicitly denied a unified past; it had no single, authoritative text; its own premises prevented any single agency or group from establishing an official formulation. Its early history was tempestuous. From the struggle over the Constitution to the Civil War and beyond, American political history was in considerable degree a conflict between rival versions of the American ideology.

In rejecting the Beardian thesis that American history turns on a continuous, essentially unchanging division between two antithetical ideologies, historians for many years closed their eyes to all ideological conflicts. We are only now discovering how seriously Americans took the differences of principle that arose within the framework of a common ideology as they strained to enact its cloudy imperatives. To understand the passion and ferocity of early American politics is to see how desperately convinced Americans were that the very survival of the Union depended on the triumph of the true version of its basic ideals. Torn loose from primordial unity and committed to finding a new solidarity in a set of beliefs they knew they had as yet only begun to realize, the Americans revealed their enormous

[25] Jacob Cooke, ed., *The Federalist* (Middletown, Conn., 1961), 351-52.
[26] On this point Ralph Barton Perry's classic treatise, *Puritanism and Democracy* (New York, 1944), is still worth reading.

dependence on ideology by quarreling chiefly over its implications and man-
dates.[27] In sum, the terrible fears and anxieties that embittered political life
in the Jeffersonian period reflected not only the frailty and the ambiguities
of the national ideology but also the psychological vulnerability of a people
who had little else to hold them together.

Though fluctuating from year to year, the tensions within the American
and Protestant ideologies persisted; they were intrinsic. The stress on a common purpose clashed in both cases with an unrelenting opposition to con-
solidated power. In the American ideology the differentiating thrust of
individualism pulled against the leveling belief in equality. Above all, the
American ideology was beset with contradiction because its basic task of
building solidarity was not compatible with the competitive, acquisitive
values the ideology also legitimized. In spite of these enduring strains, however, the main trend in the pursuit of an American identity from the time
of Thomas Jefferson to the time of Abraham Lincoln was a strengthening
of its power and a deepening of its emotional resonance.

Still thin and uncertain in the 1790s, ideological unity may have reached
its fullest development around the middle of the nineteenth century, about
100 years after its rebirth in the Great Awakening. It was the erosion
of traditional loyalties by mobility and acquisitiveness that left Americans
dependent on ideology for their sense of identity, and by the mid-nineteenth
century the dispersion of population had attained awesome proportions.
Travelers noticed that a truculent, gasconading patriotism was especially
characteristic of newly settled parts of the country, but everywhere ideological commitment compensated to some extent for the weakness of local ties.
The American, observed Alexander Mackay in 1849,

exhibits little or none of the local attachments which distinguish the European.
His feelings are more centered upon his institutions than his mere country. He
looks upon himself more in the light of a republican than in that of a native of
a particular territory. . . . Every American is thus, in his own estimation, the
apostle of a particular political creed, in the final triumph and extension of which
he finds both himself and his country deeply involved. . . .[28]

---

[27] John R. Howe, Jr., "Republican Thought and the Political Violence of the 1790's,"
American Quarterly, XIX (Summer 1967), 147-65; Richard Buel, Jr., *Securing the
Revolution: Ideology in American Politics, 1789-1815* (Ithaca, 1972).

[28] Henry Steele Commager, ed., *America in Perspective: The United States through
Foreign Eyes* (New York, 1947), 112-13. See also Nils William Olsson, ed., *A Pioneer
in Northwest America, 1841-1858: The Memoirs of Gustaf Unionius* (Minneapolis, 1950),
48; Timothy Flint, *Recollections of the Last Ten Years, Passed in Occasional Residences
and Journeyings in the Valley of the Mississippi, from Pittsburgh and the Missouri to the
Gulf of Mexico, and from Florida to the Spanish Frontier; in a series of letters to the Rev.
James Flint, of Salem, Mass.* (Boston, 1826), 204-06. There is very likely a connection,

The strengthening of ideological bonds in the first half of the nineteenth century came about partly through the development of rituals and symbols. Beginning with relatively unadorned, disembodied ideologies, Americans developed two crucial sets of rituals: on one side, the camp meeting and associated devices for mass conversions; on the other side, the annual electioneering carnival of conventions and torchlight parades. Ideological mobilization was further assisted by the elaboration of symbols, such as the portrait of George Washington, the eagle, and the flag. By the 1860s flagpoles in American towns were said to be almost as common as the chimneys on houses.[29] The unifying abstractions acquired by these means a compelling concreteness.

Meanwhile the dominant ideologies also advanced by raising their goals. On many fronts aspirations soared in the nineteenth century. Instead of viewing the American polity as an uncertain experiment, patriotic spokesmen elevated it to an ultimate, indissoluble necessity.[30] Instead of seeing only a new beginning for mankind, many now thought they could attain a state of total righteousness. Instead of anticipating a gradual betterment of society, reformers now insisted on immediate liberation.[31] Instead of waiting for the American example to be imitated, more and more citizens clamored for direct action to hasten the triumph of freedom and Christianity in benighted parts of the country and beyond its expanding frontiers. Ironically, this escalation of ideological demands was largely responsible for bringing the greatest schism in American life to a violent climax. As the desire for ideological unity increased, slavery—a flat denial of the American ideology—became less and less tolerable. In that broad sense the Civil War, like the expansionism that preceded it, was the result of a general intensification of ideological forces in nineteenth-century America.

Even before the Civil War demonstrated that ideology could not by itself

not yet understood, between the rootlessness Alexander Mackay described and the predominance of intensely felt landscapes in American painting in this period. For an indication of the scope of the problem see Barbara Novak, "American Landscape: The Nationalist Garden and the Holy Book," *Art in America*, LX (Jan. 1972), 46-57.

[29] Michel Chevalier, *Society, Manners and Politics in the United States: Being a Series of Letters on North America* (Ithaca, 1961), 306-10; [James Dawson Burn], *Three Years Among the Working-Classes in the United States during the War* (London, 1865), 116-17.

[30] Paul C. Nagel, *One Nation Indivisible: The Union in American Thought 1776-1861* (New York, 1964), 13-144.

[31] Laurence Veysey, ed., *The Perfectionists: Radical Social Thought in the North, 1815-1860* (New York, 1973). But perfectionism was not confined to radicals, as can be seen in Timothy L. Smith, *Revivalism and Social Reform In Mid-Nineteenth-Century America* (New York, 1965), 103-34. For a discussion of interconnections between the religious and political crusades of this period—between evangelical Protestantism and nationalist expansionism—see John Higham, *From Boundlessness to Consolidation: The Transformation of American Culture 1848-1860* (Ann Arbor, 1969).

permanently hold the country together, another system of integration was emerging. The new pattern was one of technical unity. By that I mean a reordering of human relations by rational procedures designed to maximize efficiency. Technical unity connects people by occupational function rather than ideological faith. It rests on specialized knowledge rather than general beliefs. It has had transforming effects in virtually every sphere of life. As a method of production, technical integration materialized early in the factory system. As a structure of authority it has taken the form of bureaucracy. As a system of values, it endorses a certain kind of interdependence, embodied in the image of the machine. Technical relations are machinelike in being impersonal, utilitarian, and functionally interlocking.[32] Since the Civil War the growth of technical unity has been the most important single tendency in American social history; and its end is not yet in sight.

Before the twentieth century few articulate Americans recognized a serious incompatibility between their ideological principles and their eager elaboration of technical networks. As early as the 1790s, according to Alexander Hamilton, it was often remarked that the genius of the American people included "a peculiar aptitude for mechanic improvements. . . ."[33] There was also a peculiar enthusiasm for such improvements. The industrialization of New England and the middle Atlantic states went forward unopposed by the machine wrecking of Luddites or the moral indignation of Tories. Even the troubled response to technology of an occasional Nathaniel Hawthorne or Herman Melville pales in comparison with the outrage of a Thomas Carlyle or a John Ruskin. America's affection for the machine, accompanied as it was by a cheerful submission to industrial discipline, cannot be explained simply by economic incentives or by pointing to the prevalence of materialistic attitudes in American society. In nineteenth-century America even the critics of materialism—the intellectuals who, generation after generation, assailed luxury and acquisitiveness as the

[32] Robert A. Nisbet, The Social Bond: An Introduction to the Study of Society (New York, 1970), 244-49; and Robert Nisbet, "The Impact of Technology on Ethical Decision-Making," Jack D. Douglas, ed., The Technological Threat (Englewood Cliffs, N.J., 1971), 39-54. See also Daniel Bell, "Technology, Nature and Society: The Vicissitudes of Three World Views and the Confusion of Realms," American Scholar, 42 (Summer 1973), 385-404; and Daniel Bell, The Coming of Post-Industrial Society: A Venture in Social Forecasting (New York, 1973).

[33] Harold C. Syrett, ed., The Papers of Alexander Hamilton (17 vols., New York, 1961-), X, 256. On the further development and display of this aptitude in the nineteenth century, see Marvin Fisher, Workshops in the Wilderness: The European Response to American Industrialization, 1830-1860 (New York, 1967), 46-75; and the illuminating documents in Carroll W. Pursell, Jr., Readings in Technology and American Life (New York, 1969).

deadliest national evils—rarely implicated technology in their indictment.[34]

One cause, generally overlooked, for the responsiveness of Americans to technical values was their ideological cast of mind. As ideologists, Americans from the outset were attuned to universal principles and to their implementation in programs of action. Ideology had largely emancipated Americans from the matrix of primordial life. It had dissolved the entanglements of tradition—the local particularistic identities—which elsewhere have constituted the principal obstacle to industrialization and modernization. Moreover, an ideological orientation taught Americans to internalize their norms in the form of conscience and thus freed them to a great extent from dependence on other persons or external institutions.[35] Their ends already infixed in their hearts, Americans adopted technical means without fear of personal loss. Thus technical integration spread under the shelter of the American ideology; and the resulting innovations were embraced as ever more powerful instruments for attaining familiar goals. Throughout the nineteenth century what Leo Marx has called the technological sublime reverberated in American rhetoric. Acclaiming the arrival of the "Mechanical Epoch," American spokesmen invested it with millennial promise. Technological progress quickens the mind, uplifts the masses, and demonstrates the superiority of republican government. In subjugating matter through the aid of mechanism, man comes more and more to resemble God.[36]

The origins of the technical order run back to the thirteenth century and before. But not until the middle of the nineteenth century do we find the

[34] This distinction has been obscured by the tendency of many American intellectuals in recent decades to make technology, industrialism, urbanization, and materialism virtual equivalents of one another. Leo Marx's sensitive and evocative book, *The Machine in the Garden: Technology and the Pastoral Ideal in America* (New York, 1964), contributed to the blurring of historical perspective by treating the machine in a highly metaphoric context, embracing a contrast between city and country and ultimately between head and heart. On that level of generality it becomes difficult to discriminate the intellectuals who were deeply concerned about technological power from those who were not. See Theodore R. Marmor, "Anti-Industrialism and the Old South: The Agrarian Perspective of John C. Calhoun," *Comparative Studies in Society and History*, IX (July 1967), 377-406.

[35] Nathan Rosenberg, *Technology and American Economic Growth* (New York, 1972), 25-36, 44-50, lists many other factors that contributed to the rapid rate of technological change in the United States in the nineteenth century. Some of Nathan Rosenberg's factors —a "utilitarian bent in American society," the "absence of inhibiting institutions," and a high level of education—may be regarded as consequences of the dominant ideologies.

[36] Charles Sanford, *The Quest for Paradise: Europe and the American Moral Imagination* (Urbana, Ill., 1961), 157-73; Perry Miller, *The Life of the Mind in America from the Revolution to the Civil War* (New York, 1965), 275-313; Hugo A. Meier, "Technology and Democracy, 1800-1860," *Mississippi Valley Historical Review*, XLIII (March 1957), 618-40. Of special interest is Timothy Walker's reply to Thomas Carlyle, "Defense of Mechanical Philosophy," reprinted in Pursell, ed., *Readings in Technology in American Life*, 67-77.

TABLE I

INVENTIONS IN PROPORTION TO POPULATION, 1800–1960[37]

Years	Total number of patents issued for inventions	Number of patents per 10,000 population	Percent increase or decrease
1800–1809	911	1.7	
1810–1819	1,998	2.8	64
1820–1829	2,697	2.8	0
1830–1839	5,605	4.4	57
1840–1849	5,508	3.2	− 27
1850–1859	19,591	8.4	163
1860–1869	71,679	22.1	163
1870–1879	124,672	31	40
1880–1889	195,104	39	26
1890–1899	221,277	35	− 10
1900–1909	304,696	40	14
1910–1919	381,198	41	3
1920–1929	414,923	39	− 5
1930–1939	442,856	36	− 8
1940–1949	307,634	23	− 36
1950–1959	425,990	28	22

Sources: United States Bureau of the Census, *Historical Statistics of the United States: Colonial Times to 1957* (Washington, 1960), 607–08; and *Historical Statistics . . . Continuation to 1962* (Washington, 1965), 85-86.

various strands (rationality, specialization, etc.) coming together in a social pattern that extended beyond the factories. In the 1850s, amidst a surge of urbanization and industrialization, technical integration became a significant force in American life. The railroads, the first big corporations, developed the elaborate administrative arrangements necessary to coordinate the flow of traffic and to supervise their personnel. In government a similar organization of large bodies of people within a strictly graded hierarchy of ability and authority was beginning in the urban public school systems and in urban police forces. A key figure was the civil engineer, who designed and managed complex projects for cities and private corporations alike. Trained in the new polytechnic institutes and scientific schools and imbued with a professional spirit, engineers rose to the status of planners and administrators.[38] Another key figure was the inventor. During the decade before the Civil War the rate of innovation—as measured by the number of inventions patented annually—made an astonishing leap, proportionately the largest in the nineteenth or twentieth centuries (see Table I).

[37] The decline in the rate of growth of patent office business in the twentieth century, as shown in Table I, is discussed in Alfred B. Stafford, "Is the Rate of Invention Declining?" *American Journal of Sociology*, LVII (May 1952), 539-45.
[38] Alfred D. Chandler, Jr. "The Coming of Big Business," C. Vann Woodward, ed., *The Comparative Approach to American History* (New York, 1968), 223-25; Michael B. Katz, *Class, Bureaucracy, and Schools: The Illusion of Educational Change in America*

This, of course, was only a beginning. A gradual but relentless diffusion of technical values went forward throughout the succeeding decades. The two most influential social philosophers of the post-Civil War era, Herbert Spencer and Henry C. Carey, were both prophets of a technical culture. For all of their differences on economic policy, Spencer and Carey shared a common commitment to a rational social order of interlinking specialists. Both argued that man progresses through the growth of occupational differentiation and the correlative forms of association that result. The evolutionary process develops specialization on one hand and interdependence on the other.[39] Nature is an evolving bureaucracy.

Accordingly, Spencer argued, successful adaptation requires habits of mind that are orderly and systematic, yet also innovative. Those were precisely the intellectual habits the new educational institutions of postwar America inculcated. At the lower level, urban public school systems taught regularity, punctuality, and above all acceptance of a rigid grading of students by ability and age. Simultaneously, the value of innovation was instilled at a higher level: the secularized universities enshrined an ideal of critical thinking in place of the older dependence on eternal verities.[40] At all levels of urban culture, Americans were learning to think more matter-of-factly about cause and effect. There is no clearer index of the spread of technical values than the increasing use of statistics as a basis for analysis and decision making.[41] To give but one example, the United States census

(New York, 1971), 56-104; David Tyack, "Bureaucracy and the Common School: The Example of Portland, Oregon, 1851-1913," *American Quarterly*, XIX (Fall 1967), 475-98; Roger Lane, *Policing the City: Boston 1822-1885* (Cambridge, Mass., 1967), 95-105; Raymond H. Merritt, *Engineering in American Society 1850-1875* (Lexington, Ky., 1969); Daniel H. Calhoun, *Professional Lives in America: Structure and Aspiration 1750-1850* (Cambridge, Mass., 1965), 56-58, 186-97. For a detailed, illuminating study of one of the mid-century pioneers in technical integration—the first American to focus intensively on what he called in 1854 "the science of management"—see Alfred D. Chandler, Jr., *Henry Varnum Poor: Business Editor, Analyst, and Reformer* (Cambridge, Mass., 1956).
[39] Robert L. Carneiro, "Structure, Function, and Equilibrium in the Evolutionism of Herbert Spencer," *Journal of Anthropological Research*, 29 (Summer 1973), 77-95; Henry C. Carey, *Principles of Social Science* (3 vols., New York, 1858-1860); Arnold W. Green, *Henry C. Carey, Nineteenth Century Sociologist* (Philadelphia, 1951), 55, 79-80. Herbert Spencer was a civil engineer before he became a social philosopher, and his philosophy can be understood as an application to nature of the principles of organization he learned in managing a railroad.
[40] Katz, *Class, Bureaucracy, and Schools*; Robert L. Church, "Introduction," Paul Buck, ed., *Social Sciences at Harvard, 1860-1920: From Inculcation to the Open Mind* (Cambridge, Mass., 1965), 1-17. The best compilation of Spencer's educational writings is in Andreas M. Kazamias, ed., *Herbert Spencer on Education* (New York, 1966).
[41] James Willard Hurst, *Law and the Conditions of Freedom in the Nineteenth-Century United States* (Madison, 1967), 73-74; Daniel J. Boorstin, *The Americans: The Democratic Experience* (New York, 1973), 165-213.

of 1850, sometimes called the first modern census, was contained within one volume; the census of 1900 filled ten.

In that matter-of-fact age of technical knowledge, it was not long before a subtle but unmistakable deflation of ideological thinking became evident. The dominant ideologies depended on an idealistic world view; they assumed that ideas shape events. In a technical world, however, a preoccupation with means has tended to take the place of the ends those means were originally designed to serve. One notices a despiritualization of life, visible already in the 1850s but more marked after the Civil War. Both painting and literature revealed a loss of heroic affirmation, together with a refinement of technique.[42] The clinical point of view that shaped the superbly articulated novels of Henry James and the objective canvasses of Thomas Eakins stemmed from technical values quite as much as did the philosophy of Spencer. Likewise in popular literature the sphere of the ideal contracted. Triumphing over one's own moral shortcomings dwindled as a primary theme in best-selling novels; the challenge of external barriers came to the fore. Similarly the emphasis on moral teaching in children's textbooks declined drastically between 1840 and 1880.[43] In the handbooks on success a comparable shift occurred a little later. By the end of the nineteenth century getting ahead seemed to require a panoply of techniques more than a set of principles.[44] The whole ideological framework receded, and utilitarian rules took over part of the function ethical absolutes had performed.

The American ideology also suffered a special disadvantage. It asserted that America is uniquely entrusted with humanity's ideals and hopes. In a technical age, however, American intellectuals became more humble about the limitations of their own spare culture and more aware of common problems emerging in all industrial societies. For solving those problems the insufficiency of the old republican faith became painfully apparent.[45] By

[42] David C. Huntington, *Art and the Excited Spirit: America in the Romantic Period* (Ann Arbor, 1972), 23-26.
[43] Richard de Charms and Gerald H. Moeller, "Values Expressed in American Children's Readers: 1800-1950," *Journal of Abnormal and Social Psychology*, LXIV (Feb. 1962), 136-42. My understanding of the themes in popular fiction rests on an unpublished analysis by Raymond Detter of the thirty best-selling novels by American authors published between 1841 and 1874, as listed in Frank Luther Mott, *Golden Multitudes: The Story of Best Sellers in the United States* (New York, 1947), 306-10.
[44] Richard Weiss, *The American Myth of Success: From Horatio Alger to Norman Vincent Peale* (New York, 1969), 11-14. For an early example, reprinted in 1970 with a valuable introduction by Annette K. Baxter, see "Business Habits: Qualifications Essential to Success," *The Universal Self-Instructor and Manual of General Reference* (New York, 1883), 484-86.
[45] Some parts of this transition are noticed in John Tomsich, *A Genteel Endeavor: American Culture and Politics in the Gilded Age* (Stanford, Cal., 1971), 88; Frederic Cople Jaher, *Doubters and Dissenters: Cataclysmic Thought in America, 1885-1918* (New

the 1890s society seemed to be tearing apart, and the American ideology was in need of reconstruction.

It is a commonplace of current historiography that the first two decades of the twentieth century brought a dramatic advance of complex organizations depending on specialized knowledge. Consequently, a "bureaucratic orientation" triumphed in American politics. The hallmarks of the period were the entry of the scientific expert into the governmental process at all levels and the diffusion of "scientific management" in industry. "Efficiency" promised a remedy for personal inadequacies as well as social injustices. So salient has this perspective become that many historians no longer take very seriously the Progressive era's rampant evangelism, its romantic celebration of freedom, equality, and heroism.[46] For too long, it is true, the old-fashioned rhetoric of the progressives obscured the calculus of their social engineering. Nevertheless, in a long-term perspective, the distinctive feature of the period from 1898 to 1918 is not the preeminence of democratic ideals or of bureaucratic techniques, but rather a fertile amalgamation of the two. An extraordinary quickening of ideology occurred in the very midst of a dazzling elaboration of technical systems. Instead of continuing to retreat as technical relations expanded, the old ideological framework was temporarily revitalized. For a time it seemed that a modernized Americanism and a social gospel could be the moving spirit of a technical society.[47] After World War I that hope waned; and we have yet to deal adequately with its failure.

York, 1964); Richard L. Rapson, *Britons View America: Travel Commentary, 1860-1935* (Seattle, 1971), 174-77.

[46] Samuel Haber, *Efficiency and Uplift: Scientific Management in the Progressive Era 1890-1920* (Chicago, 1964); Samuel P. Hays, *Conservation and The Gospel of Efficiency: The Progressive Conservation Movement, 1890-1920* (Cambridge, Mass., 1959); Joel H. Spring, *Education and the Rise of the Corporate State* (Boston, 1972); Jerry Israel, ed., *Building the Organizational Society: Essays on Associational Activities in Modern America* (New York, 1972). I am particularly indebted to the key book in this mode, Robert H. Wiebe, *The Search for Order: 1877-1920* (New York, 1967). I have differed from Robert Wiebe not only in trying to rescue the large kernel of truth in the older interpretation of progressivism but also in adopting a longer time perspective. Wiebe's concentration on dramatic change in a single decade at the turn of the century overlooks the gradual development of a technical order during the preceding fifty years. There was no "revolution in identity," no "Revolution in Values," no "intellectual revolution," and perhaps no "revolution that fundamentally altered the structure of politics and government early in the twentieth century." Wiebe, *Search for Order*, 113, 133, 145, 181. A longer perspective also permits a fuller appreciation of the ideological factor in America's "search for order." Wiebe argues that before the bureaucratic "revolution" America lacked cohesion; it was "a society without a core." *Ibid.*, 12. This judgment depends on the presupposition that national integration is to be found only in and through a complex organizational structure. Having defined integration as bureaucratic, Wiebe naturally finds none prior to the appearance of his bureaucrats. I suspect his book might have been less subject to these criticisms if it had not been confined to a fixed, limited span of time by the requirements of a series—another bureaucratic phenomenon!

[47] For arguments that the ideological revival was Protestant as well as nationalist and

The revival of ideology at the turn of the century released more than one kind of political energy. Progressivism, in the conventional sense of middle-class reform, contained only part of that energy. Some of it took the form of imperialism; some of it was expressed in an ideological kind of racism; some of it went into the remarkable upsurge of an American socialism. This last is a particularly revealing sign of the ideological passion of the Progressive era, for Marxist ideologies had until then failed to penetrate beyond small immigrant groups. The socialism of Eugene Debs, effervescent rather than doctrinaire, seems to have gained a mass following because it was a vehicle of the ideological revival. The American ideology was undergoing a reconstruction which enabled socialism to offer itself as a new version of a familiar faith, a new means of realizing the old dream of a promised land.[48]

Two alterations were basic to the renewal of the American ideology in the Progressive era. The first was a revised definition of freedom. Like socialists, the leading progressive intellectuals interpreted individual rights as a function of participation rather than autonomy. Not the absence of legal restraint but the capacity to share as widely as possible in the common good of the whole society makes us free and equal. Secondly, progressive intellectuals thought, scientific techniques can take the place of universal apriori principles. To identify the common good, we may rely on scientific inquiry. Since it is both flexible and objective, science can build a self-correcting mechanism into the American ideology. Moreover, science implements the concept of freedom through participation. Collaborative by their very nature, science and technology are extending the communications network, which in turn is widening a common life.[49] From the point of view of many progressives and most socialists, democracy and technical rationality were interdependent.

It was an exciting vision, and the disillusions that engulfed the ideological renaissance after 1918 did not destroy it completely. Most thought-

that the two were closely connected, see Robert T. Handy, *A Christian America: Protestant Hopes and Historical Realities* (New York, 1971), 128, 139; Winthrop S. Hudson, *American Protestantism* (Chicago, 1961), 124-27; Jean B. Quandt, "Religion and Social Thought: The Secularization of Post-millennialism," *American Quarterly*, XXV (Oct. 1973), 390-409.

[48] R. Laurence Moore, *European Socialists and the American Promised Land* (New York, 1970), 195-200.

[49] For an excellent synthesis, see Otis L. Graham, Jr., *The Great Campaigns: Reform and War in America, 1900-1928* (Englewood Cliffs, N.J., 1971). On the role of science and technology, see Sidney Kaplan, "Social Engineers as Saviours: Effects of World War I on Some American Liberals," *Journal of the History of Ideas*, XVII (June 1956), 347-69; Ronald C. Tobey, *The American Ideology of National Science, 1919-1930* (Pittsburgh, 1971); Jean B. Quandt, *From the Small Town to the Great Community: The Social Thought of Progressive Intellectuals* (New Brunswick, 1970).

ful Americans still believe in harnessing scientific-technical methods to
democratic ideals. What we have lost is any belief in an inner affinity between the two, such that together they can unite a divided society. What the
progressives hailed as complementary we must wrestle with as contradictions; for technical integration has tended in the long run to replace ideological unity instead of reinforcing it.

I have already mentioned in a cursory way one reason why that is so. The
utilitarian effectiveness of technical relationships made an over-arching faith
seem less important. This is not just a problem of means and ends. Moral
commands yielded to functional requirements not only because of the
demonstrable effectiveness of the latter for immediate purposes, but also
because specialization has separated one part of the culture from another
in a new way. In the twentieth century every activity has developed, more
and more, its own conceptual basis. Thus an increasing segmentation of
society weakens the hold of those universal beliefs that are the linchpins
of ideological unity.

A second reason for the incompatibility of the two types of unity has to
do with the particular values affirmed by the American ideology. Contrary
to what the progressives supposed, technical organization is essentially undemocratic. Not equal rights but the hierarchical articulation of differentiated
functions is its working principle. The more complex the knowledge required for maintaining a system, the further the professional expert is
detached from the common life and the more the centers of power are
hidden from public view.[50] It is not surprising that the technological utopias,
from Saint-Simon to B. F. Skinner, have abolished conflict and choice by
subordinating everyone else to a technical élite.

A widespread, overt consciousness of the opposition between ideals and
techniques emerged in the United States in the 1920s. Henry Adams' *Education* sounded the keynote: we have passed from unity to multiplicity, from
the Virgin to the Dynamo, from an age of faith to an age of uncontrollable
technological power.[51] Folk heroes like Henry Ford and Herbert Hoover
might insist that the partnership of machines with American ideals was
stronger than ever, but the passion of their advocacy betrayed a spreading
doubt. In different ways various groups repudiated the progressive synthesis.
Disillusioned writers described a mechanized, routinized society which

[50] Jacques Ellul, *The Technological Society* (New York, 1964), 263-89. See also
H. H. Gerth and C. Wright Mills, eds., *From Max Weber: Essays in Sociology* (New
York, 1958), 196-244.
[51] Henry Adams, *The Education of Henry Adams: An Autobiography* (Boston, 1918),
was the top nonfiction best seller in 1919. See Alice Payne Hackett, *70 Years of Best
Sellers, 1895-1965* (New York, 1967), 119.

204

turned humane values and national ideals into bitter travesties. For John Dos Passos, Elmer Rice, and Aldous Huxley technocracy crushed ideology or perverted it.[52] In contrast to these wounded idealists, many academic intellectuals kept an enthusiastic allegiance to the technical order, but in doing so they too sacrificed any long-range social goals. By insisting that science is strictly a method, the rapidly expanding social sciences tended to relieve themselves of concern with values, political programs, and ideologies.[53] A similar disjunction between ideals and techniques appeared in the popular culture of the time. Between 1905-1909 and 1925-1928 the proportion of articles published in general American magazines on topics relating to applied science increased more than sevenfold. The proportion of articles dealing with religion, philosophy, and pure science markedly declined. So we observe a common trend after World War I in American literature, in the social sciences, and in public opinion. The ideological bonds that had united Americans in the nineteenth century slackened, while technical integration accelerated. "The machine process," a young academic administrator glibly declared in 1924, "has captured practically every field of men's behavior."[54]

Since the 1920s the United States has moved farther in the same direction but not steadily or irreversibly. A second ideological revival welled up in the mid-1930s. It lasted, like the first, for about twenty years, and during that time it mitigated the compulsions of technical authority. Again, as in the Progressive era, the revival produced a reassertion of democratic ideals, an upsurge of nationalism, and a return to religion. Among its exemplars were Lewis Mumford, Reinhold Niebuhr, and Ralph Ellison. The revival

[52] John Dos Passos, *Three Soldiers* (New York, 1921); Elmer Rice, *The Adding Machine* (Garden City, 1923); Aldous Huxley, *Brave New World* (London, 1932); and Aldous Huxley, "The Outlook for American Culture: Some Reflections in a Machine Age," *Harper's Monthly Magazine*, CLV (Aug. 1927), 265-72. Some indications of the breadth of this concern in the 1920s are in: Edward J. O'Brien, *The Dance of the Machines: The American Short Story and the Industrial Age* (New York, 1929); John M. Clark, "The Empire of Machines," *Yale Review*, XII (Oct. 1922), 132-43; "The Great Theme," *Saturday Review of Literature*, II (May 8, 1926), 765; Gilbert Seldes, "The Machine Wreckers," *Saturday Evening Post*, CC (July 23, 1927), 27, 149-53. The most searing, as well as the first, of these attacks on the technical order came from Randolph Bourne, "Twilight of Idols," *Untimely Papers* (New York, 1919), 114-39.

[53] Edward A. Purcell, Jr., *The Crisis of Democratic Theory: Scientific Naturalism & the Problem of Value* (Lexington, Ky., 1973), 25-29, 103-04; John Chynoweth Burnham, "The New Psychology: From Narcissism to Social Control," John Braeman, Robert H. Bremner, and David Brody, eds., *Change and Continuity in Twentieth-Century America: The 1920's* (Columbus, Ohio, 1968), 351-98.

[54] Lawrence K. Frank, "An Institutional Analysis of the Law," *Columbia Law Review*, XXIV (May 1924), 495. See also *Recent Social Trends in the United States: Report of the President's Research Committee on Social Trends* (2 vols., New York, 1933), I, 393-96.

infused into history and the social sciences a renewed belief in the primary importance of ideas, norms, and values. But the content of this second revival—the principles and programs it espoused—was never as sharply defined as the substance of the progressive revival had been. From the outset this latter-day idealism had to serve the defensive purposes of global warfare. Plunging from one crisis to another, its spokesmen could not fix on a clear set of goals.[55] Shriveled remnants of the American ideology fell increasingly into the hands of demagogues and cold warriors. Eventually, battered intellectuals were glad to announce the end of ideology.[56] As ideological passions cooled, however, the emptiness and desolation of a technocratic world were felt more crushingly than ever before.

The experience of the last few years has not demonstrated that ideology is alive and well, only that it is still in demand. Looking back, it is possible to conclude that the age of ideology has indeed passed. Perhaps, in the long perspective of world history, the ideological age will prove to be only an intermediate stage between the primordial community and a thoroughly technical society. An alternative conclusion, however, seems to me equally possible and more attractive.

Conceivably, a deeper examination of historical experience than I have here attempted may reveal a continuing struggle to bring the primordial, the ideological, and the technical dimensions of culture into some kind of workable counterpoise with one another. American history suggests that none of these linkages can stand alone and that an alliance between any two of them will also fail. The efforts of racists and ethnic nationalists to save primordial solidarity by imposing an overlay of ideological unity have never been wholly successful. The efforts of progressives to save ideological unity by undergirding it with technical structures have also broken down. But each of these adhesive forces—the primordial, the ideological, and the technical—has something to contribute to our complex society; and each of them survives within it. If we can discover how to align the technical with the primordial so that each offsets the other, and give to ideology the task of challenging both, we may raise to a new level one of the great and enduring principles of our ideological heritage: the importance of diversity, the value of countervailing power.

[55] Purcell, Crisis of Democratic Theory, 135-231; Richard H. Pells, Radical Visions and American Dreams: Culture and Social Thought in the Depression Years (New York, 1973); Warren Susman, "The Thirties," Stanley Coben and Lorman Ratner, eds., The Development of an American Culture (Englewood Cliffs, N.J., 1970), 179-218.
[56] Daniel Bell, The End of Ideology: On the Exhaustion of Political Ideas in the Fifties (Glencoe, Ill., 1960); Robert E. Lane, "The Decline of Politics and Ideology in a Knowledgeable Society," American Sociological Review, 31 (Oct. 1966), 649-62.

1

The Mobilization of Immigrants in Urban America*

by John Higham

Early in the twentieth century sociologists inaugurated the scholarly study of immigrant communities in urban America. A whole new world came into view, especially well disclosed in the masterpiece by William I. Thomas and Florian Znaniecki, *The Polish Peasant in Europe and America.*[1] Historians, however, paid no heed. The discovery of the immigrant as a major theme in American history was made later, in the 1920s, and made by historians with no interest in urban sociology. It was made not in great cities like Chicago or New York but rather in midwestern state universities by young scholars still close to a small-town or rural background, who had gained their essential vision of American history from Frederick Jackson Turner. Between the two world wars the "Turnerverein" (as it was affectionately called) was so preeminent in our discipline that a Greek from Milwaukee, Theodore Saloutos, made his reputation as a student of American agriculture and shifted only in the 1950s to the history of his own forebears. The immigrants who fired the

*This paper was originally presented at a conference at St. Olaf College, October 26–27, 1984, on "Scandinavians and Other Immigrants in Urban America." The present article is a revised version of the paper as it was published in the proceedings of that conference.

3

imagination of historians in the 1920s and 1930s were those
whose odyssey could be understood as part of the westward
movement—people who belonged to the earth like Ántonia
Shimerda in Willa Cather's Nebraska and Per Hansa struggling to endure the Dakota plains. The pioneers of American
immigration history, above all Marcus Lee Hansen and
Theodore Blegen, gave an international sweep to the Turnerian theme of the impact of the natural environment on the
people it receives. This approach connected American history
with European history; yet it left the familiar motifs of the
American story undisturbed.[2]

A specifically urban approach to immigration history—
by which I mean a focus on processes of social interaction in
a dense and complex milieu—awaited the discovery of urban
sociology and anthropology by historians whose own roots
were in the great cities. By the 1940s a new generation, for
whom the Turnerian vision of the American past would no
longer suffice, was emerging from the graduate schools.
Among these "asphalt flowers" (to use the sobriquet some
Turnerites applied to them) was Oscar Handlin. His doctoral
dissertation, *Boston's Immigrants*, published in 1941, offered a
model of how the insights and methods of sociology could
be adapted to the materials of American history. Guided by
a sociological understanding of ethnic communities, Handlin
looked—as no historian had before—at how immigrants
coped with the process of urbanization and how a major city
changed under the stress of their coming.[3]

After this superb beginning, progress was curiously
slow. In the next two decades only one comparable monograph attempted, as Handlin's had, to embrace the multiethnic structure of an American city at a significant moment
of transition; and this second effort was an implicit warning
of the difficulty of the task, for it touched on too many disparate matters to make a strongly focused argument. The
tremendous complexity of the modern American city discouraged comprehensive studies. An adequate successor to
Boston's Immigrants materialized only in 1962, when Handlin's
student, Moses Rischin, published *The Promised City*, but

limited his subject to the experience of a single ethnic group, the eastern European Jews.[4]

Several more of Handlin's early students studied immigrants in urban or industrial contexts, as did some of Merle Curti's.[5] Gradually scholars overseas — activated by the spread of American Studies and the widening horizons of modern history — were attracted to the history of European emigration. Sources were close at hand, and the subject touched their own national histories in vital ways. Although foreign scholars have written mostly about the backgrounds and movement of emigrants, their contribution has been essential and is being continually enlarged.[6] Leadership, however, remained in the United States, and in the late 1950s it visibly waned.

Addressing this problem some years ago, Rudolph Vecoli ventured a partial explanation. In that expansive era after World War II, Vecoli pointed out, dazzling opportunities for academic careers were opening up for urban Catholics and Jews who could identify themselves with a professoriat that had previously been out of reach. Instead of studying their own origins, these newly arrived academics demonstrated their fervent commitment to the goal of assimilation by giving ethnic history a wide berth.[7] To this I would add a further thought. The process of assimilation was in actuality proceeding so rapidly and widely in the 1950s that even some scholars who were *not* escaping from their origins became doubtful of the enduring significance of ethnic differences. In the atmosphere of the late 1950s I myself found ethnic history less interesting than I had a decade earlier, and moved away from it.

Another factor that retarded the development of immigration history in the 1950s and 1960s was the paradigm that shaped the general contours of American historiography during those decades. Reacting against an earlier fascination with deep-cutting social conflicts, leading historians now reveled in discovering underlying uniformities and similarities.[8] By incorporating the immigrants within a national consensus, historians stripped away much of their differentness.

If young scholars were first attracted to the story of the immigrants — as I was — because it vibrated with dramatic social contrasts, a perspective that reduced the salience of those contrasts could only be discouraging.

Three examples suggest how the erosion occurred. During the 1950s Oscar Handlin turned against the view of the immigrant as an ousider, "a foreign element injected into American life."[9] Instead, he cast the immigrant as a type of American, undergoing as all Americans have a painful but liberating transition to modernity and freedom. By the 1960s Handlin was writing mostly about the American character and American institutions, and so were his students.

One of the earliest of those students, Rowland Berthoff, had begun by studying British and Slavic coal miners in America. In 1960, after some years of unexciting toil, Berthoff found his own way to display the whole of American history against a medieval background. He has never gone back to the mines.[10] At the University of Minnesota two years later Timothy L. Smith launched a wide-ranging study of eastern European immigrants with special reference to their assimilation. His chief contribution was to trace the immigrants' pursuit of the American dream back to predisposing experiences in Europe, experiences that made their entry into an American mainstream virtually foreordained.[11] This approach stimulated some valuable research, but it yielded a history that was peculiarly free from conflict. After a decade of study of the history of migration, Smith returned to the history of religious beliefs.

Thus for several decades the leading scholars in American immigration history emitted an ambivalent message. They called for research in a new field that seemed strikingly different from what historians had customarily studied, yet the lessons they extracted from it simply reinforced the conventional wisdom. Historians brought a new group of characters onto the stage; but the new characters usually behaved in accordance with traditional scripts. Immigration historians needed a perspective that could accentuate the distinctiveness and therefore the differentness of their subjects.

Not until the late 1960s did such perspectives become widely available. Against a tumultuous background of riots and protests the consensus paradigm was severely shaken. A new insistence on the power and persistence of the ethnic bond came to the fore.

Again social scientists led the way. Nathan Glazer and Daniel P. Moynihan inaugurated in 1963 a sustained critique of the melting-pot idea, a critique that became more and more insistent in the late sixties and early seventies. *Beyond the Melting Pot* argued that Americans are not and never have been a single people. Ethnic differences, originating in peculiar cultural inheritances, become fortified in the course of time by diverse economic and political allegiances. Ethnic groups survive not only as cultural vehicles but also as interest groups.[12] Here was a perspective that young historians, disillusioned with the promise of assimilation and aroused by the collapse of consensus, had been waiting for.

The resulting production of specialized scholarship on dozens of American ethnic groups has been abundant; and most of this outpouring has concentrated on the urban world from which our younger historians now largely derive. Even some of the earliest immigrant groups — the Palatine Germans and the French Huguenots — have now been studied in urban settings.[13] It is not easy to say what general conclusions these studies yield, but four special features that many of them share may be identified.

1. Intra-ethnic conflicts. Historians during the last fifteen years have diligently explored many disputes and rivalries within groups previously seen as more cohesive: struggles between generations among the Japanese, between tongs and other rival societies among the Chinese, between secular nationalist and Roman Catholic leaders among the Poles, between Uptown and Downtown Jews, between socialist Finns and church Finns, and so on.[14] Ethnic scholarship flourished in the 1970s as a means of particularizing identities. It exposed the cleavages that abstract ideological labels had obscured — labels such as American, Catholic, Indian, Negro, or even German-American and Italian-American. What mattered now was the tangible community of shared experience within sub-groups like Italian-American working-class women or the members of a German Catholic parish. Accordingly, serious scholarship did not often substitute an idealized ethnic nationalism for the Americanism it was undercutting. Some of the more fervent ethnic studies programs failed to appreciate the double-edged character of this particularizing imperative which made the divisions within an ethnic sector as vivid and significant as its overall identity. But a recognition that internal conflict is part of the life of every community was widely characteristic of the scholarship of this period.

2. *Contrasting responses of different ethnic groups to the American milieu.* Until the 1960s immigration historians had generally avoided making comparisons between ethnic groups. Such comparisons were thought to be invidious, potentially inflammatory, and misleading in view of the presumed dominance of environment in human affairs. *Boston's Immigrants* had featured a striking cultural contrast between the Irish and the Yankees, but Handlin had thereafter shifted to a more inclusive style of generalization, and the contrast was not followed up. But the pluralist mood of the 1960s finally legitimized the explicit examination of ethnic differences, and Glazer and Moynihan in *Beyond the Melting Pot* provided a bold example of the attractions as well as the dangers of such inquiries.

Simultaneously the opportunity materialized to probe these ethnic responses to American life at an altogether new level of scholarly rigor. The sudden popularity of quantitative methods, which historians had not hitherto used, enabled them to investigate the strategies of different groups in a way that demanded a hearing. The ethnocultural school of political historians, springing from the pioneering work of Lee Benson and Samuel P. Hays in the early 1960s, made clear how the cultural and religious traditions of various groups affected their political behavior.[15] From the point of view of the immigration historian much of this work had an important limitation. It was designed to explain how the American political system has worked; it was not intended to contribute to a larger history of the ethnic groups, and thus it did not probe the relation of politics to other aspects of their communal life. But historians who are primarily interested in ethnicity have begun to do just that.[16]

Another quantitative discipline that has encouraged the comparative study of ethnic groups is historical demography. Beginning with Stephan Thernstrom's doctoral dissertation, *Poverty and Progress* (1964), historians learned how to use unpublished census schedules and other records of private life to reconstruct the decisions that immigrants and others made about the size and character of their families, the education of their children, and the work they did. Thernstrom showed that the Irish differed significantly from the older American working class in the trade-off they made between education and the acquisition of property. Josef Barton then showed that the Slovaks differed in similar ways from Italians and Rumanians, and so on.[17]

These quantitative studies of mobility and adaptation addressed a central question that had fueled immigration history from the beginning. How have immigrants joined in the American pursuit of success, and to what avail? Measuring the material and social advancement of one generation over the previous one was extremely fashionable for a few years but then seemed increasingly out of place in a climate of opinion that scorned the old myths of assimilation and progress. After the mid-seventies a reaction against mobility studies set in. This happened, I believe, because such studies demonstrated too much success to fit the prevailing critique of the melting pot. Mobility studies had been born out of a sympathy for failure as much as a respect for success; they had offered a means of putting defeat and achievement side by side. Pluralistic historians cooled rapidly toward such studies when Andrew Greeley and Thomas Sowell used them to demonstrate that all ethnic groups succeed in America sooner or later.[18]

3. *A search for ethnic continuities.* In challenging the homogenizing myth of the American melting pot, immigra-

tion historians in the last two decades have looked hard for
distinctive traditions, customs, and capabilities that did not
yield easily to assimilative pressures but instead sustained a
group in its encounter with a new and alien land. None of our
immigration historians has produced a study of cultural continuity that is as powerful as Lawrence Levine's *Black Culture
and Black Consciousness* or as imaginative as Herbert Gutman's
The Black Family in Slavery and Freedom,[19] but many have
worked along the same lines. Some have examined sympa-
thetically the continuities imbedded in religious beliefs and
institutions. Others have shown how sturdily the immigrant
family coped with the shocks of migration and how strongly
it molded the next generation. In what may be the finest book
in this mode, *From Italy to San Francisco*, Dino Cinel takes a dialectical approach to continuity and change, pointing to ways
in which Italian emigrants strove to hold on to a crumbling
world and in doing so found the strength to make a new
one.[20]

Numerous historians have traced ethnic continuities into
the sphere of work — some to explain the immigrants' choice
of occupations, others to account for the way workers
responded to the kind of discipline they encountered in factories and mines. Especially influential has been Herbert Gutman's theory that what he calls "premodern values," brought
to industrial America by a constant influx of newcomers, account for much of the resistance of workers to employer
demands.[21]

4. The relation of ethnicity to class. The fascination of many
historians in the late 1960s and 1970s with questions of exploitation and injustice inevitably called attention to the
problematic relation between ethnic loyalties and class struggles. Following up ideas that Gutman borrowed from E. P.
Thompson, historians of labor and of radicalism have probed
diligently for the contributions specific ethnic groups have
made to wider movements of social protest.[22] This line of inquiry meets considerable resistance from more traditional
Marxists, who regard the emphasis on culture and ethnicity
as romantic traditionalism and propose that labor history

should concern itself more largely with political and economic power.[23]

While labor historians have disagreed about the importance of ethnicity, as a group they have been fully aware of the significance of the issues it poses for them. Immigration historians have been more parochial. Few of them, at least until recently, have looked squarely at the problem of class. In the 1980s this situation has begun to change. Independently of one another, John Bodnar and Olivier Zunz have proposed what seem to me exciting new interpretations of the coalescence of previously distinct ethnic groups into a white working class in the twentieth century.[24] Their interest in class *formation* can lead us beyond the labor historian's preoccupation with class *antagonisms*. Nevertheless, it remains true that immigration historians, unlike their colleagues in labor history, have not yet joined in any ongoing debate or theoretical argument on the interaction in American history between ethnicity and class. Why this is so deserves an explanation.

A simple answer might be that the influence of Marxism and other economic theories has long given labor history an aggressively interpretive edge that immigration history does not have. Immigration history has drawn on the less systematic concepts of empirical sociology. For immigration historians the basic question has always been the question of assimilation—the extent and direction of it, resistance to it, and myths about it.[25] In asking this question immigration historians have ordinarily concentrated on the immigrants' behavior and have tended to view American society "as a constituted and integral whole."[26] Understanding the changing structure of the larger society has not been, for immigration historians, a major objective. For labor historians it has.

As a means of contrasting the intellectual antecedents of two fields that now find themselves occupying common ground in the study of the American city, this explanation will do well enough. But something more should be said to account for the special condition of immigration historiography in the 1960s and 1970s. Historians of American ethnic groups during those years were simply less interested in the shape and structure of the host society than their predecessors had been. Under the spur of the ethnic revival, historians turned inward. Each tended to become a specialist in one particular group. In studying the chosen group, scholars reaped a harvest of knowledge about specific ethnic institutions, responses, and attainments. As to how those phenomena might have altered a larger context, very little was said.

The exceptional attraction of this internal approach to immigration history in the period just past becomes dramatically apparent in looking back at the four features of the period that I have just reviewed. The study of intra-ethnic conflicts, the comparative study of immigrant reactions to the American environment, and the search for ethnic continuities: all three of these features gave priority to what was happening within the experience of particular groups. The fourth feature — relating ethnicity to class — leads outward from the ethnic community to the larger society; but most of that job was not done by immigration historians. All in all, it seems fair to say that during the ethnic revival the scholars who opened to us so much of the inner world of the immigrants left their impact on America largely unexamined. In the 1980s a renewed assessment of how immigration and ethnicity have affected other aspects of American life belongs near the top of the agenda of immigration historians.

II

Rather than survey the numerous ways in which the impact of immigrants on urban America needs reappraisal, I have chosen in the remainder of this essay to dwell on one that has never received the attention it deserves. People make themselves felt in a society on many different levels, some complex and subtle, others blatantly obvious; some fully intentional, others unplanned and unforeseen. The most forceful and outspoken demands for power or influence occur when previously apathetic or uninvolved people are aroused to feverish activity and intense commitment. This is what I mean by ethnic mobilization. It is a good place to begin to look at the immigrant as a causal agent in American history.

In recent years the concept of mobilization has come into fairly widespread use in political science and sociology to designate the process by which submerged elements in society attain political consciousness and begin to make political demands.[27] Historians have occasionally employed the term "ethnic mobilization" in talking in a very general way about the formation of group consciousness. One speaks, for example, of the "ethnic mobilization of what became America's immigrant peoples" as beginning "in their homelands."[28] For my purpose ethnic mobilization does not refer to the genesis of ethnic consciousness or to its earliest political expression. Instead, I have in mind a more advanced stage of militancy.

Not every ethnic group in America has experienced a militant phase, nor have all sections of a group participated in the militancy when it occurs. But mobilization can be a contagious process, and I shall therefore concentrate on those dramatic occasions in American history when two or more ethnic minorities have joined in a common struggle. On such occasions mobilization sweeps across some ethnic boundaries, then stops at others, and thus reveals like a bolt of lightning the geography of discontent. To study ethnic mobilization as historians have studied other recurrent phenomena, watching it rise and fall, spread and contract, and take new forms as it taps new demands, is to observe how insecure minorities have striven at certain times to shape the course of history.

Since mobilization requires an internal change in the people it activates, one might suppose that it should have attracted considerable interest during the ethnic revival. That it did not may be partly attributable to the conventions that govern the writing of ethnic histories. The prevailing historiographical convention assumes that each group has its own separate history. That history is thought to consist of certain prescribed stages, which vary little from one group to another. The common pattern begins with the origins of the group, the reasons for its departure from the homeland, and

the form its migration took. The second stage is the creation
of a community: finding an area of settlement, gaining a
livelihood, and transplanting essential institutions. In the
third stage the ethnic community matures. The historian accordingly devotes successive chapters to a topical treatment
of various aspects of its developed life. The fourth and last
stage concerns the survival and/or decline of the ethnic group
in later generations. Mobilization can sometimes be discovered, if the reader ferrets it out, in aspects of the third stage
and even the fourth; but the overall sequence of stages does
not lead us to expect it. Quite the reverse: the history of each
single group unfolds through an inner dialectic of growth
and adaptation. Mobilization, however, springs from external incitements that strike a group in a particular state of ethnic readiness. To study mobilization is to study the foreign
relations of ethnic groups with one another. It is to move
decisively beyond the particularistic parameters of the immigration history inspired by the ethnic revival.

To readers of Scandinavian background a warning is in
order. In what follows, the Finns are the only Scandinavian
nationality who play a prominent role. Other Scandinavians
are conspicuous by their near-invisibility. Although further
investigation may show that I have unjustly neglected some
Norwegian or Swedish involvement in inter-ethnic mobilization, on the surface the very limited participation of Scandinavian Americans in the great episodes of ethnic assertive-
ness seems an important and hitherto unnoticed feature of
their American experience.

III

Mobilization depends crucially on leadership. It is hardly surprising that the earliest significant mobilization of European
minorities occurred in the sphere in which a vigorous inter-
ethnic leadership first came into being. Only in their religion
did the immigrants in antebellum America have a leadership
willing and able to challenge existing institutions. In the
1840s and 1850s Catholic immigrants rallied behind their
priests and bishops to oppose the Protestant character of pub-

lic education in towns and cities where they were sufficiently numerous to have some effect.

Surprisingly little is known about Catholic efforts to alter the public schools in the mid-nineteenth century or about the counter-mobilization of urban Protestants in the Know-Nothing movement. Although we now have good studies of the development of public education in those years and some valuable political analysis of the Know-Nothing party,[29] the basic confrontation of Catholic and Protestant has not been reexamined on a national scale since Ray Billington wrote *The Protestant Crusade* in 1938. What we know is that a tremendous surge in the growth of the Catholic population—increasing 142 percent in the 1840s alone—coincided with a growing belief among older Americans in the necessity of a unified public school system to maintain a stabilizing morality in a highly volatile society. The common school emerged in the mid-nineteenth century as one of the essential symbols of American nationality. Immigrant Catholic leaders, however, loathed the state schools that threatened to separate children from their parents and their pastors. In the early 1850s Catholic clergy and the Democratic legislators who represented them began to agitate for a cessation of Bible-reading in public schools and the allocation of a share of the public school funds to parochial schools so that the taxes Catholics paid could be used to support their own institutions.[30]

Nearly everywhere these demands were repelled. In the cities Protestants remained in control of the public schools. Although this first mobilization seemed to fail, the bloodshed and animosity it produced taught both sides a lesson in pragmatic accommodation. Catholic authorities were much more cautious thereafter about taking political initiatives. School boards, for their part, gradually made the public schools more attractive to Catholic parents by informal concessions on curricula and textbooks.[31]

Another major mobilization of immigrants in defense of their culture occurred from 1889 to 1893. This time the immigrant coalition was wider than it had been in the 1850s.

German Lutherans were roused and joined forces with Irish, German, Polish, and French-Canadian Catholics. The basic alignment of immigrants upholding their specific heritage against Protestant nationalists who insisted on greater cultural uniformity was unchanged, but the issues were broader. Prohibition was at least as important as the school question, which entailed for many Lutherans and Catholics a special struggle to retain their language. But the chief difference between the mid-century phase and this later phase of cultural mobilization was the strictly defensive character of the latter. By 1889 the immigrants were simply protecting the institutions they had painfully built in the preceding decades.

Why did the school problem revive in the late eighties, unprompted by the kind of initiatives that immigrant leaders had taken in the 1850s? One explanation stresses Anglo-Protestant alarm at a vigorous expansion of the Catholic school system, which the bishops had ordered at the Third Plenary Council of Baltimore in 1884.[32] Another explanation, one that accounts better for the prominence of German Protestants in the new mobilization, is that the outside world was closing in on ethnic enclaves in a sudden, unexpected way.

Two sets of demands for greater state control of private life converged on Republican state legislators in the late 1880s. One set, originating among evangelical Protestant women and reformers, called for some form of local or statewide prohibition of the liquor traffic. According to Richard Jensen, the prohibition question became the paramount local issue, year in and year out, throughout most of the Midwest and large parts of the East.[33] A second set of demands, though less noisy, was actually more explosive. It came from professional educators who wanted more effective supervision and centralization in education. Compulsory school laws, already enacted in half the states, had never been enforced. At least partly to enforce school attendance and prevent child labor, Illinois and Wisconsin in 1889 enacted laws requiring children to attend a school approved by their local board of education. The laws further stipulated that certain basic subjects should be taught in English.[34] To ethnic groups whose survival might depend on the local autonomy American institutions had always allowed, prohibition and the regulation of private schools seemed frontal attacks on their culture and their rights as parents.

The new school legislation envisaged only limited regulation. Why it deeply outraged vast numbers of immigrants may be hard to understand unless one bears in mind the wider alarm in late nineteenth-century America over a loss of independence and a decline in local autonomy. Old-stock Americans as well as immigrants felt that great forces beyond their control were invading their communities.[35] The intrusive, centralizing state that evangelical Republicans sponsored presented to Catholic and Lutheran minorities a threat similar to that which the "trusts" were beginning to pose to other Americans. Through the Democratic party the immigrants rallied to defend their "personal liberty."

Their triumph was stunning but short-lived. Beginning in 1889 with dazzling victories in Iowa and New Jersey, the Democrats swept state after state where temperance and school issues were central. They repealed the new school laws in Illinois and Wisconsin, turned back the prohibition movement, and in 1892 rolled up huge majorities in German, Swedish, Italian, Polish, and Bohemian districts.[36] For the time being, the parochial schools and the saloons were safe. After repelling the Republican onslaught, though, the immigrant coalition quickly broke up. Quarrels between the major ethnic groups within the Catholic Church, having subsided somewhat with the united front of the early nineties, flared up with new bitterness. In politics the depression of 1893 sidetracked evangelical moral reform and turned attention to national economic issues on which there was no ethnic consensus.[37] The party loyalties of many immigrant voters weakened. When the depression lifted, the political system of the northern states was firmly in the grasp of a nationally oriented middle class. In most of the larger cities outside the South the Republican party had gained a clear predominance. Among the ethnic groups that had supported the

Democratic party so vigorously in the early nineties voting now declined substantially; the newer immigrants entering the United States voted even less.[38] The mobilization of ethnic dissent by a major political party was out of the question for a generation.

So the cultural battles of the nineteenth century subsided in a tolerable truce, and ethnic militancy shifted to different terrain. While the political defense of religion and culture slackened, many immigrants threw themselves into movements for control of the workplace. They endeavored to mobilize as a class. Whether to join in the struggle or to stand aloof was the first critical decision that the new immigrants from southern and eastern Europe had to make after deciding to stay in America.

At least from the 1840s European immigrants had decisively shaped the American labor movement. Since many northern European immigrants arrived in America with experience in industrial crafts and with a well developed class consciousness, they joined trade unions readily and rose quickly to leadership. The Germans, for example, comprised 36 percent of the Chicago trade unions in 1886, though they were only 22.5 percent of the Chicago working class.[39] But while the immigrants brought stamina and dedication to American unions, disharmony between ethnic groups discouraged industry-wide organization. Working-class action was confined to the narrow and immediate objectives of autonomous craft unions. In 1897 just 2 percent of those gainfully employed outside of agriculture were organized.

By the turn of the century this modest figure doubled; a momentous change was under way. Between 1897 and 1919, two great waves of unrest rippled through the motley ranks of semiskilled and unskilled workers from southern and eastern Europe. Total union membership in the United States soared from 447,000 to more than five million, or about 16 percent of the labor force outside of agriculture.[40] The first of the two waves of unrest, extending from 1897 to 1904, began among the Slavic coal miners in the anthracite fields of eastern Pennsylvania, where the uncharacteristic perseverance of the strikers apparently owed a good deal to a legacy of peasant insurgency which rebellious priests who formed the Polish National Catholic Church brought from Galicia.[41] The second wave began in 1909 among immigrant steel workers at McKees Rock, Pennsylvania, and among Jewish and Italian women in the shirtwaist shops of New York. Here again the embattled workers had at the outset, within their own ethnic groups, leaders who brought experiences and radical convictions from the Old World. The McKees Rock workers included several veterans of European radical movements, who constituted themselves an executive committee to stiffen the equivocal stand of the American skilled workers. The shirtwaist-makers gained the backing of the rising socialist movement on the lower East Side and most especially of new emigrés who came to America after the failure of the Russian Revolution of 1905.[42]

To stress radical leadership is inevitably to call attention to the gathering strength of the Socialist party during these years, and particularly to the importance of its foreign language federations. The largest of the federations, proportionately, were Finnish, Slovenian, and Jewish. They grew not because of, but almost in spite of, the national leadership of the Socialist party, which did little in the early years of the twentieth century to cultivate its new-immigrant constituencies. Their activation sprang directly from European socialism through the migration of young Marxist firebrands who, on fleeing to the United States to escape arrest or military service, established the first socialist clubs and newspapers for their respective nationalities.[43] World War I brought this immigrant radicalism to a culmination. The foreign language federations swelled to 35 percent of Socialist party membership in 1917, then to 53 percent in 1919. Carried over into peacetime, the apocalyptic mood of the war years nerved the immigrant masses to attempt against all odds to unionize the steel industry.[44] When the great steel strike of 1919 failed, immigrant radicalism collapsed. The era of class mobilization was over.

How shall we account for the fervent militancy of those

years? Obviously the presence of dynamic leadership will not by itself explain the tremendous response that came forth from hundreds of thousands of vulnerable little people, who put their livelihood, and in some cases their lives as well, on the line. Historians are far from having answers to such questions, but there may be an intriguing clue in the curious fact that a third type of ethnic mobilization emerged in the climactic years of class mobilization and reached a peak at the same time. This was nationalist mobilization.

At various times in American history members of one or another ethnic group have organized to affect the destiny of their homeland.[45] These efforts may be intense, but ordinarily they occur separately and have only scattered, episodic effects. The First World War was unique in exciting passionate nationalist movements among a dozen ethnic groups simultaneously, each resonating to the others and all together awakening in the usually fatalistic immigrant masses a level of collective expectation that was unprecedented. Thousands of Poles, Serbs, Czechs, Slovaks, and Jews returned to the Old World to fight for the nationalist cause, many of them in special units whose exploits were followed eagerly by their compatriots in America. Although the number of German-American publications declined, the rest of the foreign-language press increased about 20 percent between 1914 and 1918. Nationalist heroes like Ignace Paderewski, the famous Polish pianist, and Thomas Masaryk, the exiled philosopher-statesman of the Czechs, toured American cities. In Washington ethnic lobbying designed to influence the peace settlement became, for Jewish Zionists, Ukrainians, Yugoslavs, Italians, Greeks, and others, a new style of politics.[46]

None of these mobilizations was more impressive than that of eastern European Jews in behalf of a Jewish homeland in Palestine. For almost two decades before World War I little Zionist societies had been helpless in the face of the Jewish immigrants' overwhelming preoccupation with their new American home. "America is our Zion," intoned the principal Jewish spokesmen, to which the socialists added, "The world is our fatherland." But the outbreak of war created such enormous needs for relief, both in Palestine and in eastern Europe, that anxiety about divided loyalties was swept aside. In this context of concern for fellow Jews dislocated by war, Zionism acquired an American relevance. Linking itself with the Wilsonian ideal of national self-determination, the goal of a Palestinian homeland for Jews suddenly seemed almost as American as apple pie. It gained the endorsement of President Wilson, widespread public sympathy, and the fervent support of the Jewish immigrant masses, who began through Zionism to exercise a new influence in American Jewish affairs.[47]

Similarly among American blacks the First World War transformed a previously inconsequential ethnic nationalism into a spectacular mass movement. Through Marcus Garvey the flickering vision of an African homeland suddenly became, in the black ghettoes of America, a palpable prospect. Like the socialist agitators who came in the same years from southern and eastern Europe, Garvey arrived in 1916 from Jamaica to proselytize among West Indians in Harlem. His primary object was to gain support for a conservative racial improvement society he had founded at home. Only after the United States entered the war did Garvey comprehend the messianic power of the nationalist idea. Identifying Africa as the subjugated homeland of blacks everywhere, Garvey began to link the redemption of his race in America to the creation of a powerful black state in Africa. "The Irish, the Jews, the East Indians and all other oppressed peoples are getting together to demand from their oppressors Liberty, Justice, Equality," he pointed out, "and we now call upon the four hundred millions of Negro People of the world to do likewise."[48] Before Garvey, the principal black protest movements had not reached much beyond an educated elite. It remained for a flamboyant Jamaican immigrant — attuned to the international scale of the ethnic ferment in American cities — to galvanize a million urban blacks into collective action.[49]

One of the attractions of nationalist mobilization was the usually welcome visibility it gave to ethnic groups yearning for greater recognition on the crowded stage of American life. Rallying opinion and raising funds for overseas projects produced countless public demonstrations: receptions for representatives from the homeland, mass meetings to pass resolutions and secure pledges, musical festivals to display a cultural heritage, and, above all, parades. In reporting these events, general-circulation newspapers were sometimes noticing for the first time the local presence of an entire community that had earlier been largely invisible.[50] After the United States entered the war, government agencies worked to orchestrate the ethnic campaigns in the interest of a united war effort; that led to still greater visibility. When Liberty Loan officials in 1918 organized a monster Fourth of July parade up Fifth Avenue in New York, the notion of demonstrating the loyalty and affinity of every nationality to the American cause proved so popular that the original roster of forty-four participating groups expanded to sixty-four. A ten-hour procession, numbering altogether 109,415 marchers and 158 bands, included American Indians, Haitians, Liberians, Japanese, Zionists for the Jewish Nation, Parsees, Russians, Carpathians, and Americans of German Origin. The Poles won first prize for the best floats, but the judges also commended the Assyrians, the Bolivians, and the Americans of German Origin.[51]

In this wartime tumult of reverberating patriotisms, what scope was left for the mobilization of a working class along lines of economic self-interest? The standard view of American history, with its heavy emphasis on the repression of dissent during the war years, suggests that class action was sharply contained. It is true that the war brought governmental intervention and manipulation here too; but whether that vitiated labor's organizing drive is another question. While federal authorities scourged the socialists and syndicalists who opposed the war, the great majority of unions received unprecedented governmental support. After a pause on the eve of the war, the mobilization of immigrant labor resumed at a high level through unionization of war industries. The appointment of many labor leaders to governmental boards and commissions gave the labor movement a new kind of civic recognition, which prompted some unions to claim (to the disgust of employers) that Uncle Sam was on their side.[52]

Even the illiberal aspects of wartime nationalism did not immediately dampen the fervor of class mobilization. To be sure, nationalism competed against a radical class consciousness for the loyalty of the immigrant masses; a deadly enmity divided nationalists from socialists in many ethnic groups. But the rivalry temporarily stimulated both forms of consciousness. In the 1917 municipal elections Socialist candidates running on anti-war platforms made heavy gains in large industrial cities like New York, Chicago, and Cleveland, where European immigrants were strongly entrenched.[53] The class and nationalist mobilizations of the Progressive Era drew a common strength from a basic urge to change the world. Both movements inspired a collective vision—one promising to realize in a new way the old dream of America, the other to redeem the homeland as well. The two awakenings shared a millennial hope, and thus each contributed to the ambiance in which the other flourished.

It is little wonder, then, that ethnic radicalism and ethnic nationalism went down in a common defeat in 1919 and 1920. For a decade thereafter both labor union membership and the number of strikes dwindled year by year.[54] Within the various ethnic groups radical organizations withered; nationalist agitation virtually collapsed. Even the Zionist movement, now greatly shrunken, survived only by becoming a purely philanthropic venture. Most historians have attributed the decline of radicalism to repression, while blaming war-weariness and factional quarrels for the fading of homeland issues.[55] But simultaneous demobilization on both fronts points also to a common cause: a general surrender of grandiose ideals.

What remained for the immigrants and their children was their lives in America. Although limited in many ways by prejudice, poverty, and cultural barriers, the southern and eastern European groups gradually acquired—through home ownership, naturalization, and education—a modicum of sta-

bility and social integration. By the end of the 1920s a second
generation, born in America, substantially outnumbered the
immigrants themselves in most of the new-immigrant communities. As the second generation moved out of the narrow
world of its parents, it became the spearhead of the last and
greatest mobilization of European immigrants. To use the
language of the day, this was a mobilization of New Americans, pushing for wider access and fuller acceptance in the
world around them.[56]

The origin of this last mobilization lay in an experience
no previous generation of European immigrants had under-
gone. The New Americans grew up in a country that had
turned decisively against large-scale immigration, a country
that no longer wanted any more of their kind. The American-
born children of the immigrants felt the stigma of inferiority
more keenly than their parents, for the children were largely
Americanized and had little consciousness of an older heritage.[57] Thus the New Americans sought dignity and inclu-
sion, and to a remarkable degree during the 1930s and 1940s
they attained these goals. They succeeded in part because
their dissatisfactions converged with the economic discontent
of other significant groups. But that convergence in turn was
fashioned by the instrumentalities of earlier ethnic mobilizations, now reshaped and connected: the Democratic party
and the labor movement.

The new mobilization began in 1928 as a powerful revival of opposition to prohibition on the part of urban
Democrats. Astute observers could sense, however, that the
immense enthusiasm for Alfred E. Smith in the cities where
the foreign stock congregated expressed not only a cultural
protest against "puritan" morality but also a wider yearning
to escape from social subordination and to claim for their
own kind a full civic recognition. "Here is no trivial conflict,"
wrote Walter Lippmann. "Here are the new people, clamor-
ing . . . and the older people, defending their household
goods. The rise of Al Smith has made the conflict plain, and
his career has come to involve . . . the destiny of American
civilization."[58]

If the dramatic urban turnout for Smith had simply been a cultural mobilization in defense of a traditional way of life, it would have ended with the repeal of prohibition and the onset of new issues, just as the mobilization of the late 1880s dissipated in 1893. This time, however, the mobilization did not end. The turnout for Democratic candidates in the foreign-stock districts of major cities continued to soar, especially through an outpouring of new voters who had been too apathetic or too young to vote before 1928.[59] Even the foreign-language press, in which Republican interests were strongly entrenched, moved decisively into a reconstructed Democratic party. The number of foreign-language Republican newspapers dropped from 57 percent of those identifying with some party in 1923 to 40 percent in 1932. Over the same span of time socialist and other radical journals declined from 30 to 16 percent of the total. Democratic newspapers increased from 11 percent to 43 percent. Four years later, in 1936, the Democratic preponderance became overwhelming.[60]

In recapturing many cities from Republican control the New Americans contributed a crucial element to the election of Franklin D. Roosevelt. Victory at the polls supplied the impetus to resume unionization of the mass-production industries. Roosevelt's triumph in 1932 led swiftly to a federal guarantee of the right of workers to organize and bargain through their own representatives. This awakened the ravaged unions and stirred in unorganized workers a fitful, uncertain courage to test anew their collective strength. "The President wants you to join the union," organizers told the Slavic miners in the Appalachians.[61]

But a second and stronger demonstration of electoral might was necessary to unleash a major economic mobilization. When labor unrest in 1933–1934 produced only minimal changes, aspiration and militancy flowed back into the political system. Not until Roosevelt's spectacular reelection in 1936 by majorities that reached from 70 to 80 percent in the most heavily ethnic cities did the New Americans become fully conscious of their power.[62] Just two weeks after the

election, mass sit-down strikes began in the automobile industry. During the following year the American labor movement made the greatest gains in its history.[63]

In contrast to previous ethnic mobilizations, that of the
New Americans is difficult to classify. Its varied initiatives
appeared sometimes as cultural, sometimes as political, sometimes as economic. They often blended indistinguishably
with those of other disadvantaged elements that were also
bent on reducing inequalities of power and origin. Yet the
basic concern of the New Americans was not equality. It was
incorporation, and that is why the militant self-assertion that
impelled their mobilization was infused with a passionate
Americanism. The Congress of Industrial Organizations appealed to workers with fluttering American flags and patriotic songs that invoked visions of national fraternity. Even
the Communists enthusiastically adopted the language of
Americanism. In 1936 the *New York Times* noted that the unrest in the steel industry was part of the same "nation-
building . . . process" that was putting husky young men
with Slavic and Italian names on the leading college football
teams. The workers in the steel mills, the *Times* reflected,
were growing more discontented as they grew more
American.[64]

To view the industrial and political struggles of the
1930s in this ethnic perspective goes far toward clarifying the
paradoxical mixture of conservatism and protest that distinguished the American New Deal among the major responses
in the Western World to the Great Depression.

Notes

[1]William I. Thomas and Florian Znaniecki, *The Polish Peasant in Europe
and America*, 5 vols. (Chicago, 1918).

[2]Allan H. Spear, "Marcus Lee Hansen and the Historiography of Im-
migration," in *Wisconsin Magazine of History*, 44 (Summer, 1961), 258–268;
Carlton C. Qualey, "Marcus Lee Hansen," in *Midcontinent American Studies
Journal*, 8 (Fall, 1967), 18–25. A more sympathetic account, full of new in-
formation and insight, is Moses Rischin, "Marcus Lee Hansen: America's
First Transethnic Historian," in Richard L. Bushman *et al.*, eds., *Uprooted*

Americans: Essays to Honor Oscar Handlin (Boston, 1979), 319–347. For Blegen's rural sympathies see especially his collected essays, *Grass Roots History* (Minneapolis, 1947), and his personal memoir, "The Saga of Saga Hill," in *Minnesota History*, 29 (December, 1948), 289–299. Another member of this early group of immigration historians was George M. Stephenson, who like Hansen came from a small town in Iowa and was a student of Frederick Jackson Turner. Stephenson's *A History of American Immigration, 1820–1924* (Boston, 1926), although the first survey of the subject by a professional historian, was less important than his later work, *The Religious Aspects of Swedish Immigration: A Study of Immigrant Churches* (Minneapolis, 1932).

[3]For a fuller assessment of Oscar Handlin's *Boston's Immigrants: A Study of Acculturation* (Cambridge, Massachusetts, 1941) see my review of the revised edition (Cambridge, 1959) in *New England Quarterly*, 32 (September, 1959), 411–413.

[4]Moses Rischin, *The Promised City: New York's Jews 1870–1914* (Cambridge, Massachusetts, 1962), is reexamined as a classic work in *American Jewish History*, 73 (December, 1983). Compare with Robert Ernst, *Immigrant Life in New York City, 1825–1863* (New York, 1949).

[5]Handlin's students included Rowland T. Berthoff (discussed below), Arthur Mann, Barbara M. Solomon, and J. Joseph Huthmacher. On Curti's interest in the immigrant theme see Merle Curti and Kendall Birr, "The Immigrant and the American Image in Europe, 1860–1914," in *Mississippi Valley Historical Review*, 37 (September, 1950), 203–230. Among Curti's students who were drawn to immigration history were Edward G. Hartmann, Rudolph Vecoli, A. William Hoglund, and myself.

[6]The special contribution of overseas scholars is suggested in *Perspectives in American History*, 7 (1973), titled "Dislocation and Emigration: The Social Background of American Immigration."

[7]Rudolph Vecoli, "Ethnicity: A Neglected Dimension of American History," in Herbert J. Bass, ed., *The State of American History* (Chicago, 1970), 70–88. I have also relied on Vecoli's indispensable historiographical conspectus, "European Americans: From Immigrants to Ethnics," in William H. Cartwright and Richard L. Watson, Jr., eds., *The Reinterpretation of American History and Culture* (Washington, D.C., 1973), 81–112.

[8]John Higham, *History: Professional Scholarship in America* (Baltimore, 1983), 212–232.

[9]Oscar Handlin, "Immigration in American Life: A Reappraisal," in Henry Steele Commager, ed., *Immigration and American History: Essays in Honor of Theodore C. Blegen* (Minneapolis, 1961), 10. This essay elaborates programatically the point of view Handlin first stated in *The Uprooted: The Epic Story of the Great Migrations that Made the American People* (Boston, 1951).

[10]Rowland Berthoff's early work was *British Immigrants in Industrial America, 1790–1950* (Cambridge, Massachusetts, 1953) and "The Social Order of the Anthracite Region, 1825–1902," in *Pennsylvania Magazine of*

28   John Higham

History and Biography, 89 (July, 1965), 261–291; the later work began with
"The American Social Order: A Conservative Hypothesis," in *American
Historical Review*, 65 (April, 1960), 495–514.

[11]Timothy L. Smith, "New Approaches to the History of Immigration
in Twentieth-Century America," in *American Historical Review*, 71 (July,
1966), 1265–1279; "Immigrant Social Aspirations and American Education, 1880–1930," in *American Quarterly*, 21 (Fall, 1969), 523–543; "Religion and Ethnicity in America," in *American Historical Review*, 83 (December,
1978), 1155–1185.

[12]Nathan Glazer and Daniel P. Moynihan, *Beyond the Melting Pot: The
Negroes, Puerto Ricans, Jews, Italians, and Irish of New York City* (Cambridge,
Massachusetts, 1963). See also Glazer's later reflections on the book and the
context in which it was written: "Pluralism and Ethnicity," in *Journal of
American Ethnic History*, 1 (Fall, 1981), 43–55.

[13]Stephanie Grauman Wolf, *Urban Village: Population, Community, and
Family Structure in Germantown, Pennsylvania, 1683–1800* (Princeton, 1977);
Jon Butler, *The Huguenots in America: A Refugee People in New World Society*
(Cambridge, Massachusetts, 1983).

[14]Roger Daniels, "The Japanese," and Robert F. Berkhofer, Jr., "Native
Americans," in John Higham, ed., *Ethnic Leadership in America*, (Baltimore,
1978), 36–63, 119–149; Stanford M. Lyman, *Chinese Americans* (New
York, 1974); Victor R. Greene, *For God and Country: The Rise of Polish and
Lithuanian Ethnic Consciousness in America 1860–1910* (Madison, Wisconsin,
1975); Arthur A. Goren, "Jews," in Stephan Thernstrom, ed., *Harvard Encyclopedia of American Ethnic Groups* (Cambridge, Massachusetts, 1980),
571–598: Michael G. Karni and Douglas J. Ollila, eds., *For the Common
Good: Finnish Immigrants and the Radical Response to Industrial America* (Superior, Wisconsin, 1977). See also articles in June Drenning Holmquist, ed.,
They Chose Minnesota: A Survey of the State's Ethnic Groups (St. Paul, Minnesota, 1981).

[15]Lee Benson, *The Concept of Jacksonian Democracy: New York as a Test
Case* (Princeton, 1961); Samuel P. Hays, *American Political History as Social
Analysis* (Knoxville, Tennessee, 1980); Samuel T. McSeveney, "Ethnic
Groups, Ethnic Conflicts, and Recent Quantitative Research in American
Political History," in *International Migration Review*, 7 (Spring, 1973), 14–33.

[16]Edward M. Levine, *The Irish and Irish Politicians* (Notre Dame, 1966);
Ronald H. Bayor, *Neighbors in Conflict: The Irish, Germans, Jews, and Italians
of New York City, 1929–1941* (Baltimore, 1978); Edward R. Kantowicz,
Polish-American Politics in Chicago, 1880–1940 (Chicago, 1975).

[17]Stephan Thernstrom, *Poverty and Progress: Social Mobility in a
Nineteenth-Century City* (Cambridge, Massachusetts, 1964) and *The Other
Bostonians: Poverty and Progress in the American Metropolis, 1880–1970* (Cambridge, Massachusetts, 1973); Josef Barton, *Peasants and Strangers: Italians,
Rumanians, and Slovaks in an American City* (Cambridge, Massachusetts,
1975); Thomas Kessner, *The Golden Door: Italian and Jewish Immigrant Mobility in New York City, 1880–1915* (New York, 1977); Clyde and Sally

Griffen, *Natives and Newcomers: The Ordering of Opportunity in Mid-Nineteenth-Century Poughkeepsie* (Cambridge, Massachusetts, 1978). See also John Bodnar, Roger Simon, and Michael P. Weber, *Lives of Their Own: Blacks, Italians, and Poles in Pittsburgh, 1900–1960* (Urbana, 1982), and Jay P. Dolan, *The Immigrant Church: New York's Irish and German Catholics, 1815–1865* (Baltimore, 1975).

[18]Andrew M. Greeley, *The American Catholic: A Social Portrait* (New York, 1977); Thomas Sowell, *Ethnic America: A History* (New York, 1981).

[19]Lawrence Levine, *Black Culture and Black Consciousness: Afro-American Folk Thought from Slavery to Freedom* (New York, 1977); Herbert Gutman, *The Black Family in Slavery and Freedom, 1750–1925* (New York, 1976).

[20]Randall M. Miller and Thomas D. Marzik, eds., *Immigrants and Religion in Urban America* (Philadelphia, 1977); Richard L. Ehrlich, ed., *Immigrants in Industrial America, 1850–1920* (Charlottesville, 1977); Dino Cinel, *From Italy to San Francisco: The Immigrant Experience* (Stanford, 1982).

[21]Herbert Gutman, *Work, Culture, and Society in Industrializing America: Essays in American Working-Class and Social History* (New York, 1976); Wayne G. Broehl, Jr., *The Molly Maguires* (Cambridge, Massachusetts, 1965). On occupational choices, see Caroline Golab, *Immigrant Destinations* (Philadelphia, 1978); Virginia Yans-McLaughlin, *Family and Community: Italian Immigrants in Buffalo, 1880–1930* (Ithaca, 1978); Humbert S. Nelli, *The Business of Crime: Italians and Syndicate Crime in the United States* (Chicago, 1976).

[22]Eric Foner, "Class, Ethnicity, and Radicalism in the Gilded Age: The Land League and Irish-America," in Foner's *Politics and Ideology in the Age of the Civil War* (New York, 1980), 150–200; Dirk Hoerder, ed., *American Labor and Immigration History, 1877–1920s: Recent European Research* (Urbana, 1983); Melvyn Dubofsky, *When Workers Organize: New York City in the Progressive Era* (Amherst, Massachusetts, 1968). See also David Brody's pioneering monograph, *Labor in Crisis: The Steel Strike of 1919* (New York, 1965).

[23]David Montgomery, "Gutman's Nineteenth-Century America," in *Labor History*, 19 (Summer, 1978), 416–429; Elizabeth Fox-Genovese and Eugene D. Genovese, "The Political Crisis of Social History: A Marxian Perspective," in *Journal of Social History*, 10 (Winter, 1976), 205–220.

[24]John Bodnar, "Immigration, Kinship, and the Rise of Working-Class Realism in Industrial America," in *Journal of Social History*, 14 (September, 1980), 45–65, and *Workers' World: Kinship, Community, and Protest in an Industrial Society, 1900–1940* (Baltimore, 1982); Olivier Zunz, *The Changing Face of Inequality: Urbanization, Industrial Development, and Immigrants in Detroit, 1880–1920* (Chicago, 1982).

[25]Notice, for example, the title of Milton Gordon's extremely influential theoretical essay, *Assimilation in American Life: The Role of Race, Religion, and National Origins* (New York, 1964). The renewed importance of alternative theories of assimilation in the general studies published in the last several years is noted in John Higham, "Current Trends in the Study of

Ethnicity in the United States," in *Journal of American Ethnic History*, 2 (Fall, 1982), 5–15.

[26]John B. Jentz and Hartmut Keil, "From Immigrants to Urban Workers: Chicago's German Poor in the Gilded Age and Progressive Era, 1883–1908," in *Vierteljahrschrift für Sozial- und Wirtschaftsgeschichte*, 68 (1, 1981), 97.

[27]Karl Deutsch, "Social Mobilization and Political Development," in *American Political Science Review*, 55 (September, 1961), 493–514; Hubert M. Blalock, Jr., *Toward a Theory of Minority-Group Relations* (New York, 1967), 109–133, 139–142, 176–180.

[28]Smith, "Religion and Ethnicity in America," 1165–1167.

[29]Recent scholarship is expertly synthesized in Carl F. Kaestle, *Pillars of the Republic: Common Schools and American Society, 1780–1860* (New York, 1983). On nativism, see Michael F. Holt, "The Politics of Impatience: The Origins of Know-Nothingism," in *Journal of American History*, 60 (September, 1973), 309–331; and Jean H. Baker, *Ambivalent Americans: The Know-Nothing Party in Maryland* (Baltimore, 1977).

[30]Holt, "Politics of Impatience," 323–324; Vincent P. Lannie, "Alienation in America: The Immigrant Catholic and Public Education in Pre-Civil War America," in *Review of Politics*, 32 (October, 1970), 503–521. See also "The Catholic Church Blunders, 1850–1854," a commonly overlooked chapter in Ray Allen Billington's *The Protestant Crusade, 1800–1860: A Study of the Origins of American Nativism* (New York, 1938), 289–321. My statistics on Catholic population are from Gerald Shaughnessy, *Has the Immigrant Kept the Faith? A Study of Immigration and Catholic Growth in the United States, 1790–1920* (New York, 1925), 189, which shows for the 1840s the highest growth rate of any decade in the nineteenth or twentieth centuries.

[31]Charles Shanabruch, *Chicago's Catholics: The Evolution of an American Identity* (Notre Dame, 1981), 24–25, 28–30; James W. Sanders, *The Education of an Urban Minority: Catholics in Chicago, 1833–1965* (New York, 1977), 22–25, 125. See also Kaestle, *Pillars of the Republic*, 170–171. The bloodiest incident is reported by Wallace S. Hutcheon, Jr., "The Louisville Riots of August, 1855," in *Register of the Kentucky Historical Society*, 1971, 150–172.

[32]Daniel F. Reilly, *The School Controversy (1891–1893)* (Washington, D.C., 1943); Sanders, *Education*, 33–35.

[33]Richard J. Jensen, *The Winning of the Midwest: Social and Political Conflict, 1886–1896* (Chicago, 1971), 70. See also Paul Kleppner, *The Third Electoral System, 1853–1892: Parties, Voters, and Political Cultures* (Chapel Hill, 1979), 298–356.

[34]Shanabruch, *Chicago's Catholics*, 59–62; *Proceedings of the National Educational Association, 1891*, 393–398; Roger E. Wyman, "Wisconsin Ethnic Groups and the Election of 1890," in *Wisconsin Magazine of History*, 51 (Summer, 1968), 269–294. For a concurrent struggle in Massachusetts, see Robert H. Lord *et al.*, *History of the Archdiocese of Boston in the Various Stages of Its Developments, 1604 to 1943*, 3 (New York, 1944), 110–133.

[35]Here I have adapted and extended the familiar argument in Robert

H. Wiebe's *The Search for Order, 1877–1920* (New York, 1967), 44–55.

[36]John M. Allswang, *A House for All Peoples: Ethnic Politics in Chicago, 1890–1936* (Lexington, Kentucky, 1971), 25–33; Jensen, *Winning of the Midwest*, 89–177; Thomas C. Hunt, "The Bennett Law of 1890: Focus of Conflict Between Church and State in Education," in *Journal of Church and State*, 23 (Winter, 1981), 69–93.

[37]Shanabruch, *Chicago's Catholics*, 76, 93–104; Frederick C. Luebke, "German Immigrants and American Politics: Problems of Leadership, Parties, and Issues," in Randall Miller, ed., *Germans in America: Retrospect and Prospect* (Philadelphia, 1984), 67–68.

[38]Paul Kleppner, *Who Voted? The Dynamics of Electoral Turnout, 1870–1980* (New York, 1982), 57–58, 68–80; Carl N. Degler, "American Political Parties and the Rise of the City: An Interpretation," in *Journal of American History*, 51 (June, 1964), 46–49. See also the detailed case study in Marc Lee Raphael, *Jews and Judaism in a Midwestern Community: Columbus, Ohio, 1840–1975* (Columbus, 1979), 123–128.

[39]Hartmut Keil, "The German Immigrant Working Class of Chicago, 1875–90: Workers, Labor Leaders, and the Labor Movement," in Dirk Hoerder, ed., *American Labor and Immigration History, 1877–1920s: Recent European Research* (Urbana, 1983), 162–163; David Montgomery, "The Irish and the American Labor Movement," in David Noel Doyle and Dudley Edwards, eds., *America and Ireland, 1776–1976: The American Identity and the Irish Connection* (Westport, Connecticut, 1980), 205–218. There are perceptive overviews in Mike Davis, "Why the U.S. Working Class Is Different," in *New Left Review*, September–October, 1980, 3–44, and David Brody, "Labor," in Stephan Thernstrom, ed., *Harvard Encyclopedia of American Ethnic Groups*, (Cambridge, Massachusetts, 1980), 609–618.

[40]Leo Wolman, *The Growth of American Trade Unions 1880–1923* (New York, 1924), 33, 85. My percentages are calculated from figures on non-farm workers in United States Bureau of the Census, *Historical Statistics of the United States, Colonial Times to 1970* (Washington, D.C., 1975), 134.

[41]Victor R. Greene, *The Slavic Community on Strike: Immigrant Labor in Pennsylvania Anthracite* (Notre Dame, 1968), 106, 141, 155; Ewa Krystyna Hauser, "Ethnicity and Class in a Polish American Community" (Ph.D. dissertation, The Johns Hopkins University, 1981), 13–27, 71–85.

[42]Melvyn Dubofsky, *We Shall Be All: A History of the Industrial Workers of the World* (Chicago, 1969), 203–205; Irving Howe, *World of Our Fathers* (New York, 1976), 290–304.

[43]Charles Leinenweber, "The American Socialist Party and 'New' Immigrants," in *Science and Society*, 32 (Winter, 1968), 1–25; Melvyn Dubofsky, "Success and Failure of Socialism in New York City, 1900–1918: A Case Study," in *Labor History*, 9 (Fall, 1968), 361–375; Karni and Ollila, *For the Common Good*, 14–15, 65–71, 94–95, 132, 168–175. A similar beginning of Croatian socialism in America is described in *Radnicka Straza*, August 12, 1910, and January 7, 1914, in Chicago Foreign

Language Press Survey, Reel 8, I E (Immigration History Research Center, University of Minnesota).

[44]Nick Salvatore, *Eugene V. Debs, Citizen and Socialist* (Urbana, 1982), 285–286; David Brody, *Labor in Crisis: The Steel Strike of 1919* (Philadelphia, 1965), 71–75, 113–114.

[45]For example, Thomas N. Brown, *Irish-American Nationalism, 1870–1890* (Philadelphia, 1966).

[46]Joseph P. O'Grady, ed., *The Immigrants' Influence on Wilson's Peace Policies* (Lexington, Kentucky, 1967); Robert E. Park, *The Immigrant Press and Its Control* (New York, 1922), 309–312; M. M. Stolarik, "The Role of American Slovaks in the Creation of Czecho-Slovakia, 1914–1918," in *Slovak Studies*, 8 (1968), 7–82; Kantowicz, *Polish-American Politics*, 110–115.

[47]Melvin I. Urofsky, *American Zionism From Herzl to the Holocaust* (Garden City, New York, 1975), 117–245; Naomi W. Cohen, *American Jews and the Zionist Idea* (n.p., 1975), 3–24.

[48]Circular [1918], reproduced in Robert A. Hill, ed., *The Marcus Garvey and Universal Negro Improvement Association Papers*, 1 (Berkeley, 1983), 315.

[49]According to the best available estimate, Garvey's movement at its height enrolled a million members in the United States and perhaps as many more in other countries. Its only rival as a protest organization, the National Association for the Advancement of Colored People, reached a peak of 91,000 members around the same time. Emory J. Tolbert, *The UNIA and Black Los Angeles: Ideology and Community in the American Garvey Movement* (Los Angeles, 1980), 3.

[50]Hauser, "Ethnicity and Class," 165–168.

[51]American Scenic and Historic Preservation Society, *Twenty-Fourth Annual Report, 1919*, 125–129; George Creel, *How We Advertised America* (New York, 1920). There is a particularly vivid record of ecstatic mobilization in the pages of the Czech-American daily, *Denni Hlasatel*, 1917–1918, in Chicago F. L. Press Survey, Reel 2, I G.

[52]Alexander M. Bing, *War-Time Strikes and Their Adjustment* (New York, 1921), 236–240; Wolman, *Growth*, 34–37.

[53]A. William Hoglund, "Breaking with Religious Tradition: Finnish Immigrant Workers and the Church, 1890–1915," in Karni and Ollila, eds., *For the Common Good*, 30–41, 58–59; James Weinstein, *The Decline of Socialism in America, 1912–1925* (New York, 1969), 145–162.

[54]United States Census Bureau, *Historical Statistics*, 178–179; Irving Bernstein, *The Lean Years: A History of the American Worker, 1920–1933* (Boston, 1960), 83–143, 334–357.

[55]Allswang, *House for All Peoples*, 117–118; William Preston, Jr., *Aliens and Dissenters: Federal Suppression of Radicals, 1903–1933* (Cambridge, Massachusetts, 1963).

[56]Louis Adamic, "Thirty Million New Americans," in *Harper's*, 169 (November, 1934), 684–694; United States Census Bureau, *Historical Statistics*, 116–118. How the initiative of second-generation immigrant workers

gradually enabled the older first-generation Slavs to overcome fear and submissiveness is sensitively examined by Peter Friedlander, *The Emergence of a UAW Local, 1936-1939: A Study in Class and Culture* (Pittsburgh, 1975).

[57]Louis Adamic's impressions on this point were very widely shared, as Richard Weiss points out in "Ethnicity and Reform: Minorities and the Ambience of the Depression Years," in *Journal of American History*, 66 (December, 1979), 583-584.

[58]Quoted in J. Joseph Huthmacher, *Massachusetts People and Politics 1919-1933* (New York, 1969), 154.

[59]For evidence of the mobilization of a new generation of voters in heavily "ethnic" cities, see Kristi Andersen, *The Creation of a Democratic Majority, 1928-1936* (Chicago, 1979), 30-38, 105-114.

[60]"Analysis of Foreign Language Publications . . . 1923," and Press Release, Foreign Language Information Service, November 7, 1932, in Archives of American Council for Nationalities Service (Immigration History Research Center, University of Minnesota); *New York Times*, August 10, 1936, 6.

[61]Irving Bernstein, *Turbulent Years: A History of the American Worker 1933-1941* (Boston, 1969), 37-46, 92-171, 217-316.

[62]Sidney Fine, *Sit-down: The General Motors Strike of 1936-1937* (Ann Arbor, 1969), 96, 330-332, 338-341.

[63]United States Census Bureau, *Historical Statistics*, 178.

[64]Roy Rosenzweig, " 'United Action Means Victory': Militant Americanism on Film," in *Labor History*, 24 (Spring, 1983), 274-288; *New York Times*, July 10, 1936, 18.

ETHNIC DIVERSITY, COSMOPOLITANISM AND THE EMERGENCE OF THE AMERICAN LIBERAL INTELLIGENTSIA

DAVID A. HOLLINGER
State University of New York at Buffalo

IN 1916 RANDOLPH BOURNE EXPRESSED THE HOPE THAT ETHNIC DIVERSITY would enable the United States to develop a style of life and thought more fulfilling than that of any of the single, national cultures of Europe and America. Exactly at the point in history when the majority of native-born Americans were the most anxious about the cultural effects of massive immigration from Eastern and Central Europe, Bourne depicted this immigration as a unique opportunity for Americans to liberate themselves from "parochialism," and to develop in themselves a truly "cosmopolitan spirit."[1] His denunciation of contemporary chauvinism was of virtually no importance in a national political context; public policy was influenced rather by those who wanted to assimilate immigrants into a preexisting American norm, and to drastically limit additional immi-

---

[1] Randolph Bourne, "Trans-National America," *Atlantic,* 118 (1916), 86–97, rpt. Carl Resek, ed., *War and the Intellectuals: Essays by Randolph Bourne, 1915-1919* (New York: Harper & Row, 1964), 107–23. Since Bourne was destined to become a cultural hero to so many intellectuals, his advocacy of this view is especially pertinent to an inquiry into the development of the intelligentsia. A handful of other writers, less well-known, expressed similar views in the 1910s, e.g., Horace J. Bridges, *On Becoming an American: Some Meditations of A Newly Naturalized Immigrant* (Boston, 1919), esp. 117–21, 135–49. Ironically, the British immigrant Bridges used the term "cosmopolitanism" to denote exactly the view that he and Bourne were against, the eradication of cultural differences in the interest of a narrowly homogeneous society. Bridges was aware of the semantical problem, and proposed "Internationalism" as a more appropriate term for the overcoming of provincialism in the interests of merging many cultures "into a distinctive American civilization which shall transcend them all" (see esp. 120, 148).

239

gration.[2] Yet Bourne's articulation of the cosmopolitan ideal was with, rather than against, the drift of history when his efforts are viewed in another context: the emergence of a national, secular, ethnically-diverse, left-of-center intelligentsia.

This intelligentsia had become a prominent feature in American life by the end of the 1940s.[3] Its most obvious leaders included Edmund Wilson, Lionel Trilling, and Dwight Macdonald, among men of letters; David Riesman and Daniel Bell among social scientists; and Reinhold Niebuhr and Sidney Hook among philosophical essayists. The discourse of this intelligentsia was largely institutionalized in the liberal arts divisions of several major universities and in such journals of opinion as the *New Republic*, the *Partisan Review*, *Commentary*, the *Nation*, and, more recently, the *New York Review of Books* and the *New York Times Book Review*. So influential was this intelligentsia during the 1940s, 1950s, and 1960s that most Americans who thought of themselves as "intellectuals" were either members of it, or part of its audience.[4] Although the precise extent of this community of discourse can be a matter for argument,[5] persons who identify with it recognize one another so readily that some sociologists have described "intellectuals" as virtually an "ethnic group."[6] The analogy is ironic in view of the diversity of the actual ethnic origins of these intellectuals. In Bourne's time, leaders of American "high culture" were predominantly Anglo-Saxon and Protestant, not only in origin but in their sense of what it meant to be an American; by mid-century, this leadership was approximately half Jewish and half "WASP,"[7] and its two halves

[2]On nativism in the 1910s, see John Higham, *Strangers In the Land: Patterns of American Nativism, 1860-1925* (New Brunswick: Rutgers Univ. Press, 1955), 158-93. The editor of the *Atlantic* was shocked by Bourne's lack of allegiance to the "English instinct" and the "Anglo-Saxon ideal," but decided to publish the "utterly mistaken" article because it seemed "the ablest and certainly the most interesting" thing that his protégé, Bourne, had written; Ellery Sedgwick to Bourne, March 30, 1916, Bourne MSS, Columbia University Special Collections.
[3]The term "intelligentsia," it could be argued, ought to be reserved to distinguish radical literati from "mandarins." This usage would be true to the word's most conventional association, with the Russian intellectuals of the mid-nineteenth century. Yet the term has developed a broader meaning in recent years, especially in the United States. The Webster-Merriam *Third International Dictionary* counts as an *intelligentsia* any "class of well-educated, articulate persons constituting a distinct, recognized, and self-conscious stratum within a nation and claiming or assuming for itself the guiding role of an intellectual, social, or political vanguard."
[4]For a representative and widely read example of this presumption, see "The Intellectual: Alienation and Conformity," the final chapter of Richard Hofstadter's *Anti-Intellectualism in American Life* (New York: Knopf, 1963), 393-432, esp. 394.
[5]For an attempt to pursue this question in detail, and to discover who are the "top 70" American intellectuals, see the amusing, but seriously intended book by the sociologist Charles Kadushin, *The American Intellectual Elite* (Boston: Little, Brown, 1974), esp. 28-30.
[6]Milton Gordon, *Assimilation in American Life* (New York: Oxford Univ. Press, 1964), 224-32, and "Marginality and the Jewish Intellectual," in Peter I. Rose, ed., *The Ghetto and Beyond* (New York: Random House, 1969), 477-91.
[7]Certainly, there were a number of prominent intellectuals whose origins were neither Jewish

worked in concert to serve values that were distinctly aloof from conventional ethnic particularism of any species. Indeed, the potentially obvious, but rarely spelled-out cosmopolitanism of the mid-century intelligentsia is a key to the latter's historical development.

The "cosmopolitanism" to which I refer is the desire to transcend the limitations of any and all particularisms in order to achieve a more complete human experience and a more complete understanding of that experience. The ideal is decidedly counter to the eradication of cultural differences, but counter also to their preservation in parochial form. Rather, particular cultures and subcultures are viewed as repositories for insights and experiences that can be drawn upon in the interests of a more comprehensive outlook on the world. Insofar as a particular ethnic heritage or philosophical tradition is an inhibition to experience, it is to be disarmed; insofar as that heritage or tradition is an avenue toward the expansion of experience and understanding, access to it is to be preserved.

Bourne believed that a process of cultural cross-fertilization was underway, especially among young people: "It is not uncommon for the eager Anglo-Saxon" in college to "find his true friends not among his own race but among the acclimatized German . . . Austrian . . . Jew . . . Scandinavian or Italian," for such persons "are oblivious to the repressions of that tight little society in which the Anglo-Saxon so provincially grew up." These immigrants, in turn, were experiencing a transformation, for contact with Anglo-Saxons expanded their own cultural horizons. This process seemed especially productive when young Jewish intellectuals were involved; Bourne specifically praised the contributions of Felix Frankfurter, Horace Kallen, Morris R. Cohen, and Walter Lippmann.[8]

Bourne was far from alone in espousing cosmopolitanism and in believing that Jews were more useful to the cause than were other immigrants. Floyd Dell was grateful that Davenport, Iowa, had so many descendants of the immigration of 1848, especially Jews, for it created a more liberated, intellectual environment. A pivotal influence on Dell was a heretical rabbi who ministered mostly to "Gentiles, Socialists and Atheists."[9] The

---

nor Protestant Anglo-Saxon, including, for example, the Yugoslavian immigrant Louis Adamic, the black James Baldwin, and such Catholics (or one-time Catholics) as James Burnham, C. Wright Mills, and James Agee. Yet in absolute numbers, there is no doubt that the bulk of the intelligentsia descended from either the Jewish immigration from Eastern Europe or the older American "WASP" tradition.

[8] Randolph Bourne, "The Jew and Trans-National America," *Menorah Journal*, 2 (1916), 277–84, rpt. Resek, 124–33. Cf. Bourne's references to Lippmann, Frankfurter, and Harold Laski in his letter to Alyse Gregory, November 10, 1916, Bourne MSS. Cf. to Bourne, Thorstein Veblen, "The Intellectual Preeminence of Jews in Modern Europe," *Political Science Quarterly*, 1919, rpt. Max Lerner, ed., *The Portable Veblen* (New York: Viking Press, 1948), 467–79.

[9] Floyd Dell, *Homecoming* (New York, 1933), esp. 121, 170, 192.

Nebraskan Alvin Johnson, who prided himself on his "prosemitism," was
excited by the opportunities afforded by Columbia University for meeting
and learning from "unlike types."[10] Lincoln Steffens rejoiced in the
expanded horizons he and his journalistic colleagues obtained by keeping
tabs on Abraham Cahan and the cultural life of the Lower East Side.[11]
Hutchins Hapgood's *Spirit of the Ghetto* explored in detail the intuition
that what made the East European Jews remarkable was their passionate
intellectuality, their determination to pursue abstract ideas about art,
metaphysics, and political economy to ultimate and universal conclusions.[12]
And the young Edmund Wilson was inspired by what he identified as the
"cosmopolitanism" of Paul Rosenfeld, who was, according to Wilson,
never defensive about his "catholic interest in art and life," and who introduced Wilson to "a whole fascinating world, united though international,
of personality, poetics, texture, mood."[13]

Perhaps it is no surprise to learn that an ideal of cosmopolitanism was
somehow involved in the legendary efforts of the 1910s and 1920s to
transcend the limitations of Victorian literary tastes, commercial civilization, superpatriotism, and "Puritanism." Yet "cosmopolitanism," unlike
"alienation," is not a central concept in the very works that have made the
history of these revolts against American conventions so familiar.[14] Alienation may have been real enough as a *condition*, but those who experienced
it and those who have since written about it have sometimes depicted it, mis-
leadingly, as an ideal, or value, or doctrine. Attention to the proverbial
alienation of people like Bourne, Dell, Van Wyck Brooks, John Reed,

[10]Alvin Johnson, *Pioneer's Progress: An Autobiography* (New York: Viking Press, 1952),
11, 127.

[11]Lincoln Steffens, *Autobiography* (New York: Harcourt Brace, 1931), 318.

[12]Hutchins Hapgood, *The Spirit of the Ghetto* (New York: Funk and Wagnalls, 1909; rpt.
1965), esp. 47–52. Cf. Hapgood, *A Victorian in the Modern World* (New York, 1939), esp.
144–45. That Hapgood's revealing *Spirit of the Ghetto* has not been more thoroughly analyzed
and absorbed into the canon of American cultural history is an index of the extent to which
scholarly writing about the relations of Gentiles and Jews has been dominated by the question
of anti-Semitism. On the tendency of scholarship to overlook manifestations of cordiality in
relations between ethnic groups, see Rudolph J. Vecoli, "European Americans: From Immigrants to Ethnics," *International Migration Review,* 6 (1972), 414, 416, 434.

[13]Edmund Wilson, *Classics and Commercials* (New York: Farrar and Strauss, 1950), 503–
05.

[14]Daniel Aaron, *Writers on the Left* (New York: Harcourt Brace, 1961); Christopher Lasch,
The New Radicalism in America, 1889-1963: The Intellectual as a Social Type (New York:
Knopf, 1965); Henry F. May, ed., *The Discontent of the Intellectuals* (Chicago: Rand
McNally, 1963); Frederick J. Hoffman, *The Twenties: American Writing in the Postwar
Decade* (New York: Viking Press, 1955); John P. Diggins, *The American Left in the Twentieth
Century* (New York: Harcourt Brace, 1973); and Hofstadter, *Anti-Intellectualism.* These his-
torians are not always oblivious to the cosmopolitan impulse; for example, Henry F. May's
The End of American Innocence: A Study of the First Years of Our Own Time, 1912-1917
(New York: Knopf, 1959), although it is couched in other terms, offers a very helpful ex-
ploration of this impulse in Bourne's generation (see esp. 279-301).

Harold Stearns, Max Eastman, and Ezra Pound has tended to obscure their actual values, especially their cosmopolitanism.

What is often termed the "alienation" of the literary radicals and expatriates of the 1910s and 1920s is their antiprovincialism, the obverse side of the coin of cosmopolitanism. The heart of the matter was expressed in "Provincialism the Enemy," an essay of 1917 by the greatest expatriate of all, Ezra Pound. "The bulk of the work of Henry James's novels is precisely an analysis of, and thence a protest against all sorts of petty tyrannies and petty coercions," explained Pound, who linked James with Flaubert and Turgenev in the great "struggle against provincialism." Whatever these authors protest about "artistic detachment or any theories of writing," warned Pound, their work has ultimately been in the fight against provincialism, and their weapon "has largely been the presentation of human variety." Insofar as this literary tradition has a social counterpart, it is found, Pound explained, in the nations that most recognize "diversity," especially France and England, with their great capitals of Paris and London. What defects France has can be traced to its provinces; Napoleon, for example, was the "incarnation" of the "ever damned spirit of provincialism," and "only a backwoods hell like Corsica could have produced him." The ideal circumstance for the advancement of culture would be a tunnel from London to Paris; this would "make for a richer civilization, for a completer human life." In the process, the differences between the two cities would be attractively accentuated, and "nothing," concluded Pound "is more valuable than just this amicable accentuation of difference, and of complementary values."[15]

It was appropriate that the iconoclast Pound should refer to Henry James, for the latter represented a tradition that the young intellectuals of the 1910s and 1920s were reasserting and radically enlarging. The standard "literary culture" of nineteenth century America included a guarded, genteel cosmopolitanism that attributed to upper-class Europeans a life more complicated, expansive, and fulfilling than James, for example, believed could be generated by purely American experience.[16] Although James himself was unnerved and offended by the actual working-class immigrants he encountered in New York, many native-born Americans of his generation had trusted that out of the diversity of European races and cultures a unified, superior society could be created in the United States. This older "cosmopolitan nationalism" was virtually eclipsed by resurgent

---

[15] Ezra Pound, "Provincialism the Enemy," *New Age,* 22 (1917), 269, 289, 309.
[16] For a helpful overview of the cosmopolitan aspirations within the genteel tradition, see Howard Mumford Jones, *The Age of Energy: Varieties of American Experience, 1865–1915* (New York: Viking Press, 1971), 259–300. For James in this context, see esp. *The Portrait of a Lady* (New York, 1881).

nativism in America at large, just when the young intellectuals were taking up the tradition among themselves.[17]

If antiprovincialism pushed Pound toward expatriation, it led others to the apparently opposite strategy of "cultural nationalism." The latter outlook, as formulated by Van Wyck Brooks, Lewis Mumford, and Harold Stearns, was less a criticism of non-American art and letters than it was an attempt to bring to their own national culture an intensity and scope comparable to that of European civilization. They looked to a new intelligentsia to manifest a more diverse, more broadly based emotional and intellectual existence, and they were eager for this cause to be advanced by persons of any ethnic origin.[18]

H. L. Mencken's onslaughts against American chauvinism did not spare even the newest of Ellis Island arrivals, but his scorn for them derived from values very similar to Bourne's. Mencken condemned the immigrants for the speed with which they dropped their heritage and transformed themselves into the average American boob.[19] What to Bourne was a robust hope—that immigrants would retain enough of their own past to enrich American life—was to the more cynical Mencken a lamentably unlikely prospect.

If the concept of alienation has tended to obscure the reality of the cosmopolitan ideal as held by cultural critics in America, especially those of Anglo-Saxon stock who became prominent before 1930, then the concept of "assimilation" has tended, analogously, to obscure the cosmopolitan ideal as held by intellectuals of Jewish origin.[20] Certainly, this ideal has been more widely attributed to Jews than to others,[21] but more emphasis needs to be given to the fact that when Jewish immigrants and their children responded avidly to classics of American literature, this response was part of a larger discovery of modern and Western culture generally. The so-called

[17]For the tradition of "cosmopolitan nationalism" and its decline, see Higham, *Strangers,* 20–23, 63, 97, 110, 120, 124, 251, 304. For James's reaction to the Yiddish ghetto, see Henry James, *The American Scene* (New York, 1907), 131–35.

[18][Van Wyck Brooks,] "Where Are Our Intellectuals," *Freeman,* 2 (1920), 53–54; Harold Stearns, "America and the Young Intellectuals," *Bookman,* 3 (1921), 42–48; Lewis Mumford, "The American Intelligentsia," *World Tomorrow,* 8 (1925), 200–01; Mumford, conversation with author, Amenia, New York, June 21, 1974. Cf. Susan J. Turner, *A History of The Freeman: Literary Landmark of the Early Twenties* (New York: Columbia Univ. Press, 1963), esp. 25, 62–67; and Floyd Dell, *Intellectual Vagabondage: An Apology for the Intelligentsia* (New York, 1926).

[19]H. L. Mencken, *Prejudices: Third Series* (New York: Knopf, 1922), 35–36.

[20]E.g., Allen Guttmann, *The Jewish Writer in America: Assimilation and the Crisis of Identity* (New York: Oxford Univ. Press, 1971).

[21]Indeed the concept of the "cosmopolitan Jew" has long been a stereotype of adulation (e.g., Isaac Deutscher, *The Non-Jewish Jew* [New York: Hill & Wang, 1968], 24–41) and of anti-Semitism (e.g., the writings of G. K. Chesterton).

"Americanization" of the East European Jews, in particular, was an extension, indeed an explosive flowering of the *haskalah*, the "romantic enlightenment" already underway within the Pale of Settlement in the nineteenth
century. Memoirs of intellectual life on the Lower East Side establish beyond doubt that newly-liberated Jews grasped simultaneously for Marx and
Horatio Alger, George Eliot and Washington Irving, Voltaire and Benjamin
Franklin.[22] True, the settlement houses did tend to present Western civilization as filtered through the genteel tradition, but the most self-consciously
intellectual of the immigrants were not interested in substituting a new parochialism for the one left behind; instead, they aimed to "possess" for
themselves, as Morris R. Cohen put it in 1902, all the benefits of "the Age
of Reason," of modern life generally.[23]

Cohen was the first Russian-born Jew to become a member of the
American Philosophical Association, a regular contributor to the *New Republic*, and a prominent secular moralist. To a generation of immigrant's
sons at the City College of New York, he was a cultural hero, the
preeminent exemplar of success as an American intellectual. Typed though
he was by his admirers and his critics as "the Paul Bunyan of the Jewish Intellectuals,"[24] Cohen was determined to be a thinker, not a "Jewish
thinker" nor even an "American thinker"; he opposed both Zionists and the
killers of Sacco and Vanzetti as parochial tribalists. It was this insistent
cosmopolitanism that defined the terms on which Cohen was "assimilated":
not only was he first introduced to American intellectual life and then in-
ducted into it by patrons who were, themselves, critics of American parochialism—Thomas Davidson, William James, and two German Jews of
Cohen's generation, Felix Frankfurter and Walter Lippmann—but he soon
became a symbol of cosmopolitanism for Anglo-Saxons such as Bourne,
Oliver Wendell Holmes, Jr., and John Herman Randall, Jr.[25]

To emphasize "cosmopolitanism" as opposed to "alienation" or
"assimilation" is therefore not merely a semantical gesture. This change in

[22]E.g., Morris R. Cohen, *A Dreamer's Journey* (New York: Free Press, 1949), 74, 85–86,
94–99, 166–67; Joseph Epstein, *Let There Be Sculpture* (New York, 1940), esp. 8–13; cf.
Moses Rischin, *The Promised City: New York's Jews, 1870–1914* (Cambridge, Mass.: Harvard Univ. Press, 1962), esp. 130–31, 209.

[23]Morris R. Cohen, "The East Side," *Alliance Review*. 2 (1902), 451–54; Cohen, *Journey*,
98.

[24]E.g., the use of this phrase by Morris Friedman, "The Jewish College Student: New
Model," in Elliot Cohen, ed., *Commentary on the American Scene* (New York, 1953), 282.

[25]Bourne, "Jew and Trans-National America," 133; "The Holmes-Cohen Correspondence,"
in Leonora Cohen Rosenfield, *Portrait of A Philosopher: Morris R. Cohen in Life and Letters*
(New York: Harcourt Brace, 1962), 313–60; John Herman Randall, Jr., "Annual Meeting of
the Eastern Division of the American Philosophical Association," *Journal of Philosophy*. 23
(1926), 37–38.

emphasis gets us closer to the dynamics of the process whereby the intelligentsia comes into being. It would not be enough even to say that persons alienated from one heritage were assimilated into a group alienated from another heritage; it was the affirmative dimension, the cosmopolitan ideal, that made rapport between the two ethnic types possible. In this view, the intelligentsia that came fully into its own in the 1940s was formed primarily by the merger of two, originally autonomous revolts against two distinctive provincialisms, and what mattered most about the Jewish immigrants was not their ethnicity, nor even their inherited devotion to learning, but their impatience with the limitations of ethnic particularism. Certainly, the ethnicity of the Jews appealed to some Anglo-Saxons in search of counter models to the apparent deficiencies in their own upbringings,[26] but this function could often be performed by the ethnicity of Italians, Slavs, and other immigrant groups. What made the young Jewish intellectuals so pivotal in the development of the intelligentsia was the depth and authenticity of their revolt against the constraints of the East European Ashkenazim, and the universalist tone of that revolt. The "American" discourse of the sons of Harvard—and of Davenport, Iowa—into which the heirs of the *haskalah* were "assimilated" was a discourse with cosmopolitan aspirations of its own, aspirations that were in turn reinforced and intensified by liberated Jews.

Among the most liberated of the Jews was Joseph Freeman. Bewildered by the dissolution of traditional Jewish culture and unpersuaded by the claims of its religion, the adolescent Freeman tried to find an identity for himself in the tradition of Western, secular literature, especially that of the Enlightenment and of the English romantics. Hostile to the commercialism of his father, he yearned for a means to distance himself from the ethos of the Jewish businessman. His life began to fit together at the age of sixteen, when he discovered *The Masses:* somewhere in "mysterious Greenwich Village" there were "native Americans who had integrated the conflicting values of the world." At the center of the *Masses* group was Max Eastman, himself married to a Jewish woman, as Freeman was quick to note. When Freeman and his Jewish friends gazed at Eastman, they "at last . . . saw Shelley plain." Here was the embodiment, "in sensuous outline," of the "New Spirit of the Intelligentsia": the prematurely white-haired Eastman "looked Beauty and spoke Justice." Freeman followed *The Masses* in its flight "from Moses and Jesus to Venus and Apollo," and found in that flight other "souls," like himself, "in rebellion against puritan bondage." And when Freeman actually joined the staff of the *Liberator,* the postwar successor of *The Masses,* he rejoiced that "Nordic Americans" like Eastman and Floyd Dell did not make him suffer for his Jewish origins: "I felt that on

---

[26] E.g., Gilbert Seldes, "The Demoniac in the American Theatre," *Dial,* 75 (1923), 303–08.

a small scale the *Liberator* group represented that ideal society which we all wanted, that society in which no racial barriers could possibly exist." By the time he worked for the *Liberator,* Freeman had come to feel that he and his friends were "no longer, culturally, Jews"; rather, they were "Westerners initiated into and part of a culture which merged the values of Jerusalem, Egypt, Greece and ancient Rome with the Catholic culture of the Middle Ages, the humanistic culture of the Renaissance, the equalitarian ideals of the French Revolution, and the scientific concepts of the nineteenth century." To this they added "socialism," which seemed to them "the apex" of Western culture.[27]

While in sheer numbers it was East European Jews like Freeman and Cohen who would eventually make up the "Jewish half" of the intelligentsia, the early stages of the accommodation were facilitated by a small but influential group of Jews of German origin, whose families had immigrated, in most cases, two or three generations before. An index of their importance is the fact that about half of the earliest editors of the *New Republic* and *Seven Arts*—perhaps the two most influential journals in the early development of the intelligentsia—were German Jews: Walter Lippmann, Walter Weyl, James Oppenheim, Waldo Frank, and Paul Rosenfeld. Even Bourne and Brooks, whose names are always associated with *Seven Arts,* were comparative latecomers to the enterprise; and only when they joined the magazine was it relieved, as Oppenheim put it, "of the onus of being non-Anglo-Saxon."[28]

The German Jews were more assimilated and generally well-off than their East European counterparts; many had grown up on the Upper West Side and had spent their summers in Atlantic City. Rosenfeld and Frank were graduates of Yale, Lippmann of Harvard; Rosenfeld had even gone to a military academy in the Hudson Valley.[29] Yet Bourne and Edmund Wilson were aware of, and pleased by, cultural capacities that seemed to distinguish such Ivy League Hebrews from Gentile peers. And when Rosenfeld spoke of Bourne, he praised him as one Anglo-Saxon American "not yet ready to renounce the Elizabethan heritage of liberty," and a person whose "multitudinous interests" made him a "salon" in and of himself.[30] Brooks appealed to Rosenfeld as a mixture of "Harvard blandness" with the critical ideal of

[27] Joseph Freeman, *An American Testament: A Narrative of Rebels and Romantics* (New York: Farrar and Rinehart, 1936), esp. 28, 49, 61, 65, 160–61, 246.

[28] James Oppenheim, "The Story of the *Seven Arts*," *American Mercury,* 20 (1930), 156–64, esp. 158. On the background of Lippmann and Weyl, see Charles Forcey, *Crossroads of Liberalism* (New York: Oxford Univ. Press, 1961), 56–58 and 91–93. For the marginally "foreign" perspective of the chief *New Republic* editor, Herbert Croly, see Forcey, 12.

[29] Sherman Paul, "Introduction" to Paul Rosenfeld, *Port of New York* (Urbana, Ill.: Univ. of Illinois Press, 1961), ix. *Port of New York,* a collection of essays, was originally published in 1924.

[30] Paul Rosenfeld, "Randolph Bourne," *Dial,* 75 (1923), 546, 552, 555.

Taine and Herder; Brooks was, Rosenfeld observed, a truly "cosmo-politan" critic.[31]

Horace Kallen, too, was German-born, and it was his earliest for-mulation of the theory of "cultural pluralism" that helped inspire Bourne's manifesto of 1915.[32] Kallen was a leading critic of the "100 per cent Ameri-canism" that would use the "melting pot" not to create a new national mix-ture, but to melt down immigrant stock into a substance malleable enough to be molded into a traditional Anglo-Saxon American.[33] Kallen contributed in some ways to the growth of the cosmopolitan ideal, but his outlook differed importantly from the vision of Bourne and of most of the members of the nascent intelligentsia. Kallen, a Zionist, tended to favor the retention of parochial loyalties almost for their own sake; he was not so much for cross-fertilization as for the harmonious cooperation and mutual enrichment of clearly defined, contrasting, durable ethnic units.[34] Bourne shared some of Kallen's hope that a plurality of particularistic interests could function as countervailing forces in the social order in general, yet Bourne's scope was more limited: Bourne was moved by the idea of a com-munity of intellectuals, a complex, yet unified, single discourse to which a variety of contingent particularisms would make their distinctive contribu-tions. He was more willing than Kallen to see the immigrants themselves undergo cultural changes. Moreover, Kallen's attempt to speak about the ethnic composition of American society as a whole gave his program a more broadly political character than was characteristic of the ethnic at-titudes of most intellectuals, a few of whom defended continued, massive immigration but most of whom expressed their cosmopolitanism more locally and quietly, in the social relationships of a community in-the-making. And in this more private sphere Kallen, like other German Jews, was active in the growth of the community; it was in Kallen's Wisconsin living room, for example, that New Yorkers Bourne and Eastman first met each other.

Hence by the late 1920s and 1930s, sons of East European immigrants had the opportunity of following the lead not only of former *Landsleuter*

---

[31]Rosenfeld, *Port of New York*, 20, 47–48, 62.

[32]Horace Kallen, "Democracy Versus the Melting Pot," in *Culture and Democracy in the United States* (New York, 1924), 67–125. The essay appeared originally in the *Nation*, 100 (1915), 191–94, 217–20.

[33]The figure of the "melting pot" was used in support of radically contrasting social policies concerning immigrants, some of which were very close to the "cultural pluralism" Kallen viewed as antithetical to the "melting pot." These ambiguities are very helpfully discussed by Philip Gleason, "The Melting Pot: Symbol of Fusion or Confusion?" *American Quarterly*, 16 (1964), 20–46.

[34]E.g. Kallen, *Culture and Democracy*, 124–25. See also the exchange over Zionism between Morris R. Cohen and Kallen: Cohen, "Zionism: Tribalism or Liberalism," *New Republic*, 18 (1919), 182–83; Kallen, "Zionism: Democracy or Prussianism," *New Republic*, 18 (1919), 311–13.

like Cohen and Freeman or of halfway figures like Lippmann and Rosenfeld, but of Anglo-Saxons whose own outlook had been influenced by the presence in America of Jewish intellectuals. By the time Alfred Kazin and Lionel Trilling were growing up, they could take as their "American" model Edmund Wilson, who had himself learned so much from Rosenfeld. Kazin and Trilling were attracted by Wilson's wide-lensed surveys of modernism and of Marxism, but they were most fascinated by Wilson as the incarnation of the great tradition of Greenwich Village. Kazin in the 1930s identified explicitly with Bourne, Brooks, and the New York of 1912;[35] Trilling consciously "signalized" his own "solidarity with the intellectual life" itself by taking an apartment in the Village just across the way from where Wilson himself could be seen each evening, working at his desk. Trilling saw Wilson as the embodiment of the least provincial aspects of the Village; from Wilson one got a "whiff of Lessing at Hamburg, of Sainte-Beuve at Paris."[36]

The young Kazin saw himself as simultaneously an American studying American literature and a Jew fulfilling, through his criticism, a vaguely Jewish "mission to humanity." He attributed his drive to create to his ethnic heritage, yet felt he had emancipated himself from the cultural content of that heritage; he had been most influenced by "Blake, Melville, Emerson, the seventeenth-century English religious poets, and the Russian novelists," none of whom, he said in 1944, had any "direct associations" with Jewish culture. As for the latter entity, he believed it indistinguishable, in its contemporary form, from middle-class chauvinism of any sort.[37]

As a graduate student in the late 1920s Trilling had contributed to the *Menorah Journal*, but by the end of the 1930s had come to lament as "provincial and parochial" all such efforts at "realizing one's Jewishness." The issue was not that of "escaping" Jewish origins, Trilling explained, but of taking one's life for what it was. "I cannot discover anything in my professional intellectual life" traceable to a specifically Jewish background, said Trilling, and "I should resent it if a critic of my work were to discover in it either faults or virtues which he called Jewish."[38]

[35] Alfred Kazin, *Starting Out in the Thirties* (Boston: Little, Brown, 1965), 5, 136–37.
[36] Lionel Trilling, *A Gathering of Fugitives* (Boston, 1956), 49–51. Cf. Irving Howe's characterization of Wilson in "The New York Intellectuals: A Chronicle and A Critique," *Commentary*, 46 (1968), 31, and James Burckhardt Gilbert's account of Wilson's influence on Phillip Rahv and William Phillips, in Gilbert's *Writers and Partisans: A History of Literary Radicalism in America* (New York: Wiley, 1967), 99. Cf. also, Kazin's description of how Malcolm Cowley appeared to him in 1934; *Thirties*, 15–17.
[37] Alfred Kazin, "Under Forty: A Symposium on American Literature and the Younger Generation of American Jews," *Contemporary Jewish Record*, 7 (1944), 12; Kazin, *Thirties*, 86.
[38] Lionel Trilling, "Under Forty," 15–17; Trilling, "Introduction" to Robert Warshow, *The Immediate Experience* (New York: Doubleday, 1962), 14 (to associate with a "Jewish"

Educated Americans in general received Kazin's *On Native Grounds* and Trilling's *The Liberal Imagination* as helpful analyses of the American social imagination, as works that made available to all a more enlightened perspective on the intellectual experience of the previous half century. Opinion on these books today is somewhat more divided,[39] but the attention they commanded in the 1940s and 1950s is an important episode in what Leslie Fiedler has hyperbolically called "the great take-over by Jewish-American writers" of a task "inherited from certain Gentile predecessors, urban Anglo-Saxons and midwestern provincials of North European origin," the task of "dreaming aloud the dreams of the whole American people."[40] The lives of Kazin and Trilling were caught up in the dialectic of ethnic diversity and cosmopolitanism; in the course of working out their own relation to the life of the mind in America, they achieved a critical ambience that persons far removed from Morningside and St. Nicholas Heights responded to as eagerly as Kazin and Trilling had once responded to the example of Edmund Wilson. But when Kazin and Trilling had read *Axel's Castle,* they were, by their own testimony, acutely aware that they were Jews and that Wilson was not. To the Americans of various backgrounds later inspired by *The Liberal Imagination* and *On Native Grounds* such distinctions were far less important, when they were noticed at all. Among the reasons for this change was the more complete integration, in the intervening years, of the discourse of the intelligentsia.

It was partly on account of Joseph Stalin that this integration proceeded as quickly as it did. The issues of the 1930s were new and immediate to Malcolm Cowley as well as to Alfred Kazin, to Dwight Macdonald as well as to Sidney Hook.[41] However one resolved one's own attitude toward Stalin, the act of doing it was the first traumatic intellectual and moral experience that the old Ivy Leaguers and the New York Jews went through together. The struggle against each other and against the non-Leftist world over issues that seemed frighteningly important created bonds of antagonism and of friendship that cemented together the community of discourse

---

magazine would be, for Trilling, a "posture and a falsehood"). Cf. Trilling, "Afterword" to Tess Slesinger, *The Unpossessed* (New York, 1934; reprint edition with Trilling's comments, New York, 1967), 316–24.

[39] As representative of the recent reassessment of Trilling, see Roger Sale, "Lionel Trilling," *Hudson Review,* 25 (1973), 241–47.

[40] Leslie Fiedler, *To the Gentiles* (New York: Stein & Day, 1972), 183. Cf. Howe, "New York Intellectuals," 30–31, and David T. Bazelon, "A Writer Between Generations," in Bazelon, *Nothing But a Fine Tooth Comb* (New York: Simon & Schuster, 1969), 17–47, esp. 18–22.

[41] On the attraction of intellectuals of Jewish origin to the Communist movement, see the essay by Daniel Aaron, "The Jewish Writer and Communism" *Salmagundi,* 1 (1965), 23–36. This piece is an important supplement to Aaron's more general study of the appeal of Communism, *Writers on the Left.* The essay is reprinted in Rose, ed., *Ghetto and Beyond,* 253–69.

of the 1940s, 1950s, and 1960s. Trilling probably exaggerated only very slightly when he observed in 1967 that the experience of participating in, or responding to Stalinism "created the American intellectual class as we know it."[42]

To a remarkable extent, the argument over Stalinism was carried out within the terms of the cosmopolitan ideal. Was or was not Marxism the most fully comprehensive, the least culture-bound analysis of society? Was the Soviet Union fulfilling or betraying the universalism of the Marxist vision? Was the enlistment of artists "on the side of the worker" a step beyond the conceptual prison of individual idiosyncracy, a step into a truly international movement that would eventually open up all of life's opportunities to all human beings; or, was such enlistment a callow enslavement to a new parochialism in which the freedom to grow and to experiment at will was repressed? Did the Popular Front Against Fascism afford an opportunity for the expansion of experience through rapport with folk and bourgeois cultures, or was the Popular Front, by virtue of its uncritical support for potential allies of the Soviet Union, a program for the stagnation of the intellect and for the covert preservation of unregenerate nationalism?

The most influential answers to the questions of the 1930s were those offered by the *Partisan Review*. Indeed, the story of how the anti-Stalinist writers gathered around the *Partisan Review* after 1937 and used it to perform a job of intellectual demolition on the Popular Front has assumed the proportions of a legend comparable to that associated with Bourne's attacks on John Dewey during World War I.[43] Although the *Partisan Review* group came together on the immediate basis of attitudes toward politics and literature, not attitudes toward ethnicity, the composition of the editorial board was an index of how the ethnic foundation of the intellectual community had shifted since the days of *Seven Arts*. The old Ivy League tradition was still represented, this time by Yale men Dwight Macdonald, F. W. Dupee, and George L. K. Morris, but the editors of Jewish origin— Philip Rahv and William Phillips—were products of the East European immigration, Rahv having actually been born in Russia. The other founding editor, Mary McCarthy, was a lapsed Catholic from Seattle. The opposing "Stalinists" were similarly constituted ethnically, but it was the *Partisan Review* that won the argument, and so decisively that its writers virtually established their own outlook as the ideological basis for the cultural criticism done by the intelligentsia for the subsequent two or three decades.

[42]Trilling, "Afterword" to *Unpossessed*, 324.
[43]An especially vivid memoir is in Dwight Macdonald, *Politics Past: Essays in Political Criticism* (New York: Viking Press, 1970), 9–14. Cf. Gilbert, *Writers and Partisans*, 155–233, and Richard H. Pells, *Radical Visions and American Dreams: Culture and Social Thought in the Depression Years* (New York: Harper & Row, 1973), 334–46.

It was in a context of anti-Stalinism and anti-Fascism, therefore, that the *Partisan Review* writers drew upon the cosmopolitan ideal, as in Harold Rosenberg's classical formulation of it in 1940.

In "The Fall of Paris," Rosenberg commented on the loss of "the laboratory of the twentieth century," first to the Popular Front and then to the Nazis. Before anti-Fascist unity had filled Paris with sympathy for "the conventional, the sententious, the undaring, the morally lax," and before Hitler had shut things down completely, this "cultural Klondike" had been the home of "the searchers of every nation."

> Released in this aged and bottomless metropolis from national folklore, national politics, national careers; detached from the family and the corporate taste; the lone individual, stripped, yet supported on every side by the vitality of other outcasts with whom it was necessary to form no permanent ties, could experiment with everything that man has within him of health or monstrousness. . . .

Its hospitality created by "a tense balance of historical forces, preventing any one class from imposing . . . its own restricted forms and aims," Paris was the "only spot where necessary blendings could be made and mellowed." In Paris, "no folk lost its integrity: on the contrary, artists of every region renewed by this magnanimous milieu discovered in the depths of themselves what was most alive in the communities from which they had come." Only this "international of Culture" could enable "American speech to find its measure of poetry and eloquence," only ideas spreading from here "could teach a native of St. Louis, T. S. Eliot, how to deplore in European tones the disappearance of centralized European culture—and a modern rhetoric in which to assault Modernism." And while the capital of the international culture is now gone, modernity in the arts survives "as solid evidence that a creative communion sweeping across all boundaries is not out of the reach of our time."[44]

Although it would be an exaggeration to say that New York took the place of Paris as the cultural capital,[45] the temporary ascendancy of Hitler in Europe suddenly transformed America, as Kazin put it in 1942, into "a repository of Western Culture" in a world overrun by its enemies.[46] This

[44]Harold Rosenberg, "The Fall of Paris," *Partisan Review*, 7 (1940), 440–48; reprinted in Rosenberg, *The Tradition of the New* (New York: The Horizon Press, 1960), 209–20. Cf. F. W. Dupee, "The Americanization of Van Wyck Brooks," *Partisan Review*, 6 (Summer 1939), 69–85, esp. 76–77, 81, 83, 85. On cosmopolitanism as a factor in Dupee's inability to work with the *New Masses*, where he had been before switching to the *Partisan Review*, see Gilbert, *Writers and Partisans*, 174.

[45]On the need for a cultural capital of some kind, and the relation of this need to American expatriation to Paris, see the illuminating essay by Warren Susman, "The Expatriate Image," in Cushing Strout, ed., *Intellectual History in America* (New York: Harper & Row, 1968), 2:145–57.

[46]Kazin, *On Native Grounds* (New York: Harcourt Brace, 1942; abr. ed. Doubleday, 1956), 380.

impression was not simply a general one; it had the specific reinforcement of the new intellectual migration. However parochial and nativist American society remained in the 1930s and early 1940s, it at least managed to accept a number of the prominent political dissenters and non-Aryan physicists, philosophers, and psychoanalysts driven out of Central Europe.[47] The presence in America of spirits like Thomas Mann, Jacques Maritain, and Albert Einstein, noted Kazin, intensified one's pride in trying to create here "a new cosmopolitan culture."[48] Values once associated with Europe, especially Paris, now had no physical, geographical, social foundation more solid than that provided by the United States. Suddenly, America did not seem so outrageously provincial. This is the context in which we must see the legendary patriotism of the intelligentsia in the Cold War era.

With varying degrees of certainty and enthusiasm, the intelligentsia of the 1940s and 1950s believed that the United States had become a viable, if imperfect embodiment of the cosmopolitan ideal. This "nationalism" triumphed only when it was felt to be distinct from the sensibility of the same name that had been so firmly rejected by the likes of Bourne, Cohen, and Rosenberg. The superiority of America to the Soviet Union was partially described in terms of the greater freedom and diversity that seemed to characterize American society. One needs neither to quarrel with nor to affirm the appropriateness of this assessment to understand that much of its persuasiveness derived from the actual social circumstances of the intelligentsia at the time: its members had come out of their various "exiles"—expatriation, the Diaspora, displacement from contemporary Europe—to find not simply "America," but to find each other. Feeling, in each other's presence, that cosmopolitanism was substantially a fact, they could not only choose sides in the Cold War, but could even show selective appreciation for American provincialism. The life depicted in *Let Us Now Praise Famous Men* was in no way a threat and could be drawn upon as a source of insight, in accordance with the cosmopolitan ideal.[49] The same could be felt about even Brooklyn or the Lower East Side: *A Walker in the City* could scarcely have been written until its author was utterly secure not simply as an American, but as a cosmopolitan.[50]

If the intelligentsia as a whole found it easier by the 1940s to accept American identity, so, too, did many of its Jewish members find themselves

[47]See Donald Fleming and Bernard Bailyn, eds., *The Intellectual Migration, 1930–1960* (Cambridge, Mass.: Harvard Univ. Press, 1969).

[48]Kazin, *On Native Grounds*, 380.

[49]James Agee and Walker Evans, *Let Us Now Praise Famous Men* (Boston: Houghton Mifflin, 1941).

[50]Alfred Kazin, *A Walker in the City* (New York: Harcourt Brace, 1951). On the generation of "Jewish intellectuals" who began their careers in the mid-1940s, there are two especially revealing memoirs: Bazelon, "A Writer Between Generations," and Norman Podhoretz, *Making It* (New York: Random House, 1967), 83–102.

moved to assert their ethnic identity after 1945, when the full dimensions of the European holocaust became known. For some, this assertion amounted to a qualified, if not open affirmation of parochialism. Ben Hecht, for example, underwent an intensive "conversion" to a religious and ethnic tradition that had played almost no part—even privately—in the first forty-nine years of his life.[51] Yet the "Jewishness" more commonly acknowledged was of a sort that could, like the patriotism of the period, be made compatible with the cosmopolitan ideal. Norman Podhoretz, for example, appreciated the liberation achieved by Trilling's generation, but was troubled by the absence of any representatives of Judaism in the international "Republic of Letters" to which his Columbia education of the 1940s had introduced him. Yet in 1954, when two highly respected, nonsectarian critics seriously proposed the admission of the Yiddish classics to this Republic, Podhoretz was ambivalent: while reading the texts offered by Irving Howe and Clement Greenberg, Podhoretz was "oppressed more powerfully than ever before by the feeling that very little of this has anything to do with that part of me which reads English, French, and Russian fiction, and everything to do with that part of me which still broods on the mystery of my own Jewishness." The pleasure of reading Yiddish literature was not, Podhoretz reluctantly concluded, that of reading "good fiction," it was rather "the pleasure of Old World charm and quaintness, titillating but not challenging, and therefore not to be taken too seriously." What irony, he exclaimed, "that this should be the effect of a literature which more than any other demands to be taken with the most apocalyptic seriousness!"[52] Podhoretz, by "accepting" (instead of rejecting) Yiddish literature as parochial, participated in no simple "return" to a clearly delineated, but dormant entity called the Jewish tradition. Associations with Jewish life that had once been impediments to growth were now avenues to expansion. Once it appeared possible to delve into an aspect of sensibility associated with Jews, without thereby cutting off other experiences, such explorations became more attractive.

To say that the mid-twentieth century intelligentsia had managed to absorb a certain amount of patriotism and an ambiguous element of ethnic identification into its system of values is not, of course, to make a judgment about the viability of this integration. One could, perhaps, object that the intelligentsia was not "really" cosmopolitan, but was merely another intellectual province, blind to issues that it should be confronting and

[51]Ben Hecht, *A Guide for the Bedeviled* (New York, 1944), esp. 3, 44, 60, 64, 78–79; Ben Hecht, *A Child of the Century* (New York, 1954).
[52]Norman Podhoretz, "Jewish Culture and the Intellectuals," in Irving Malin and Irwin Stark, eds., *Breakthrough: A Treasury of Contemporary Jewish-American Literature* (Philadelphia, 1964), 301–11.

oblivious to values that a larger view of life would compel it to recognize. Yet this is merely to carry on the argument within the intelligentsia's own terms, to criticize its members for a "parochial" failure to live up to the cosmopolitan ideal.[53] Quarrels of this sort over the practical meaning of commonly held, abstract ideals are endemic to any community of discourse and are to be distinguished from disagreements over the validity of fundamental values, such as the cosmopolitan ideal. Disagreements of the latter variety did appear in the mid-1960s.

The intelligentsia could not avoid being affected by a series of abrupt changes in its political environment, beginning with the expulsion of whites from civil rights organizations by black separatists. This was followed quickly by an upsurge of vehement ethnic particularism among "white ethnics," whose festering resentment at the attention blacks had been given during the civil rights era was now intensified by the specter of "black power." In the meantime, Israel's Six-Day War against its Arab enemies inspired a greater number of American Jews to take an active interest in the fortunes of Israel and to take their own "Jewish ethnicity" more seriously. These pressures impinged upon the intelligentsia, moreover, exactly at a time when it was being divided—often violently—over the Vietnam War and the growth of the New Left, divisions that were not directly related to the rise of particularism, but which sharpened the general feeling that the intellectual community was experiencing a shake-up.

Simultaneously, the cosmopolitan ideal was put on the defensive in an episode internal to the intelligentsia: the controversy over Hannah Arendt's *Eichmann in Jerusalem*. In this book Arendt—herself a refugee from Hitler's Europe—criticized the response Jewish leaders had made when confronted with persecution and genocide.[54] Arendt was accused of making the victims of Nazi terror look worse than the terrorists. Dwight Macdonald, one of the most determined defenders of the cosmopolitan ideal, complained that some Jewish writers were pulling their punches when it came to assessing the behavior of Jewish leadership; Daniel Bell was guilty of a "cop-out," insisted Macdonald, when Bell invoked a special standard for the evaluation of Jews.[55]

By the early 1970s it was clear that *Commentary,* under the leadership of a much-changed Norman Podhoretz, had moved decisively toward both Jewish particularism and political conservatism, while the *New York*

[53]Christopher Lasch, *The Agony of the American Left* (New York: Random House, 1969), esp. 58, criticizes the intelligentsia in precisely this way.
[54]Hannah Arendt, *Eichmann in Jerusalem* (New York: Viking Press, 1964).
[55]Dwight Macdonald, "Hannah Arendt and the Jewish Establishment," *Partisan Review.* 32 (1964), reprinted in Macdonald, *Discriminations: Essays and Afterthoughts. 1938-1974* (New York: Viking Press, 1974), 317.

Review of Books resisted both of these trends.[56] The relative merits of parochialism and cosmopolitanism, as competing ideals, were now openly debated within the intelligentsia.[57] Irving Howe, whose cosmopolitanism had once been as principled as Dwight Macdonald's, admitted that the cause of Israel had led him to modify his outlook.[58] Meanwhile, the upswing of ethnic patriotism was promoted in other contexts by Michael Novak, a Catholic writer of Slavic origin, and by Harold Cruse's influential *The Crisis of the Negro Intellectual.*[59]

Whatever the eventual fate of the cosmopolitan ideal among American intellectuals, the ascendancy of that ideal from the mid-1910s through the mid-1960s entailed certain beliefs about the spiritual capacities of individuals and of subcultures. The opportunities presented by life were felt to be broader than a choice between various particularisms (whether in the form of ideologies, religious traditions, or folkways). It was believed possible for human beings of diverse experience to put together a perspective on the world more authentic, reliable, and satisfying than any perspective generated by the intensification of a narrowly constricted range of experience. There was no reason in principle, it was assumed, why an individual could not have Whitman's "multitudes" within him or her and yet be able to achieve the stability required to enjoy those multitudes and to set priorities among them; similarly, it was hoped that a subculture could be complex and variegated without losing its integrity. In other words, the cosmopolitan ideal implicitly attributed to people the ability to confront, absorb, and profit from experience not only qualitatively different from, but *quantitatively greater* than that of any given provincial existence.

It makes sense, therefore, that the ascendancy of the cosmopolitan ideal should correspond so neatly to the era in which American intellectuals were the most conscious of the difference between "intellectuals" and other people, and that the epoch should be flanked on either end by periods in which "elitism" was suspect even among intellectuals. The point is not that either of these two conditions of early- and mid-twentieth century America was the "cause" of the other, but that cosmopolitanism, as opposed to mere pluralism, is difficult to maintain as a prescription for society at large unless one is willing—as most American intellectuals have not been—to attribute

---

[56]Of the various attempts to provide an overview of the "split" in the intelligentsia reflected in the outlook of these two journals, Peter Steinfels, "The Cooling of the Intellectuals: The Case of *Commentary* and *The New York Review of Books,*" *Commonweal.* 94 (May 21, 1971), 255–61, is especially cogent.

[57]E.g., the exchange between Robert Alter and George Steiner in *Commentary.* 49 (1970), 4–14.

[58]Irving Howe, "Thinking the Unthinkable about Israel," *New York Magazine* (December 24, 1973), 44–45, 48–52.

[59]Michael Novak, *The Rise of the Unmeltable Ethnics* (New York: Macmillan, 1971): Harold Cruse, *The Crisis of the Negro Intellectual* (New York: Morrow, 1967).

to the general population a prodigious capacity for growth. The cosmopolitan ideal commanded the widest allegiance from American intellectuals when it was implicitly understood to be their peculiar possession, when members of the intelligentsia did not feel obliged—as many of them did after the mid-1960s—to adopt values that could be justified in the wider context of general social theory.[60]

The recognition of the nature and role of the cosmopolitan ideal has been impeded, ironically, by a preoccupation with this very distinction between intellectuals and other Americans. The concepts of "alienation" and "assimilation" cannot help but entail, as a starting point, the "given" world of the official, majority culture of the United States. Studies of the history of intellectuals are thereby inclined to revolve around a single, needlessly narrow question: to what extent, and for what reasons, have intellectuals of various descriptions been estranged from, integrated into, or apologists for the established moral and political order of the society?[61] Commentaries on this question are destined, it would seem, to become variations on the Odyssean theme of withdrawal and return that has defined the autobiographies of so many intellectuals themselves, especially Malcolm Cowley's *Exile's Return*.[62] This theme is far from unimportant, but so, too, is the system of values that made the intelligentsia not simply a collectivity of persons with similar experiences but an interacting community of discourse.[63]*

[60]The same obligation was felt in the 1930s when some intellectuals did go beyond the "more-cosmopolitan-than-thou" frame of argument to repudiate the cosmopolitan ideal itself. This repudiation was most common among those willing to accept the discipline of the Communist Party, as in the case of Michael Gold, author of the *locus classicus* of the anticosmopolitan strain in the 1930s, "Wilder: Prophet of the Genteel Christ," *New Republic*, 64 (1930), 266-67.

[61]This preoccupation informs, and has an unfortunately constricting effect on even *Radical Visions and American Dreams*, the recent learned study of the intelligentsia in the 1930s by Richard Pells, whose findings are nevertheless compatible with the argument of this essay.

[62]Malcolm Cowley, *Exile's Return* (New York: Viking, 1934; rev. ed., New York, 1951). Cf. one of the latest examples of the genre, William Barrett, "The Truants: 'Partisan Review' in the 40's," *Commentary*, 57 (June, 1974), 48-54, esp. 53-54.

[63]Lasch's *New Radicalism* considerably advanced the study of the intelligentsia, but the book is weakened by its highly abstract aim: to chart the growth of a collectivity of *individuals* who manifest the general social characteristics (e.g., detachment, reliance upon the mind in work and play) that presumably distinguish "an intellectual" from other individuals (see esp. ix-xi). At times, Lasch's account of the experience of particular intellectuals can be read as a commentary on certain value conflicts within a community of discourse, but the authenticity of these conflicts and of the community divided by them is muted by Lasch's tendency to depict these arguments merely as occasions for the triumph of a single and generic "social type."

*A draft of this article was read at the Annual Meeting of the Organization of American Historians, April 18, 1974, at Denver, Colorado. For critical suggestions I am indebted to the following persons: Alexander N. Block, John P. Diggins, Michael Frisch, Richard Gillam, Samuel Haber, Marcus Klein, Thomas C. Leonard, Laurence A. Schneider, Mark Shechner, and Ronald G. Walters.

The Integration of Italian Immigrants into the United States and Argentina: A Comparative Analysis

HERBERT S. KLEIN

ARGENTINA AND THE UNITED STATES were the two nations that absorbed the largest number of Italian immigrants during the period of Europe's greatest intercontinental migration. Both began to attract Italians on a large scale from the decade of the 1880s, and both continued to accept them in large numbers until the outbreak of World War I and again in the early 1920s. Although the timing, intensity, and peak of Italian immigration differed somewhat in the two nations, their migration flows occurred within largely similar bounds. Yet, despite this common historical evolution, Italian integration and mobility within the two societies differed markedly during the first generation and continues to differ substantially to the present day. The dual aim of this very preliminary survey is to determine the nature of this differing experience of mobility and to suggest factors that explain its evolution. This will involve a study of the regional origins of the Italian immigrants as well as their comparative American integration in terms of occupational distribution, social mobility, and relative wealth.

The sharp differences in the Italian immigrant experience within Argentina and the United States were fully perceived by both the immigrants themselves and virtually all contemporary observers. Most contemporary analysts stressed the relative economic conditions in the two host countries as the main explanatory factor. But in more recent years several alternative causal models have been proposed.[1] A cultural model emphasizing the attitudes and background of the arriving migrants has again become popular among historians.[2] Among econo-

I would like to thank several friends for their criticism and advice during various stages of this study. These include Marcello Carmagnani, Roberto Cortes Conde, Torcuato and Tamara Di Tella, Michael Edelstein, Stanley Engerman, Michael Katz, Harriet Manelis Klein, Edward Malefakis, Nicolás Sánchez-Albornoz, and John Thompson.

[1] For a good survey of this literature, see J. D. Gould, "European Inter-Continental Emigration, 1815–1914: Patterns and Causes," *Journal of European Economic History*, 8 (1979): 593–639.

[2] In the United States, the cultural emphasis can be found in such recent studies as Stephan Thernstrom's *The Other Bostonians: Poverty and Progress in an American Metropolis, 1880–1970* (Cambridge, Mass., 1973), and Thomas Kessner's *The Golden Door: Italian and Jewish Immigrant Mobility in New York City, 1880–1915* (New York, 1977). For the older economic model, see, for example, Robert F. Foerster, *The Italian Emigration of Our Times* (Cambridge, Mass., 1919); and Humberto Nelli, *The Italians in Chicago, 1880–1930* (New York, 1970).

mists, debate about bias in labor markets has led to a series of alternative hypotheses to explain immigrant integration. U.S. economic historians have debated the existence of prejudice against immigrants in determining wage differentials and have even suggested regional wage and labor-market variations as important explanatory variables.[3] Finally, recent work on international migrations has led to the elaboration of a dual labor-market model. This postulates a basic demand function in advanced industrial societies for unskilled labor entering into high-risk and low-status occupations and industries, a market only supplied by nonnative migrants. The emphasis in the dual labor-market theory on immigrant strategies in relation to status and savings in the mother and host countries is especially relevant to the Italian experience.[4]

Testing both the older and more recent models found in the literature on migration and integration requires surveying statistical materials to determine the regional differences within Italy, the differences in the migration streams to Argentina and the United States as seen by American immigration officials, and the differences in the rates of occupational and social mobility in the host countries.

ALTHOUGH ARGENTINA AND THE UNITED STATES were the two primary countries of Italian immigration in the Americas between 1880 and 1914, the flows of Italian migrants to their shores differed over time. It was Brazil and Argentina that initially were the primary targets of Italian migrants, with the United States running a poor third. In the 1870s, and through most of the 1880s, Argentina was the primary zone of reception. By the late 1880s, with the abolition of slavery and the massive shift to subsidized Italian workers in the expanding coffee fields of São Paulo, Brazil temporarily emerged as the primary immigration zone despite the steady increase in Italian migration to both the United States and Argentina. But the hardships imposed on the Italian coffee workers led the Italian government to oppose Brazilian subsidization, and by the early 1900s Italian migration to Brazil was halved, while it continued to increase to the other two states.[5] By 1900 the

---

[3] The debate began with Robert Higgs's "Race, Skill, and Savings: American Immigrants in 1909," *Journal of Economic History*, 31 (1971): 420–28. Higgs stressed that, once differences in skills, literacy, and length of residence are controlled for, there was no discrimination in wage payments to immigrants. For work that supports Higgs's position, see Peter J. Hill, "Relative Skill and Income Levels of Native and Foreign-Born Workers in the United States," *Explorations in Economic History*, 12 (1975): 47–60; Peter R. Shergold, "Relative Skill and Income Levels of Native and Foreign-Born Workers: A Re-Examination," *ibid.*, 13 (1976): 451–61; Martha Norby Fraundorf, "Relative Earnings of Native and Foreign-Born Women," *ibid.*, 15 (1978): 211–20; and Michael B. Tannen, "Women's Earnings, Skill, and Nativity in the Progressive Era," *ibid.*, 19 (1982): 128–55. Only Paul L. McGouldrick and Michael B. Tannen have disagreed, arguing that a 10 percent wage differential between southern and eastern Europeans and the older immigrants and native-born can still be seen even after controlling for skill, literacy, and length of residence; McGouldrick and Tannen, "Did American Manufacturers Discriminate against Immigrants before 1914?" *Journal of Economic History*, 37 (1977): 723–46. For a discussion of regional differences in labor markets within the United States, see Gordon W. Kirk and Carolyn T. Kirk, "The Immigrant, Economic Opportunity, and Type of Settlement in Nineteenth-Century America," *ibid.*, 38 (1978): 226–34.

[4] See Michael J. Piore, *Birds of Passage: Migrant Labor and Industrial Society* (Cambridge, Mass., 1979).

[5] For a good survey of Italian immigration to Brazil, see Angelo Trento, "Miseria e speranze: L'Emigrazione italiana in Brasile, 1887–1902," in José Luiz del Rio, ed., *Lavoratori in Brasile* (Milan, 1981). Also useful are Franco Cenni, *Italianos no Brasil* (São Paulo, 1975); and Antonio Franceschini, *L'Emigrazione nell'America del Sud* (Rome, 1908), chaps. 4–5. On the history of the early experimentation with immigrant labor and the transition

TABLE 1

Estimate of Annual Italian Migration to the Americas, 1876–1914

Period	Argentina	Brazil	United States	Other	Total
1876–80	8,871	3,722	2,675	11,067	26,335
1881–85	26,532	8,371	14,952	8,527	58,382
1886–90	51,769	34,739	34,094	9,818	130,420
1891–95	31,117	65,981	41,319	8,374	146,791
1896–1900	42,247	50,064	61,546	7,152	161,009
1901–05	55,702	40,021	199,670	11,702	307,095
1906–10	91,217	20,652	266,220	13,826	391,915
1911–14	62,799	25,954	250,745	22,296	361,794

SOURCE: Istituto Centrale di Statistica, *Bolettino mensile de Statistica* (Gennaio, 1975), Anno 5, n. 1, Appendix 2: "Espatriati e Rimpatriati, anni 1876–1973," pp. 254–55. These statistics represent the latest Italian effort to measure migration and appear to be a judicious blend of the older DGS and CGE (Statistical Bureau and Emigration Commissariat) series. For a useful critique of these earlier series, see Marcello Carmagnani and Giovanna Mantelli, "Fonti quantitative italiane relative all'emigrazione italiana verso l'America Latina (1902–1914)," *Annali della Fondazione Luigi Einaudi*, 9 (1975).

United States had finally emerged as the major recipient of Italians arriving in America. Once this domination was achieved, it was never challenged. As of the outbreak of World War I, the United States had absorbed close to 70 percent of all immigrants going to these three primary American host countries. (See Table 1.)

Not only was the timing of the flows different among the three receiving countries, but the regional origins of the immigrants were also varied, which reflected changing regional interest in the overseas migration process, as southerners, especially, became more committed to overseas migration in the last decade of the nineteenth century and the first two decades of the twentieth century.[6] But equally there were within the regions of Italy clearly marked preferences for specific American countries, which also influenced the flow of migrants.

Even in the earliest stages of the massive migration period, southern Italians showed special interest in the United States and less interest in Argentina; equally, while northern and central Italian migrants went to the United States, they showed a more general interest in Argentina as their destination (see Table 2). As the

---

from slave to free workers, see Emília Viotti da Costa, *Da senzala à colônia* (São Paulo, 1966); and Warren Dean, *Rio Claro: A Brazilian Plantation System, 1820–1920* (Stanford, 1976). The best study to date on the economic life of the immigrants is Thomas Holloway, *Immigrants on the Land: Coffee and Society in São Paulo, 1886–1934* (Chapel Hill, 1980). Finally, for an interesting comparative treatment of the distortions in the immigration flow caused by Brazilian subsidization, see Chiara Vangelista, "Inmigrazione, structtura produttiva, e mercato del lavoro in Argentina e in Brasile (1876–1914)," *Annali della Fondazione Luigi Einaudi*, 9 (1975): 197–216; also see her *La Braccia per la fazenda: Immigrati e "caipiras" nella formazione del mercato del lavoro paulista (1850–1930)* (Milan, 1982).

[6] Pre–World War I regional divisions are used throughout: northern Italy comprises Piemonte, Liguria, Lombardia, and Veneto; central Italy comprises Emilia, Toscana, Marche, Umbria, and Lazio; and southern Italy comprises the remaining peninsular divisions and the islands.

TABLE 2
Regional Origins of Italian Immigrants, 1876–1930

Period	Percentage from Northern Italy	Percentage from Central Italy	Percentage from Southern Italy
Argentina			
1876–78	66	6	28
1884–86	66	9	25
1894–96	44	16	39
1904–06	32	20	48
1907–09	31	14	55
1910–14	31	14	54
TOTAL, 1876–1930	41	12	47
TOTAL IMMIGRANTS, 1876–1930	988,235	281,577	1,116,369
United States			
1876–78	41	11	47
1884–86	12	3	85
1894–96	7	5	88
1904–06	9	12	79
1907–09	9	14	78
1910–14	11	14	75
TOTAL, 1876–1930	11	9	80
TOTAL IMMIGRANTS, 1876–1930	564,345	460,227	4,034,204

NOTE: The regional divisions used here are those in effect before 1919—that is, northern Italy includes Piemonte, Liguria, Lombardia, and Veneto; central Italy includes Emilia, Toscana, Marche, Umbria, and Lazio; and southern Italy includes the remaining peninsular divisions plus the islands.

SOURCES: Commisariato Generale dell'Emigrazione, *L'Emigrazione italiana dal 1910 al 1923* (Rome, 1926), 832–49; and Associazione per la sviluppo dell'industria nel mezzogiorno [hereafter, SVIMEZ], *Statistiche sul mezzogiorno d'Italia, 1861–1953* (Rome, 1954), 118.

volume of southern migration continued, however, it appears that southerners were discriminating more in the areas of destination, and thus the percentage going to South America increased considerably, while the ratio going to the United States declined. This was occurring as overall southern Italian migration was increasing steadily (see Table 3). Thus, prior to World War I, sharp regional preferences were beginning to break down as all regions sent migrants to all American states. But this

TABLE 3

Regional Origins of the Transatlantic Italian Immigrants, 1876–1914

Period	Percentage from Northern Italy	Percentage from Central Italy	Percentage from Southern Italy	Total Number of Transatlantic Migrants	Transatlantic Migrants as a Percentage of All Migrants
1876–79	61	6	33	99,722	24
1880–84	45	7	48	254,750	35
1885–89	39	11	50	514,949	54
1890–94	32	11	57	566,260	51
1895–99	29	11	60	787,521	54
1900–04	13	12	74	1,265,632	53
1905–09	15	13	71	2,012,774	60
1910–14	17	14	69	1,861,644	57
TOTAL, 1876–1914	26	10	64	7,363,252	55

NOTE: The regional divisions used here are those that obtained prior to 1919.

SOURCE: Commisariato Generale dell'Emigrazione, L'Emigrazione italiana dal 1910 al 1923, passim.

process never reached total equality, and the United States undoubtedly received more southern Italians than did Argentina overall, although both countries had immigration flows from all three Italian regions.[7]

With southern Italians accounting for 80 percent of the total immigration of Italians to the United States in the 1876–1930 period, and only 47 percent to Argentina, it is worth exploring the regional variations between the two major Italian regions of the *nord* (central and northern districts) and the *mezzogiorno* (southern departments) to determine the nature of the differences, if any, that existed between the migrants from these two basic regions within Italy. What becomes apparent from this comparison is that Italy itself was made up of so many complex, even intraregional, economic and social structures that the statistics reveal relatively little variation across regions despite the fact that the *mezzogiorno* was clearly less developed than the *nord*.

Thus a comparative analysis of the major demographic variables reveals only modest variation between the *nord* and *mezzogiorno*. In terms of age structure and civil status, there is virtually no difference between the two regions. Age at marriage, birth rates, and even size of families were all quite similar across Italy. It is only in such categories as still births, infant mortality, crude death rates, and average heights that we can begin to see a distinction between the two zones. Evidently, the *mezzogiorno* was not as healthy a region as the *nord*, not in terms of climate but rather because of differences in wealth. This is obvious from the 1928 income differentials. It is also apparent from the wide differences in educational opportunities in the two regions, which found expression in the extreme difference in literacy rates. (See Table 4.)

But, despite the wealth-poverty distinction, one is still surprised by the relatively modest variation in most of the demographic and even the economic statistics. Especially surprising is the commonality of the divisions by major occupational categories of the economically active populations. Thus, while there was obviously an important *nord-mezzogiorno* distinction, it is not as sharp as the one found today in most Third World countries, which have an advanced-backward regional split.

Moreover, as many commentators have stressed, there was a tendency for selectivity of immigrant groups in all zones. It was obviously not the poorest and least prepared groups that migrated from either the *nord* or the *mezzogiorno*. Equally, given the very complex land, labor, and social arrangements within each region, it is not surprising that peasants or urban dwellers—north, center, or south—came from quite similar backgrounds and experiences. All recent studies stress that the immigrant groups usually came from the better situated and more mobile upper elements of the working classes in all regions, thus tending toward a homogenization of immigrants, despite the regional variations that did exist.[8]

---

[7] For useful surveys of the changing directions of Italian migration in this period and its context within a century of intense Italian migration, see Luigi Favero and Graziano Tassello, "Cent'anni di emigrazione italiana (1876–1976)," in Gianfausto Rosoli, ed., *Un Secolo di emigrazione italiana* (Rome, 1978), 9–63; and Ercole Sori, *L'Emigrazione italiana dall'unità alla seconda guerra mondiale* (Bologna, 1979), chap. 2.

[8] Sori, *L'Emigrazione italiana*, 295–96; and J. S. McDonald, "Some Socio-Economic Differentials in Rural Italy, 1902–1913," *Economic Development and Cultural Change*, 7 (1958).

TABLE 4

Comparative Characteristics of the Italian Population

	Nord	Mezzogiorno
AGE STRUCTURE (1901)		
0–14 years	34 percent	35 percent
15–39 years	37 percent	36 percent
40–59 years	19 percent	20 percent
60+ years	10 percent	10 percent
SEX RATIO (1901)		
Male to Female	100.5	96.8
VITAL STATISTICS (1910–12)		
Crude Birth Rate	31.4	34.0
Age-Specific Birth Rate per 1000 women, 14–45	269	271
Still Births per 1000 live births	39.8	43.6
Infant Mortality (deaths under 1 year per 1000 live births)	137.4	147.3
Crude Death Rate	18.5	21.9
Natural Growth Rate	12.9	12.2
CIVIL STATUS (1901)		
Single	33 percent	30 percent
Married	54 percent	57 percent
Widowed	13 percent	12 percent
FAMILY STRUCTURE (1913–14)		
Average Age at Marriage (Males)	27.6 years	27.1 years
Average Age at Marriage (Females)	23.8 years	23.3 years
Average Size of Family (1911)	4.8 persons	4.1 persons
HEIGHT OF MALE CONSCRIPTS	165.03 cm.	161.83 cm.
TOTAL POPULATION		
1881	17.3 million	11.2 million
1901	19.7 million	12.7 million
1911	21.4 million	13.3 million
ESTIMATED NET MIGRATION LOSS		
1881–1901	1,250 thousand	930 thousand
1901–11	787 thousand	859 thousand
DISTRIBUTION OF MALE WORKFORCE, 1901		
Agriculture	57 percent	62 percent
Industry	25 percent	21 percent
Transportation	4 percent	4 percent
Commerce	6 percent	5 percent
Other	8 percent	8 percent
INDEX OF AVERAGE PER CAPITA INCOME, 1928 (Italy = 100)	117.2	69.5
ILLITERACY RATE, 1901		
Persons above 5 years of age	33.9 percent	68.1 percent

SOURCES: SVIMEZ, *Statistiche sul mezzogiorno, passim*; and Istituto Centrale di Statistica, *Sviluppo della popolazione italiana dal 1861 al 1961* (Rome, 1965), 56–63, 301.

TABLE 5
Argentine and U.S. Immigrant Occupations (as a Percentage), 1876–1910

Occupation	Argentina (1876–1909)		United States (1899–1910)	
	Italians	All Immigrants	Italians	All Immigrants
AGRICULTURAL WORKERS AND FARMERS: *agricultores*	68	56	33	25
UNSKILLED DAY LABORERS: *jornaleros*	13	18	43	36
SKILLED AND SEMI-SKILLED WORKERS: *artesanos y artistas*	10	12	16	22
MERCHANTS: *comerciantes*	2	5	1	2
OTHER PROFESSIONS: *varios professiones*	6	9	6	16
NUMBER OF IMMIGRANTS, OCCUPATION LISTED	1,475,073	2,644,642	1,768,281	7,049,010
NUMBER OF IMMIGRANTS, NO OCCUPATION LISTED	208,888	436,906	516,320	2,506,717

SOURCES: Direccion Nacional de Migraciones, *Memorias Anuales, 1899–1910*; and U.S. Immigration Commission [Dillingham Commission], *Reports*, volume 3: *Statistical Review of Immigration, 1820–1910* (Washington, 1911), 98–178.

The question therefore remains as to what differences actually existed in the stream of migrants arriving in the two American nations. Differences were, in fact, noted by U.S. and Argentine immigration officials. Thus the moderate variations between migrants from the *nord* and those from the *mezzogiorno* seen in the Italian statistics are far more exaggerated in the American data. Argentina, for example, appears to have received far more agricultural workers and far fewer day laborers than did the United States. While farmers and farm laborers made up just a third of the Italians arriving in the United States, they made up over two-thirds of the Italians arriving in Argentina. Equally, while day laborers were the dominant occupational group of immigrants arriving in the United States, they made up only 13 percent of the arrivals in Argentina. (See Table 5.) This difference in the labeling of unskilled workers probably reflects the relative timing of the two migration streams. Up until the 1890s there was an overwhelming predominance of agricultural workers listed among the unskilled emigrating Italians, whereas after 1900 this imbalance tended to disappear as both groups of occupations were more nearly equal in representation among the male migrants leaving Italy. (See Table 6.)

But the entire distinction between nonfarm unskilled laborers and farm workers may have been rather artificial to begin with. Even as late as 1911, 60 percent of the male labor force in Italy was still engaged in agriculture. As the leading contemporary expert on Italian immigration noted at the time, the majority of unskilled workers, no matter what their designation, in fact came from the rural population and should equally be counted as agricultural laborers.[9] Thus, it can be assumed that most of the arriving *giornaliere* (*jornaleros*, or "day laborers") were of agricultural origin and could have been employed in farm work. It is justifiable, then, to place these two groups together when assessing skilled and unskilled occupations of arriving immigrants in the two American nations. When this is done, the combined totals of farm and day laborers are quite similar in the two host countries: 81 percent for Argentina and 76 percent for the United States. What makes for the major differences between Italians going to Argentina or the United States, then, is not so much the relative importance of unskilled, skilled, and professional workers, which did not differ significantly, but between the number of unskilled workers listed as doing agricultural or day labor.

What this distinction signifies is, however, difficult to assess fully. As Roberto Cortes Conde has recently pointed out for Argentina, the mobility of workers

TABLE 6

Occupations of Italian Adult Male Migrants (as a Percentage), 1876–1910

Period	Agricultural Laborers and Farmers	Unskilled Day Laborers	Skilled Construction Workers	Industrial Workers and Artisans	Liberal Professions	Other and Unknown
1876–78	42	21	16	12	0.7	8
1884–86	50	23	12	8	0.6	6
1894–96	45	26	17	6	0.6	5
1904–06	36	32	13	12	0.3	7
1907–10	35	33	13	11	0.4	7

NOTE: "Adult" is here defined as fifteen or more years old.

SOURCE: Francesco Coletti, *Dell'emigrazione italiana* (Milan, 1912), 55.

between the categories of urban day laborers and construction workers on the one hand and agricultural laborers on the other was quite high at the end of the nineteenth century. There seemed little difficulty in Argentina, at least, of *jornaleros* passing over temporarily into *peones* in the rural sector during harvest periods, particularly when there was unemployment in the construction and urban sectors.[10] In the United States this possibility does not appear to have occurred. In Argentina the high cost of attracting native Argentine workers out of subsistence and into commercial agriculture contrasts with the situation in the United States, in which Americans were fully integrated into commercial farming and expanding demand was met with a native-born labor force. Thus the undifferentiated nature of these two occupational categories, implicit in the Italian and Argentine experience, could

[9] In 1912 Francesco Coletti declared that he and all other analysts at that time found that "laborers, day laborers, and the like come in large part from the rural classes and for that reason should be added to the category of agricultural laborers in order to account fully for the rural contingent in the emigrant stream"; Coletti, *Dell'emigrazione italiana* (Milan, 1912), 56.

[10] Cortes Conde, *El Progreso argentino, 1880–1914* (Buenos Aires, 1979), 197–204.

not be tested in the United States because of the competition of the native-born in the agricultural market.[11]

Whatever the real differences may have been between these occupational definitions, it is worth stressing that those going to Argentina reflected quite closely all foreign immigration going to that country, just as the occupational breakdown of those going to the United States reflected all foreign immigrations in that period (see Table 5). In both cases, Italians were either more heavily agricultural workers or day laborers than the total migration group. But in both cases, for Italians and total immigration, there appears a much greater stress in one country on agriculturalists and in another on unskilled day laborers.

Migrants bound for Argentina were apparently more literate than those headed to the United States (although the figures are not quite comparable); but the majority of immigrants in both streams was literate, just as the majority of the Italian population, according to the census of 1901, was literate. Immigrants to both American republics, however, apparently were somewhat more literate as a group than the entire Italian population (see Tables 4, 7, and 8). This finding, as well as the higher percentage of skilled workers noted even for the U.S.-bound immigrants, seems to support the assertion of recent studies that it was the more skilled and educated of the laboring classes in both societies that migrated.[12]

In terms of demographic characteristics, there were differences between the immigrants to the United States and Argentina. Although immigrant groups were dominated by working-age males, the U.S.-bound Italians were considerably more so. But higher repatriation of Italian males than Italian females led to an approximately equal sex ratio in both resident Italo-American communities by 1914 and 1920 respectively (see Tables 7 and 8).[13] In both cases, however, this ratio was still considerably higher than that for the respective native-born populations, just as the mean age of the Italian-born immigrants in both countries was on average ten to fifteen years older than that of the American-born populations.[14]

[11] In 1910 the South and the North Central states together had 85 percent of the farm population (as well as 80 percent of all farm acreage and the total value of all farms) but only 20 percent of the Italian population. Moreover, since three-quarters or more of the Italians lived in urban areas, probably no more than sixty thousand Italian immigrants worked in the agricultural heartland of the United States. In contrast, 69 percent of the native-born population lived in these two regions. U.S. Bureau of the Census, *Thirteenth Census of the United States . . . , 1910*, 1 (Washington, 1913): 800, and *Historical Statistics of the United States, Colonial Times to 1970*, 1 (2d edn., Washington, 1976): 90–92, 458.

[12] For the Italian background experiences of selected U.S.-bound immigrants, see John W. Briggs, *An Italian Passage: Immigrants to Three American Cities, 1890–1930* (New Haven, 1978), chap. 1; and Virginia Yans-McLaughlin, *Family and Community: Italian Immigrants in Buffalo, 1880–1930* (New Haven, 1978), chap. 1.

[13] The only detailed study of the age, sex, and civil status of repatriated immigrants is the model demographic analysis by Massimo Livi Bacci for Italians returning from the United States. He concluded that in the period 1909–28 a much higher percentage of the repatriates was male than was the original U.S.-bound group of immigrants: the sex ratio of the repatriates was 734 males per 100 females, and that for the immigrants was 234 per 100 females. The repatriates were more likely than the immigrants to be single young adults, and they were far more likely to have come from the most recently arrived group of immigrants. Whereas 90 percent of the repatriated Italians had resided in the United States fewer than ten years, only 43 percent of the foreign-born Italians in 1930 had resided in the United States fewer than twenty years. See Livi Bacci, *L'Inmigrazione e l'assimilazione degli italiani negli Stati Uniti secondo le statistiche demografiche americane* (Milan, 1961), chap. 4.

[14] República Argentina, *Tercer censo nacional de . . . 1914*, 10 vols. (Buenos Aires, 1916), 1: 143. In the United States in 1910, the mean age differential was approximately the same at thirteen years; U.S. Bureau of the Census, *Historical Statistics of the United States*, 19.

TABLE 7
Characteristics of Italian Immigrants and First-Generation Italo-Americans
in Comparison to All Immigrants, 1899–1910

	Northern Italians	Southern Italians	All Italians	All Immigrants
OCCUPATIONAL STRUCTURE.				
Professionals	1 percent	<1 percent	<1 percent	1 percent
Skilled Workers	20 percent	15 percent	16 percent	20 percent
Farm Laborers	19 percent	34 percent	32 percent	23 percent
Day Laborers	48 percent	8 percent	9 percent	19 percent
Other	12 percent	8 percent	9 percent	19 percent
SEX RATIO (Male to Female)				
Immigrants, 1899–1910 ·	361.2	367.5	366.5	227.8
Immigrants, 1893–1914			325.0	
Resident Foreign-Born, 1910			190.6	131.1
AGE STRUCTURE				
Immigrants, 1899–1913				
Under 14 years	9 percent	12 percent	11 percent	12 percent
15–44 years	87 percent	82 percent	83 percent	82 percent
45+ years	4 percent	6 percent	6 percent	5 percent
Resident Foreign-Born, 1920				
Under 15 years	9 percent	12 percent	11 percent	12 percent
15–44 years			70 percent	56 percent
45+ years			25 percent	40 percent
ILLITERACY RATE				
Persons above 14 years	12 percent	54 percent	47 percent	27 percent
FINANCIAL CONDITION				
Average Savings upon Arrival of Those Declaring Income	$30.76	$17.14	$19.45	$28.95
Those Arriving with Less than $30.00, 1899–1903	37 percent	7 percent	n/a	18 percent
Those Arriving with Less than $50.00, 1904–1914	14 percent	6 percent	n/a	14 percent

SOURCES: U.S. Immigration Commission, *Reports*, 3: 47, 84, 95, 350; Massimo Livi Bacci, *L'Emigrazione e l'assimilazione degli italiani negli Stati Uniti secondo le statistiche demografiche americane* (Milan, 1961), 103; and U.S. Bureau of the Census, *Thirteenth Census of the United States. . . , 1910*, 1 (Washington, 1913): 866, and *Historical Statistics of the United States from Colonial Times to 1972*, 1 (Washington, 1975): 16–17.

TABLE 8

Characteristics of Italian Immigrants and First-Generation Italo-Argentines
in Comparison to All Immigrants, 1893–1914

	All Italians	*All Foreign-Born Residents*
AGE STRUCTURE		
Resident in 1914		
Under 15 years	7 percent	10 percent
15–44 years	61 percent	66 percent
45+ years	32 percent	25 percent
Immigrants, 1893–1909		
Under 13 years	15 percent	15 percent
13+ years	85 percent	85 percent
SEX RATIO (Male to Female)		
Immigrants, 1893–1909	267.8	260.6
Resident Foreign-Born, 1914	171.2	166.7
CIVIL STATUS (Residents, 1914)		
Single	27 percent	36 percent
Married	65 percent	57 percent
Widowed	8 percent	7 percent
ILLITERACY RATE (Residents, 1914)		
Persons 7 years and older	36 percent	32 percent

NOTE: Data are missing for age of immigrants for five years—1901–03 and 1905–06.
SOURCES: República Argentina, *Tercer censo nacional de . . . 1914*, 10 vols. (Buenos Aires, 1916),
passim; and Direccion General de Immigración, *Resumen estadistico del movimiento en la República
Argentina años, 1857–1924* (Buenos Aires, 1925), 19, and *Memorias Anuales, 1899–1910*.

HOW CAN THE DIFFERENCES between the regional similarities in Italy and the very
sharp differences between the two migration streams of Italians arriving in America
be explained? It has been argued that the cultural differences between Latin and
Catholic Argentina and Protestant and English-speaking United States attracted
different kinds of immigrants. Such differences may have influenced some of the
elite liberal professionals among the Italian migrants—no more than 1 to 2 percent
in either immigrant stream—but cannot explain the self-selection among the mass
of immigrants. Clearly, the forms of agricultural production were not dissimilar in
the Argentine pampas and the U.S. plains. Wheat production technology was

identical and was easily adopted by the immigrants. In fact, Italian agricultural laborers in South America were required to adapt to coffee plantation agriculture and cattle ranching, both new technologies for them. Within the North American context, they could readily have developed any special skills needed to handle the cereal or other agricultural production techniques then available. Even in industrial pursuits, the world of U.S. industrial activity was not dissimilar to the northern Italian experience of the time, nor did it require a highly trained work force. In short, there was neither a cultural nor a technological impediment to any specific type of Italian immigration, nor was southern or northern Italian work experience very different from what might be required in similar situations in the United States or Argentina.

It would appear, then, that it was primarily differing labor markets within the United States and Argentina that exercised an attraction for distinct types of immigrants and thus distorted the streams of Italians flowing to the New World. Each local economy provided different incentives, and Italians responded to those incentives. As contemporaries were well aware, the relative availability of land in Argentina and its relative scarcity in the United States was one major factor. The second was the relative demand of a beginning industrial plant in Argentina and the concomitant new urban expansion compared to an older and established industrial plant in the United States with its fully elaborated urban complex. Finally, the history of previous immigrations meant that the relative importance of Italian immigrants differed in important respects within the two countries.

In Argentina, the Italians were among the first massive group of immigrants to arrive and could establish immigrant norms of integration. They both dominated the foreign-born group and even formed a substantial minority in the total population (they were 39 percent of the foreign-born residents and 12 percent of the entire population in 1914). In contrast, Italians in the United States were late arrivals and in 1910 ranked fourth among foreign-born, accounting for just under 10 percent of the foreign-born but 1.5 percent of the national population. Although Italians increased in importance to second place among the foreign-born by 1920, the concurrent growth of the native population meant that Italians still accounted for only 1.5 percent of the entire U.S. population. Moreover, of the other major immigrant groups, those accounting for over a million migrants, only the Poles and the Russians were like the Italians in being "new immigrants" of the post-1880 period. The equally important Germans and Irish came well before 1880.[15] Both the Polish and Russian migrants brought the same skills as the Italians, and the first- and second-generation Germans and Irish were already well established before the arrival of the Italians. Indeed, newly arrived Italians could often obtain only those jobs scorned by the native-born and the second-generation children of immigrants. Nor were there any major opportunities in the Eastern half of the United States—by then the oldest industrial sector of the country—for innovative industrial development.[16]

[15] *Historical Statistics of the United States*, 105–09.
[16] In 1910 only 11 percent of the Italian immigrants lived in the Middle West industrial states (East Northcentral region), whereas 72 percent were confined to the Northeast. New York State alone had over one-

All this was perfectly evident to both the northern and southern Italians who migrated. Thus, the perceptions they held of the two labor markets determined their decisions to migrate, their willingness to remain in the country, and their ideas about developing a local community. Even patterns of savings and investment were largely determined by their perceptions of the possibilities within the two labor markets.

In the United States, this meant that the immigrants were overwhelmingly single males going into day laborer positions within the urban centers. Italians arrived just as the modernization (lighting, urban rail transport, sanitation, and the like) of the North American cities was occurring. These opportunities, along with more traditional aspects of mining, railroad and highway construction, and housing, all provided excellent labor markets for the Italians. Given the high wages, especially in comparison to those in Italy, the majority of the Italians were able to return to Italy as planned, and thus the development of the local community was considerably slowed. Given the relatively higher wages of manual labor in North America, Italians, unlike native-born Americans, were willing to concentrate on immediate income and ignore both long-term investments in human capital for themselves or their families in America and the low-status assignment of these jobs. This basic decision, even for those who remained, meant that savings, if not repatriated, were placed in factors that were not directly related to long-term occupational mobility—investing more in housing than education, for example. For the first generation, this was a clearly thought-out alternative, as repatriated savings became the basis for occupational mobility at home.

Such a strategy based on short-term expediency was also apparent for many Argentine migrants, as the repatriation figures suggest. Thus, between 1880 and 1920 roughly equal ratios of Italians returned from Argentina as had returned from the United States during this period (or approximately 51 percent for Argentina to approximately 54 percent for the United States).[17] But, given the differing market opportunities in land, commerce, and industry, the possibilities for those who remained in America were greater in Argentina than they were in the United States. Thus investments in land, stores, factories, and children's education were seen to have a high payoff in the long run and to be worth sacrificing immediate consumption or security to obtain. Given the more closed nature of the U.S. market, such sacrifices were not as readily justified. Thus, just as

---

third of the Italian-born immigrants. U.S. Bureau of the Census, *Thirteenth Census of the United States, . . . 1910*, 800, 804. In Argentina, however, all foreign-born residents, including the Italian immigrants, were concentrated in the litoral region, which was the center of both commercial agriculture and all industrial activity. Cortes Conde, *El Progreso argentino, 1880–1914*, 70.

[17] I calculated the rate of return from the United States using Livi Bacci's differing decennial estimates for the period 1880–1920 to obtain an overall ratio; *L'Inmigrazione e l'assimilazione*, 35. I calculated the overall estimate of return from Argentina using the data in Dirección General de Inmigración, *Resumen estadístico del movimiento migratorio en la República Argentina, años 1857–1924* (Buenos Aires, 1925), 8. Recent Italian government statistics, which began to be compiled only in 1905, show even higher trends of repatriation for the period 1905–1920 than the estimates of Livi Bacci for the United States, but these statistics correspond more closely with the official Argentine figures. See Instituto Centrale di Statistica, *Bollettino mensile di Statistica* (Gennaio, 1975), Anno 5, Appendix 2: "Espatriati e Rimpatriati, anno 1876–1973," 255, 263. Because of his detailed calculations for birth and death rates and his reliance on censused resident populations, I prefer Livi Bacci's figures. On the difficulties involved in estimating these rates, see J. D. Gould, "European Inter-

the differences in the labor markets help explain the differences in the characteristics of the arriving migrants, these same variables are fundamental to explaining the savings and investment strategies of those who did not repatriate themselves and their earnings. This in turn goes a long way toward explaining the relative rates of mobility and integration within the two societies.[18]

To assess more fully these relative rates, it would be ideal if we could compare the differences in the occupational structure, in land ownership, and in ownership of the means of production. Unfortunately, such a comparable set of figures does not yet exist for either society. Moreover, in each nation different sets of materials exist, which are not quite comparable. In Argentina, for example, there are excellent ownership data by the first part of the twentieth century, but comparatively poor occupational data. In the case of the United States, there exist excellent occupational and income data, but ownership data are poor. Equally, although much of the Argentine data is national in scope, most of the U.S. data is found only in sample surveys of selected regions. But it will be argued, as this analysis proceeds, that enough material exists to make a rough approximation of mobility in the two societies.

THE MAIN ATTRACTION FOR MANY ITALIAN IMMIGRANTS going to Argentina was the relative availability of land and the possibility of entering the role of independent farmer. Although traditionally it was assumed that a few Argentines monopolized the land market, it has recently been shown that an open land market existed in Argentina from at least 1880 onward. At the same time, the stock of cultivated land after 1880 was increasing by an extraordinary 10 percent per year.[19] Although the relative returns between renting and owning may have favored the former activity to the discouragement of property ownership, there is little question that Italians became farm owners in unusually large numbers for such a recently arrived immigrant group.

Native Argentines naturally continued to monopolize the land market, but, as the data of the 1914 census indicate, a remarkably large proportion of Italians

Continental Emigration—The Road Home: Return Migration from the U.S.A.," *Journal of European Economic History*, 9 (1980): 79–87. Brazilian-bound Italian immigrants also repatriated at comparable rates during the period 1901–20; see G. Mortara, "A imigração italiano no Brasil e algumas caracteristicas do grupo italiano de São Paulo," *Revista Brasileira de Estadistica*, 11 (1950): 325.

[18] Even in political terms, the Italian experience differed strongly in the two societies, as studies of radical politics and labor organization show; see Samuel L. Baily, "The Italians and Organized Labor in the United States and Argentina, 1880–1910," *International Migration Review*, 1 (1967): 55–66. It is worth pointing out, however, that for the Italians who remained in America, their social integration with the native population proceeded in roughly comparable rates for both Argentina and the United States. Although historians have debated the relative cultural homogeneity or acculturation of the Italian immigrant communities, demographic studies for both Argentina and the United States suggest that Italians moved very rapidly toward native national norms in rates of fertility and nuptiality and also that they intermarried with the native-born populations at ever-increasing rates. See Livi Bacci, *L'Immigrazione e l'assimilazione*, chap. 6; and Samuel L. Baily, "Marriage Patterns and Immigrant Assimilation in Buenos Aires, 1882–1923," *Hispanic American Historical Review*, 60 (1980): 32–48.

[19] Cortes Conde, *El Progreso argentino*, 239. In contrast, U.S. farm acreage grew by only 4.6 percent in the entire decade 1901–10; U.S. Bureau of the Census, *Historical Statistics of the United States*, 457.

succeeded in owning land.[20] Italians were consistently the second most important group of landowners in cereal and cattle production and were especially successful in grain farming. In fact, Italian-born immigrants within Argentina did extremely well in landownership in general throughout the republic. As of the 1914 census, 25 percent of the Italians twenty or more years of age owned some type of property, a figure close to the national norm and only slightly below that for native-born Argentines. Italians also did far better than the Spaniards, who were almost as numerous and were the second most important immigrant group in the nation. (See Table 9.)

This high general rate of property ownership among Italians is partially explained by their extremely high rates of ownership of urban commercial and industrial property. As of a special census for Buenos Aires in 1909, Italians owned 38 percent of the 28,632 commercial establishments in the city. They were the single largest group of owners of these firms and held double the number owned by native Argentines. All this occurred when they represented only 22 percent of the city's population.[21] Furthermore, most commentators have stressed that the Italian immigrants participated in industrial activity not only as skilled workers but even more so as entrepreneurs.[22] Unfortunately for our purposes, the 1914 census does not break down firm ownership by nationality; it simply provides data for all foreigners as a group as well as for all Argentine nationals. Given the rate of Italian ownership of property above their percentage in the total population, it can be assumed that the Italians held minimally 40 percent of the foreign corporations—their share of the foreign-born urban population—and thus owned at a minimum 26 percent of the 48,779 industrial firms listed in the 1914 census.[23] In fact, they most probably did even better than that, since it is the assumption of all

---

[20] The nature of rural land ownership by immigrants is a much-debated issue in Argentine historiography. Reflecting the traditional viewpoint, James Scobie stressed the inability of the immigrants, especially the Italians, to gain control over the land they farmed; Scobie, *Revolution in the Pampas: A Social History of Argentine Wheat, 1860–1910* (Austin, 1964), 31. Roberto Cortes Conde has challenged this view in the first systematic study of the rural land market for this period. He has shown the existence of a thriving land market in the pampas throughout the period of heavy immigration. Cortes Conde, *El Progreso argentino*, chap. 3. The national statistics, moreover, all support the assertion that Italians were able to become landowners, even able to join the supposedly closed ranks of the cattle ranchers. Although land ownership was not democratically distributed among all groups, Italians did extremely well considering their recent arrival and their initial lack of capital. This same mythology of immigrant inability to purchase the lands they worked has also appeared in Brazilian historiography, where it was assumed that Italians suffered even more discrimination. But recent, systematic studies show that even in the heart of the coffee zones Italians were unusually successful in obtaining commercial agricultural lands; see Holloway, *Immigrants on the Land*, chap. 6; and Thomas W. Merrick and Douglas H. Graham, *Population and Economic Development in Brazil, 1800 to the Present* (Baltimore, 1979), 111–12.

[21] Alberto B. Martinez, ed., *General Census of the City of Buenos Aires of 1909*, 1 (Buenos Aires, 1910): 130–34; and James R. Scobie, *Buenos Aires: Plaza to Suburb, 1870–1910* (New York, 1974), 260.

[22] In the census of 1914, foreign workers accounted for 53 percent of the workforce in commercial establishhments and 50 percent of the labor in industrial plants; they accounted for 66 percent of the owners of commercial property and 74 percent of the industrial owners; see Gino Germani, *Política y sociedad en una época de transición* (Buenos Aires, 1962), 195. For a fine analysis of the predominant role of foreign-born residents in the advanced industrial sectors of the nation in 1914, see Gustavo Beyhaut et al., "Los Inmigrantes en el sistema ocupacional argentino," in Torcuato Di Tella, ed., *Argentina, sociedad de masas* (Buenos Aires, 1965), 85–124.

[23] República Argentina, *Tercer censo nacional de ... 1914*, 8: 246. In the industrial census of 1935, foreigners still owned 54 percent of the 50,985 industrial establishments whose owners' nationality was known. And of this total, Italians controlled 41 percent of the foreign-owned firms and thus 22 percent of all such companies. See Oscar Cornblidt, "Inmigrantes y empresarios en la política argentina," Instituto Torcuato Di Tella, Doc. de Trabajo, no. 20 (Buenos Aires, 1966), 27.

TABLE 9
Property Ownership by Nationality (as a Percentage) in Argentina, 1914

Nationality	Rural Population			Total Population		
	Relative Importance in Rural Population	Non-Ranch Rural Property Owners	Ranch-Owners (Estancieros)	Relative Importance in Adult Population	Relative Importance among Property Owners	Adults Owning Property
ARGENTINES	77.7	59.4	77.8	51.8	62.2	32.4
ITALIANS	8.7	21.0	6.4	20.2	18.9	25.1
SPANIARDS	6.4	6.4	4.7	16.3	9.7	15.9
RUSSIANS	1.2	3.0	0.6	1.7	0.9	13.9
URUGUAYANS	0.7	0.8	0.9	1.7	1.2	20.6
FRENCHMEN	0.7	2.6	2.4	1.9	2.0	29.5
OTTOMANS	n/a	n/a	n/a	1.2	0.7	16.1
AUSTRO-HUNGARIANS	0.6	2.1	0.8	0.7	0.8	30.5
ENGLISHMEN	0.3	0.4	1.1	0.6	0.4	17.6
GERMANS	0.3	0.6	0.5	0.6	0.4	19.7
SWISS	0.2	0.8	0.8	0.3	0.4	44.2
ALL OTHERS	3.2	2.9	4.0	3.1	1.6	14.3
TOTAL POPULATION IN CATEGORY	3,359,737	72,429	66,561	4,016,739	1,074,964	4,016,739

NOTE: Adult here means more than nineteen years of age. To compensate for the age bias between the native-born and immigrant populations (nationals were on average fifteen years younger than foreigners in 1914), I have taken persons age twenty and above as the basis for my calculations for "Relative Importance in Adult Population" and "Adults Owning Property." In doing so, I had to estimate the adult-age population for four national groups—Russians, Ottomans, Austro-Hungarians, and Swiss—since these were grouped together with "Other Nationals" in the age classifications of the census of 1914. I have used the figure obtained for this general category as the estimator for the four unknown nationalities.

SOURCE: República Argentina, *Tercer censo national de ... 1914*, 2: 395–96, 3: 295–309, 4: 68, 5: 837, and 6: 679.

274

contemporary and later commentators that Italians dominated the manufacturing sector.

Concentrating on rural land ownership and entrepreneurial activity unquestionably yields the best indices of capital accumulation and, ultimately, of social mobility. Further support for the social mobility of Argentina's Italian immigrants could be obtained from data on the occupational distribution of the population; unfortunately, however, the Argentine statistics for this period break down the occupational structure of the skilled work force only by the simple division of foreign and national jobholders for each category. Foreigners in Argentina, who represented only 30 percent of the total population in 1914, dominated almost all of the skilled occupational categories. Among the liberal professions, they were less well represented but usually came out at or below their 30 percent representation in most fields of endeavor. They even represented 35 percent of the capitalists (*rentistas*) of the nation.[24]

By any standards, these general indices of ownership and occupational distribution attest to the very rapid integration of the resident Italian population into the national economy. Although half of the Italian immigrants returned to Italy, those who chose to remain in Argentina found ready investments for their savings and had little difficulty in achieving rapid economic and social mobility. Italian-born Argentine residents were well represented in every occupation of the nation and were generally over represented in the category of land owners. Even in that most Argentine of all occupations, that of cattle-ranch owner, Italians could be found. Although the available data are obviously not as complete or as comparable as one would like, they all point in the same direction of extraordinary success for a people who had only just entered the national economy and were still overwhelmingly of the first generation.

THE UNITED STATES DID NOT OFFER THE SAME OPPORTUNITIES for Italian immigrants that Argentina did. In studying the mobility of Italians in the United States during the same period, we immediately run into the problem of comparability of data. In the U.S. censuses of this period and even in the special Congressional and Bureaus of the Census and of Labor studies, no relevant figures are provided on land ownership, one of the key variables we were able to analyze in the Argentine case. Moreover, even in the occupational distribution data, there are problems. These national statistical problems, however, are somewhat compensated for by the existence of numerous samples of the population, which have been studied both by U.S. government agencies and by later social scientists. Thus, samples of families nationally and of male workers in large urban centers on a local level will provide much of the basis for the following discussion.

What these disparate sources reveal is that, in the first decade of the twentieth century, the "New Immigrants" were consistently in the lowest paying and lowest status jobs in the United States. Moreover, when the New Immigrant category is

[24] República Argentina, *Tercer censo nacional de ... 1914,* 4: 382–97.

broken down into nationalities, it was found that Italians were consistently at the lowest end of the scale. Although some economic historians have recently argued that this wage and status differential was due to lower skill levels, lack of English, and short-term length of residence in the United States, statistics concerning second-generation Italians—that is, children of Italian-born parents—also reveal extremely low rates of social mobility for these persons of Italian descent who are literate and have lived their entire lives in the United States.

What both the Dillingham Immigration Commission *Reports* of 1909 and the Labor Commissioner's survey of 1903 reveal is that Italians consistently were at the bottom in family income and of male and even female income in contrast to all other foreign-born workers. In each case they were lower than two-thirds of the New Immigrants and in most cases were at the very bottom of the scale. Even home ownership, sometimes a heavy investment for immigrants in the lower ends of the occupational scale, was a distinctly minor factor among the Italians. Where the Italians showed a positive feature was in their capacity to save. Italians, if this very small 1903 national sample is to be accepted, were probably among the very best savers among immigrant groups. (See Table 10.) This characteristic, which we will return to in later discussions, tells us a great deal about Italian attitudes toward savings and toward repatriation to Italy. It also reveals an unwillingness to sacrifice repatriation of savings at the cost of local investments.

A well-drawn sample of Italians in New York City from the heart of the Italian districts at the beginning of this century reveals the same patterns found in the national surveys. Comparing occupational stratification between the Italians and the Russian Jews, who arrived at the same time as the Italians to the United States, reveals just how different the Italian mobility experience had become. The Russian Jews were, of course, at the other extreme from the Italians in terms of repatriation, being the classic case of the immigrants who could not return to Europe and were therefore concerned most completely with "making it" in America. By 1905 in New York City, the Russian Jews already had reduced their numbers in unskilled and semi-skilled occupations to 19 percent as contrasted to 58 percent of the Italians who remained in these occupational categories (see Table 11). Obviously, this is an extreme comparison, and, in contrast to the Polish immigrants, the Italians would not appear in such an unfavorable light. Nevertheless, it does reveal just how skewed the occupational distribution of these Italians were and why they were consistently coming in with the lowest incomes.

The question to be asked in this context is why the Italians consistently had the lowest rates of income, ownership, and job skills. Clearly, there was extreme prejudice against Italians in the United States, especially those considered to be from southern Italy. The *Reports* of the Immigration (or Dillingham) Commission of 1910 are especially flagrant in the racist attacks on southern Italians. But more important than the discrimination, which tended to exist in every American society that received foreign immigrants, were the preferences of the Italians themselves and the nature of the labor market they entered.

Italians deliberately concentrated their activity on insecure and unskilled laboring jobs, which had short-term potential for high savings. They also tended to

TABLE 10
Comparative Economic Status of Immigrant Workers
in the United States, 1903 and 1909

	Italians		All Foreign Born	
SURVEY OF 1903				
Mean Annual Family Income	$611	(256)	$711	(10,279)
Percentage of Homeowning Families	12%		24%	
Percentage of Savings (Income/Expenses)	7%		4%	
SURVEY OF 1909				
Mean Annual Family Income	$595	(1,963)	$704	(13,825)
Mean Annual Income of Males (18+)	$417	(3,553)	$455	(22,938)
Mean Annual Income of Females (18+)	$235	(320)	$284	(2,386)
Percentage of Homeowning Families	19%	(2,258)	22%	(15,551)

SOURCES: For the 1903 survey, see U.S. Commissioner of Labor, *Eighteenth Annual Report, 1903* (Washington, 1904), *passim*; and, for the 1909 survey, see U.S. Immigration Commission, *Reports*, 1: 407–12, 468.

concentrate in those regions and cities where such jobs were most abundant and tended to shun the states of the Middle West, for example, where the industrial core of the nation was developing, and the South, where their market was restricted by a native black and white labor force in abundance. The limited availability of farm occupations, which grew at a slower rate than the rest of the labor force, also offered few attractions. In contrast, construction, railroad, manufacturing, and trade jobs were increasing faster than the rate of increase of the labor force.[25] Thus Italians concentrated in all of these more expansive occupations, except manufacturing. In the United States as in Argentina this strategy paid off. With average daily wages of laborers varying from $1.25 to $1.50 per day, and with steamship fares costing on average $15 to $20 per person for steerage class from Europe to the United States, it is no wonder that the Italian response to the U.S. labor market was so elastic.[26] Over time, moreover, real wages in the United States, as in Argentina, were on the rise for most of the period from 1880 to the first decade of the twentieth century.[27]

[25] U.S. Bureau of the Census, *Historical Statistics of the United States*, 139, 144–45.

[26] Gould, "European Inter-Continental Emigration, 1815–1914," 611–15; Philip Taylor, *The Distant Magnet: European Emigration to the U.S.A.* (New York, 1971), chap. 8; and Sori, *L'Emigrazione italiana*, chap. 8.

[27] Between 1890 and 1914 real wages, both hourly and daily, increased by over 30 percent in manufacturing, and from 1880 to 1914 real wages rose by 48 percent for all nonfarm labor; Albert Reese, *Real Wages in Manufacturing, 1890–1914*, National Bureau of Economic Research (Princeton, 1961), 120; and U.S. Bureau of the Census, *Historical Statistics of the United States*, 164–65.

Thus the response of Italians to U.S. labor market conditions helps explain their relative concentration in certain low-status, economically remunerative jobs. But, in their very response to that market, the half of the migrants who decided to remain and construct a new community found themselves, through the result of their timing and concentration, in a poor position to compete with both other immigrant groups and native-born Americans. The concentration of Italians in the urban centers of the Northeastern states of the United States was a negative influence on their future rates of mobility. As a recent survey of occupational mobility and location concludes, "Opportunity for migrants in the nineteenth century was greatest in young, small communities outside the Northeast."[28] This locational disadvantage still influenced social mobility into the first decade of the new century

TABLE 11

Occupational Distribution of Immigrant Heads of Households
in New York City, 1905

Occupational Category	Percentage of Italians	Percentage of Russian Jews
HIGH WHITE COLLAR	2	15
LOW WHITE COLLAR	18	31
SKILLED	22	35
SEMI-SKILLED	16	18
UNSKILLED	42	2
TOTAL IMMIGRANT HEADS OF HOUSEHOLDS	1,015	963

SOURCE: Thomas Kessner, *The Golden Door: Italian and Jewish Immigrant Jewish Mobility in New York City, 1880–1915* (New York, 1977), 52, 60.

as well. The decision of Italians therefore to concentrate in the oldest regions (72 percent lived in the Northeastern states in 1910) and primarily in urban areas (78 percent) in the long run had a negative impact on their potential social and economic mobility.[29] That this decision to concentrate in the urban Northeast was a reasonable one in terms of earning potential for unskilled laborers in turn became a

[28] Kirk and Kirk, "The Immigrant," 231–32.
[29] By 1920, 84 percent of the Italian-born residents of the United States lived in urban areas, and 73 percent lived in the Northeast. This was the highest concentration in this region for any immigrant group. When first- and second-generation Italians are added together, their concentration in the Northeast in 1920 rises to 81 percent. Niles Carpenter, *Immigrants and Their Children, 1920* (Washington, 1927), 368, 372. On the occupational distribution of Italians and their relatively limited role in U.S. agriculture, especially in contrast to their much larger role in Argentine and Brazilian agriculture, see Foerster, *The Italian Emigration of Our Times*.

negative factor in their possibility for advancement once a permanent community had been established. This in turn helps explain the relative low rates of mobility that we have seen for the Italians compared to other New Immigrant groups. Thus, the relative importance of the Italians within the labor force, their late arrival in North America, and their consequent concentration in low-status, unskilled jobs tended in the aggregate to make the mobility of Italians in the United States quite different from their experience in Argentina.

When Italians finally settled, they found high-status jobs blocked to them, they found agricultural lands in the hands of native-born Americans or other immigrants, and they found most of the industrial establishment fully in the control of native-born Americans and rapidly moving toward monopoly situations. This does not mean that there were not pockets of rapid mobility for some Italians. The 9 percent of the Italians who were listed as living in the West in 1910 clearly had much in common with the Italians who went to Argentina. Arriving early in the settlement process, they quickly entered into farming and wine production and soon had rates of mobility that were probably quite comparable to those in Argentina. But for the majority of Italians their concentration of settlement in the older regions of the United States meant that long-term mobility, even for the second generation, was at a much lower level than that experienced by other immigrant groups of both the New and Old migrations. Italians did not do well comparatively in terms of occupational, educational, or social mobility.

An analysis of the U.S. census of 1950, for example, shows that first- and second-generation Italians had the highest percentage of unskilled, nonfarm laborers and the lowest percentage of professionals of all major immigrant groups. Only the Poles had fewer white-collar workers, and only the Irish had fewer in the skilled craftsmen category. (See Table 12.) This pattern of lower mobility among Italians is even more evident in a detailed study in 1950 of first- and second-generation immigrants in Boston, a major center of Italian migrants. Italians were the least well off of all major ethnic groups in the city, having on average the least schooling, the fewest high-status white-collar workers, and the lowest income.[30]

Thus, even as late as a generation following the end of massive immigration from Italy, Italians had not achieved a significant rate of mobility in the United States, compared not only to native white North Americans but even to all other immigrant groups. Yet, by 1920, almost half of the so-called Italian *stock*, as defined by the census, was born in the United States, a figure that rose to over two-thirds of those of Italian origin in the United States by 1950. Clearly, the Italians in Argentina had achieved a position in the professions, in land ownership, and in industry by 1914 not achieved by their contemporary migrants to the United States by 1950.

[30] Stephan Thernstrom, *The Other Bostonians: Poverty and Progress in the American Metropolis, 1880–1970* (Cambridge, Mass., 1973), 172. Even as late as 1960, a U.S. Bureau of the Census survey of second-generation males shows that, of all the so-called New Immigrants from Southern and Eastern Europe, Italian Americans had the lowest percentage of professionals among all age groups, including the youngest (those from twenty-five to thirty-four years of age); Stanley Lieberson, *A Piece of the Pie: Blacks and White Immigrants since 1880* (Berkeley and Los Angeles, 1980), 330.

TABLE 12

Comparative Nonfarm Occupational Structure (as a Percentage)
for the Major Immigrant Groups in the United States, 1950

Occupation of Employed Males	Native American Whites	Germans	Italians	Poles	Irish
PROFESSIONALS	9	9	6	7	10
MANAGERS AND SUPERVISORS	12	15	11	9	12
CRAFTSMEN AND FOREMEN	23	28	22	23	20
OPERATIVES	24	20	30	33	18
CLERICAL, SALES, AND SERVICE	22	22	22	19	33
DAY LABORERS	8	6	9	8	6
TOTAL NUMBER OF EMPLOYED MALE IMMIGRANTS	21,217,560	1,096,620	1,118,940	721,710	569,370

NOTE: Given the high concentration of native whites and the extremely low participation of most immigrants in agriculture, I decided to show only nonfarm labor (for which all occupational unknowns have been deleted).

SOURCE: E. P. Hutchinson, *Immigrants and Their Children, 1850–1950* (New York, 1956), 335–49.

THIS VERY PRELIMINARY SURVEY OF COMPARATIVE ITALIAN IMMIGRATION reveals several important themes. The Italians who migrated to Argentina and the United States were concerned with accumulating savings through the higher wages available in the Americas. In most cases, the immigrants assumed that those savings would be invested back in Italy either in land or other economic activities so as to improve their economic and social standing.

In the Argentine situation the relative economic opportunities were such that many immigrants were attracted to invest their savings in the local economy. Skilled artisans and professionals, moreover, were more drawn to the Argentine situation because of the tremendous expansion of both agriculture and industry. Since the Italians were the premier immigrant group and in fact accounted for some 14 percent of the national population, their potential for investment of their savings in America was extraordinary. The fact that so many still returned to Italy is testimony to the tremendous commitment of most immigrants to return to the mother country.

Overall, the same factors of wage differentials and high savings potential pulled Italians in even larger numbers to the United States. Here the opportunities for unskilled labor were extraordinary, although jobs in heavy industry and agriculture were far less available than they were in the Argentine. But the labor market for low-status, unskilled workers was expanding so rapidly that the Italians found even their competition with other immigrant groups no impediment to a rapid accumulation of savings. That the majority of them returned to Italy is testimony to their successful analysis of the market conditions open to them. But, for those who stayed, the relative closure of higher-status jobs and the earlier strategies that had

280

stressed current income and repatriation of savings over local investment in land or education reduced occupational mobility. Second-generation Italians were still more heavily concentrated in unskilled and manual labor jobs than were most other major immigrant groups. Although third-generation Italian-Americans were becoming indistinguishable from native-born North Americans, the process of assimilation took much longer in the United States than it did in Argentina. Most importantly, it was the relative structure of the individual labor markets of the host countries that determined the patterns of integration and mobility of the immigrants who remained. No significant factors in the Italian origin of the immigrants, or in their cultural make-up, can as fully explain the social and economic history of the Italians in the Americas.

Beyond the Great Divide:
Immigration and the Last Frontier

MOSES RISCHIN

S INCE 1945, American historians have been hastening to overtake a world-centered United States. Seeking a world audience, they can no longer view their country as an innocent adolescent nation which has been engaged in a trans-Atlantic feud with an authoritarian European parent. Increasingly, the United States has become a premier trustee and guarantor of civilization, burdened with all the ironies and ambiguities that accompany its new condition. Looking outward, the nation's historians inevitably have come to look inward; and a new cosmopolitanism is gradually being introduced to the reassessment and rewriting of American history.[1]

Nowhere is the hiatus between the older and the new historiography more challenging and more interesting than west of the Rockies in the thirteen latter-day original states, which include Alaska and Hawaii—the much touted racially aloha laboratory of democracy. No aspect of the history of the new West is more crucial to American self-understanding and more universal in interest than the virtually unexplored story of the accommodation and interaction of its diverse peoples and the implications of the severance or perpetuation of group and personal ties with the places of their origin elsewhere in America or abroad.[2] No region of the United States has

Mr. Rischin is professor of history in San Francisco State College.

[1] See John Higham, "The Construction of American History," John Higham, ed., *The Reconstruction of American History* (New York, 1962), 10-11; Earl Pomeroy, "The Changing West," Higham, *The Reconstruction of American History*, 64-81; Earl Pomeroy, "Old Lamps for New: The Cultural Lag in Pacific Coast Historiography," *Arizona and the West*, II (Summer 1960), 107-26; Mario S. De Pillis, "The Conceptual Crisis in the Historiography of the American West," paper delivered at the meeting of the Organization of American Historians in Kansas City, April 1965.

[2] See Earl Pomeroy, *The Pacific Slope: A History of California, Oregon, Washington, Idaho, Utah, and Nevada* (New York, 1965), 253-92; Rodman Wilson Paul, "Mining Frontiers as a Measure of Western Historical Writing," *Pacific Historical Review*, XXXIII (Feb. 1964), 25-34; and especially Henry Nash Smith, "Mark Twain as an Interpreter of the Far West: The Structure of *Roughing It*," Walker D. Wyman and Clifton B. Kroeber, eds., *The Frontier in Perspective* (Madison, 1957), 205-28. For Hawaii, see

·42·

seen from its beginnings so great and so varied a mingling of peoples, and
nowhere has the need for a sense of history and identity been more nakedly
and more decisively felt.[3] Yet for most Americans the new West only recently has become a palpable social reality. Its history, in many critical aspects, became meaningful only after the closing of the frontier, where ironically most histories of the West end. In 1890 this region contained only
five percent of the country's population, and these people were distributed
over nearly forty percent of its land area. To historians east of the Rockies,
with a few notable exceptions, the West beyond the West, except at the
level of gold-prospecting and geopolitics, has continued to seem a distant
backwater, as remote from the central concerns of America as was Australia
from Great Britain.

The history of the far-western region has been singularly recent and contemporary, even by the standards of the new nations; and its place in
American history has been so stylized and parochialized that it has come to
represent the ultimate in American historical discontinuity. Increasingly,
the myth of the new American West provided psychological and inspira-
tional relief from the compelling dilemmas of a complex industrial society
which was profoundly at odds with its individualistic agrarian and democratic traditions. For those who vainly resisted the dissolution of an older
America, the Far West has offered a retreat and panacea. There cowboys,
Indians, outlaws, buffalo hunters, prospectors, and other children of nature
countered the discontents of civilization.[4] Given the hyper-American excep-
tionalist role which the Far West was fated to play, no understanding, insight, or relevance to the continuities with the American non-West and
western civilization could be expected to arise. Western historians were
yea-sayers, thrice-over. Both spatially and chronologically, the Far West was
thrice removed from the European civilization that traditionally served as
the foil for the writing and interpretation of the American story. As a result, this region has borne the glory and the burden of a triple myth, the
American, the western, and the new western; and its history has inevitably
been one-sided.

especially Romanzo Adams, *Interracial Marriage in Hawaii* (New York, 1937), 316-17;
Andrew W. Lind, *Hawai'i's Japanese: An Experiment In Democracy* (Princeton, 1946),
19-20, 62-97.
   [3] See Page Smith, *The Historian and History* (New York, 1964), especially pp. 232-49;
C. Page Smith, "The Pacific Coast: A Study of Southern California," *Current History*, 40
(May 1961), 291-96; Joseph Boskin, "Associations and Picnics as Stabilizing Forces in
Southern California," *California Historical Society Quarterly*, XLIV (March 1965), 17-26.
   [4] Henry Nash Smith, *The Virgin Land* (New York, 1957), 291; Earl Pomeroy, *In
Search of the Golden West: The Tourist in Western America* (New York, 1957); Kent
Steckmesser, *The Western Hero in History and Legend* (Norman, 1965).

Immigration history, in every respect except for the goal of individual opportunity, the antithesis of pure American and western history, inevitably fell victim to amnesia. Of course, the very subject of immigration has been central, indeed obsessive, to western history and has produced some of its most distinguished imaginative and historical writing. But scholarship and veneration have been limited to the pilgrim years. The Far West's Jamestown has been at Donner Pass, its Massachusetts Bay in the Salt Lake Valley. In the study of no other region of the United States does the term immigration, except when applied to Asiatics, almost exclusively denote internal land migration. In no other region, and most especially in California where "the West has come to a focus,"[5] did the early settler seek so avidly and so desperately to quick-freeze the pioneer era into a super-American past. Perhaps no other region shifted more abruptly from heroic epic years to statistical drift years, from manifest destiny to the "Great Barbecue." Yet no other region's total history is so contemporary, falling just below the horizon of living memory, and so relevant and instructive for an understanding of the present.

The very rapidity and intensity of change in a region so vast with a population so new and so elusive, so mobile and so diverse, so contemptuous of antecedents and yet so hungry for a past, has made it difficult for the historian to find his bearings. The analytical intelligence, which has been the hallmark of the outstanding historians in stabler and older regions, has been notably deficient here. Easterners and far easterners, southwesterners and midwesterners, immigrants and sons of European immigrants and transmigrants, and those from south of the border as well as north, have swarmed over this intellectually uncharted land. But "Middletown," "Yankee City," "Southern Town," and "Jonesville" have not been matched by a major study of "Western City," for sociologists have been as delinquent as historians. Less ambitious sociological studies of western communities have been noticeably few, except, ironically, for studies of Japanese relocation centers, utopian colonies, and, of course, Indian villages, which never have been in sufficient supply to satisfy the anthropologists.[6] Even Carey

---

[5] Pomeroy, *The Pacific Slope*, vi.

[6] Ruth D. Tuck, *Not With the Fist: Mexican-Americans in a Southwest City* (New York, 1946) and Walter Goldschmidt, *As You Sow* (New York, 1947) are the best of the limited sociological studies. See Alexander H. Leighton, *The Governing of Men: General Principles and Recommendations Based on Experience at a Japanese Relocation Camp* (Princeton, 1945), a study of the Japanese relocation center at Poston, Arizona; Leonard J. Arrington, *The Price of Prejudice: The Japanese-American Relocation Center in Utah During World War II* (Logan, 1962); Robert V. Hine, *California's Utopian Colonies* (San Marino, 1953); Ray Allen Billington, *America's Frontier Heritage* (New York, 1966), 182-84; Dorothy Johannsen, "A Working Hypothesis for the Study of Migrations," *Pacific Historical Review*, XXXVI (Feb. 1967), 1-12.

McWilliams, who popularized the cause of the nation's minorities in a sé-
ries of books based on the western scene, produced a truncated story because his concerns were to programmatic and his historical research too per-
functory to allow for depth or for balance. But the editor of the *Nation*
has had no counterpart among western historians, who are invariably
strangers themselves to the Far West. What Rowland Berthoff has recently
written of the Pennsylvania anthracite region is not without application to
both far-western society and to its historians. "The story is one of groups,
classes, institutions, and individuals so equivocally related as to be mutually
unintelligible and quite heedless of each other. The region had plenty of
groups, classes, institutions, and notable personages, to be sure, but it is
hard to find among them any functional design of reciprocal rights and du-
ties, the nuts and bolts which pin together a stable social order."[7]

Even John D. Hicks, whose comments in the early 1930s on the cosmopolitan sources of culture in the Middle West revealed keen insight and a
sense of historical complexity, failed to sustain his interest upon crossing
the Great Divide. Although he objected to a parochial Hispanophilia,
Hicks offered no alternative conception. In 1945, shortly after coming to
California, he saluted San Francisco, site of the founding of the United
Nations, as the true gateway to the Orient and to Latin America; but curiously, he ignored that immigrant city's proverbial boast that it harbored
the spirit of every land, that provincialism alone was a stranger within the
Golden Gate.[8] Today, the San Francisco Public Library does not maintain a
single foreign-language newspaper file, although about thirty foreign-language and ethnic weeklies are still published in the Bay area. The fiction is
maintained that the earthquake and fire of 1906 destroyed most of the early
foreign-language newspaper files of this historic spiritual and intellectual
metropolis of the West. But the file of San Francisco's oldest Italian newspaper, founded in 1859, was extant in North Beach until recently; and
there are complete files, at their respective newspaper offices, of the currently published Danish (1882-) and Italian (1910-) papers.[9] Needless

---

[7] Carey McWilliams, *Brothers Under the Skin* (Boston, 1943), 7-49; Rowland Berthoff,
"The Social Order of the Anthracite Region, 1825-1902," *Pennsylvania Magazine of History and Biography*, LXXXIX (July 1965), 261-62.

[8] John D. Hicks, "The Development of Civilization in the Middle West, 1860-1900,"
Dixon Ryan Fox, ed., *Sources of Culture in the Middle West: Backgrounds versus Frontier*
(New York, 1934), 85; John D. Hicks, "California in History," *California Historical
Society Quarterly*, XXIV (March 1945), 7-16; John D. Hicks, "History in California,"
California Historical Society Quarterly, XXXVI (June 1957), 107-16; Harr Wagner, ed.,
Notable Speeches by Notable Speakers of the Greater West (San Francisco, 1902), 356.

[9] Joseph Giovinco, a graduate student at San Francisco State College, reported that until
1964 a complete file of *La Voce Del Popolo* was available in the offices of *L'Italia*. A
change in location led to the discarding of the file. The author of this paper has con-

to say, the city at the Golden Gate is representative, not exceptional, in its indifference to the social complexities of its own past.

Oblivious to the possibilities for research in social history, far-western historians have repeatedly taken the casual impressions of a curious trio for chapter and verse. The tendency to cite the tourist James Bryce, the displaced person Henry George, and the exile Josiah Royce to document the greater Americanization of European immigrants in the West has obscured the vigorous nativism that flourished in the region from its inception and the equally vigorous continuity of group diversities.[10] The conspicuously immigrant background of many of the leaders of far-western nativism has also contributed to a remarkable insensitivity on the part of historians to the extreme conformist pressures that prevailed. It is hardly surprising that Father James Bouchard, an American Indian who visited "the City" in the 1880s, prudenty camouflaged his origins when he lashed out at the Chinese with the vigor and abandon of a second-generation American.[11] The candid Yankee authors of San Francisco's earliest history, which had been published in 1855, minced no phrases in their commitment to an Anglo-Saxon manifest destiny.

Both [the French and German] races have played a prominent part in the industrial history of San Francisco, and in that of California generally. Their numbers are very large in the various mining districts; while, as we have seen they form a considerable proportion of the population of the city. They are not the dominant spirits of the place—for these are of the true American type that ever cry *go ahead*!—but they help to execute what the national lords of the soil, the restless and perhaps unhappy people of progress contrive. The character of a man may at least partially be inferred from his "drinks." The true Germans dote on *lager-bier*—and they are a heavy, phlegmatic, unambitious race; the French love light wines—and they are as sparkling, yet without strength or force of character; the genuine Yankee must have a burning *spirit* in his multitudinous draughts—and he is a giant when he begins to work, tearing and

ducted a survey of the foreign-language press resources of the Bay area and has corresponded and spoken with archivists and historians in Montana, Nevada, Oregon, and Washington.

[10] Pomeroy, *Pacific Slope*, 262-89; William Hanchett, "The Question of Religion and the Taming of California, 1849-1854," *California Historical Society Quarterly*, XXXII (June 1953), 122-23; John Higham, "The American Party, 1886-1891," *Pacific Historical Review*, XIX (Feb. 1950), 38; L. E. Fredman, "Broderick: A Reassessment," *Pacific Historical Review*, XXX (Feb. 1961), 41. For a later period see Gloria Waldron, "Anti-Foreign Movements in California, 1919-1929" (doctoral dissertation, Univerity of California, Berkeley, 1955).

[11] John Higham, *Strangers in the Land* (New Brunswick, 1955), 228; Roger Daniels, *The Politics of Prejudice: The Anti-Japanese Movement in California and the Struggle for Japanese Exclusion* (Berkeley, 1962), 24, 28; William Preston, Jr., *Aliens and Dissenters* (Cambridge, 1963), 152-80; John B. McGloin, *Eloquent Indian: The Life of James Bouchard, California Jesuit* (Stanford, 1949), 172-86.

trampling over the *impossibilities* of other races, and binding them to his absolute, insolent will.[12]

Hinton R. Helper's *Land of Gold*, also published in 1855 and recently reproduced as a hoax under the title *Dreadful California*, revealed that antislavery advocate's loathing not only for Negroes but also for most non-Anglo-Saxon peoples—a feeling that was clearly shared by many nineteenth-century Americans.

Yet nearly half a century later, Josiah Royce, although insisting on the indifference of the Californian to family tradition, avowed that in childhood even he had appreciated three types of hereditary distinctions in addition to his own—the Chinese, the Mexican, and the Irish. Most westerners, however, conceded Royce, were more catholic in their prejudices and showed a "hearty American contempt for things and institutions and people that were stubbornly foreign."[13] Even the statue of Father Junipero Serra, contributed to the Hall of Statuary in the Capitol, conformed to the code of a dime western by transforming California's diminutive patron saint into a tall, lean westerner. By contrast, Douglas Tilden's sculpture of 1908, given by James D. Phelan to San Francisco's Golden Gate Park, realistically portrayed him as a smallish, plump figure. Even Earl Pomeroy in the first major synthesis of far-western history devoted only three pages to the European ethnics and reserved his landmark discussion for the region's conspicuously different and naked victims of barbaric violence—not to speak of prejudice—the Orientals and the Mexicans.[14]

Clearly, in the Far West more than in other regions, the dynamics of group life have remained unexplored and poorly understood—indeed, as invisible in works of formal history as they have been visible in life. The author of the most comprehensive article on immigration to California before 1870, Doris M. Wright, concluded that the state was "as American as the rest," that its "cosmopolitanism was more apparent than real," and that there was nothing more to add.[15]

[12] Hinton R. Helper, *Land of Gold* (Baltimore, 1855); Hinton Helper, *Dreadful California*, Lucius Beebe and Charles M. Clegg, eds., (Indianapolis, 1948); Frank Soulé and others, *The Annals of San Francisco* . . . (New York, 1855), 464-65; Louis B. Wright, *Culture on the Moving Frontier* (Bloomington, 1955), 123-67; Edward McNall Burns, *David Starr Jordan: Prophet of Freedom* (Stanford, 1953), 66-72.

[13] Josiah Royce, *Race Questions, Provincialism, and Other American Problems* (New York, 1908), 206-07; Josiah Royce, *California: From the Conquest in 1846 to the Second Vigilance Committee in San Francisco: A Study of American Character* (New York, 1948), 218.

[14] See Theodore Maynard, *The Long Road of Father Serra* (New York, 1954), 291; Maynard J. Geiger, *The Life and Times of Fray Junipero Serra, O. F. M., or The Man Who Never Turned Back (1713-1784)* (2 vols., Washington, 1959), II, 272-73; Pomeroy, *The Pacific Slope*, 262-92.

[15] Doris Marion Wright, "The Making of Cosmopolitan California: An Analysis of

In the last few years, however, an upsurge of historical scholarship indicates a growing interest in the plurality of origins, institutions, and group memories that have been native to the West. More than a dozen scholars have analyzed a wide range of ethnic groups; and while they have produced many excellent studies, they have by no means exhausted the field. In addition, Francis Weber has compiled the first collection of documents of California Catholic history; John McGloin has completed a biography of Archbishop Alemany; Allan Breck has published a book on the Jews of Colorado; William J. Parish has contributed an insightful study of the pioneer Jews of New Mexico; and work is in progress on histories of the Jews of Los Angeles, the Mother Lode country, and San Francisco.[16]

Immigration, 1848-1870," *California Historical Society Quarterly*, XIX (Dec. 1940), 323-43, XX (March 1941), 65-79; Marion Clawson, "What It Means To Be a Californian," *California Historical Society Quarterly*, XXIV (June 1945), 139-61.

[16] William Mulder, *Homeward to Zion: The Mormon Migration from Scandinavia* (Minneapolis, 1957), 248; P. A. M. Taylor, *Expectations Westward: The Mormons and the Emigration of their British Converts in the Nineteenth Century* (Ithaca, 1966); Kenneth O. Bjork, *West of the Great Divide: Norwegian Migration to the Pacific Coast, 1847-1893* (Northfield, Minn., 1958); see A. P. Nasatir, ed., *A French Journalist in the California Gold Rush: The Letters of Etienne Derbec* (Georgetown, Calif., 1964), for a masterful introduction to French materials; Clifford Bissell, "The French Language Press in California," *California Historical Society Quarterly*, XXXIX (March-Dec. 1960), 1-18, 141-73, 219-62, 311-53; Joseph Giovinco, "Democracy and Banking: The Bank of Italy and California's Italians" is soon to be published in the *California Historical Society Quarterly*; Andrew Rolle's pioneer work on the Italians of the West is soon to be published by the University of Oklahoma Press; Frederick Bohme has completed a doctoral dissertation on the Italians of New Mexico; Frederick G. Bohme, "The Portuguese in California," *California Historical Society Quarterly*, XXXV (Sept. 1956), 233-52; Wayne S. Vucinich, "Yugoslavs in California," *Historical Society of Southern California Quarterly*, XLII (Sept. 1960), 287-309; Gunther Barth, *Bitter Strength: A History of the Chinese in the United States 1850-1870* (Cambridge, 1964); T. Scott Miyakawa is directing a projected history of the Japanese, "The Japanese in the United States 1860-1960"; see also Daniels, *The Politics of Prejudice*, 1-15; Leonard Pitt, *The Decline of the Californios: A Social History of the Spanish-Speaking Californians, 1846-1890* (Berkeley, 1966); Manuel P. Servín, "The Pre-World War II Mexican-American: An Interpretation," *California Historical Society Quarterly*, XLV (Dec. 1966), 325-38; Rudolph M. Lapp, "The Negro in Gold Rush California," *Journal of Negro History*, XLIX (April 1964), 81-98; Rudolph M. Lapp, "Negro Rights Activities in Gold Rush California," *California Historical Society Quarterly*, XLV (March 1966), 3-20; Robert G. Athearn, *Westward the Briton* (New York, 1953); Oscar C. Winther, "English Migration to the American West, 1865-1900," *Huntington Library Quarterly*, XXVII (Feb. 1964), 159-73; Charles Bateson, *Gold Fleet for California: Forty-Niners from Australia and New Zealand* (East Lansing, 1964); Jay Monaghan, *Australians and the Gold Rush* (Berkeley, 1966); Lancaster Pollard, "The Pacific Northwest," Merrill Jensen, ed., *Regionalism in America* (Madison, 1951), 187-212; Francis J. Weber, *Documents of California Catholic History (1784-1963)* (Los Angeles, 1965); John B. McGloin, *California's First Archbishop* (New York, 1966); Allan D. Breck, *A Centennial History of the Jews in Colorado: 1859-1959* (Denver, 1960); William J. Parish, *The Charles Ilfeld Company: A Study of the Rise and Decline of Mercantile Capitalism in New Mexico* (Cambridge, 1961); Robert Levinson, a doctoral candidate at the University of Oregon, is preparing a dissertation on the pioneer Jews of the Mother Lode country to 1880. Organized early in 1967, the Western Jewish History Center of the Magnes Museum in Berkeley promises to become a major archive of materials documenting the history of the Jews of the West.

Most exciting, perhaps, of all recent scholarly developments has been the fresh confrontation with the history of the Mormons. Symptomatic no less than symbolic of western history, the story of the Mormons is being explored with a new depth and perspicacity by both Mormon and gentile scholars. The Mormon Historical Association, organized in San Francisco in December 1965, the quarterly, *Dialogue: A Journal of Mormon Thought*, launched in the spring of 1966, and thoughtful articles by half a dozen younger and older scholars reflect an intellectual poise, sophistication, and candor that augur a new secularization of the Mormon posture. A breakthrough in appreciation and understanding of this strategic historic group may well provide a new sense of the continuities and discontinuities in western social history and their implications for all groups.[17]

The reason for the blind spot in western history is not difficult to understand; it is simply the extreme extension of a traditional American exceptionalism. Presumably, in an area distant from the corrupt older America, the troublesome provincialisms of race, region, religion, and nationality that divided and redivided Europe and nearly destroyed the United States could be happily forgotten. The far-westerner's anxiety to bring order out of chaos, his passion to establish a regional identity vis-à-vis the East, and his avidity for cultural unity are both commendable and comprehensible. Perhaps it would be best to ignore the immediate pasts of immigrants from all the states and all the source countries so that they might all the more readily become Americans and golden westerners. Indeed, a region and a people without a history seemingly might best select a new identity by claiming for itself a near legendary and unique past. The appeal of such a prospect in California is suggested by the founding in 1850 of the Society of California Pioneers, followed two decades later by the establishment of the Native Sons of the Golden West, the Native Daughters, the California Historical Society, and the Southern California Historical Society. At the turn of the century the process culminated in the dedication of the Bancroft Library, topped by Herbert E. Bolton's interfaith cathedral to a *Nuevo Mundo*.[18]

Indeed for new westerners, a self-conscious regionalism virtually became psychologically mandatory in the early years of the twentieth century. And like other American regionalisms, it found historian-trumpeters of a re-

[17] Leonard J. Arrington, "Scholarly Studies of Mormonism in the Twentieth Century," *Dialogue*, I (Spring 1966), 15-28; Leonard J. Arrington, ed., "Reappraisals of Mormon History," *Dialogue*, I (Autumn 1966), 23-46; Rodman W. Paul, "The Mormons as a Theme in Western Historical Writing," *Journal of American History*, LIV (Dec. 1967), 511-23.

[18] Ruth Teiser, ed., *This Sudden Empire California: The Story of the Society of California Pioneers 1850 to 1950* (San Francisco, 1950), ix-x, 3-10; John Walton Caughey, *California* (2nd ed., Englewood Cliffs, 1953), 540-41.

gional declaration of cultural independence. The Spanish and Hispanic past, however remote and quixotic they may appear to contemporaries, provided not only a plausible claim to uniqueness but also a mystique and a golden age. Bolton and his Hispanophile colleagues who dominated the western academic empire inevitably seized upon a pseudo identity that found sanction in the popular mind even as it provided both color and a common denominator to the researches of diverse rootless scholars who were isolated physically and professionally from the American mainstream. For them, Bolton projected reassuringly a greater American synthesis "to Parkmanize," as he romantically declared, the history of the Spanish settlements, without incorporating Parkman's anti-Catholicism. To Catholic historians, at odds with the secular and Protestant American cultural and intellectual climate of the nineteenth century, Bolton's romance with the Spanish borderlands proved especially inviting, prompted scholarly good fellowship, and seemed to redress the historic American anti-Catholic prejudice while buttressing and giving respectability to an American Catholic identity. "The American story need no longer be an unrelieved, and in that measure, an unhistorical, Anglo epic," is the way one of Bolton's leading Catholic students, John Francis Bannon, recently summed up the virtues of the Bolton school.[19] Clearly, Bolton's famous course, "The History of the Americas," auspiciously inaugurated in 1920, made a clean break with older American history no less than with European history beneath a banner of wider American horizons. Indeed, until the coming of Frederick L. Paxson from Wisconsin in 1932, the Berkeley department uniquely boasted three "American" historians, Charles E. Chapman, Herbert E. Priestly, and Bolton; Eugene McCormac alone professed a narrower "United States" history. But Paxson's doctoral dissertation, *The Independence of the South American Republics*, published in 1903, identified even that "United States" historian with Bolton's Berkeley school.

To a later generation, the cross, sword, and gold-pan school of history could only seem eccentric and escapist. "The Spanish colony of upper California . . . was . . . virtually without significance in world history until it was annexed by the United States of America," asserted John Hawgood in the Thirteenth Montague Burton International Relations Lecture. Bolton "gave a specious appearance of significance to a program of fragmentary research," concluded John Higham, a leading student of American historiog-

[19] Pomeroy, *In Search of the Golden West*, 34; Cecil Robinson, *With the Ears of Strangers: The Mexican In American Literature* (Tucson, 1963), 135-61; Herbert E. Bolton, *Wider Horizons of American History* (New York, 1939), 149-91; John Francis Bannon, ed., *Bolton and the Spanish Borderlands* (Norman, 1964), 4, 9; see especially Peter Masten Dunne, *Black Robes in Lower California* (Berkeley, 1952), vii-ix.

raphy. Indeed, even Bolton's loyal disciples have reluctantly conceded that their mentor's focus on colonial history no longer seems relevant.[20]

Yet, if Bolton contributed little that has enlarged the historical understanding of the United States, there is no denying that he sang to the hearts of thousands of students, undergraduates and graduates alike, who found regional and pan-American fellowship in an arcane yet benign hemispheric past that gave the new American West a claim to cultural parity with, if not superiority to, the older regions. Successive Bolton festschrifts reflected an extreme adulation that is unparalleled in academic life. The lonely Royce at Berkeley a generation earlier would have appreciated this yearning for community.[21] Perhaps representative of Bolton's disciples and suggestive of the complexities of their backgrounds, personalities, and their needs is George P. Hammond, Bolton's successor as director of the Bancroft Library. Significantly, Hammond, like the great historian of immigration Marcus Hansen, is of Danish origin and still writes and speaks Danish fluently. As a young scholar, Hammond, like Hansen, was interested in German colonization plans in the nineteenth century; but to him like to many others of diverse antecedents, Bolton's magnetic Spanish-American empire proved irresistible.[22]

If the story of the Far West is to acquire the national and international attention that it merits, its scholars will have to acquire new viewpoints and stir up fresh and imaginative research. Historians will have to reckon with the key insights not only of Frederick Jackson Turner but also with the counterpoint of his student, Hansen, who viewed immigration, like the frontier, as a continuum extending from Europe to America and who "set himself the task of describing and explaining the European migration to North America as a dynamic and continuing process both at its source and on the immense continent where its forces found play." Hansen's transcontinental no less than his trans-Atlantic sweep is most strikingly apparent in his posthumously published study of the two-way migration across the Ca-

[20] John Hawgood, *California as a Factor in World History in the Last Hundred Years* (Nottingham, 1949), 1; John Higham and others, *History* (Englewood Cliffs, 1965), 41; John W. Caughey, "Herbert Eugene Bolton," Wilbur R. Jacobs, John W. Caughey, and Joe B. Frantz, *Turner, Bolton, and Webb: Three Historians of the American Frontier* (Seattle, 1965), 66-67; Lewis Hanke, ed., *Do The Americas Have a Common History? A Critique of the Bolton Theory* (New York, 1964), 14-49.

[21] See George P. Hammond, ed., *New Spain and the Anglo-American West: Historical Contributions Presented to Herbert Eugene Bolton* (2 vols., Lancaster, 1932); Adele Ogden and Engel Sluiter, eds., *Greater America: Essays in Honor of Herbert Eugene Bolton* (Berkeley, 1945).

[22] George P. Hammond to the author, Sept. 10, 1965; see Marcus L. Hansen, *German Schemes of Colonization Before 1860* (Northampton, 1924); George Hammond, "German Interest in California Before 1850" (master's thesis, University of California, Berkeley, 1921).

nadian-American border; and it even embraced, if but peripherally, the Far
West. His work remains the only immigration study to encompass the continent. Conceived as a three-part project, shared with American and Canadian demographers and population experts, and supported by the Carnegie
Foundation, it represents the most comprehensive effort to chart the international comings and goings of the immigrants of two nations. Despite a
certain superficiality, it is still the only major work of scholarship suggestive of the scope and complexity of the immigrant diffusion in the Far
West.[23]

Neither Hansen nor Turner, however, was a thesis-bound scholar, whatever the limitations of their disciples. Some thirty years ago, Hansen, taking a cue from Turner, called for a comparative social history that would
rise above the isolationist guild jurisdictions which have divided European
from American history.[24] The Charles Warren Center for Studies in American History at Harvard and the Center for Immigration Studies at the University of Minnesota are fulfilling the hopes of both Hansen and Turner
by transcending the cultural barriers that have traditionally bisected history
departments. Their example should encourage similar endeavors in other
regions, especially in the Far West where the challenge of comparative historical study holds out unusual perspectives. The history of the Far West,
and of California especially, offers unparalleled opportunities for national
as well as international self-knowledge. For this region, in all but the political sense, is a new nation fashioned out of a multiplicity of racial, religious, regional, and ethnic groups unmatched elsewhere in the United
States.[25]

A few years ago a student echoed David Potter in an eloquent and perceptive statement of the ongoing meaning of the immigrant heritage in
California.

[23] Marcus Hansen and John B. Brebner, *The Mingling of the Canadian and American
Peoples* (Toronto, 1940), vii; R. H. Coats and M. C. Maclean, *The American-Born in
Canada: A Statistical Interpretation* (Toronto, 1943); Leon E. Truesdell, *The Canadian
Born in the United States: An Analysis of the Statistics of the Canadian Element in the
Population of the United States 1850 to 1930* (Toronto, 1943).
[24] Marcus L. Hansen, "Remarks," Fox, *Sources of Culture in the Middle West*, 108-10;
Everett E. Edwards, comp., *The Early Writings of Frederick Jackson Turner* (Madison,
1938), 63; see Solomon F. Bloom, *Europe and America* (New York, 1961), for an
imaginative probing of mutuality.
[25] Harvard University, *Charles Warren Center For Studies in American History, First
Annual Report, June 30, 1966*; The University of Minnesota, Immigrant Archives, "A
Progress Report and A Review of Policy, Dec. 31, 1965"; Commonwealth Club of California,
The Population of California (San Francisco, 1946) and Warren S. Thompson, *Growth
and Changes in California's Population* (Los Angeles, 1955) suggest the wealth of
readily accessible demographic data. During the past five years, the author has had the
privilege of reading over 200 family histories by Californians which only begin to suggest the diversity of the American experience here.

Becoming an American is a spiritual journey. Every group in America—Irish, Jewish, Southern, or Japanese—feels that its experiences as a group have set it off from the rest of America. We speak of first, second, and third generation Americans, but we never think of applying these terms to New Englanders or Southerners. My people have lived in the South for more than two hundred years. There were Mitchells in the House of Burgesses and the Revolutionary Conventions before the War with England. There were Elmores from Virginia who fought with Greene's men in South Carolina and saw Cornwallis surrender at Yorktown. Yet I am the first American in my family. It seems symbolic that all groups, no matter how different, have to go through the same experience to become Americans. We must love and hate our group, be ashamed and proud of our past; be nostalgic for home, yet strive to be free. Sometimes it seems Americans not only had to create America, they had to create Americans.

Changing one's location in space does not change one's identity; it is the experiences one finds there. For me California was a step into the world, and my experiences there have made me an American.[26]

The rediscovery of America and the world in the new West by historians provides them with a superb opportunity for appreciating the social forces that have been shaping and reshaping the country for over a century. The Immigration Act of October 3, 1965, which provides for a flexible world quota, officially scraps both the racist national origins basis of quota allocation and the pan-American mystique. (Ironically, it establishes a quota for the Western Hemisphere.) Therefore, mission has triumphed over manifest destiny in ways not quite anticipated.[27] Now is the time for a mature and sophisticated understanding of far-western social and immigration history and for a candid exploration of a complex web of reciprocal relations in a region once but no longer peripheral to the American historical experience.

[26] Jane Mitchell, "Family History" (history research paper, University of California, Los Angeles, 1964); David M. Potter, "The Quest for the National Character," Higham, *The Reconstruction of American History*, 197-220; see Oscar Handlin, *The Americans: A New History of the People of the United States* (Boston, 1963), for an acute impressionistic interpretation of the influence of migration upon the American people.

[27] Edward P. Hutchinson, "The New Immigration: An Introductory Comment," *Annals of the American Academy of Political and Social Science*, 367 (Sept. 1966), 1-3; U. S. Statutes at Large, V (1965), 79, 911-21; Frederick Merk, *Manifest Destiny and Mission in American History: A Reinterpretation* (New York, 1963), 3, 261-66.

The Spectrum of Jewish Leadership in Ante-Bellum America

JONATHAN D. SARNA

STUDENTS OF AMERICAN ETHNIC LEADERSHIP have three basic conceptual models within which to organize their data. The first is based upon *source* of authority. Kurt Lewin pioneered this approach, distinguishing between leaders from the center "who are proud of the group, who wish to stay in it and to promote it," and those who are marginal, interested in moving out of the group, in short, "leaders from the periphery." John Higham further refined these categories into (1) received leadership, "leadership *over* an ethnic group," (2) internal leadership, "leadership that arises *within* the group and remains there," and (3) projective leadership, "leadership *from* an ethnic group . . . [that] affects its reputation without being directly subject to its control."[1]

The second model derives from conscious leadership *strategy*. Higham, in an earlier, now apparently rejected formulation, adapted Gunnar Myrdal's famous typology and divided leadership into two basic polar types: (1) leadership of accommodation, in this case accommodation to America, and (2) leadership of protest, resistance to accommodation. This model, as Higham later realized, applies best to leaders of persecuted groups, like American Indians and blacks. Still, the paradigm has broader implications since it relates action to ideology. Leaders, the model claims, either look favorably on America and encourage acculturation, or do the opposite.[2]

Finally, there is a third model which examines leadership *function*. Some ethnic leaders preserve tradition; others promote change. Most, as Victor Greene has pointed out, simultaneously do both. They unconsciously serve as mediating brokers, or to use Greene's terminology, "traditional progressives." They seek to maintain the old ways, even as they act as agents of the new.[3]

These three classification schemes are not the only ones possible, nor are they mutually exclusive. In at least two unfortunate ways, however, they are alike. First, they are static models, requiring that leaders be pigeonholed into one or another preexisting categories. Second, they are elite models, ignoring, though less in Greene's case than the others, the relationship between leaders and led.

295

The model proposed in this essay seeks to overcome both of these problems by positing a "spectrum of leadership" rather than just another series of categories. On a spectrum, leaders can be placed in relationship to one another and change over time can be graphed. Furthermore, the spectrum approach clarifies the relationship between leaders and led by revealing that those at the top and those on the bottom share a common set of tensions and aims. Viewed from this perspective, an ethnic group divides into traditionalist leaders and followers, assimilationist leaders and followers, and people arrayed at various points in between. The spectrum of leaders mirrors the spectrum of followers—and vice versa.

To test this model, I have examined ethnic leadership in America's ante-bellum Jewish community. This may seem an odd choice, considering Nathan Glazer's comment that "between the 1840s and the 1880s the American Jewish community was a remarkably homogeneous one."[4] Glazer, however, is mistaken. The two decades before the Civil War, and for that matter the two decades that followed its outbreak, saw many of the same kinds of subethnic ("Bayer" vs. "Pollack"); religious (Radical Reform, Moderate Reform, Orthodox); and social tensions manifested in later years. Many called for unity and worked to secure it, but they never succeeded. A contemporary view of American Jewry in 1861, found in the *Occident*, the first major Jewish newspaper in America, tells the story. "There is actually no union between the natives of Poland and Germany nor even between those born in this country if their parents happened to be attached to one or the other modes of worship."[5]

My survey of ante-bellum Jewish leadership is limited, for the sake of simplicity, to a discussion of four people who represented four different ideological positions. Two of the four were rabbis; two not.[6] Two of them were "major opinion leaders"—the central Jewish communal figures of the day—two of them more peripheral. If leaders may broadly be defined as "individuals who exercise decisive influence over others within a context of obligation or common interest,"[7] then all four men were leaders, for all in one way or another exercised active or passive influence over some of their fellow Jews. All four men served as role models: their activities received publicity, and others learned from them.

There is no anachronism in speaking about a "Jewish community" during this period. Research has shown that Jews in various states corresponded with one another, exerted themselves as a group in time of crisis, and by the end of our period could boast of several newspapers and a central Board of Delegates. Long before the Civil War, Jews were viewed as a separate community, and saw themselves as such. Admittedly, the

Jewish community differed both from "racial minority" communities, and from geographically based ethnic communities. Still, minority groups in general share much in common. So long as obvious differences are kept in mind, parallels between Jews and others can prove revealing.[8]

The initial leader I am going to discuss is Abraham Rice [Reiss (1800?–1862)], generally considered the first properly ordained rabbi in America. Rice emigrated from Bavaria in 1840, and after short stints in New York and Newport, he was invited to serve as rabbi of Nidche Israel (the Baltimore Hebrew Congregation). He quickly came into conflict with his congregants, lashing out against those who violated the Sabbath and employed Masonic rites at funerals. But his efforts to punish these deviations came to naught. His railings against other sins—from intermarriage and dietary law violations to prayer abbreviation and mixed dancing—were apparently no more successful. In 1847, Rice considered leaving America for the Holy Land, but decided to remain. His mission, stated in 1840, was to "introduce the pure Orthodox faith into the country." In 1849, Rice resigned from the rabbinate, promising to "fight the battle of the Lord" as a private citizen. He became a merchant, but continued to teach, hold services in his house, issue rabbinic opinions, and agitate on behalf of traditional Judaism. He briefly resumed the pulpit at Nidche Israel in 1862, but died shortly thereafter.[9]

Rice was not a major ethnic leader in terms of followers or direct influence. He received notice—the *New York Herald* once dubbed him "Grand Rabbi of the United States"—and a few congregants, notably young Aaron Friedenwald, later a pioneering American ophthalmologist, venerated him.[10] His importance, however, lies not so much in his impact as in his ideological function. To ante-bellum American Jews he symbolized tradition in the extreme. They viewed him as a "defender of the faith" committed to preserving all aspects of Judaism in the face of outside pressure. To many, Rice may have served as a negative example, a foil against which they measured their own acculturation. Yet, they respected Rice as "leader of the opposition," even if they did not follow in his ways. Rice's opposition stance should not be seen as a "protest" against America. To the contrary, he appreciated the country's free institutions. He rather felt that Jews should accommodate themselves to their new land in a very different way. "I conduct myself as I did in days of old in my native country," he reassuringly wrote to his teacher in Germany.[11] No doubt he wished that his fellow Jews would do the same.

This wish remained unfulfilled. Instead, most Jews acculturated, following the ways of their neighbors. Jewish leaders generally supported acculturation in principle, although they debated among themselves how many concessions to make to the outside world. A few notables, however, championed thoroughgoing assimilation. For obvious reasons, assimilationists did not become leaders of the Jewish community: they did not support the community's continued existence. As leaders who happened to be Jewish, however, assimilationists exercised considerable passive influence over the Jewish community. Theirs is an example of projective leadership: once they won recognition in the larger community their fellow Jews took notice of them. Thoroughgoing assimilationists no more represented a mainstream position than did traditionalist defenders of the faith. Most Jews rejected both extremes. But Jews who sought success in the outside world certainly had assimilationist role models from which to choose.

The most prominent Jewish assimilationist in ante-bellum America was Judah P. Benjamin (1811–1884): brilliant lawyer, senator from Louisiana, and then, during the Civil War, attorney general, secretary of war, and finally secretary of state of the Confederacy. Benjamin married a Catholic, Natalie St. Martin, in 1833, and his only daughter was raised in her mother's faith. But Benjamin did not convert—except perhaps on his deathbed—and his Judaism was a matter of public knowledge. Enemies spoke of "Judas Iscariot Benjamin" or "Benjamin the Jew." Jews sought to prove that this most successful of their coreligionists maintained some tenuous connection with his ancestral faith.[12]

The stories told of Benjamin's Jewish activities—including quoted pro-Jewish statements, a supposed Yom Kippur sermon, and legends of his attending various synagogues—all prove spurious. Bertram Korn, who thoroughly investigated the evidence, concluded flatly that "Benjamin had no positive or active interest in Jews or in Judaism."[13] Jews, however, had considerable interest in Benjamin, and understandably took pride in his achievements. They fashioned a mythical Benjamin—a Jewishly conscious Benjamin—in order to blunt the assimilationist message that rang out from his life's story. "If Jews intermarry and follow in the ways of the Gentiles they can succeed handsomely" was the lesson that Judah Benjamin's life really projected. If, in the case of Benjamin, mythologizers later refashioned that lesson, there always were other Jewish assimilationists, like August Belmont, whose life stories could demonstrate the original point.

Benjamin and Rice represent something close to the polar extremes. The one, a secular leader, projected a message of wholehearted assimilation; the other, a religious leader, openly demanded thoroughly traditional identification. Each of these positions found support in the Jewish community, but for most American Jews neither choice by itself was acceptable. They sought both to identify as Jews *and* to integrate into American society. Unsurprisingly, their role models—the men quite generally viewed as the two greatest Jewish leaders of the ante-bellum period— were men who insisted that some sort of synthesis was possible. One could, they claimed, be active Jews and active citizens at the same time.

The leaders I refer to were Mordecai M. Noah (1785–1851) and Isaac Leeser (1806–1868). They were the Jewish "opinion leaders" of their day, widely respected by their coreligionists throughout the country. Noah was a New York journalist-politician, at different times consul at Tunis, sheriff of New York, and Grand Sachem of Tammany Hall, a man who was intimate with leading figures in the Jacksonian period and well-known in non-Jewish circles. He was active in Congregation Shearith Israel; he once tried to establish a Jewish colony ("Ararat") on Grand Island, New York; he was president of the Hebrew Benevolent Society; and most important of all, he served as a representative Jew in the eyes of leading Christians. Simply by virtue of his position he demonstrated that in America, one could openly and simultaneously be a leader in the political world and in the Jewish one.[14]

Leeser, by contrast, was a religious leader, a *chazan*, first at Congregation Mikve Israel in Philadelphia, and somewhat later at Congregation Beth El Emeth in the same city. He founded and edited the *Occident*; he was actively involved in Jewish education and the publication of Jewish textbooks; he translated prayerbooks and the Bible into English for a Jewish audience; and he played a leading part in the major Jewish activities and organizations of his day. Outside Philadelphia, however, non-Jews hardly knew of his existence. His life and work were mainly within the context of his own minority group. He sought to defend his faith, but unlike Rice, he worked to Americanize Judaism so that it might be more accessible and appealing.[15]

The ante-bellum American Jewish community thus had two primary leaders. They derived their authority from different sources, held certain similar goals, and operated in quite different spheres. Unsurprisingly, major issues arose that brought them into conflict.

The most interesting dispute between the two men was occasioned by Mordecai Noah's 1844 Restoration Address, delivered to a mostly Christian audience, in which Noah urged missionaries to work for the restoration of Jews in their *unconverted* state to the Holy Land. Noah asked missionaries to hold off their conversionist efforts, and to rely "on the fulfillment of the prophecies and the will of God" to determine who would convert and which messiah would come. Pending the end of days, he did not believe that these ultimate theological differences should pose an obstacle to close Jewish-Christian cooperation.[16]

Isaac Leeser, when he read this speech, was horrified. He was devoting his life to creating books and institutions aimed at protecting Jews from Christian encroachments. How dare a Jewish leader—even one significantly older and better known than himself—call on Jews and missionaries to work together. Leeser thundered his disapproval: "With conversionists as such we cannot, as Jews, enter into any league . . . if they grant us any favors they do it for the sake of a return."[17]

The acerbic clash demonstrates the fierce tension between the "integrationist" and the "traditionalist" even within the narrower spectrum containing only widely respected ethnic leaders. Noah called for harmony and cooperation with Christian America; Leeser feared for Jewish group identity. The same array of forces took place during a subsequent clash over Sunday blue laws. Leeser, eager to strengthen Jewish Sabbath observance, opposed the laws since they wrought great hardships on Jews who either had to violate their Sabbath or lose one full day of business a week. He believed that the Constitution's religious liberty clause protected Jews from having to make this heartrending choice. Noah, on the other hand, feared the implications of a Jewish-Christian battle over this issue. He defended the blue laws' constitutionality, terming them "mere local or police regulation[s]," and warned Jews not to "disturb the Christian by business or labor on his Sabbath." He concluded that the question "ought not to have been raised" in the first place. To his mind, the threat which the Sabbath issue posed to intergroup relations far exceeded any possible threat to the integrity of Judaism itself.[18]

Over the years, Leeser and Noah also clashed about other issues, but their areas of agreement are just as important. When Jews faced threats, internally or externally, the two could be found working together in their defense. Similarly, both favored Jewish education, and both were staunch supporters of Jewish charities. Broadly speaking, both men saw the need to preserve Jewish identity while both understood that Americanization was essential. No disagreement existed over basics; clashes occurred only when these two goals came into conflict. Then decisions had to be made based on the weight attached to each goal: how much identity would be sacrificed for how much integration. At that point it became clear that each man held to a different scale of values.

This brief survey of American Jewish leadership in the ante-bellum period suggests two broad conclusions. First, it should be clear that great advantages accrue from an open and dynamic model of ethnic leadership. By viewing leadership as a full spectrum stretching from "completely traditionalist" on the one hand to "thorough-going assimilationist" on the other we can more accurately classify leaders, and show how they changed over time. Leaders arrayed themselves along different points on this spectrum, and shifted their positions as circumstances changed. Most of the best known minority group leaders, like Noah and Leeser, mediated between tradition and change, and never moved far from the middle of the spectrum. But others, not generally as well known, like Rice, took extreme positions. Uncompromising assimilationists or traditionalists may have found few adherents; indeed, as in the case of Benjamin, they may only have exercised leadership passively by setting examples which others followed. Nevertheless, they form part of the history of ethnic leadership, and so deserve recognition. In fact, their extreme positions probably helped to define the "middle of the road" where most people felt more comfortable.

Second, the tradition/assimilation spectrum shows that leaders and led both were grappling with precisely the same basic dilemmas. Leaders gave expression to tensions over Americanization which immigrants and their children confronted—but did not solve—in their daily lives. Most immigrant and ethnic groups looked approvingly on a range of popular leaders, wth varying conflicting outlooks on problems of tradition and change, because they offered a range of potential alternatives to choose from. Thus, mid-nineteenth century Irish, German and Swedish immigrants looked for guidance to assimilationists like Congressman Mike Walsh, Senator Carl Schurz and pioneer Hans Mattson as well as to traditionalists like Archbishop John Hughes, Lutheran Church leader C.F.W. Walther, and Pastor T.N. Hasselquist.[19] They learned that disagreements existed at all levels, even among leaders. Leadership tensions merely reflected life tensions—and they were irresolvable. By contrast, on matters of security—the battle against hatred and discrimination—major leaders were agreed. On such issues their followers were united as well.

Alone, no ethnic leader ever satisfactorily embodied, much less integrated, the collective hopes, fears and problems which played so great a part in immigrant and ethnic life. For this reason, no ethnic community ever enjoyed a single, universally acknowledged spokesman, regardless of what outsiders may have believed. As a group, however, leaders succeeded far better. They defined complicated issues, represented diverse interests, and ultimately forged an informal polity within which debate took place. Leaders never solved the contradiction between tradition and assimilation, nor could they have. But they did present to their followers the range of options that America held open to them. Individuals had then to make critical choices on their own.

NOTES

1. Kurt Lewin, *Resolving Social Conflicts* (New York, 1948), pp. 190-197; John Higham, "Leadership" in *Harvard Encyclopedia of American Ethnic Groups*, ed. Stephan Thernstrom (Cambridge, Mass., 1980), pp. 642-47.

2. John Higham, ed., *Ethnic Leadership in America* (Baltimore, 1978), pp. 1-18; Higham, "Leadership," p. 646; Gunnar Myrdal, *An American Dilemma* (New York, 1944).

3. Victor Greene, "'Becoming American': The Role of Ethnic Leaders—Swedes, Poles, Italians, and Jews," in *The Ethnic Frontier*, eds. Melvin G. Holli and Peter d'A Jones (Grand Rapids, Mich., 1977), pp. 144-175. See also, Judith R. Kramer, *The American Minority Community* (New York, 1970), pp. 129-34; Nicholas Tavuchis, *Pastors and Immigrants: The Role of a Religious Elite in the Absorption of Norwegian Immigrants* (Hague, 1943); Josef Barton, *Peasants and Strangers* (Cambridge, Mass., 1975), pp. 71-72; Yonathan Shapiro, *Leadership of the American Zionist Organization, 1897-1930* (Urbana, Ill., 1971); S.N. Eisenstadt, "Place of Elites and Primary Groups in the Absorption of New Immigrants in Israel," *American Journal of Sociology*, 57 (1951-52): 222-231; and Alvin M. Gouldner, *Studies in Leadership* (New York, 1950).

4. Nathan Glazer, "The Jews," in *Ethnic Leadership*, p. 21. On Jewish leadership, see also Edwin Wolf II, "Leadership in the American Jewish Community," in *The American Jew: A Reappraisal*, ed. Oscar Janowsky (Philadelphia, 1972), pp. 363-72; and Daniel Elazar, *Community and Polity* (Philadelphia, 1976).

5. *Occident*, 18 (1861), p. 245; cf. Rudolf Glanz, *Studies in Judaica Americana* (New York, 1970), pp. 187-202; Moshe Davis, *Yahadut Amerika Be-Hitpathutah* (New York, 1951), pp. 218-88; and more generally Allan Tarshish, "The Rise of American Judaism," (Ph.D. diss., Hebrew Union College, 1935).

6. Religious and ethnic leaders are not readily separable in the case of Jews, since most Jews see themselves both as members of the Jewish people and as adherents to the Jewish religion. See Charles Liebman, *The Ambivalent American Jew* (Philadelphia, 1973), pp. 3-22; and more generally Timothy Smith, "Religion and Ethnicity in America," *American Historical Review*, 83 (December 1978): 1155-85; and Randall M. Miller and Thomas D. Marzik, eds., *Immigrants and Religion in Urban America* (Philadelphia, 1977).

7. Higham, "Leadership," p. 642.

8. Rufus Learsi [Israel Goldberg], *The Jews in America: A History* (New York, 1972), pp. 53-89; Malcolm H. Stern, "The 1820s: American Jewry Comes of Age," in *A Bicentennial Festschrift for Jacob Rader Marcus*, ed. Bertram W. Korn (Waltham, Mass., 1976), p. 539-49; and Abraham J. Karp, *The Jewish Experience in America* (Waltham, Mass., 1969), vols. 2 and 3.

9. Israel Tabak, "Rabbi Abraham Rice of Baltimore," *Tradition*, 7 (Summer 1965): 100-120; Moshe Davis, "Igrot Hepekidim Veha'amarchalim Meamsterdam," in *Salo Baron Jubilee Volume*, Hebrew section, eds. Saul Lieberman and Arthur Hyman (Jerusalem, 1974), pp. 95-103; Leon A. Jick, *The Americanization of the Synagogue 1820-1870*

(Hanover, N.H., 1976), pp. 70-74; Isaac M. Fein, *The Making of an American Jewish Community* (Philadelphia, 1971), pp. 54-57; and [New York] *Sunday Times and Noah's Weekly Messenger* (28 February 1847), p. 2.

10. *New York Herald*, 29 September 1845; Fein, *Making of an American Jewish Community*, p. 58.

11. Tabak, "Rabbi Abraham Rice," p. 102.

12. Bertram W. Korn, "Judah P. Benjamin as a Jew," *Eventful Years and Experiences* (Cincinnati, 1954), pp. 79-97; idem, *The Early Jews of New Orleans* (Waltham, Mass., 1969), pp. 187-90, 226-28, 232-33; Richard S. Tedlow, "Judah P. Benjamin," in *Turn to the South: Essays on Southern Jewry*, eds. Nathan M. Kaganoff and Melvin I. Urofsky (Charlottesville, Va., 1979), pp. 44-54.

13. Korn, "Judah P. Benjamin as a Jew," p. 93.

14. Jonathan D. Sarna, *Jacksonian Jew: The Two Worlds of Mordecai Noah* (New York, 1980), esp. 119-42; see pp. 220-222 for earlier studies.

15. Book-length studies of Leeser include: Lance J. Sussman, "'Confidence in God': The Life and Preaching of Isaac Leeser (1806-1868)" (Ordination thesis, Hebrew Union College, 1980); Maxine S. Seller, "Isaac Leeser: Architect of the American Jewish Community" (Ph.D. diss., University of Pennsylvania, 1965), and E. Benet, "An Evaluation of the Life of Isaac Leeser" (Ph.D. diss., Yeshiva University, 1959). See also Jick, *Americanization of the Synagogue, passim*; Bertram W. Korn, "Isaac Leeser: Centennial Reflections," *American Jewish Archives*, 19 (1967): 127-41; Maxwell Whiteman, "Isaac Leeser and the Jews of Philadelphia," *Publications of the American Jewish Historical Society*, 48 (1959): 207-44; and Henry Englander, "Isaac Leeser," *Central Conference of American Rabbis Yearbook*, 28 (1918): 213-52.

16. Mordecai M. Noah, *Discourse on the Restoration of the Jews* (New York, 1845); Sarna, *Jacksonian Jew*, pp. 152-56.

17. Quoted in *Occident*, 2 (1845), p. 605; 3 (1845), pp. 29-35; Maxine Seller, "Isaac Leeser's Views on the Restoration of a Jewish Palestine," *American Jewish Historical Quarterly*, 58 (September 1968): 118-35.

18. *Occident*, 6 (1848), pp 186-93, 302, 367-8; Seller, "Isaac Leeser, Architect of the American Jewish Community," p. 145; Morris U. Schappes, ed., *Documentary History of the Jews in the United States 1654-1875* (New York, 1971), pp. 279-81; Sarna, *Jacksonian Jew*, p. 134.

19. In addition to items cited above in notes 1-3, see appropriate articles in the *Dictionary of American Biography*, and A.F. Ander, *T.N. Hasselquist*, (Rock Island, Ill., 1931); Vincent P. Lannie, *Public Money and Parochial Education: Bishop Hughes, Governor Seward, and the New York School Controversy* (Cleveland 1968); Lars Ljungmark, "Hans Mattson's *Minnen*: Swedish American Monument," *Swedish Pioneer Historical Quarterly*, 29 (1978): 57-68; Claude M. Fuess, *Carl Schurz, Reformer* (New York, 1932).

THE SIGNIFICANCE OF IMMIGRATION IN AMERICAN HISTORY

ARTHUR MEIER SCHLESINGER
State University of Iowa

ABSTRACT

The peopling of America considered as a means of relieving pressure of population in Europe. The two grand themes of American history are, properly, the influence of immigration upon American life and institutions, and the influence of the American environment upon the everchanging composite population. The first voyage of Columbus, an Italian, with a crew of Spaniards, an Irishman, an Englishman, and an Israelite, prefigured the subsequent movement. Even the people of the thirteen English colonies were a mixture of racial breeds. While the religious motive has been stressed in the history of American colonization, the economic urge sent scores of thousands. Jamestown, the Penn Colony typical, not solitary. Desire to be rid of criminals and paupers accounts for other streams of emigration, perhaps to the extent of one-half the white emigrants during the larger part of the colonial period. Franklin deplored the arrival of Germans in Pennsylvania—"generally the most stupid of their own nation." Puritan and Scotch-Irish variations. The non-English strains as factors making for independence. Later phenomena of interracial influence before and after the Civil War.

The New World was discovered by a man who was trying his utmost to find an older world than the one he had sailed from. If Columbus had known that he had failed to reach the fabled Orient, he would have died a bitterly disillusioned man. Yet, in the judgment of history, the measure of his greatness is to be found in the fact that he committed this cardinal blunder, for thereby he and the later explorers opened up to the crowded populations of Europe an egress from poverty and oppression for many centuries to come. The ratio between man and land became changed for the whole civilized world, and there opened up before humanity unsuspected opportunities for development and progress. On account of political disturbances in Europe and the difficulties of ocean travel, the full possibilities of this epochal change were only gradually developed; and the effects were thus distributed through the last four centuries of world-history. But the event itself stands forth as one of the tremendous facts of history. So far as the human mind can foresee, nothing of a similar nature can ever happen again.

71

The great *Völkerwanderungen*, set in motion by the opening up of the Western Hemisphere, have been essentially unlike any earlier migrations in history, and in comparison with them most of the earlier movements of population were numerically insignificant. In a large sense, all American history has been the product of these migratory movements from the Old World. Since the red-skinned savage has never been a potent factor in American development, the whole history of the United States and, to a lesser degree, of the two Americas is, at bottom, the story of the successive waves of immigration and of the adaptation of the newcomers and their descendants to the new surroundings offered by the Western Hemisphere. Thus the two grand themes of American history are, properly, the influence of immigration upon American life and institutions, and the influence of the American environment, especially the frontier in the early days and the industrial integration of more recent times, upon the ever-changing composite population.

Columbus's first voyage of discovery was a strange foreshadowing of the later history of the American people, for, in a very real sense, his voyage may be considered an international enterprise. Acting under the authority of Spain, this Italian sailed with a crew consisting of Spaniards, one Irishman, an Englishman, and an Israelite. These nationalities were later to enter fully into the rich heritage which this voyage made possible to the world. In the next two centuries the nations of Europe, large and small, sought to stake out colonial claims in America, not with entire success from an imperialistic point of view, but with the result that cultural foundations were laid whose influence may still be traced in the legal systems, customs, and institutions of many parts of the United States today. A familiar illustration is afforded in the case of Louisiana, where the continental civil law, instead of the English common law, governs domestic relations and transfers of property as a reminder of the days when the French and the Spanish owned the land.

It is, perhaps, not generally understood that even the people of the thirteen English colonies were a mixture of racial breeds. This was due, in part, to the English conquest of colonies planted by rival European powers along the Atlantic Coast, but was the result more largely of abundant immigration from various parts of the world after the original settlements had been well established. A Colonial Dame or a Daughter of the American Revolution might conceivably have nothing but pure Hebrew blood or French or German blood in her veins.   During the first century of English colonization, the seventeenth, the English race was the main contributor to the population, the Dutch and French Huguenot contributions being less important.   These racial elements occupied the choice lands near the coast, and thus compelled the stream of immigration of the eighteenth century to pour into the interior, a significant development in view of the different character and great numbers of these later settlers.

While the religious motive has properly been stressed in the history of colonization, it should not be overlooked that the economic urge, operating independently or as a stiffening to religious conviction, sent many scores of thousands fleeing to American shores.   We need not wink at the fact that the immigrants of colonial times were actuated by the same motives as the immigrants today, namely a determination to escape religious or political oppression and a desire to improve their living conditions.   To make this generalization strictly applicable to immigration in our own day, one might wish to reverse the order of statement, although the Russian Jews and the Armenian refugees are conspicuous examples of the contrary.

The earliest English settlement, that at Jamestown, was sent out by an English trading corporation which was interested primarily in making profits for the stockholders of the company out of the industry of the settlers.   To cite another example, William Penn was a canny Quaker who, after the first settlements were made in his dominion of Pennsylvania, lost no opportunity to stimulate immigration artificially, for the resulting enhancement of real estate values meant an increased income for him.   He advertised his lands widely throughout Europe, offering large tracts at nominal prices and portraying the political and religious advantages of residence under his rule.   In anticipation of later practices, he maintained paid agents in the Rhine Valley, who were so successful that within a score of years German immigrants numbered almost one-half of the population.

Another source of "assisted immigration" was to be found in the practice of European nations to drain their almshouses and jails into their colonies; it has been estimated that as many as fifty thousand criminals were sent to the thirteen colonies by Great Britain. Due allowance must, of course, be made for a legal code which condemned offenders to death for stealing a joint of meat worth more than one shilling! Perhaps one-half of all the white immigrants during the larger part of the colonial period were unable to pay their expenses. They came "indentured" and were auctioned off for a period of service by the ship captains in payment for their transportation. Another element of the population, perhaps one-fifth of the whole in the eighteenth century, consisted of Guinea negroes who became emigrants to the New World only through the exercise of superior force. A well-known historian is authority for the statement that probably one-third of the colonists in 1760 were born outside of America.

Men of older colonial stock viewed the more recent comers with a species of alarm that was to be repeated with each new generation of the American breed. Benjamin Franklin declared that the German immigrants pouring into Pennsylvania "are generally the most stupid of their own nation. . . . . Not being used to liberty they know not how to make modest use of it." They appear at elections "in droves and carry all before them, except in one or two counties. Few of their children know English." The familiar objections to immigration on grounds of non-assimilability, pauperism, and criminality originated during these early days, leaving for later and more congested times the development of arguments derived from the fear of economic competition.

The preponderance of English settlers in the first century of colonization served to fix governmental institutions and political ideals in an English mold and to make English speech the general language of the colonists. In the subsequent colonial period most of New England retained its purely English character because of the Puritan policy of religious exclusiveness; but into the other colonies alien racial elements came in great numbers and left their impress on native culture and, in a less measure, on American speech. It is instructive to remember that the great English Puritan migration did not exceed twenty thousand, whereas more than one hundred and fifty thousand Scotch-Irish Presbyterians settled in the colonies in the eighteenth century. Unlike the Puritans the Scotch-Irish were to be found in nearly five hundred settlements scattered through all the colonies on the eve of the Revolution; and being everywhere endowed with a fierce passion for liberty, they served as an amalgam to bind together all other racial elements in the population. The Germans, who also came in large numbers, localized their settlements in western New York, and particularly in the western counties of Pennsylvania, where they gave rise to the breed which we call the Pennsylvania Dutch. A recent student of the subject estimates that, at the outbreak of the War for Independence, about one-tenth of the total population was German and perhaps one-sixth Scotch-Irish.

Since the best sites near the coast were pre-empted, these races for the most part pushed into the valleys of the interior where they occupied fertile farm lands and acted as a buffer against Indian forays on the older settlements. Combining with the native whites in the back country, they quickly developed a group consciousness due to the organized efforts of the English-American minorities of the seaboard to minimize the influence of the frontier population in the colonial legislature and courts, and in the case of the abortive Regulator uprising in North Carolina they invoked civil war to secure a redress of grievances. Eventually their struggle proved to be the decisive factor in establishing the two American principles of equality before the law and of representation upon the basis of numbers. When the disruption with Great Britain approached, the non-English strains of the back country lent great propulsive force to the movement for independence and republican government. They were probably the deciding factors in Pennsylvania and South Carolina, where the ties of loyalty binding the colonists were especially strong.

Other racial strains made a deep impress upon the history of the times. Someone has pointed out that eight of the men most prominent in the early history of New York represented eight non-English nationalities: Schuyler, of Dutch descent; Herkimer, whose parents were pure-blooded Germans from the Rhine Palatinate; John Jay, of French stock; Livingston, Scotch; Clinton, Irish; Morris, Welsh; Baron Steuben, Prussian; and Hoffman, Swedish. Of the fifty-six signers of the Declaration of Independence, eighteen were of non-English stock and, of these, eight were born outside of the colonies. Joseph Galloway, the Pennsylvania loyalist, declared before a committee of the House of Commons in 1779 that in the patriot army "there were scarcely one-fourth natives of America,—about one-half Irish, the other fourth were English and Scotch." This statement fails to do justice to the other foreign-born soldiers who fought in the War for Independence.

Throughout the period of national independence, immigration continued to exert a profound influence on the development of American institutions, political ideals, and industrial life. Within ten years of the adoption of the Constitution, immigration received unwelcome recognition as wielding a democratizing influence on American life. The Federalist party, dominated by aristocratic sympathies, was determined to deal a deathblow to the heresy known variously as mobocracy or democracy; and so it passed the Alien and Sedition Acts and the Naturalization Law in 1798 for the purpose of preventing aliens from cultivating this dangerous doctrine in the United States. The party did not survive this legislation.

Beginning with the year 1820 the numbers of foreigners migrating into the United States each decade mounted rapidly, passing the half-million mark during the thirties and rising above the two and a half million mark in the decade of the fifties. The racial strains represented in this migration were essentially the same as during colonial times, the Teutonic and the Celtic. The high-water mark in the period before the Civil War was reached when the tide of immigration brought to American shores, in the late forties and early fifties, huge numbers of famine-stricken Irish, and great numbers of German liberals, who fled Germany because of the outcome of the Revolution of 1848. The United States was still predominantly agricultural, and the Germans and other north Europeans, attracted by the abundance of cheap government land, tended to move westward into the upper Mississippi Valley, whereas the Irish were likely to remain in the eastern cities or go out into the construction camps. Virtually all the western states perceived the advantages of immigration as an agency for developing their resources; and emulating the example of William Penn they were not backward in appropriating money and establishing agents in Europe to furnish prospective emigrants with all possible information as to the soil, climate, and general conditions of the country. Colonies of European peasants began to be established in many parts of the West—at one time it appeared that Wisconsin might become exclusively a German state.

By their disinclination for agricultural pursuits, the Irish found themselves in a position to play an important part in the rapid physical development of the country in the twenties and the thirties. Those were the years during which roads, canals, and public works were being constructed upon an extensive scale and the first railroads were being projected. The hard manual labor for these enterprises was performed mainly by the Irish. The congestion of foreigners in the eastern cities led to increases in pauperism, intemperance, and prostitution; and these conditions gave great impetus to the numerous movements for humanitarian reform which characterized the thirties. In 1838 it was estimated that more than one-half of the paupers in the country were of foreign birth. Better housing conditions, a more humane legal code, prohibition, women's rights—all these reforms were urgently advocated by writers and speakers who, in subsequent years, devoted their attention almost exclusively to the greatest social injustice of all, slavery.

As a result of the heavy immigration of the forties and fifties, political corruption became an important factor in American politics for the first time. The newly arrived foreigner fell an easy prey to the unscrupulous native politician; and fraudulent naturalization papers, vote buying, and similar practices became so notorious that a probe committee of Congress declared in 1860:

"It is well known to the American people that stupendous frauds have been perpetrated in the election of 1856, in Pennsylvania, by means of forged and fictitious naturalization papers." President Buchanan wrote that "we never heard until within a recent period of the employment of money to carry elections." Much of the immigrant labor came in under contract to private corporations, and the decade of the fifties saw the first effective employment of arguments against immigration based upon the plea that the lower standard of living of the foreigners made it impossible for native laborers to compete with them.

These considerations, added to the preponderance of Roman Catholics among the Irish immigrants, led to the growth of a powerful movement against immigration, which is without parallel in American history. Calling themselves Native Americans, political parties were formed in New York and other eastern cities to prevent the election of foreign-born citizens to office; and ten years later, in 1845, a national organization was effected with more than one hundred thousand members. In 1850 the movement assumed the guise of a secret organization under the name, known only to the initiate, of The Supreme Order of the Star Spangled Banner. Outsiders lost no time in dubbing the members "Know Nothings," since the rank and file, when asked regarding the mysteries of the order, invariably replied: "We know nothing." Due perhaps to the disturbed state of politics in the fall of 1854 and the hesitancy of many citizens to take a definite stand on the slavery question as reopened by the Kansas-Nebraska Act, the party enjoyed phenomenal success, carrying six states and failing in seven others only by a narrow margin. But two years later, with a presidential ticket in the field, the party showed little strength, having succumbed to the growing popular absorption in the slavery controversy. Several attempts were made after the Civil War by secret societies and minor parties to revive nativist feeling but with a notable lack of success, although, as we shall see presently, nonpartisan political agitation during the same period has resulted in the passage of certain restrictive measures by the federal government.

In the period prior to the Civil War the stream of immigration had been turned from the South by the Mason and Dixon line, for the free laborers of Europe could not profitably compete with the slave laborers of the South. Nearly all the immigrant guidebooks published before the Civil War warned Europeans against the presence of slavery and the strongly intrenched caste system in that section. This avoidance had serious results for the South, as some economists of that section foresaw, for it practically precluded that diversification of industry which a plentiful supply of cheap white labor would have rendered possible. Thus the economic system of the South came to rest more and more exclusively upon a single prop, and the control of southern policy fell into the ambitious hands of the cotton planters. Furthermore, the native southern stock, left to itself, interbred, and the mass of the whites were deprived of the liberalizing influences of contact with persons and ideas from other parts of the world. The first federal law restricting immigration was passed during this period when the act of 1807 forbade the future introduction of negro slaves; but this law came too late to avert the evil consequences flowing from the earlier unrestricted importation of blacks.

Meanwhile, the European peasants and workingmen, predisposed against slavery by temperament and economic interest, had massed themselves in the North and helped to stiffen the tolerant public sentiment of that section against an institution that was an anachronism in Europe. Who can estimate of what vital consequence it was to the future of a united country that, in the eventful decade prior to the outbreak of the Civil War, the foreign population of the United States increased 84 per cent? In the actual fighting, foreign-born soldiers played a notable part, although many of them had fled Europe to escape compulsory military service. It is perhaps generally known that the militia companies formed among the Germans in Missouri, especially in St. Louis, were pivotal in saving that state for the Union in the early months of the war; but it is not so well known that both the Germans and the Irish furnished more troops to the federal armies in proportion to their numbers than did the native-born northerners.

Immigration entered a new phase in the years following the Civil War. Prior to this time the immigrants had been of racial strains very closely related to the original settlers of the country. Indeed, from one point of view, the American people in this period of their history were merely a making-over, in a new environment, of the old English race out of the same elements which had entered into its composition from the beginning in England. With the great industrial expansion in America after the war and the opening of many steamship lines between the Mediterranean ports and the United States, new streams of immigration began to set in from Southern and Eastern Europe; and this new invasion with its lower standards of living caused a reduction in the old Teutonic and Celtic immigration from Western Europe. The change began to be apparent about 1885, but it was not until 1896 that the three currents from Austria-Hungary, Italy, and Russia exceeded in volume the contributions of the United Kingdom, Germany, and Scandinavia.

On the Pacific Coast a new situation also arose, due to the first coming of thousands of Chinese laborers in the fifties and sixties. California became transformed into a battleground for a determination of the issue whether the immigrant from the Orient or from the Occident should perform the manual work of the Pacific Coast. In this connection it is suggestive that the notorious Dennis Kearney, arch-agitator of the sand lots against the Chinese immigrant, was himself a native of the County Cork. The victory ultimately fell to the European immigrant and his American offspring in this conflict as well as in the later and more familiar one with the Japanese immigrant. The considered judgment of Americans of European origin seems to be that no Asiatic strain shall enter into the composite American stock or make its first-hand contribution to American culture.

Far more important than this problem has been the effect of the latter-day influx from Europe upon American development and ideals. Since 1870 twenty-five million Europeans have come to the United States as compared with possibly one-third of that number in the entire earlier period of independent national existence. These immigrants have contributed powerfully to the rapid exploitation of the country's natural resources and to the establishment of modern industrialism in America. Some of them became farmers, settling in distinct colonies on the fertile lands of the upper Mississippi Valley; the greater number bore the brunt of the manual labor of building the railroads as well as of performing most of the unskilled work in the mines and the great basic industries of the country.

A characteristic of the latter-day immigration has been the fact that approximately one-third of the immigrants have returned to their places of origin. This has created a restless, migratory, "bird of passage" class of laborers, lacking every interest in the permanent advance of the American working class and always competing on a single-standard basis. The swarming of foreigners into the great industries occurred at considerable cost to the native workingmen, for the latter struggled in vain for higher wages or better conditions as long as the employers could command the services of an inexhaustible supply of foreign laborers. Thus, the new immigration has made it easier for the few to amass enormous fortunes at the expense of the many and has helped to create in this country for the first time yawning inequalities of wealth.

Most sociologists believe that the addition of hordes of foreigners to the population of the United States has caused a decline in the birth-rate of the old American stock, for the native laborer has been forced to avoid large families in order to be in a position to meet the growing severity of the economic competition forced upon him by the immigrant. This condition, joined to the tendency of immigrant laborers to crowd the native Americans farther and farther from the industrial centers of the country, has caused the great communities and commonwealths of the Atlantic seaboard, about whose names cluster the heroic traditions of revolutionary times, to change completely their original characters. Puritan New England is today the home of a population of whom two-thirds were born in foreign lands or else had parents who were. Boston is as cosmopolitan a city as Chicago; and Faneuil Hall is an anachronism, a curiosity of bygone days left stranded on the shores of the Italian quarter. In fifteen of the largest cities of the United States the foreign immigrants and their children outnumber the native whites; and by the same token alien racial elements are in the majority in thirteen of the states of the Union.

When President Wilson was at the Peace Conference, he reminded the Italian delegates that there were more of their countrymen in New York than in any Italian city; and it is not beside the point to add here that New York is also the greatest Irish city in the world and the largest Jewish city.

Whatever of history may be made in the future in these parts of the country will not be the result primarily of an "Anglo-Saxon" heritage but will be the product of the interaction of these more recent racial elements upon each other and their joint reaction to the American scene. Unless the unanticipated should intervene, the stewardship of American ideals and culture is destined to pass to a new composite American type now in the process of making.

Politically the immigration of the last half-century has borne good fruit as well as evil. The intelligent thoughtful immigrant lacked the inherited prejudices of the native voter and was less likely to respond to ancient catchwords or be stirred by the revival of Civil War issues. The practice of "waving the bloody shirt" was abandoned by the politicians largely because of the growing strength of the naturalized voters, of which group Carl Schurz was, of course, the archtype. In place of this practice arose a new one, equally as reprehensible, by which the major parties used their appointments to office and their platform professions to angle for the support of naturalized groups among the voters. Racial groupings became important pawns in the political game as played by astute politicians. Blaine is said to have lost the Irish vote and with it the presidency because an indiscreet supporter prominently identified his name with opposition, to "Rum, Romanism, and Rebellion"; and in the next presidential election both parties found it expedient to insert in their platforms forthright declarations in favor of home rule for Ireland! The so-called "hyphenated American" has become a familiar figure in the last few years merely because the Great War has made native-born citizens take serious cognizance of the polyglot political situation; and the activity of the German-American Alliance in the campaign of 1916 is an illustration of how dangerous to the national welfare the meddling of racial divisions among the voters may become.

To the immigrant must also be assigned the responsibility for the accelerated growth of political and industrial radicalism in this country. While most of the newcomers quietly accepted their humble place in American society, a minority of the immigrants consisted of political refugees and other extremists, embittered by their experiences in European countries and suspicious of constituted authority under whatever guise. These men represented the Left Wing in their revolt against political authority in Europe just as three centuries earlier the Pilgrims comprised the Left Wing in their struggle against ecclesiastical authority.

Since radicalism is a cloak covering a multitude of dissents and affirmations, the influence of these men may be traced in a wide variety of programs of social reconstruction and movements for humanitarian reform. The first Socialist parties in the United States were organized by German-Americans in the years following the Civil War; and political Socialism, in its type of organization, terminology, and methods of discipline, can hardly yet be said to be fully acclimated to the New World. Violence and anarchism were first introduced into the American labor movement in the eighties by Johann Most and his associates, the greater number of whom, like Most himself, were of alien birth; and the contemporaneous I.W.W. movement finds its chief strength in the support of the migratory foreign-born laborer. Even the Non-partisan League may not be hailed, though some would so have it, as a product of an indigenous American Socialism, for this organization originated and has enjoyed its most spectacular successes in a western commonwealth in which 70 per cent of the people were natives of Europe or are the children of foreign-born parents.

The new immigration from Southern and Eastern Europe, with its lower standard of living and characteristic racial differences has intensified many existing social problems and created a number of new ones, particularly in the centers of population. The modern programs for organized and scientific philanthropy had their origin very largely in the effort to cure these spreading social sores. Out of this situation has also grown a new anti-immigration or nativist movement, unrelated to similar phenomena of earlier times and indeed regarding with approval the very racial groups against which the earlier agitation had been directed. This new movement has functioned most effectively through non-partisan channels, particularly through that of organized labor, and has commanded strong support in both parties. Whereas immigrants had virtually all been admitted without let or hindrance down to 1875, a number of laws have been passed since then with the primary purpose of removing the worst evils of indiscriminate immigration, the severest restriction being the literacy test affixed in 1917. This contemporary nativism cannot justify its existence by reason of the large proportion of aliens as compared with the native population, for, as Professor Max Farrand has recently shown, immigration was on a proportionately larger scale in colonial times than during the last fifty years. It owes its being, doubtless, to the tendency of the latter-day immigrants to settle in portions of the country that are already thickly populated and to the fact that the Americans of older stock can no longer find relief from industrial competition by taking up government land in the West.

No modern people is compounded of such heterogeneous elements as the American. It is not fantastic to believe that, during three centuries of history, these alien breeds have not only profoundly influenced American manners, culture, institutions, and material progress but have also been largely responsible for distilling that precious essence which we call American idealism. The bold man falters when asked to define American idealism, but three of its affirmative attributes are assuredly a lyric enthusiasm for government by the people, an unwavering toleration of all creeds and opinions, and, in more recent times, a deep abiding faith in pacific foreign relations. The great mass of immigrants came to the New World to attest their devotion to one or all of these ideals—they came as protestants against tyranny, intolerance, militarism, as well as against economic oppression. Nor is more concrete evidence lacking to show that neither they nor their sons rested until these great principles were firmly woven into the fabric of American thought and political practice.

During the last five years the United States has risen to a position of world-leadership in a sense never realized by any other country in history. Sober reflection convinces one that this was not an accident due to one man's personality; it grew out of the inevitable logic of a situation which found the United States an amalgam of all the peoples at war. Although the old stocks continued belligerent and apart in Europe, the warring nations instinctively turned for leadership to that western land where the same racial breeds met and mingled and dwelt in harmony with each other. Observers in Europe during the war testify to the willingness with which all classes of people in the various countries were ready to hearken to and follow the country whose liberal spirit they knew from the letters of their friends in America or from their own experiences there. In the great world-drama President Wilson played a predestined part; by reason of his position as spokesman of the American people he was the historic embodiment of the many national traditions inherent in a nation formed of many nations. This would seem to foreshadow the rôle which, for good or ill, the United States is fated to play in the future. Those who, in the discussions over the proposed League of Nations, are advocating the return of the United States to a position of isolation and irresponsibility have failed to grasp the significance of immigration in American history.

New Approaches to the History of Immigration in Twentieth-Century America

Timothy L. Smith*

THE once promising field of immigration studies has fallen upon hard times. Several able scholars who entered it with enthusiasm ten or twenty years ago have recently abandoned it. Yet the obvious importance of immigrants and their children in the urbanization of America in the twentieth century makes an understanding of their history more vital than ever before. The popularity of general works such as Will Herberg's *Protestant, Catholic, Jew* (Garden City, N. Y., 1960), Samuel Lubell's *Future of American Politics* (New York, 1956), and Nathan Glazer's and Daniel Moynihan's *Beyond the Melting Pot* (Cambridge, Mass., 1963) attests the importance that social workers, religious leaders, urban planners, and politicians attach to the theme. How then are we to explain the flight from a field of scholarship whose pioneer practitioners won an audience as significant as the makers and the readers of such books?

One reason, certainly, is the blight of ethnic parochialism, which has done far more damage to studies of twentieth-century immigrants than of earlier ones. The great migrating groups of the nineteenth century—the Irish, Germans, Swedes, and Jews—arrived early enough and in sufficient numbers to play significant roles in the economic and social development of major urban or agricultural regions. The history of any one group, therefore, seemed worth a lifetime of study by several competent scholars, willing to search out both the European background and the American experience of the group. But a solid book about Rumanians, Lithuanians, or Croatians seems hardly as promising a way for a young historian to launch his career today. Indeed, most of the immigrant peoples of the twentieth century gain significance in American history chiefly from the fact of their settlement alongside other nationalities with whom they shared closely parallel experiences in housing, employment, and social adjustment.

* The author of *Revivalism and Social Reform in Mid-Nineteenth-Century America* (Nashville, Tenn., 1957), Mr. Smith is interested primarily in American social history. He is a professor of history and education at the University of Minnesota.

1265

Studying these diverse groups together, however, magnifies a second, already serious problem: language skills. Few of today's American graduate students are masters of a single Eastern European tongue. An occasional one may set out to learn Polish, perhaps, especially if as a child he heard his grandparents speak it. But if we tell him he needs Czech and Lithuanian as well to understand the northern Slavs, or that a competent study of Ashtabula, Gary, or Joliet, or of immigrant workers in coal mining or automobile manufacturing may also involve sources in Hungarian, Finnish, Croatian, and Italian, he is understandably dismayed.

An even more serious barrier is the scattered and unorganized condition of source materials. Public librarians, even in such centers as Pittsburgh, Cleveland, Chicago, and New York, have long since despaired of keeping broad and continuous files of the scores of immigrant periodicals and almanacs or the thousands of books and pamphlets published in their own cities. The multiplicity of languages involved, the lack of staff members competent to handle more than one or two of them, and the difficulty of demonstrating the worth of any single publication were doubtless more important than prejudice against recent immigrants in producing this situation. The most substantial university Slavic collections, at Harvard, Princeton, Indiana, and Berkeley, have, moreover, concentrated upon the history of the Slavs in Europe, not in America. Thus, important files of periodicals and manuscripts have recently been destroyed, and others have been sent piecemeal to Europe. The scholar who works on any of the twentieth-century immigrant groups must spend untold hours simply locating material and negotiating for permission to use it, realizing at the same time that it must remain in private hands, out of the reach of other scholars who might retrace and correct his steps or cut a new path. A broad-scale program to collect and organize in one or more of the major university libraries a wide sample of the publications, organizational records, and personal papers of every immigrant nationality from Central, Eastern, and Southern Europe and from the Near East seems necessary.

Should even these major technical problems be solved, yet another cause of the crisis in immigration history would beset us: the intellectual and emotional involvement of historians in a cluster of value-laden arguments over cultural pluralism and the meaning of Americanization, over the nature of Anglo-Saxon domination and of religion's social role. Several of the premises that underlie much research in the history of recent immigration reflect this involvement. Americanization appears chiefly in these studies as a native Protestant scheme to engineer cultural and social uniformity. Economic exploitation of the newcomers seems an inevitable concomitant of the cultural. And the immigrants themselves, uprooted from their homes in the Old World, appear predestined to be strangers in the New. Their history, as thus far written, is a story of alienation and conflict. Organizations and individuals whose function was not unity and defense, but assimilation, seem somehow like the good black Sambos and the Uncle Toms of Negro history —worthy of notice chiefly by way of contrast with those who nurtured and preserved their nationality's contribution to a culturally plural America.

In this paper, therefore, I wish to suggest approaches to immigration history that lay frank stress upon assimilation, both cultural and structural, rather than ethnic exclusiveness. The approaches require comparative and quantitative studies employing the tools and the perceptions of both the older social history and the newer behavioral sciences. The suggestions are my own, but they arise out of an extensive investigation that Clarke Chambers, Hyman Berman, and I have recently concluded of the social history of the Minnesota iron mining towns. Two sets of findings seem to offer important suggestions for future studies of urban immigrants: one group centers upon the integrative factors at work in this particular kind of small-town environment; the other deals with the relationships between local and national structures of social organization.

The Vermilion and Mesabi iron lands were a virgin wilderness until 1884. Those who settled there in the following thirty years came from a wide spectrum of Eastern, Southern, and Western European backgrounds. The nature of mining operations required them to locate in a dozen small towns and some forty-odd tiny villages. Here face-to-face relationships prevailed, as in their homelands. But the structure of law and custom was Anglo-Saxon, midwestern, and thoroughly capitalistic. The population, moreover, was in both language and religion as polyglot as Chicago; and economic life, far more than in great cities, depended heavily upon giant corporations like United States Steel or Pickands-Mather, whose headquarters were in faraway Cleveland, Pittsburgh, and New York.[1] In this particular kind of small-town environment, cultural islands grounded in sentiments of nationality could not withstand the assimilating effects of shared experience.

The close segregation of residences according to ethnic patterns, for example, simply did not occur. All that happened was that in larger towns

[1] George O. Virtue, *The Minnesota Iron Ranges* (Washington, D. C., 1909), 345–53, provides statistics based upon mining company records that are either no longer in existence or inaccessible to scholars.

workers from Eastern and Southern Europe were spread out at random through the poorer neighborhoods. English-speaking families, many of whom were immigrants from Canada, Scotland, or Cornwall, occupied the best homes available, with Irish, Germans, and Scandinavians scattered in between.[2] Under these circumstances, marriage across ethnic lines occurred frequently from the beginning; immigrant wives established informal contacts with others of different nationalities more often than in cities; and children found it impossible to identify the mixed culture of the street and the neighborhood school with their parents' Old World traditions.[3] The consequence was an astonishingly rapid adjustment of all groups to prevailing American folkways, and a surprising degree of structural assimilation as well, in business partnerships, civic activities, religious worship, and recreation.

Should not studies of immigrants in cities concentrate more upon the life histories of families who settled in multiethnic neighborhoods and passed rapidly into associations and activities geared to interest rather than ethnicity? Given the unbalanced sex ratios, the pursuit of wives outside their own nationality among the men who were first to arrive created many families whose language was necessarily English. Did such families later exercise a mediating role among newcomers of the father's nationality? Scattered evidence from literary sources presently available—family histories, immigrant almanacs and guidebooks, and the obituary columns of the foreign-language press—offers fruitful points to begin such studies. And urban parish records, school surveys, and census reports beckon to the student with an interest in quantification.

A second finding was that in these small towns Roman Catholic congregations functioned socially as ethnic melting pots, while those serving Protestant immigrants often nurtured a specific Old World tradition. Except for the separate Italian parishes founded after 1906 at Hibbing and Eve-

[2] See, e.g., Minnesota Fourth Decennial Census, 1895, MS schedules for Saint Louis County, 119–22 (for McKinley residents, Minnesota State Archives); lists of petitioners for sidewalk and sewer improvements in Eveleth City Council, "Minute Book" for 1913 and 1914, Eveleth City Clerk's office; and addresses of heads of families of the Russian Orthodox congregation in Chisholm in 1922 in M. H. Godfrey to John H. McLean, Sept. 21, 1922, Oliver Iron Mining Company, Executive Files, Minnesota Historical Society.
[3] Saint Louis County, MS marriage record book, for Tower, 1886–1890, courthouse, Duluth, Minn., records 134 marriages, of which 16 seem, from the rough estimate possible from names alone, to have crossed ethnic lines. See also *Narodni Vestnik* [National Herald], Sept. 28, 1911, Immigrant Archives, University of Minnesota Library, recording the marriage of a Slovene girl to a son of Mining Superintendent Charles Trezona; MS marriage records of St. John the Baptist Roman Catholic Church (Polish-Slovenian), Virginia, for 1909, in the parish office showing 4 of 28 marriages were exogamous, and for 1916, showing 5 of 18; and the same for the Presbyterian church, Virginia, in the church office, for 1926–28, showing only 10 of 42 marriages were endogamous, each of these being between partners both of whom were either Finns or Scandinavians.

leth, the Slovene church at Eveleth, and the one at Virginia called, marvelously, the Polish-Slovenian church, the rule in range towns from Ely to Calumet was one Roman Catholic parish, serving Irish, Germans, Slavs, and Italians. Among Protestant congregations in the village of Virginia alone, by contrast, were a Norwegian, a Swedish, a German, and three Finnish Lutheran groups; two Baptist churches, one Finnish, the other Swedish; a Norwegian and a Swedish Methodist; an English Methodist and an Episcopal congregation, which divided between them not only the native Americans of those faiths but the immigrant mining captains from Cornwall; and a Presbyterian congregation serving both persons born in the United States and Scots and Scotch-Irish who had recently arrived from the British Isles and Protestant Canada.[4]

Many studies of Roman Catholic newcomers in cities have dealt in one way or another with the Americanizing influence of Irish bishops, of course. But few have explored the dynamics of congregational life. How many and exactly what kinds of interethnic congregations existed among Roman Catholics in large cities such as Chicago? When national parishes emerged among Slavs and Italians, whose memories were bound to a particular Old World village, precisely how did these congregations nurture a sense of national identity among their membership? How did ethnic lodges and mutual benefit societies affect the pattern of personal relationships in mixed and national parishes? And what different roles did non-Irish priests play when they served congregations of their own, of another, or of several language groups? How did these differences affect the establishment and operation of parochial schools? To these and other important questions we have almost no answers. Not just some mystic drive toward Catholic unity, but specific measures and circumstances have shaped the emerging community of Roman Catholics in American cities.

As for Protestants, the need for answers to analogous questions seems even greater. Which of the millions so labeled in numerous studies were in fact members of immigrant Protestant congregations: Italian, Swedish, or German Baptist; Norwegian, Finnish, Welsh, or German Methodist; Danish, Finnish, or Lithuanian Lutheran; Hungarian Reformed; or Italian Waldensian? And how, precisely, did their adjustment to the dominant culture differ from that of immigrants of other faiths? To assume the existence of a national community of white Protestants, as Herberg and Gerhard

[4] Information on ethnic origins of Roman Catholic congregations is most easily available from anniversary histories, an extensive file of which is in the Immigrant Archives. For Protestant churches, range town newspapers may be supplemented by the William Bell Papers, Minnesota Historical Society, and Oliver Iron Mining Company, Executive Files.

Lenski appear to do, may be far less defensible than to stress the steadily increasing identification of Roman Catholics or of Jews with their general religious heritage. Certainly a much closer analysis of what Lenski calls *The Religious Factor* (Garden City, N. Y., 1963), in his comparison of social attitudes among Detroit Catholics, Jews, white Protestants, and Negro Protestants, would be possible from a study of, say, Hungarian Catholics, Hungarian Jews, and Hungarian Protestants who settled simultaneously in that city, or of Slovak Catholic and Reformed congregations in Cleveland, or of Rumanians of the Baptist, Roman Catholic, Orthodox, and Jewish faiths in Chicago.

The mediating role of immigrant businessmen also stood out sharply in our study of the Minnesota towns. Most fascinating were the Slovene tavern-keepers, many of whom graduated rapidly into general merchandising, hotel ownership, or undertaking. Some were allies of the mining superintendents, provoking the socialists to a brief flirtation with temperance sentiments. Others were neutral on labor issues but a principal support of the parish church. All joined the chorus of popular complaint against Wall Street, while making for themselves a niche in the power structure of Main Street.[5] Meanwhile, the Lithuanian Jews who sold special or general merchandise to all comers, the German and Scandinavian wholesalers who profited from easy communication with major distributors in Duluth and Minneapolis, and the Danish and Norwegian bankers all served in different ways as agents of assimilation. Of special significance were the young Finnish and Slovene clerks whom most larger banks and mercantile houses employed to serve their countrymen in their native tongue; they were links "between two worlds" long before anyone thought of writing an immigrant play by that title.[6]

The go-getter spirit, the pragmatism, and the penuriousness of these businessmen mirrored every facet of what Max Weber taught us to call the Protestant ethic. We need comparative studies of such men in larger cities, if for nothing else to give Weber's hypothesis a new kind of test. The familiar combination of attitudes he described may turn out to be simply an ethic appropriate to the elite leaders of any uprooted and mobile people.

[5] See advertisements in *Amerikanski Slovenec* [American Slovene], Sept. 10, 1891, and thereafter, Immigrant Archives; similar advertisements in *Narodni Vestnik;* letter of John Movern, Eveleth, in *Proletarec* [Proletariat], Sept. 20, 1910, Immigrant Archives; and numerous letters in that and succeeding years in *Proletarec* attacking saloonkeepers who were in league with mining officials, *ibid*.

[6] A statistical study of the careers of fifty businessmen prominent on the range by 1920, who arrived there before 1901, reveals that 58 per cent of the men were foreign born and that 34 per cent were of East European extraction.

Perhaps more important, such studies would also make plain the precise manner in which businessmen led the way in adjustment to new conditions, providing both thrust and guidance for the newcomers' flight through cultural space. The considerable literature that now exists on immigrant bankers, Italian padrones, and Jewish merchants and clothing manufacturers is limited by ethnic perspectives, but it points to the relevant source materials: news and obituary columns in the ethnic press, the records of mutual benefit societies, and business records to be found in family papers. Consider, for example, a career such as that of Anton Nemanich, tavernkeeper at Joliet, Illinois, unofficial employment agent for International Harvester, and pillar of St. Joseph's Church. His enterprises in the "Nemanich block" eventually included a meat market, a mortuary, a florist shop, and a brewery. In 1904 he became national president of a Catholic Slovene benefit society, the organization chiefly responsible for maintaining ethnic feeling among that group. The anticlerical Slovenes called him king, but the Joliet community thought of him more as father, counselor, friend. On many an Easter Sunday the parents of half the children confirmed in St. Joseph's Church would ask Nemanich to serve as godfather. And the old priest himself declared that the congregation could never have become the center of the community in the early years if Nemanich and two other tavernkeepers had not insisted that unmarried newcomers must first go to Mass on Sundays if they wished to eat.[7]

Another important instrument of acculturation in the iron range towns was a broad program of social services, at first private and then increasingly public in their sponsorship. In the early years the welfare programs of the mining companies combined with scattered efforts of national missionary and local church agencies to meet pressing human needs. The medical doctors also played key roles, especially in encouraging the public schools to make health and recreation a major part of their expanding services. By 1920 the mining companies were shifting responsibility for such programs as they had sponsored to the towns and school districts, partly to put ore taxes to better use but also in response to the interest of their local superintendents. Thereafter, politics on the range became a game of balancing and harmonizing widespread local demands for services against such restraints as the companies could exercise directly or through the state legis-

[7] Interview with Father Matthias Hiti, Holy Ghost Roman Catholic parish, Waukegan, Ill., Mar. 5, 1964; files of *Amerikanski Slovenec* and *Glasilo K.S.K.J.* [Voice of the Grand Carniolian-Slovenian Catholic Union], Immigrant Archives, for the years 1904–21; *Spominski Album, Joliet, Illinois: Slovenskih Trgovcev in Obrtnikov* [Commemorative Album, Joliet, Illinois, Slovene Merchants and Tradesmen], comp. Rafko Zupanec (Joliet, 1915), 5, 6, 13; Joliet *Evening Herald*, May 31, 1910.

lature. The result in these communities was a welfare state that antedated the New Deal by a dozen years. Even the Boy Scout executives were subsidized with public school funds; municipal heat and light were available at bargain rates; and junior high schools had their own swimming pools. Both earlier and later social welfare programs were harmonizing influences that penetrated deeply into the life of immigrant families. At least partly in consequence, the parishes and mutual benefit societies limited greatly the range of services that their counterparts in larger cities provided.[8]

Students of immigration have much to learn, I think, from those at work in the new and expanding field of social welfare history, and perhaps something to teach as well. Here, too, the task of gathering and organizing a wide range of personal and organizational archives has only recently begun. In consulting these sources, however, historians of immigration should pay less attention than formerly to the social problems that these documents lay bare and more attention to the role of welfare agencies in resolving them and in hastening the adjustment of the newcomers to American life. Ethnic-oriented studies have tended to dismiss as unimportant the influence of Yankee do-gooders. But they rely too much on the testimony of idealists recorded in their moments of despair, or of immigrants who, precisely because they resisted such influences, remained prominent in the ethnic enclaves. Is not the story of other newcomers to whom welfare services provided a release from the bonds of nationality equally important and equally accessible to researchers bent on recovering it?

Finally, we have been able in these small towns to study closely the impact of public schooling upon the children of new immigrants. Roman Catholic congregations, struggling for their existence and unable in any case to harness ethnic loyalties to the clerical cart, found parochial schools impracticable, save in the two largest "melting-pot" congregations at Hibbing and Virginia. The public schools succeeded in imposing a common English culture upon children of many nationalities. The devices by which they attempted to prevent a conflict between generations were remarkably well planned. And they kindled an enthusiasm for high school and college education in the hearts of their students that has marked the history of the range

---

[8] See C. W. More, "Reminiscences of a Range Physician," *Minnesota Medicine* (Jan. 1936), 36–42; W. H. Moulton, "The Sociological Side of the Mining Industry," *Proceedings, Lake Superior Mining Institute, 1909* (Duluth, Minn., 1909), 82–98; Victor Power, mayor of Hibbing, open letter to J. A. O. Preus, state auditor, Sept. 1, 1915, Power's scrapbooks, in possession of Charles Bardessona, Hibbing; Oliver Iron Mining Company, Executive Files; see also *Daily Virginian,* Dec. 5–10, 1921, containing a running account of Oliver's public stand on welfare; and Hibbing School Superintendent, "Report," Superintendent's Office, Hibbing Schools, Feb. 1919, Sept. 1921.

towns ever since. By 1910 school enrollment in each of them except Chisholm exceeded the averages for both the state as a whole and for all towns of comparable size in the state. At Ely 97.5 per cent of the youngsters were enrolled, a record impossible without universal parental enthusiasm. And in the next decade Chisholm mastered relatively larger hindrances to become a showcase for public education for the entire upper Midwest.[9] The only comparable story now known is that of the immensely successful marriage of New York City's Jewish population to the public schools.

Have historians of immigration working in urban settings paid enough attention to the later careers of the thousands of Catholic and Orthodox children who attended public rather than parochial schools, often from choice as well as necessity? Have we given sufficient emphasis to the broad support of public education generally, and particularly of compulsory attendance laws, which came from Czech, Polish, Greek, and Italian leaders anxious to relieve their nationalities of the stigma and the handicap of ignorance? Federal census reports for 1910 indicate that in every region the percentage of children of foreign or mixed parentage enrolled in school closely approximated that for children of native-born Americans, despite the obvious social handicaps of the former group. In adult literacy statistics, moreover, the offspring of immigrants uniformly outranked the others, even in the populous Middle Atlantic and north central states, where newcomers were many and traditions of public education in the older population strong.[10]

More careful study of the zeal for schooling that these statistics suggest, and of the role of immigrant families and organizations in cultivating it, might help rid us of the notion that Americanization was an exclusively Anglo-Saxon project. And it might also reveal the bias in the widespread belief that a drive for education was the special trait of one or another ethnic group. Those who made the decision to migrate to the New World were not usually from families of superior learning or social standing, whatever their nationality. The process of self-selection turned rather upon ambition, upon a wish and a will to believe that the future was more real than the past, and upon a readiness to accept changes and make adjust-

---

[9] J. P. Vaughan, "Superintendent's Report, 1913–1914," Chisholm Schools, Superintendent's Office, and mimeographed sets of "Language Plans" for the elementary grades are the most revealing of a mass of such materials examined for this study; numerous student literary publications are also exceedingly useful. See also, in the same location, L. H. Weir, "Plans and Suggestions upon the Organization and Conduct of a System of Employment of the Free Time of the People of Chisholm, Minnesota" (multigraphed, Chisholm, 1915); Chisholm school district, "Graduates Lists" for 1926, giving occupations of one hundred outstanding high school graduates, 1908–25; and United States, *Thirteenth Census (1910)*, *Abstract . . . , with Supplement for Minnesota* (Washington, D. C., 1913), 624–28.

[10] *Ibid.*, 227–28, 245.

ments. Long before the ship on which he traveled touched the docks, many an immigrant had inquired carefully of those he met what the conditions were that he must face, the lessons he must learn to make his venture a success. Once ashore, he was staggered by the number and complexity of the things he did not know. He had to learn quickly in order to get ahead. To find countrymen who spoke his own language and would help him initially was great good fortune. For such a man, the "ethnic community" was not a room but a corridor. His ultimate objective was the fulfillment of a dream of success that owed nothing at all to Horatio Alger. If it was too late for him to make more than a start, it was not too late for his children. And for them, he knew, schooling was the key that unlocked the corridor door.

The other major category of our findings deals with the varying relationships of regional and national structures of social organization to local face-to-face groups. These also suggest that assimilation is a more useful perspective than alienation from which to approach the history of twentieth-century immigration.

Entrepreneurial historians, for example, have as yet paid insufficient attention to the subtle divergences of interest and policy between the local and the central offices of national business combinations. These divergences became especially significant in the Mesabi country, where the lords of industrial empires whose headquarters were far away directed when to open and close mines, what wages to pay, and what sorts of employees to favor. Many of the range captains, however, were themselves immigrants. Though sometimes well educated, they were usually practical men who disdained the armchair engineers of Cleveland and Pittsburgh. The experiences they shared and the sense of companionship they developed with their employees at the mines affected the immigrant worker's attitudes quite as much as his lodge or his foreign-language newspaper. Off the job, the superintendents frequently identified themselves more with the communities of which they were masters than with the corporations which they served, exerting, with the help of their wives, an influence that was not subject to statistical analysis or central control. Their tacit approval or disapproval of extensions of educational opportunity or of municipal services; their leadership in church and social welfare programs; their control of banks, or real-estate development companies; their selection of foremen from one or another ethnic group; and their personal friendship with priests, politicians, or saloonkeepers were all immensely important factors in the pace and the direction of the newcomer's integration. Studies of the local captains of industry and of the factory societies over which they presided in places like South Bend, Lorain, or Youngstown would likely yield similar conclusions, and historians of immigration have a special stake in leading the way.

The impact of national professional groups upon their members, and through them upon immigrant populations, also seems newly significant from our study of the range towns. National and regional associations of mining engineers cultivated professional and ethical standards on this frontier that set limits to both corporate policy and personal greed. Professional school administrators performed a similar function. The mining captains who dominated the early school boards knew the value of topflight administration of any large and rapidly expanding operation and outbid other districts in the state to get it. The self-conscious pride of the school superintendents they employed, not only in gleaming and well-equipped new buildings but also in the equal status they enjoyed with the all-powerful men who ran the mines, is obvious at every turn of the story. Leading members of both professions had been educated at state universities in Wisconsin, Michigan, and Minnesota, during the years when the academic environment nurtured progressivism.[11] Their tough-minded readiness to accept responsibility for social engineering poses questions that should be asked about the nature of local Americanization campaigns elsewhere as well. On the iron range, certainly, they owed less to Anglo-Saxon chauvinism than to a remarkably humane concern for an efficiently functioning society.

The roles of the three professions that dominated cultural life on nineteenth-century frontiers—the doctors, lawyers, and clergymen—varied here in ways both novel and familiar: according to the differing lengths of time that individuals served in a particular town, the strength of their local professional associations, the nature of their services, and the degree of discipline exercised by regional and national bodies. Although religious congregations were supported chiefly by their own members, grants from mission agencies in New York, Chicago, St. Louis, and the Twin Cities were sufficient to knit most local congregations into a national organization. The young clergymen and rabbis who served as their pastors were not only trained and appointed by distant denominational agencies, but tended to see their professional futures leading elsewhere.

Attorneys and doctors, by contrast, tended to identify themselves permanently with one local community and to form close professional ties within the region. The doctors early managed to establish their independ-

---

[11] A statistical analysis of the careers of three hundred business and professional men who occupied leadership positions by 1920 underlies this description of occupational groups.

ence of mining company dictation, despite their reliance upon fees from company medical plans. Private hospitals evolved into prosperous clinics which in turn financed personal investments in banks and real estate. Meanwhile, they served on school boards and in various civic and welfare enterprises. In small-town societies with a narrow range of occupations, such doctors inevitably became models to the brightest immigrant youngsters. Forty-nine graduates of the high school at Chisholm entered the medical profession before 1960, thirty of them from East European families, chiefly Slavic.[12] The life histories of comparable groups of immigrant children who first broke into the professional ranks in urban localities would reveal much about their mediating role, I believe, both within and outside the emerging ethnic communities.

As with business and professional men, so with labor, the decisive question was the relationship of local to central organizations. Leaders of local workers' associations, both formal and informal, developed attitudes different from those which national and regional unions sought to cultivate. Their work was further complicated by ethnic competition on both local and national levels, by the successful appeal of Marxism to a minority within each language group, and by the immense power that the mining companies wielded over a narrow job market. These circumstances inclined such workers' organizations as did exist toward both a greater degree of radicalism and a stronger emphasis upon ethnic loyalties than their national leaders, who were chiefly Anglo-Saxon, in theory supported.[13]

A close reading of the American workers' newspapers published in each of the Eastern European languages seems necessary before the crazy quilt pattern of American socialist history can be seen whole. And understanding that pattern, in turn, must precede any adequate analysis of the relationship between the American labor movement generally and the immigrant communities that so often frustrated and divided it. The story is difficult for doctrinaire liberals to tell objectively because the immigrants who opposed radicalism on labor issues often accepted assimilation to American culture more readily. Moreover, as in other matters covered here, the variety of the languages and the complexity of the issues require a collection of source materials that covers the entire water front. And the program of research should involve steady cooperation among scholars whose total range of interests and capabilities is very wide.

---

[12] The list taken from the Chisholm *Free Press*, May 29, 1963, was checked against school records and interviews for ethnic identifications.
[13] See translations of scores of letters published in the Slovene socialist newspapers, *Glas*

Finally, comparison of the process by which national ethnic communities emerged out of the local associations of Slovenes and Finns makes plain the contribution of immigrant leaders themselves to the process of acculturation. A large proportion of the Americans of these two nationalities settled in the Lake Superior region. Their Old World heritages contrasted sharply. The Finns were highly literate, Lutheran, and accustomed to a climate and topography similar to that of northern Minnesota, while the Slovenes were Roman Catholics from a Mediterranean land, and from one-fourth to one-half of them were illiterate. The latter, moreover, were the only European people to arrive in this country preceded by a substantial number of clergymen of their own nationality. For decades before 1890 Slovene priests had served as missionaries to the Chippewa Indians in the dioceses of Marquette and St. Cloud and as pastors of Czech and German frontier parishes there. Yet the institutions that the two nationalities fashioned to nurture group loyalty show striking parallels.

In 1889 Archbishop John Ireland appointed Joseph Buh, Slovene missionary and pastor at Tower and Ely, as vicar-general of the new diocese of Duluth. Buh was charged with the task of knitting the German and southern Slav newcomers on the iron ranges into the American, which is to say, Irish Catholic Church. He soon founded a weekly Slovene newspaper, however, and permitted students from St. Paul Seminary who assisted him during the summer to organize Slovene mutual benefit lodges in the mixed parishes of the mining towns. The idea spread rapidly to other midwestern states. After several years of discussion, delegates from these local lodges formed a national association known as the Grand Carniolian Catholic Union, with headquarters in Joliet, Illinois. An ethnic sect thus took shape by voluntary action, inside the structure of American Catholicism. Buh's weekly newspaper became the organ of the new body, issuing almanacs, pamphlets, and a dictionary, and summoning members to an annual convention at which the students from St. Paul Seminary provided national music. Letters from local units scattered from Pennsylvania to Colorado appeared in the newspaper each week, displaying the emotions that surrounded the search for a wider kinship among people who in the Old World would have remained strangers, bound to their own village and valley. Moreover, precisely as in experiences of sect formation among Protestants, tensions flowing from the conflict between local and general objectives produced an early secession and another national Slovene organization, the

---

Svobode [Voice of Liberty], 1901–1909, and *Proletarec*, by Mary Molek, curator, at Immigrant Archives; papers of Work Peoples College, Finnish IWW school at Duluth, *ibid.*

South Slavic Catholic Union, whose headquarters after 1899 were at Ely.[14]

Similarly, among Lutheran Finns, local clubs and temperance societies gave rise to congregations which, in turn, coalesced gradually into three national sects. All three were heirs of divergent tendencies within the Church of Finland, which in the Old World had been held by national law and custom in a single communion. Many independent Finnish congregations in the mining region, however, refused to join any one of these denominations. Meanwhile, the temperance societies formed national brotherhoods as well—three different ones, none of which was identified with a particular religious sect. Thereafter, competition among these various national organizations for the allegiance of newcomers pressed each toward an increasing emphasis upon Finnishness.[15]

Both Slovene and Finnish religious communities, moreover, faced a continuous challenge from socialism, whose organization and ideology nurtured in each case a separate identity. Marxist lecturers appeared in the mining country after 1899 and converted numerous Finnish "workers clubs" to their program. No less than four sects of Finnish socialists eventually emerged, each fielding its own team of itinerant evangelists, and each cultivating ethnic loyalties through newspapers and summer schools in a manner that contradicted both the theoretical and the practical internationalism of the socialist movement. The same development occurred among Slovenes after 1902, when Marxists recently arrived from the homeland gained control of a newly formed anticlerical benefit society. Thereafter, local socialist clubs and lodges serving both nationalities insulated workers and their families from the religious congregations by cultivating national music and drama and fashioning a social life entirely centered in the group. "Hall so-

[14] *Amerikanski Slovenec* is the chief source of this story, esp. articles of Oct. 14, 1892 (by F. S. Šušteršič), Oct. 30, Nov. 5, 1891 (by Ivan Pakiž, Ely), Apr. 20, 1894 (by students at St. Paul Seminary), June 28, 1895 (reprinted in *Glasilo K.S.K.J.*, Apr. 7, 1915). See also *Zgodinja Danica* [Morning Star], XLVIII (Nov. 15, 1895), 370; *Jubilejna Spominska Knjiga . . . Tridesetletnice K.S.K.J.* [Jubilee Memorial Book . . . Thirteenth Anniversary . . . Grand Carniolian-Slovenian Catholic Union . . .] (Cleveland, 1924), 19, 23, 59, *et passim;* and Joe Zavertnik, *Amerikanski Slovenski . . .* [American Slovenes . . .] (Chicago, 1925), 375, on JSKJ. (Translations of these citations, chiefly by Mary Molek, are in the Immigrant Archives.)

[15] William Rautanan, *Amerikan Suomalainen Kirkko* [The Finnish American Church] (Hancock, Mich., 1911), 241–47; Uuras Saarnivaara, *Amerikan Laestadiolaisuuden eli Apostolisluterilaisuuden Historia* [American Laestadian or Apostolic Lutheran History] (Ironwood, Mich., 1947), an English summary of which appeared the following year; J. E. Nopola, *Evangelis-Luterilainen Kansalliskirkko . . .* [Evangelical Lutheran National Church . . .] (Ironwood, Mich., 1949), 1–49, *passim;* Akseli Järnefelt, *Suomalaiset Amerikaasa* [The Finns in America] (Helsinki, 1899), 141–45; and *Kirkollinen Kalenteri . . . 1904* [Church Almanac . . . 1904] (Hancock, Mich., 1904), 64–65, 72–87. Douglas Ollila of Gustavus Adolphus College has assisted me in the translation of these references; his unpublished dissertation, done at Boston University, is the best introduction to theological phases of Finnish church history in America.

cialism" became a synonym for ethnic as much as for ideological activity.[16]

The several strands of this story offer numerous suggestions for research in immigrant history. A comparison of the effectiveness of the Roman Catholic hierarchy with that of the leaders of American socialism in restraining the growth of ethnic particularism in their midst is certainly in order; it would gain much from recent studies of the sociology of large-scale organization. The use of education as a device of indoctrination among both church and socialist groups is also obvious. But how did the consequences vary with the degree of control of local by national officers, or with the sharpness of the separation between competing associations of the same nationality? What difference did neighborhood ties with other nationalities make? Did the identification of religion with the established order in America strengthen the appeal of immigrant churches to those newcomers who sought individual material success? Did socialism, then, when organized on an ethnic basis, serve more to retard the processes of assimilation, and so to popularize cultural pluralism among the intelligentsia? Finally, how did the simple fact of a common language and national origin in the long run win out over ideological division and bring the various segments of each nationality closer together?

These and many similar questions beg for reasoned answers by students willing and able to look at immigrant history as a whole. Other legitimate and important approaches will, of course, continue to evoke studies of a much different kind from the ones recommended here. But until historians pay as much attention to the processes of assimilation as they have to the persistence of ethnic loyalties, not only in small towns, but in great cities as well, we will know only half of the story. Experiences of alienation, and the resulting crises of identity, may prove to have sprung more from rivalries and estrangements within the immigrant communities than from any pressures exerted from the outside. And the drive of the immigrant himself, moving individually as well as through organized groups toward what has often been called "Americanization," but which is better termed "urbanization," may turn out to be the central theme.

[16] See *Sosialisti* [The Socialist] (newspaper organ of the syndicalist or IWW wing of Finnish socialists), Sept. 1, 3, 1914 (describing origins of Work Peoples College, Duluth), and, for other matters, Dec. 11, June 13, 22, 1914 (on itinerant lecturers), Sept. 7, 1914 (a socialist funeral); *Työmies* [The Laborer] (organ of democratic socialism, 1904–present), Jan. 4, Feb. 1, 1910; and *Aakkosis Sosialistien Lapsilla* [A Primer for Socialist Children], ed. A. B. Makela (Hancock, Mich., n.d.). For Slovene socialism, Zavertnik covers the ground, but often inaccurately. See also Ivan Molek, "Over Hill and Dale; Autobiographical Sketches" (MS tr. by Mary Molek, Immigrant Archives), the best general source on free-thinking Slovenes in America, 247–53; the files of *Glas Svobode*, 1902–1909; *Ameriski Druzinski Koledar . . . 1935* [American Family Almanac . . . 1935] (Chicago, 1935), 141–42 *et passim;* Slovene Library Club, Ely, Minn., "Minute Books," Immigrant Archives; and tr. of letters from *Proletarec* by Molek.

Contadini *in Chicago: A Critique of* The Uprooted

RUDOLPH J. VECOLI

IN *The Uprooted*[1] Oscar Handlin attempted an overarching interpretation of European peasant society and of the adjustment of emigrants from that society to the American environment. This interpretation is open to criticism on the grounds that it fails to respect the unique cultural attributes of the many and varied ethnic groups which sent immigrants to the United States. Through an examination of the south Italians, both in their Old World setting and in Chicago, this article will indicate how Handlin's portrayal of the peasant as immigrant does violence to the character of the *contadini* (peasants) of the Mezzogiorno.[2]

The idealized peasant village which Handlin depicts in *The Uprooted* did not exist in the southern Italy of the late nineteenth century. Handlin's village was an harmonious social entity in which the individual derived his identity and being from the community as a whole; the ethos of his village was one of solidarity, communality, and neighborliness.[3] The typical south Italian peasant, however, did not live in a small village, but in a "rural city" with a population of thousands or even tens of thousands.[4] Seeking

Mr. Vecoli is assistant professor of history in Rutgers, The State University.

[1] Oscar Handlin, *The Uprooted* (Boston, 1951).

[2] The Mezzogiorno of Italy includes the southern part of continental Italy, i.e., the regions of Abruzzi e Molise, Campania, Puglia, Basilicata, Calabria, and the island of Sicily.

[3] *Uprooted*, 7-12.

[4] On south Italian society see Edward C. Banfield, *The Moral Basis of a Backward Society* (Glencoe, Ill., 1958); Robert F. Foerster, *The Italian Emigration of Our Times* (Cambridge, 1919), 51-105; Leopoldo Franchetti and Sidney Sonnino, *La Sicilia nel 1876* (2 vols., Florence, 1925); Carlo Levi, *Christ Stopped at Eboli* (New York, 1947); Leonard W. Moss and Stephen C. Cappannari, "A Sociological and Anthropological Investigation of an Italian Rural Community" (mimeographed, Detroit, 1959); Luigi Villari, *Italian Life in Town and Country* (New York, 1902); Arrigo Serpieri, *La Guerra e le Classi Rurali Italiane* (Storia Economica e Sociale della Guerra Mondiale, Pubblicazioni della Fondazione Carnegie per la Pace Internazionale, Bari, 1930), 1-21; Friedrich Vöchting, *La Questione Meridionale* (Casa per il Mezzogiorno Studi e Testi I, Naples, 1955); Phyllis H. Williams, *South Italian Folkways in Europe and America* (New Haven, 1938); Rocco Scotellaro, *Contadini del Sud* (Bari, 1955).

· 404 ·

refuge from brigands and malaria, the *contadini* huddled together in these hill towns, living in stone dwellings under the most primitive conditions and each day descending the slopes to work in the fields below.

Nor were these towns simple communities of agriculturists, for their social structure included the gentry and middle class as well as the peasants. Feudalism died slowly in southern Italy, and vestiges of this archaic social order were still visible in the attitudes and customs of the various classes. While the great landowners had taken up residence in the capital cities, the lesser gentry constituted the social elite of the towns. Beneath it in the social hierarchy were the professional men, officials, merchants, and artisans; at the base were the *contadini* who comprised almost a distinct caste. The upper classes lorded over and exploited the peasants whom they regarded as less than human. Toward the upper classes, the *contadini* nourished a hatred which was veiled by the traditional forms of deference.[5]

This is not to say that the south Italian peasants enjoyed a sense of solidarity either as a community or as a social class. Rather it was the family which provided the basis of peasant solidarity. Indeed, so exclusive was the demand of the family for the loyalty of its members that it precluded allegiance to other social institutions. This explains the paucity of voluntary associations among the peasantry. Each member of the family was expected to advance its welfare and to defend its honor, regardless of the consequences for outsiders. This singleminded attention to the interests of the family led one student of south Italian society to describe its ethos as one of "amoral familism."[6]

While the strongest ties were within the nuclear unit, there existed among the members of the extended family a degree of trust, intimacy, and interdependence denied to all others. Only through the ritual kinship of *comparaggio* (godparenthood) could non-relatives gain admittance to the family circle. The south Italian family was "father-dominated but mother-centered." The father as the head of the family enjoyed unquestioned authority over the household, but the mother provided the emotional focus for family life.

[5] The following thought, which Handlin attributes to the immigrant in America, would hardly have occurred to the oppressed *contadino:* "Could he here, as at home, expect the relationship of reciprocal goodness between master and men, between just employer and true employee?" *Uprooted,* 80.

[6] Banfield, *Moral Basis of a Backward Society,* 10. In his study of a town in Basilicata, Banfield found that both gentry and peasants were unable to act "for any end transcending the immediate, material interest of the nuclear family." On the south Italian family see also Leonard W. Moss and Stephen C. Cappannari, "Patterns of Kinship, Comparaggio and Community in a South Italian Village," *Anthropological Quarterly,* XXXIII (Jan. 1960), 24-32; Leonard W. Moss and Walter H. Thomson, "The South Italian Family: Literature and Observations," *Human Organization,* XVIII (Spring 1959), 35-41.

Among the various families of the *paese* (town), there were usually jealousies and feuds which frequently resulted in bloodshed. This atmosphere of hostility was revealed in the game of *passatella*, which Carlo Levi has described as "a peasant tournament of oratory, where interminable speeches reveal in veiled terms a vast amount of repressed rancor, hate, and rivalry."[7] The sexual code of the Mezzogiorno was also expressive of the family pride of the south Italians. When violations occurred, family honor required that the seducer be punished. The south Italian was also bound by the tradition of personal vengeance, as in the Sicilian code of *omertà*. These cultural traits secured for southern Italy the distinction of having the highest rate of homicides in all of Europe at the turn of the century.[8] Such antisocial behavior, however, has no place in Handlin's scheme of the peasant community.

If the south Italian peasant regarded his fellow townsman with less than brotherly feeling, he viewed with even greater suspicion the stranger —which included anyone not native to the town. The peasants knew nothing of patriotism for the Kindom of Italy, or of class solidarity with other tillers of the soil; their sense of affinity did not extend beyond town boundaries. This attachment to their native village was termed *campanilismo*, a figure of speech suggesting that the world of the *contadini* was confined within the shadow cast by his town campanile.[9] While this parochial attitude did not manifest itself in community spirit or activities, the sentiment of *campanilismo* did exert a powerful influence on the emigrants from southern Italy.

During the late nineteenth century, increasing population, agricultural depression, and oppressive taxes, combined with poor land to make life ever more difficult for the peasantry. Still, misery does not provide an adequate explanation of the great emigration which followed. For, while the peasants were equally impoverished, the rate of emigration varied widely from province to province. J. S. McDonald has suggested that the key to these differential rates lies in the differing systems of land tenure and in the contrasting sentiments of "individualism" and "solidarity" which they produced among the peasants.[10] From Apulia and the interior of Sicily

[7] Levi, *Christ Stopped*, 179.
[8] Napoleone Colajanni, "Homicide and the Italians," *Forum*, XXXI (March 1901), 63-66.
[9] Richard Bagot, *The Italians of To-day* (Chicago, 1913), 87.
[10] J. S. McDonald, "Italy's Rural Social Structure and Emigration," *Occidente*, XII (Sept.-Oct. 1956), 437-55. McDonald concludes that where the peasantry's "aspirations for material betterment were expressed in broad associative behavior, there was little emigration. Where economic aspirations were integrated only with the welfare of the individual's nuclear family, emigration rates were high." *Ibid.*, 454.

where large-scale agriculture prevailed and cultivators' associations were formed, there was little emigration. Elsewhere in the South, where the peasants as small proprietors and tenants competed with one another, emigration soared. Rather than practicing communal agriculture as did Handlin's peasants, these *contadini,* both as cultivators and emigrants, acted on the principle of economic individualism, pursuing family and self-interest.

Handlin's peasants have other characteristics which do not hold true for those of southern Italy. In the Mezzogiorno, manual labor—and especially tilling the soil—was considered degrading. There the peasants did not share the reverence of Handlin's peasants for the land; rather they were "accustomed to look with distrust and hate at the soil."[11] No sentimental ties to the land deterred the south Italian peasants from becoming artisans, shopkeepers, or priests, if the opportunities presented themselves. Contrary to Handlin's peasants who meekly accepted their lowly status, the *contadini* were ambitious to advance the material and social position of their families. Emigration was one way of doing so. For the peasants in *The Uprooted* emigration was a desperate flight from disaster, but the south Italians viewed a sojourn in America as a means to acquire capital with which to purchase land, provide dowries for their daughters, and assist their sons to enter business or the professions.

If the design of peasant society described in *The Uprooted* is not adequate for southern Italy, neither is Handlin's description of the process of immigrant adjustment an accurate rendering of the experience of the *contadini.* For Handlin, "the history of immigration is a history of alienation and its consequences."[12] In line with this theme, he emphasizes the isolation and loneliness of the immigrant, "the broken homes, interruptions of a familiar life, separation from known surroundings, the becoming a foreigner and ceasing to belong." While there is no desire here to belittle the hardships, fears, and anxieties to which the immigrant was subject, there are good reasons for contending that Handlin overstates the disorganizing effects of emigration and underestimates the tenacity with which the south Italian peasants at least clung to their traditional social forms and values.

Handlin, for example, dramatically pictures the immigrant ceasing to be a member of a solidary community and being cast upon his own resources as an individual.[13] But this description does not apply to the *contadini* who customarily emigrated as a group from a particular town, and, once in

---

[11] Kate H. Claghorn, "The Agricultural Distribution of Immigrants," in U.S. Industrial Commission, *Reports* (19 vols., Washington, 1900-1902), XV, 496; Banfield, *Moral Basis of a Backward Society,* 37, 50, 69.

[12] *Uprooted,* 4.

[13] *Ibid.,* 38.

America, stuck together "like a swarm of bees from the same hive."[14] After working a while, and having decided to remain in America, they would send for their wives, children, and other relatives. In this fashion, chains of emigration were established between certain towns of southern Italy and Chicago.[15]

From 1880 on, the tide of emigration ran strongly from Italy to this midwestern metropolis where by 1920 the Italian population reached approximately 60,000.[16] Of these, the *contadini* of the Mezzogiorno formed the preponderant element. Because of the sentiment of *campanilismo,* there emerged not one "Little Italy" but some seventeen larger and smaller colonies scattered about the city. Each group of townsmen clustered by itself, seeking, as Jane Addams observed, to fill "an entire tenement house with the people from one village."[17] Within these settlements, the town groups maintained their distinct identities, practiced endogamy, and preserved their traditional folkways. Contrary to Handlin's dictum that the common experience of the immigrants was their inability to transplant the European village,[18] one is struck by the degree to which the *contadini* succeeded in reconstructing their native towns in the heart of industrial Chicago. As an Italian journalist commented:

Emigrating, the Italian working class brings away with it from the mother country all the little world in which they were accustomed to live; a world of traditions, of beliefs, of customs, of ideals of their own. There is no reason to marvel then that in this great center of manufacturing and commercial activity of North America our colonies, though acclimating themselves in certain ways, conserve the customs of their *paesi* of origin.[19]

If the south Italian immigrant retained a sense of belongingness with his fellow townsmen, the family continued to be the focus of his most

[14] Pascal D'Angelo, *Son of Italy* (New York, 1924), 54.
[15] These chains of emigration are traced in Rudolph J. Vecoli, "Chicago's Italians Prior to World War I: A Study of Their Social and Economic Adjustments" (doctoral dissertation, University of Wisconsin, 1963), 71-234.
[16] On the Italians in Chicago see Vecoli, "Chicago's Italians"; U.S. Commissioner of Labor, *Ninth Special Report: The Italians in Chicago* (Washington, 1897); Frank O. Beck, "The Italian in Chicago," *Bulletin of the Chicago Department of Public Welfare,* II (Feb. 1919); Jane Addams, *Twenty Years at Hull-House* (New York, 1910); Giuseppe Giacosa, "Chicago e la sua colonia Italiana," *Nuova Antologia di Scienze, Lettere ed Arti,* Third Series, CXXVIII (March 1, 1893), 15-33; Giovanni E. Schiavo, *The Italians in Chicago* (Chicago, 1928); Alessandro Mastro-Valerio, "Remarks Upon the Italian Colony in Chicago," in *Hull-House Maps and Papers* (New York, 1895), 131-42; Harvey Warren Zorbaugh, *The Gold Coast and the Slum* (Chicago, 1929), 159-81; I. W. Howerth, "Are the Italians a Dangerous Class?" *Charities Review,* IV (Nov. 1894), 17-40.
[17] Jane Addams, *Newer Ideals of Peace* (New York, 1907), 67.
[18] *Uprooted,* 144.
[19] *L'Italia* (Chicago), Aug. 3, 1901. See also Anna Zaloha, "A Study of the Persistence of Italian Customs Among 143 Families of Italian Descent" (master's thesis, Northwestern University, 1937).

intense loyalties. Among the male emigrants there were some who abandoned their families in Italy, but the many underwent harsh privations so that they might send money to their parents or wives. Reunited in Chicago the peasant family functioned much as it had at home; there appears to have been little of that confusion of roles depicted in *The Uprooted*. The husband's authority was not diminished, while the wife's subordinate position was not questioned. If dissension arose, it was when the children became somewhat "Americanized"; yet there are good reasons for believing that Handlin exaggerates the estrangement of the second generation from its immigrant parentage. Nor did the extended family disintegrate upon emigration as is contended. An observation made with respect to the Sicilians in Chicago was generally true for the south Italians: "Intense family pride . . . is the outstanding characteristic, and as the family unit not only includes those related by blood, but those related by ritual bonds as well (the *commare* and *compare*), and as intermarriage in the village groups is a common practice, this family pride becomes really a clan pride."[20] The alliance of families of the town through intermarriage and godparenthood perpetuated a social organization based upon large kinship groups.

The south Italian peasants also brought with them to Chicago some of their less attractive customs. Many a new chapter of an ancient vendetta of Calabria or Sicily was written on the streets of this American city. The zealous protection of the family honor was often a cause of bloodshed. Emigration had not abrogated the duty of the south Italian to guard the chastity of his women. Without the mitigating quality of these "crimes of passion" were the depredations of the "Black Hand." After 1900 the practice of extorting money under threat of death became so common as to constitute a reign of terror in the Sicilian settlements. Both the Black Handers and their victims were with few exceptions from the province of Palermo where the criminal element known collectively as the *mafia* had thrived for decades. The propensity for violence of the south Italians was not a symptom of social disorganization caused by emigration but a characteristic of their Old World culture.[21] Here too the generalizations that the immigrant feared to have recourse to the peasant crimes of revenge, and that the immigrant was rarely involved in crime for profit,[22] do not apply to the south Italians.

To speak of alienation as the essence of the immigrant experience is to

[20] Zorbaugh, *Gold Coast*, 166-67. *Commare* and *compare* are godmother and godfather. See also Zaloha, "Persistence of Italian Customs," 103-05, 145-48.
[21] *The Italian "White Hand" Society in Chicago, Illinois. Studies, Actions and Results* (Chicago, 1906); Illinois Association for Criminal Justice, *Illinois Crime Survey* (Chicago, 1929), 845-62, 935-54; Vecoli, "Chicago's Italians," 393-460.
[22] *Uprooted*, 163.

ignore the persistence of traditional forms of group life. For the *contadino,* his family and his townsmen continued to provide a sense of belonging and and to sanction his customary world-view and life-ways. Living "in," but not "of," the sprawling, dynamic city of Chicago, the south Italian was sheltered within his ethnic colony from the confusing complexity of American society.

While the acquisition of land was a significant motive for emigration, the south Italian peasants were not ones to dream, as did Handlin's, of possessing "endless acres" in America.[23] Their goal was a small plot of ground in their native towns. If they failed to reach the American soil, it was not because, as Handlin puts it, "the town had somehow trapped them,"[24] but because they sought work which would pay ready wages. These peasants had no romantic illusions about farming; and despite urgings by railroad and land companies, reformers, and philanthropists to form agricultural colonies, the south Italians preferred to remain in the city.[25]

Although Chicago experienced an extraordinary growth of manufacturing during the period of their emigration, few south Italians found employment in the city's industries. Great numbers of other recent immigrants worked in meatpacking and steelmaking, but it was uncommon to find an Italian name on the payroll of these enterprises.[26] The absence of the *contadini* from these basic industries was due both to their aversion to this type of factory work and to discrimination against them by employers. For the great majority of the south Italian peasants "the stifling, brazen factories and the dark, stony pits" did not supplant "the warm living earth as the source of their daily bread."[27] Diggers in the earth they had been and diggers in the earth they remained; only in America they dug with the pick and shovel rather than the mattock. In Chicago the Italian laborers quickly displaced the Irish in excavation and street work, as they did on railroad construction jobs throughout the West.[28]

[23] *Ibid.,* 82.

[24] *Ibid.,* 64.

[25] Vecoli, "Chicago's Italians," 184-234; Luigi Villari, *Gli Stati Uniti d'America e l'Emigrazione Italiana* (Milan, 1912), 256. Villari observed that even Italian immigrants who worked as gardeners in the suburbs of Boston preferred to live with their countrymen in the center of the city, commuting to their work in the country. *Ibid.,* 224.

[26] In 1901, for example, of over 6,000 employees at the Illinois Steel works only two were Italian. John M. Gillette, "The Culture Agencies of a Typical Manufacturing Group: South Chicago," *American Journal of Sociology,* VII (July 1901), 93-112. In 1915 the Armour packing company reported that there was not one Italian among its 8,000 workers in Chicago. U.S. Commission on Industrial Relations, *Final Report and Testimony* (11 vols., Washington, 1916), IV, 3530.

[27] *Uprooted,* 73.

[28] Chicago *Tribune,* March 20, 1891; Frank J. Sheridan, "Italian, Slavic and Hungarian

The lot of the railroad workers was hard. Arriving at an unknown destination, they were sometimes attacked as "scabs," they found the wages and conditions of labor quite different from those promised, or it happened that they were put to work under armed guard and kept in a state of peonage. For twelve hours a day in all kinds of weather, the laborers dug and picked, lifted ties and rails, swung sledge hammers, under the constant goading of tyrannical foremen. Housed in filthy boxcars, eating wretched food, they endured this miserable existence for a wage which seldom exceeded $1.50 a day. Usually they suffered in silence, and by the most stern abstinence were able to save the greater part of their meager earnings. Yet it happened that conditions became intolerable, and the *paesani* (gangs were commonly composed of men from the same town) would resist the exactions of the "boss." These uprisings were more in the nature of peasants' revolts than of industrial strikes, and they generally ended badly for the *contadini*.[29]

With the approach of winter the men returned to Chicago. While some continued on to Italy, the majority wintered in the city. Those with families in Chicago had households to return to; the others formed cooperative living groups. Thus they passed the winter months in idleness, much as they had in Italy. Railroad work was cyclical as well as seasonal. In times of depression emigration from Italy declined sharply; many of the Italian workers returned to their native towns to await the return of American prosperity. Those who remained were faced with long periods of unemployment; it was at these times, such as the decade of the 1890s, that the spectre of starvation stalked through the Italian quarters of Chicago.[30]

Because the *contadini* were engaged in gang labor of a seasonal nature there developed an institution which was thought most typical of the Italian immigration: the padrone system.[31] Bewildered by the tumult of the city,

Unskilled Laborers in the United States," U.S. Bureau of Labor, *Bulletin* XV (Sept. 1907), 445-68; Vecoli, "Chicago's Italians," 279-337.

[29] D'Angelo, *Son of Italy*, 85-119; Dominic T. Ciolli, "The 'Wop' in the Track Gang," *Immigrants in America Review*, II (July 1916), 61-64; Gino C. Speranza, "Forced Labor in West Virginia," *Outlook*, LXXIV (June 13, 1903), 407-10.

[30] U.S. Commissioner of Labor, *Italians in Chicago*, 29, 44; Rosa Cassettari, "The Story of an Italian Neighbor (as told to Marie Hall Ets)," 342-50, ms., on loan to the author; Mayor's Commission on Unemployment (Chicago), *Report* (Chicago, 1914); Vecoli, "Chicago's Italians," 279-337.

[31] On the padrone system see Grace Abbott, "The Chicago Employment Agency and the Immigrant Worker," *American Journal of Sociology*, XIV (Nov. 1908), 289-305; John Koren, "The Padrone System and the Padrone Banks," U.S. Bureau of Labor, *Bulletin* II (March 1897), 113-29; S. Merlino, "Italian Immigrants and Their Enslavement," *Forum*, XV (April 1893), 183-90; Gino C. Speranza, "The Italian Foreman as a Social Agent," *Charities*, XI (July 4, 1903), 26-28; Vecoli, "Chicago's Italians," 235-278; Giovanni Ermenegildo Schiavo, *Italian-American History* (2 vols., New York, 1947-1949), I, 538-40.

the newcomers sought out a townsman who could guide them in the ways of this strange land. Thus was created the padrone who made a business out of the ignorance and necessities of his countrymen. To the laborers, the padrone was banker, saloonkeeper, grocer, steamship agent, lodging-house keeper, and politician. But his most important function was that of employment agent.

While there were honest padrones, most appeared unable to resist the opportunities for graft. Although Handlin states that "the padrone had the virtue of shielding the laborer against the excesses of employers,"[32] the Italian padrones usually operated in collusion with the contractors. Often the padrones were shrewd, enterprising men who had risen from the ranks of the unskilled; many of them, however, were members of the gentry who sought to make an easy living by exploiting their peasant compatriots in America as they had in Italy. The padrone system should not be interpreted as evidence "that a leader in America was not bound by patterns of obliga-tion that were sacred in the Old World"; rather, it was a logical outcome of the economic individualism and "amoral familism" of south Italian society.

In their associational life the *contadini* also contradicted Handlin's asser-tion that the social patterns of the Old Country could not survive the ocean voyage.[33] The marked incapacity of the south Italians for organizational activity was itself a result of the divisive attitudes which they had brought with them to America. Almost the only form of association among these immigrants was the mutual aid society. Since such societies were common in Italy by the 1870s,[34] they can hardly be regarded as "spontaneously generated" by American conditions. Instead, the mutual aid society was a transplanted institution which was found to have especial utility for the immigrants. An Italian journalist observed: "If associations have been found useful in the *patria,* how much more they are in a strange land, where it is so much more necessary for the Italians to gather together, to frater-nize, to help one another."[35] Nowhere, however, was the spirit of *cam-panilismo* more in evidence than in these societies. An exasperated Italian patriot wrote: "Here the majority of the Italian societies are formed of individuals from the same town and more often from the same parish, others are not admitted. But are you or are you not Italians? And if you are, why do you exclude your brother who is born a few miles from your

[32] *Uprooted,* 69-70.
[33] *Ibid.,* 170-71.
[34] Franchetti and Sonnino, *La Sicilia,* II, 335.
[35] *L'Unione Italiana* (Chicago), March 18, 1868.

town?"[36] As the number of these small societies multiplied (by 1912 there were some 400 of them in Chicago),[37] various attempts were made to form them into a federation. Only the Sicilians, however, were able to achieve a degree of unity through two federations which enrolled several thousand members.

The sentiment of regionalism was also a major obstacle to the organizational unity of the Italians in Chicago. Rather than being allayed by emigration, this regional pride and jealousy was accentuated by the proximity of Abruzzese, Calabrians, Genoese, Sicilians, and other groups in the city. Each regional group regarded those from other regions with their strange dialects and customs not as fellow Italians, but as distinct and inferior ethnic types. Any proposal for cooperation among the Italians was sure to arouse these regional antipathies and to end in bitter recriminations.[38] The experience of emigration did not create a sense of nationality among the Italians strong enough to submerge their parochialism. Unlike Handlin's immigrants who acquired "new modes of fellowship to replace the old ones destroyed by emigration,"[39] the South Italians confined themselves largely to the traditional ones of family and townsmen.

The quality of leadership of the mutual aid societies also prevented them from becoming agencies for the betterment of the *contadini*. These organizations, it was said, were often controlled by the "very worse [sic] element in the Italian colony,"[40] arrogant, selfish men, who founded societies not out of a sense of fraternity but to satisfy their ambition and vanity. The scope of their leadership was restricted to presiding despotically over the meetings, marching in full regalia at the head of the society, and gaining economic and political advantage through their influence over the members. If such a one were frustrated in his attempt to control a society, he would secede with his followers and found a new one. Thus even the townsmen were divided into opposing factions.[41]

The function of the typical mutual aid society was as limited as was its sphere of membership. The member received relief in case of illness, an indemnity for his family in case of death, and a funeral celebrated with pomp and pageantry. The societies also sponsored an annual ball and picnic,

[36] *L'Italia*, Oct. 23-24, 1897.
[37] Schiavo, *Italians in Chicago*, 57.
[38] Giacosa, "Chicago," 31-33; Comitato Locale di Chicago, *Primo Congresso degli Italiani all'estero sotto l'atto patronato di S. M. Vittorio Emanuele III* (Chicago, 1908).
[39] *Uprooted*, 189.
[40] Edmund M. Dunne, *Memoirs of "Zi Pre"* (St. Louis, 1914), 18. Father Dunne was the first pastor of the Italian Church of the Guardian Angel on Chicago's West Side.
[41] Comitato Locale di Chicago, *Primo Congresso; L'Italia*, Feb. 18, 1888, Oct. 21, 1899.

and, most important of all, the feast of the local patron saint. This was the extent of society activities; any attempt to enlist support for philanthropic or civic projects was doomed to failure.[42]

Since there was a surplus of doctors, lawyers, teachers, musicians, and classical scholars in southern Italy, an "intellectual proletariat" accompanied the peasants to America in search of fortune.[43] Often, however, these educated immigrants found that America had no use for their talents, and to their chagrin they were reduced to performing manual labor. Their only hope of success was to gain the patronage of their lowly countrymen, but the sphere of colonial enterprise was very restricted. The sharp competition among the Italian bankers, doctors, journalists, and others engendered jealousies and rivalries. Thus this intelligentsia which might have been expected to provide tutelage and leadership to the humbler elements was itself rent by internecine conflict and expended its energies in polemics.

For the most part the upper-class immigrants generally regarded the peasants here as in Italy as boors and either exploited them or remained indifferent to their plight. These "respectable" Italians, however, were concerned with the growing prejudice against their nationality and wished to elevate its prestige among the Americans and other ethnic groups. As one means of doing this, they formed an association to suppress scavenging, organ-grinding, and begging as disgraceful to the Italian reputation. They simultaneously urged the workers to adopt American ways and to become patriotic Italians; but to these exhortations, the *contadino* replied: "It does not give me any bread whether the Italians have a good name in America or not. I am going back soon."[44]

Well-to-do Italians were more liberal with advice than with good works. Compared with other nationalities in Chicago, the Italians were distinguished by their lack of philanthropic institutions. There was a substantial number of men of wealth among them, but as an Italian reformer commented: "It is strange that when a work depends exclusively on the wealthy of the colony, one can not hope for success. Evidently philanthropy is not the favored attribute of our rich."[45] Indeed, there was no tradition of philanthropy among the gentry of southern Italy, and the "self-made" men did

[42] Beck, "The Italian in Chicago," 23; Comitato Locale di Chicago, *Primo Congresso; L'Italia,* Aug. 24, 1889, April 28, 1906.

[43] Amy A. Bernardy, *Italia randagia attraverso gli Stati Uniti* (Turin, 1913), 293; Giacosa, "Chicago," 31; *L'Italia,* Jan. 19, 1889.

[44] Robert E. Park and Herbert A. Miller, *Old World Traits Transplanted* (New York, 1921), 104; Mastro-Valerio, "Remarks Upon the Italian Colony," 131-32; *L'Italia,* Aug. 6, 1887, April 5, 1890.

[45] *L'Italia,* Aug. 24-25, 1895; Luigi Carnovale, *Il Giornalismo degli Emigrati Italiani nel Nord America* (Chicago, 1909), 67; Comitato Locale di Chicago, *Primo Congresso.*

not recognize any responsibility outside the family. Projects were launched for an Italian hospital, an Italian school, an Italian charity society, an Italian institute to curb the padrone evil, and a White Hand Society to combat the Black Hand, but they all floundered in this morass of discord and disinterest. Clearly Handlin does not have the Italians in mind when he describes a growing spirit of benevolence as a product of immigrant life.[46]

If there is one particular in which the *contadini* most strikingly refute Handlin's conception of the peasant it is in the place of religion in their lives. Handlin emphasizes the influence of Christian doctrine on the psychology of the peasantry,[47] but throughout the Mezzogiorno, Christianity' was only a thin veneer.[48] Magic, not religion, pervaded their everyday existence; through the use of rituals, symbols, and charms, they sought to ward off evil spirits and to gain the favor of powerful deities. To the peasants, God was a distant, unapproachable being, like the King, but the local saints and Madonnas were real personages whose power had been attested to by innumerable miracles. But in the devotions to their patron saints, the attitude of the peasants was less one of piety than of bargaining, making vows if certain requests were granted. For the Church, which they had known as an oppressive landlord, they had little reverence; and for the clergy, whom they knew to be immoral and greedy, they had little respect. They knew little of and cared less for the doctrines of the Church.

Nor was the influence of established religion on the south Italian peasants strengthened by emigration as Handlin asserts.[49] American priests were scandalized by the indifference of the Italians to the Church.[50] Even when Italian churches were provided by the Catholic hierarchy, the *contadini* seldom displayed any religious enthusiasm. As one missionary was told upon his arrival in an Italian colony: "We have no need of priests here, it would be better if you returned from whence you came."[51] As in their native towns, the south Italian peasants for the most part went to church "to be christened, married or buried and that is about all."[52]

---

[46] *Uprooted*, 175-76.

[47] *Ibid.*, 102-03.

[48] Levi, *Christ Stopped*, 116-18; Leonard W. Moss and Stephen C. Cappannari, "Folklore and Medicine in an Italian Village," *Journal of American Folklore*, LXXIII (April 1960), 85-102; Banfield, *Moral Basis of a Backward Society*, 17-18, 129-32.

[49] *Uprooted*, 117.

[50] On the religious condition of the Italian immigrants, see the discussion in *America*, XII (Oct. 17, 31, Nov. 7, 14, 21, 28, Dec. 5, 12, 19, 1914), 6-7, 66, 93, 121, 144-45, 168-69, 193-96, 221, 243-46.

[51] G. Sofia, ed., *Missioni Scalabriniane in America, estratto da "Le Missioni Scalabriniane tra gli Italiani"* (Rome, 1939), 122.

[52] "Church Census of the 17th Ward, 1909," Chicago Commons, 1904-1910, Graham Taylor Papers (Newberry Library).

Because they were said to be drifting into infidelity, the south Italians were also the object of much of the home mission work of the Protestant churches of Chicago. Drawing their ministry from Italian converts and Waldensians, these missions carried the Gospel to the *contadini*, who, however, revealed little inclination to become "true Christians." After several decades of missionary effort, the half dozen Italian Protestant churches counted their membership in the few hundreds.[53] The suggestion that Italians were especially vulnerable to Protestant proselyting was not borne out in Chicago. For the *contadini*, neither Catholicism nor Protestantism became "paramount as a way of life."[54]

According to Handlin, the immigrants found it "hard to believe that the whole world of spirits and demons had abandoned their familiar homes and come also across the Atlantic,"[55] but the *contadino* in America who carried a *corno* (a goat's horn of coral) to protect him from the evil eye harbored no such doubts. The grip of the supernatural on the minds of the peasants was not diminished by their ocean crossing. In the Italian settlements, sorcerers plied their magical trades on behalf of the ill, the lovelorn, the bewitched. As Alice Hamilton noted: "Without the help of these mysterious and powerful magicians they [the *contadini*] believe that they would be defenseless before terrors that the police and the doctor and even the priest cannot cope with."[56] For this peasant folk, in Chicago as in Campania, the logic of medicine, law, or theology had no meaning; only magic provided an explanation of, and power over, the vagaries of life.

The persistence of Old World customs among the south Italians was perhaps best exemplified by the *feste* which were held in great number in Chicago. The cults of the saints and Madonnas had also survived the crossing, and the fellow townsmen had no doubt that their local divinities could perform miracles in Chicago as well as in the Old Country. Feast day celebrations were inspired not only by devotion to the saints and Madonnas; they were also an expression of nostalgia for the life left behind. The procession, the street fair, the crowds of townsmen, created the illusion of being once more back home; as one writer commented of a *festa:* "There in the midst of these Italians, with almost no Americans, it seemed

[53] Palmerio Chessa, "A Survey Study of the Evangelical Work among Italians in Chicago" (bachelor of divinity thesis, Presbyterian Theological Seminary, Chicago, 1934); Jane K. Hackett, "A Survey of Presbyterian Work with Italians in the Presbytery of Chicago" (master's thesis, Presbyterian College of Christian Education, Chicago, 1943).
[54] *Uprooted*, 117, 136.
[55] *Ibid.*, 110.
[56] Alice Hamilton, "Witchcraft in West Polk Street," *American Mercury*, X (Jan. 1927), 71; Chicago *Tribune*, Jan. 19, 1900; *L'Italia*, Oct. 3, 1903. See also Zaloha, "Persistence of Italian Customs," 158-63.

to be truly a village of southern Italy."[57] Despite efforts by "respectable" Italians and the Catholic clergy to discourage these colorful but unruly celebrations, the *contadini* would have their *feste*. After the prohibition of a *festa* by the Church was defied, a priest explained: "The feast is a custom of Sicily and survives despite denunciations from the altar. Wherever there is a colony of these people they have the festival, remaining deaf to the requests of the clergy."[58] The south Italian peasants remained deaf to the entreaties of reformers and radicals as well as priests, for above all they wished to continue in the ways of their *paesi*.

The *contadini* of the Mezzogiorno thus came to terms with life in Chicago within the framework of their traditional pattern of thought and behavior. The social character of the south Italian peasant did not undergo a sea change, and the very nature of their adjustments to American society was dictated by their "Old World traits," which were not so much ballast to be jettisoned once they set foot on American soil. These traits and customs were the very bone and sinew of the south Italian character which proved very resistant to change even under the stress of emigration. Because it overemphasizes the power of environment and underestimates the toughness of cultural heritage, Handlin's thesis does not comprehend the experience of the immigrants from southern Italy. The basic error of this thesis is that it subordinates historical complexity to the symmetrical pattern of a sociological theory. Rather than constructing ideal types of "the peasant" or "the immigrant," the historian of immigration must study the distinctive cultural character of each ethnic group and the manner in which this influenced its adjustments in the New World.

[57] *L'Italia*, July 28-29, 1894; Cassettari, "Story of an Italian Neighbor," 419. See also Zaloha, "Persistence of Italian Customs," 90-100.
[58] Chicago *Tribune*, Aug. 14, 1903.

ACKNOWLEDGMENTS

Samuel L. Baily, "The Adjustment of Italian Immigrants in Buenos Aires and New York, 1870–1914," *American Historical Review*, 88:2 (April 1983), 281–305. Courtesy of Yale University Library.

Ronald H. Bayor, "Italians, Jews and Ethnic Conflict," *International Migration Review*, 6 (Winter 1972), 377–391. Reprinted with the permission of *International Migration Review*. Courtesy of *International Migration Review*.

John Bodnar, "Immigration, Kinship and the Rise of Working-Class Realism in Industrial America," *Journal of Social History*, 14:1 (Fall 1980), 45–65. Reprinted with the permission of the *Journal of Social History*. Courtesy of Yale University Library.

A. W. Carlson, "One Century of Foreign Immigration to the United States: 1880–1979," *International Migration*, 23:3 (September 1985), 309–334. Reprinted with the permission of *International Migration*. Courtesy of Yale University Library.

Roger Daniels, "Chinese and Japanese in North America: The Canadian and American Experiences Compared," *The Canadian Review of American Studies*, 17:2 (Summer 1986), 173–187. Reprinted with the permission of *The Canadian Review of American Studies*. Courtesy of *The Canadian Review of American Studies*.

Oscar Handlin, "Historical Perspectives on the American Ethnic Group," *Daedalus* (Spring 1961), 220–232. Reprinted with the permission of *Daedalus*. Courtesy of Yale University Library.

Marcus L. Hansen, "The History of American Immigration as a Field for Research," *American Historical Review*, 32 (April 1927), 500–518. Courtesy of Yale University Library.

R. F. Harney, "The Commerce of Migration," *Canadian Ethnic Studies*, 9:1 (1977), 42–53. Reprinted with the permission of *Canadian Ethnic Studies*. Courtesy of *Canadian Ethnic Studies*.

James A. Henretta, "Social History as Lived and Written," *American Historical Review*, 84:5 (December 1979), 1293–1322. Courtesy of Yale University.

John Higham, "Hanging Together: Divergent Unities in American History," *Journal of American History*, 61 (June 1974), 5–28. Reprinted with the permission of the *Journal of American History*. Courtesy of Yale University Library.

John Higham, "The Mobilization of Immigrants in Urban America," *Norwegian-American Studies*, 31 (1986), 3–33. Reprinted with the permission of *Norwegian-American Studies*. Courtesy of George E. Pozzetta.

David A. Hollinger, "Ethnic Diversity, Cosmopolitanism and the Emergence of the American Liberal Intelligentsia," *American Quarterly*, 27:2 (May 1975), 133–151. Reprinted with the permission of *American Quarterly*. Courtesy of Yale University Library.

Herbert S. Klein, "The Integration of Italian Immigrants into the United States and Argentina: A Comparative Analysis," *American Historical Review*, 88:2 (April 1983), 306–329. Courtesy of Yale University Library.

Moses Rischin, "Beyond the Great Divide: Immigration and the Last Frontier," *Journal of American History*, 55 (December 1968), 42–53. Reprinted with the permission of *Journal of American History*. Courtesy of George E. Pozzetta.

Jonathan D. Sarna, "The Spectrum of Jewish Leadership in Ante-Bellum America," *Journal of American Ethnic History*, 1:2 (Spring 1982), 59–67. Reprinted with the permission of *Journal of American Ethnic History*. Courtesy of Yale University Library.

Arthur Meier Schlesinger, "The Significance of Immigration in American History," *American Journal of Sociology*, 27 (July 1921–May 1922), 71–85. Reprinted with the permission of *American Journal of Sociology*. Courtesy of Yale University Library.

Timothy L. Smith, "New Approaches to the History of Immigration in Twentieth-Century America," *American Historical Review*, 71:4, (July 1966), 1265–1279. Courtesy of Yale University Library.

Rudolph J. Vecoli, "*Contadini* in Chicago: A Critique of *The Uprooted*," *Journal of American History*, 51:3 (December 1964), 404–417. Reprinted with the permission of *Journal of American History*. Courtesy of Yale University Library.